THE PRESENT STATE
OF SCHOLARSHIP
IN
FOURTEENTH-CENTURY
LITERATURE

THE PRESENT STATE
OF SCHOLARSHIP
IN
FOURTEENTH-CENTURY
LITERATURE

EDITED BY
THOMAS D. COOKE

UNIVERSITY OF MISSOURI PRESS

COLUMBIA & LONDON, 1982

Library of Congress Cataloging in Publication Data
Main entry under title:

The Present state of scholarship
in fourteenth-century literature.

Rewritten papers originally presented in the spring
of 1981 at several lecture series planned by the
Committee for Medieval and Renaissance Studies of the
Graduate School of the University of Missouri-Columbia.
Includes bibliographies.
1. Literature, Medieval—Research—History—
Addresses, essays, lectures.   2.   Literature,
Medieval—History and criticism—Bibliography.
I. Cooke, Thomas Darlington, 1933-
PN681.P73   809′.023   82-2682
ISBN 0-8262-0379-5   AACR2

55, 244

PREFACE

In 1976 and 1977 the Medieval-Renaissance Committee at the University of Missouri–Columbia initiated a series of lectures on current trends and needs in the scholarship of six major sixteenth-century literatures: English, French, German, Italian, Latin, and Spanish. The six essays were later gathered together by William M. Jones and published under the title *The Present State of Scholarship in Sixteenth-Century Literature* (University of Missouri Press, 1978).

At the same time, the Medieval-Renaissance Committee at UMC began plans for similar surveys of the literatures of the thirteenth, fourteenth, and fifteenth centuries. For a number of reasons the committee decided to deal with the fourteenth century first, and so, with a generous grant from the National Endowment for the Humanities, a symposium surveying the scholarship of that century was held in Columbia on 21–22 April 1981. The essays in this volume are refined versions of the papers that were first delivered at the symposium. The volumes on scholarship in the thirteenth and fifteenth centuries are presently in the planning stage.

Although the purpose of this series of studies is to provide an overview of current scholarship, the essays have had to be selective in both the literature they survey and the scholarship on that literature; the essays are broad, but they do not attempt to be comprehensive. And because some authors bridge two centuries, arbitrary decisions had to be made on which century would be more appropriate for them. Dante, for example, is not discussed in the present volume, even though he wrote the *Commedia* in the fourteenth century, but he will be discussed in the volume on thirteenth-century literature. Although

v

that might be a questionable decision, such is the wealth of scholarship on the other two giants of fourteenth-century Italian literature, Petrarch and Boccaccio, that to attempt to survey all three in one volume would severely limit the coverage given to each author. Since the purpose, moreover, of these volumes is to survey the literature within a certain time period, the essays do pay some attention to minor works and authors. In determining the areas to be discussed, each of the six contributing scholars was provided general guidelines, but the ultimate choice of materials was determined by the unique needs of each of the six literatures.

The terminus a quo for the scholarship surveyed in these essays is 1960, which was the terminus ad quem for the study these volumes seek to supplement: *The Medieval Literature of Western Europe: A Review of Research, Mainly 1930–1960*, edited by John Hurt Fisher. Occasionally the essays in the present volume go back beyond 1960 if an important piece of scholarship was not mentioned in the Fisher collection.

My introduction to the essays attempts to provide the general reader with a brief overview of the historical background of the period, an even briefer survey of the kinds of literature the century produced, and the briefest of statements concerning the authors discussed in the essays. Those who are well versed in these matters may with confidence skip over those pages. As Dame Julian of Norwich once advised: "I am not trying to tell the wise something they know well already; but I am seeking to tell the uninstructed" (*Revelations*, chapter 9).

The chronological list of works and authors should be of interest to all readers of this volume, since I know of no other chart that attempts to provide precisely the same information, namely an indication of the kinds or genres of works written in the six different literatures. I felt that readers would profit from learning the specific genre of a work or the important genres of an author rather than merely reading a title, particularly a "foreign" title, which in many cases provides no indication of the kind of work it is. Since one dimension of the chart is comparative, generic descriptions will provide more links than individual titles. With the exception of the list of Latin writers and works, which Professor Nichols prepared, I did the basic work on the lists, but each of the contributing scholars provided me with many helpful suggestions, for which I am greatly indebted.

A debt is owed to the members of the Medieval-Renaissance Committee at UMC for initiating this project and for many forms of assistance and support both with the symposium and with the preparation of this volume: to Dean Andrew Minor, to Professors Bonner Mitchell, Edzard Baumann, the late Lloyd E. Berry, Lee R. Entin-Bates, Milton McC. Gatch, James V. Holleran, William M. Jones, Claudia Kren, Charles Nauert, Jr., Osmond Overby, John R. Roberts, Homer L. Thomas, and especially Vern G. Williamsen. We were pleased that Don H. Blount, Dean of the Graduate School at UMC, was able to open our symposium, and we were doubly honored at the symposium banquet to have the President of the University, James C. Olson, introduce our featured speaker, Robert Lopez, Sterling Professor of History at Yale University.

Besides some of the members of the Medieval-Renaissance Committee already mentioned, I would also like to thank the following colleagues at UMC for their help in making the symposium run smoothly and for their suggestions in the preparation of this volume: Benjamin Honeycutt, Sue Firestone, Martin Camargo, John Foley, Ingeborg Henderson, Daniel Gulstad, and Luitpold Wallach. Claudia Kren at UMC and John C. Moore from Hofstra University read the historical part of my introduction and made many valuable suggestions. John and Ellen Dubinski admirably performed the heroic task of proofreading all essays and doublechecking all bibliographical entries. Kyle Glover helped do some research on the introduction and chronological lists. Sue Strom and Freddy Randolph helped plan and run the symposium efficiently. Marilynn Keil typed much of this material with her usual good cheer and care.

On a lighter side, thanks are due to Dean Andrew Minor's *Collegium Musicum*, which presented a delightful banquet concert of songs and instrumental music that represented the six different medieval languages under discussion at the symposium. We were also fortunate to have had James Tyler's London Early Music Group open our symposium with a concert of medieval music.

Our largest debt is due to the National Endowment for the Humanities, which funded the symposium and some of the costs of preparing this volume for publication.

My gratitude is also extended to Kathleen Ellsbury, who, from the beginning of this project to its near-completion, was far more encouraging and understanding than she needed to be.

With its customary generosity, the Research Council at UMC helped defer some of the costs of preparing this volume for publication.

I would, finally, like to express my personal thanks to the six contributors to this volume. Their presence at the symposium in the spring of 1981 made it a delightful as well as an instructive meeting, and throughout the whole course of our venture they have treated this editor's questions, requests, and deadlines with unfailing kindness, patience, and promptness. Largely because of them, my work on this project has been a pleasant scholarly task.

T.D.C.
Columbia, Mo.
September 1982

CONTENTS

INTRODUCTION:
A HISTORICAL AND LITERARY
SURVEY OF THE FOURTEENTH CENTURY

Thomas D. Cooke

In our need to understand and to place past ages, we frequently bestow upon them labels that are attempts to summarize their essence. Not all such endeavors are mere intellectual shorthand; many are legitimate attempts to understand the controlling ideas and goals of a period, its compelling needs and moods, and even its unspoken assumptions. When we accept one label as valid for an age, we imply that the age was unified in its ideas, needs, and assumptions. When we cannot agree on a single tag for an age, or when we find contradictory tags, we conclude that the age was complex or shifting.

The complexity and instability of the fourteenth century can be seen in the number of contradictory terms that have been bestowed upon it by recent scholars. On the one hand, it has been called the calamitous age, the age of disaster and dismay, an age of apathy, of purposeless agitation, an age of skepticism, pessimism, upheaval, chaos, frustration, retrenchment, decline, insecurity, violence, misfortune and confusion, and an age of ambiguity. On the other hand, it has been called an age of discovery, change, an age of a new spirit of curiosity, the age of the first modern man (Petrarch), an age of growing optimism, a period of the first movements of modern science, and an age of maturing art, architecture, and music. Commenting specifically on the religion of the age, scholars and observers refer to it as a time of heresy, scandal, spiritual decay and destruction, and a time of continual religious controversy. Others, however, call it a profoundly religious period, the century of mystics, the age of the devout layman, and a visionary age. Still other scholars, perhaps unwilling to choose either of those two extremes, prefer to think of the fourteenth century in a broader historical context. But even here there is division. One group prefers to think of the time as the end of the Middle Ages, another as the beginning of the Renaissance, and a third group, with a dubious sense of compromise, regards it as an age of transition or as the bridge between the Middle Ages and the Renaissance.

Those conflicts in interpretation become only apparent ones, however, when we recall the unusual blend of disasters and developments that took place during that one hundred years. Early in the century wide-spread flooding throughout Europe led to general crop failure, which in turn caused famine and starvation for countless people. Throughout the century private and national wars raged, from the petty squabbles of families to the devastating Hundred Years' War between France and England. Among the results of those wars were the numerous bankruptcies of financiers who loaned money to the combatants. The national wars also led to heavy taxation on the peoples of Europe, who suffered further financial burdens from the debased coinage that resulted from the recurring depressions in economic markets. A dubious achievement of the fighting during the fourteenth century was the first use of gunpowder and cannon.

It was in the middle of the century that its most calamitous event began, the Black Death, which first occurred in 1348–1350, when it killed, it is estimated, from one-third to one-half of all the people in Europe, and it kept recurring periodically throughout the century. Reactions to the plague are a grim indication of the contradictory nature of the period. While many fervent Christians sought divine mercy by gathering together in bands of flagellants and processing through the towns of Europe beating one another with rods and lashes, other groups sought solace in riotous living, some even gathering together and dancing lasciviously in parodic imitation of the penitential flagellants.

Some lucky people, like the aristocrats in Boccaccio's *Decameron*, could flee the plague by retiring to an unaffected spot. One group that chose not to flee was the many devout and religious priests, who stayed to help the afflicted and who in turn caught the plague and died. Their deaths seriously depleted the ranks of the clergy. In addition to this quantitative reduction, the Church's reputation and prestige suffered heavily during the fourteenth century. Its monks were generally considered useless, its friars dissolute, its nuns frivolous, its priests too often absent, its bishops and cardinals too worldly, and its popes were either imprisoned in the shame of the Babylonian Captivity or in the disgrace of the Great Schism. Given such a poor example, it is little wonder that so-called heresies and heretics kept appearing, such as the licentious cult of the Free Spirit or the prophetic but cantankerous Wyclif and his followers, the Lollards. Anticlericalism was, naturally, a common attitude.

The established Church was not the only institution under fire; the secular state and its controlling upper classes were the occasional target of animosity and grievances. Revolts by Italian workers, the *Ciompi*, and the revolts of the common people, such as the *Jacquerie* in France and the Peasants' Revolt in England broke out spontaneously (and unsuccessfully) in protest against social injustices.

The insecurity that resulted from all this turmoil found its philosophical counterpart in the destruction of the Thomistic synthesis by such philosophers as William of Ockham and other Nominalists of the century. Even though the common man was neither aware of nor interested in the fine distinctions of the schoolmen, his daily life was evidence enough of mankind's precarious and unprotected position in the universe. In addition to the over-whelming, and seemingly endless threats of famine, war, and plague, there was also the more local threat of daily catastrophes for which he had little human help, such as the threat of fire (and no fire insurance), disease and accidents (and no real medicine), and lawlessness (with no real police force).

Contemplating such an array of horrors and calamities, many recent historians conclude that of all previous centuries the fourteenth is the one most like the twentieth, which, with its two global wars and the threat of another one of world-ending potential, is equally horrific. Those same historians, however, add that the fourteenth century is also like our own in the important innovations and developments that took place, which, ironically, came about either as the result of, or in spite of the disasters. For example, one result of the depressed economy and shrinking markets was the development of the more rational and orderly business practices that modern economies still depend on. The Plague accelerated the disappearance of serfdom in Western Europe, as the shortage of workers placed peasants in a strong bargaining position. The scandalous conduct of the clergy turned men away from the institutional church, for sure, but many of those disaffected souls became more devout in spite of the hierarchy, and a number found an even greater personal spiritual satisfaction in mysticism, which flourished in that century as perhaps at no other time.

Although the lower classes were unsuccessful in their attacks on the upper classes, governments of the times were becoming more representative of a wider spectrum of society. As a result of social changes and the increasing complexities of governing, bureaucracies evolved that made possible the efficient and orderly carrying out of governmental business. Nominalism, which created philosophical skepticism and ambiguity, also resulted in a belief in the importance of the particular and the empirical, and that belief in turn led to the birth of modern science and technology. Freed from an excessive worship of and dependence on the past, science made some important discoveries, particularly in theories of motion. Advances in technology led to the first reliable mechanical clocks, which, in turn, led ultimately to accurate time measurements that made possible exact scientific calculations, an essential tool of modern science. Two seemingly unrelated technological advances were to prove extremely influential: the development of reading glasses and the growing availability of paper. Combined with the fifteenth-century invention of printing, these developments brought about profound changes in the forms and audience of literature. There were also improvements in shipbuilding, which along with the perfection of the mariner's compass and the availability of more reliable maps, led to the most important event of the next century, the discovery of the New World.

The complexity and diversity of events that occurred between 1300 and 1400 find their counterpart in the literature of that period, especially the combined literatures of six different languages. Each of those fourteenth-century literatures has a special place and reputation in relationship to the rest of the literature in that language, and, as the comments of the six contributing scholars to this volume reveal, those reputations vary considerably. For fourteenth-century Italian—with Dante (whose greatness and the resulting wealth of scholarship force us to devote to him part of a future volume in this series), Petrarch, and Boccaccio—it is the century of preeminence. For English literature, with Chaucer, Langland, and the *Pearl* Poet, the second half of the century was the "first English golden age." Spanish literature of the period does quite well with Juan Manuel and Juan Ruiz, although some might still regard the period primarily as one for specialists. The quality of Latin literature of the period is "not as high as that of the centuries preceding it or following it, nor is it as high as the quality of the vernacular literatures of its time" (a severe judgment that must be tempered by the recognition of the growing acceptance throughout the century of the vernacular as a proper literary mode). German literature of the fourteenth century is an "unloved stepchild," and except for Meister Eckhart, some of its other principal writers, like Heinrich der Teichner and Oswald von Wolkenstein, may not be familiar to scholars outside the field. The French literature of the century has been viewed as a period of "embarrassing sterility," even with the work of Guillaume de Machaut and Eustache Deschamps. In spite of these varied evaluations, each of the literatures has significant merit.

One basic complexity of these literatures is the fact that fourteenth-century writers were most often multilingual. Not a few of the authors during the century wrote both in the vernacular and in Latin, and the Englishman John Gower composed major works in his native tongue, in Latin, and in French. Some authors, notably Petrarch and Boccaccio, wrote what they considered their important and enduring work in Latin and their less serious and more ephemeral literature in the vernacular. Although most modern readers now regard their vernacular writings as the more significant, scholars have established, as Professor Bergin notes, the necessity of understanding the Latin writings of those authors for a complete appreciation of their vernacular works. At the beginning of the century, Latin was generally used as the official language, but by the end of the century it had given way to native tongues. And Latin itself was changing, from a medieval Latin at the beginning to a more classical or humanistic Latin by the close of the century.

Each of the native languages was also undergoing linguistic and dialectal changes, all of which affected the literatures of the time. And there were unique language problems; one of the more unusual found in Spain, where Jewish, Christian, and Muslim cultures still coexisted.

The late fourteenth-century *Poema de José,* a Christian version of the Old Testament story of Joseph (but with the *Koran* as a principal source), was written in Romance, but transcribed in Arabic characters (a phenomenon known as *literatura aljamiada*).

The genres of the century present us with a similar array. Some genres were born in the period, a few declined, many flourished, and they all changed. Epics, for example, were being written in the fourteenth century, but hardly with the exalted results of previous centuries. It is a long way from the *La Chanson de Roland* to *Le Bâtard de Bouillon* or from the *Cantar de mio Cid* to *Las Mocedades de Rodrigo,* and even farther away is the *Baudouin de Sebourc* and Heinrich Wittenwiler's *Der Ring,* both of which transformed the earlier epic spirit into a comic counterpart. Petrarch attempted a Latin epic, *Africa,* a "failed masterpiece," and when Boccaccio did write an epic, *Teseida,* Chaucer took the story and turned it into a medieval romance, *The Knight's Tale.* One scholar argues that Boccaccio's *Decameron* is an "epic of the merchant class."

Most of the best known medieval romances were written in previous centuries, though the genre thrived in the fourteenth. From England alone some sixty have survived; besides *The Knight's Tale* Chaucer also wrote *Troilus and Criseyde,* and there is the anonymous *Sir Gawain and the Green Knight.* Boccaccio wrote three important romances, *Filocolo, Filostrato,* and *Fiammetta.* In early fourteenth-century Spain we find *El caballero Zifar* (also regarded as the first Spanish novel), as well as evidence for the composition of *Amadís de Gaula.* In France we have the grail romance, *Perceforest,* and three Alexander romances, *Les Voeux du paon, Le Restor du paon,* and *Le Parfait du paon.*

It was a creative century for lyric poetry and for the development of new poetical forms and styles. Petrarch perfected the sonnet form, while Guillaume de Machaut developed *ballades* and *rondeaux.* Chaucer experimented with several metrical styles, and he charmed iambic pentameter feet into rhymed lines that later became known as the heroic couplet. In Germany, which as Professor Glier notes was in a transitional period for the lyric, Heinrich von Meissen ("Frauenlob") and Oswald von Wolkenstein helped to effect important formal changes in lyric poetry. And in Spain, Juan Ruiz experimented widely with verse forms, using some sixteen different metrical forms in *El libro de buen amor.*

The art of storytelling flourished in the fourteenth century, particularly the art of gathering stories into collections, such as Boccaccio's *Decameron,* Sacchetti's *Trecentonovelle,* Nicole Bozon's *Contes Moralisés,* Chaucer's *Canterbury Tales,* Gower's *Confessio Amantis,* and Juan Manuel's *Conde Lucanor.* Similar to those collections, which often included tales of many different genres, were certain mixed-genre works, such as *Der Ring* by Heinrich Wittenwiler (who marked the manuscript with different colors to indicate the changing styles), *El libro de buen amor* by Juan Ruiz, *El rimado de palacio* by Pero López de Ayala, *Le Voir dit* by Machaut, and *Piers Plowman* by William Langland. Like most of the collections of tales, these mixed-genre works use a framing device of one kind or another that allows the author to tell stories, relate anecdotes, satirize political or ecclesiastical corruption, sing lyrics, write letters, depict allegorical events, travel all around the physical world and all through time, and, in short, to indulge at will his medieval muse. In a complex, shifting, and disturbed time like the fourteenth century, it is understandable and perhaps even unavoidable that the old forms would give way to new ones that were eclectic and amorphous.

Although many collections of tales and the mixed-genre works were comic and even occasionally scatological, it would be an oversimplification to label them secular works. Very little that was written in the fourteenth century was purely secular or totally nonreligious. Indeed, most writings of the time were primarily religious, and those writings come in all forms: sermons, *exempla*, saints' lives, devotionals, moral instruction, proverbs, and translations of the Bible and of other religious works. Medieval man could, of course, take even the pagan classics and turn them into something religious, as happened with the early fourteenth-century French work, *Ovide moralisé*. One of the dominant religious modes of the Middle Ages was allegory, represented in the fourteenth century by such works as *Le Pèlerinage de la vie humaine* and *Le Pèlerinage de l'ame*, both by Guillaume de Digulleville. Religious allegory itself took on different shapes; one of the more notable was the dream vision, of which the most famous fourteenth-century examples are the English poems, *Pearl*, *Piers Plowman*, and above all, the *Divine Comedy* (though not all readers would classify the *Comedia* primarily as a dream vision). There were also dream visions that were not as religiously oriented, including Chaucer's *Book of the Duchess*, an early narrative poem.

Among the best known religious writers of the fourteenth century were its mystics: in England there was Julian of Norwich, Walter Hilton, Margery Kempe, Richard Rolle, and the anonymous author of *The Cloud of Unknowing*; in Germany there were the three Dominican monks, Meister Eckhart, Johannes Tauler, and Heinrich Seuse; in Italy, St. Catherine of Siena; in Spain, Blessed Ramon Lull; and in France, Jean Gerson (who also, incidentally, openly defended the cause of women). It is commonly suggested that the scandalous nature of the institutional Church was a primary reason that so many devout people turned to mysticism for spiritual satisfaction. Whatever the cause, it is significant that the writings by these mystics often took the form of autobiographies. Indeed, two of their works, *The Book of Margery Kempe* and *Der Seuse*, are regarded as the first autobiographies in English and in German, respectively.

This impetus toward autobiography also found its way into other genres: in his *Histoire de St. Louis*, Joinville tells of his own exploits as well as those of the king, and some of the lyrics of Oswald von Wolkenstein and Machaut sing of their personal experiences. Some works are directly autobiographical, like Petrarch's *Letter to Posterity*; some more indirect, as is the claim for Richard de Bury's *Philobiblon*; and some take the posture of being partially autobiographical, such as the *Canterbury Tales* and *El libro de buen amor.*

Philosophy was still the handmaiden of theology in the fourteenth century, though it was not long to remain so. The century saw the breakdown of the Thomistic synthesis that it had inherited from the previous century. Two Franciscan friars helped to bring about that change, first Duns Scotus, a transitional figure at the beginning of the century, and later William of Ockham, whose nominalism is a main reason that the period is referred to as an age of criticism and an age of skepticism.

Drama of various kinds (liturgical drama, folk plays, miming) had been in existence for quite a long time before the fourteenth century; and a few of the more famous medieval vernacular plays (such as *Le Mystère d'Adam* and *El auto de los Reyes Magos*) first appeared in the twelfth century. It would seem likely, therefore, that by the fourteenth there would be a strong dramatic tradition throughout Europe, but existing records are generally scanty. The available sources are beset with problems or exist only in manuscripts from later centuries, so it is impossible to make many definite statements about the drama of the period. One firm and important date is 1311, when Pope Clement ratified the edict establishing the Feast of Corpus Christi, a religious celebration that eventually led to the development of great cycles of mystery plays in some countries, primarily in late fourteenth-century England. In the other European countries the Passion play dominated the religious theater. In France there

are also plays by known writers, such as Phillipe de Mézières and Eustache Deschamps, as well as the collection
of plays dealing with miracles attributed to the Virgin
Mary. There is evidence that cycles were performed in
Germany during the thirteenth century, and a number of
Passion plays and other religious dramas from the fourteenth have survived. Spain seems to have had no vernacular drama, either religious or secular, during the century,
though, as Professor Burke observes, the whole question
of medieval Spanish drama is "shrouded with enigma and
uncertainty." Evidence for any vernacular drama in Italy
is even scantier. Throughout Europe in general, whatever
the direct evidence, tangential evidence suggests that some
plays in native tongues were being performed. Of course,
with the rise of vernacular drama, there was a steady de-
crease in the number of Latin plays.

Numerous and varied are the other genres of the century. Some of the more important ones are rhetorical treatises (Dante and Deschamps), letters (Petrarch and
Catherine of Siena), biography (Boccaccio), encyclopedia
(Cecco d'Ascoli), natural history (Konrad von Megenberg),
educational treatises (Geoffroy de la Tour Landry), government policy (Dante and Phillipe de Mézières), jurispru-
dence (Cino da Pistoia), cosmography (Pierre d'Ailly),
pastoral poetry (Gerson and Petrarch), fables (*Der Edel-
stein*), debates (*Winner and Waster*), chronicles (Froissart,
Joinville, Villani, Compagni, Yáñez, Higden, Trevisa, Robert Mannyng, Kuchimeister, Elhen von Wolfhagen), and
travel literature, like Mandeville's *Voyage d'outremer*, a
work of sufficient popularity that its English and Latin
versions are considered major works in those languages.
There is also the allegorical kind of travel literature, which
charted an inward journey of the soul, like the two pilgrimage poems of Guillaume de Digulleville, the English
Pearl, Fazio degli Uberti's *Dittamondo*, and the *Divine
Comedy*.

Finally, there were two works, both written in the last

part of the century, that taken together reveal the complexity and shifting nature of fourteenth-century literature.

William Langland's *Piers Plowman* charts the spiritual journey of its hero, and in its rough combination of many different generic types and styles is a thoroughly medieval work, even looking back to a more Anglo-Saxon time for its alliterative verse form. At the end of the century, there was another work centering on a plowman, *Der Ackermann aus Böhmen*, by Johannes von Tepl. Although this scholarly dialogue between the plowman (whose wife has just died) and Death is within the range of medieval works, some of its learning and sytlistic effects are also characteristic of humanism; indeed, it is generally considered as representing the beginning of humanism in Bohemia. Instead, therefore, of being determinedly medieval like *Piers Plowman, Ackermann* looks forward to the coming Renaissance.

Such a diverse range of literature corresponds to a diverse group of writers. Taken together, the fourteenth-century authors comprise a surprisingly broad picture of medieval types and occupations. This range may not be different from what we might find in any other century, but it certainly is in keeping with a century of so many complexities and changes.

Some of the writers were of modest beginnings, like Heinrich der Teichner and Heinrich Wittenwiler; one, Boccaccio, was reportedly born out of wedlock (but later made legitimate by his father). A large number of writers were born into families of wealth and distinction, such as Nicole Bozon, Fazio degli Uberti, Pedro López de Ayala, Hugo von Montfort, and Juan Manuel, a nephew to the king. As might be expected, there were writers who chose not to lead lives in a conventional family setting. Oswald von Wolkenstein ran away from home at the age of ten and only after fourteen adventurous years did he return to claim his property. At the age of nineteen Richard Rolle also ran away from home, but to become a hermit. Ramon Lull also forsook his family and wealth, but not until midlife, in order to lead a devout and missionary life.

Indeed, many if not most of the writers of the century were formally religious, ranging from the tertiary St. Catherine of Siena (the last of twenty-five children) to the bishop and cardinal, Pierre d'Ailly. In between just about every religious vocation is represented: the hermit Rolle; the canons Guillaume de Machaut, Walter Hilton, and Konrad von Megenburg; the vicar Trevisa; the archpriest Juan Ruiz, the anchoress Dame Julian of Norwich, and the nuns Christine Ebner and Adelheid Langmann; the Franciscan friars and philosophers Scotus and Ockham; the Dominican friars and mystics Eckhart, Tauler, and Seuse; the prior Passavanti; and a rabbi, the Spaniard Shem Tov ben Titzhak Ardutiel, commonly known as Sartob de Carrión. Many were teachers and educators, and some held important posts: Jean Buridan was rector of the University of Paris, where Pierre d'Ailly and Jean Gerson were also chancellors. Some of these same men were noted preachers, particularly Ramon Lull and Gerson, and many were famous theologians: in addition to Scotus, Ockham, d'Ailly, Lull and Gerson, there was also Wyclif, Nicole Oresme, and Heinrich von Langenstein.

The rest of these authors were layfolk who were active in a wide variety of occupations. Cino da Pistoia and Eustache Deschamps practiced law. Giovanni Sercambi was an apothecary by training. A few were "businessmen," like the banker Villani or the merchant Franco Sacchetti, but more were government officials of various ranks or performed different kinds of services for people in power. Johannes von Tepl was the town clerk of Saaz in Bohemia (for twenty-eight years), and Francesco da Barberino and Tilemann Elhen von Wolfhagen were notaries. Antonio Pucci was a bell ringer and town crier in Florence. Heinrich von Meissen, Deschamps, and Uberti have all been described as courtiers (a term that could be applied to many more of these authors). Several of these writers held the high post of chancellor: Richard de Bury (of England), Phillipe Mézières (Kingdom of Cyprus), Colvaccio Salutati (Florentine Republic), and López de Ayala (Castile). Many of these writers were also involved in fighting battles or wars (religious or secular ones), such as Deschamps, Mézières, Joinville, Dante, Chaucer, and von Montfort. Although active in many different ways, Dante, along with Petrarch, was supported mainly by patrons. Some of these layfolk were also teachers: Cecco d'Ascoli taught astrology, Cino da Pistoia taught law (Boccaccio was one of his students), and Bonvesin de la Riva taught grammar. The few women writers that we know of in the fourteenth century were in religious orders, except for Margery Kempe, a wife and mother. Two of these women writers, Margery Kempe and St. Catherine of Siena, were illiterate, and composed their works by dictation.

Few of these authors seem to have had merely one occupation, but rather moved quite naturally from one position to another. After he ran away from home at the age of ten, Oswald von Wolkenstein supported himself by working as a cook, stable boy, boatman, and minstrel. Pedro López de Ayala was a page, in charge of a fleet during a naval battle, governor of Toledo, ambassador to Aragon, and chancellor of Castile. Nicole Oresme was a professor of theology, bishop of Lisieux, and chaplain and counselor to Charles V. Chaucer served as a page, soldier, customs officer (for about a dozen years), foreman in charge of maintenance at the Tower and at Westminster Hall, a member of parliament, ambassador for the crown on many occasions, a justice of the peace, and a deputy forester.

Given such a range of jobs, occupations, and duties, it should not be surprising how far and extensive were the travels of these writers, even though the reasons for those travels varied considerably, whether they were the diplomatic missions of Sir John Clanvowe, the preaching of Lull, the crusades of Joinville, the pilgrimages of Margery

Kempe, or the exile of Dante. Journeys to all parts of Europe, including the Scandinavian countries, to Africa, and to the Holy Land were not out of range for some of these writers.

The forced exile of Dante, Uberti (who spent his life in exile), and others exemplify the mixed fortunes of four-teenth-century writers. Many of them were respected, ad-mired, and celebrated in their lifetimes, especially Petrarch, crowned Poet Laureate in Rome on April 8, 1341. Others suffered such calamities as being captured in war or im-prisoned on various charges, like Lull, Joinville, Villani, Oswald von Wolkenstein, and López de Ayala (who spent two years in jail). Ramon Lull was not only imprisoned by the Moslems he was trying to convert, he was also stoned to death by them. Cecco d'Ascoli was burned alive for heresy, a charge (though not the punishment) leveled against the writings of Eckhart and Wyclif. It is possible that Chaucer was guilty of rape, and he was definitely fined two shillings once for beating up a Franciscan friar.

In spite of their misfortunes and transgressions, almost all of these writers seem to have been decent folk. Even with such bizarre behavior as Margery Kempe's loud weeping and writhing in church and her conspicuous white clothes, scholars find little to condemn in these people, with few possible exceptions, such as Juan Manual, who reportedly was unscrupulous in politics and brutal to each of his three successive wives. (Hugo von Montfort, on the other hand, was reportedly very happily married to each of his three successive wives.)

Finally, despite all the risks and dangers that accom-panied daily living in the fourteenth century, particularly for such an active group as these writers, most of them lived to an uncommonly advanced age, most well up into their fifties, sixties, or even later. Despite having taken part in the crusades and being imprisoned, Joinville lived to be ninety-three. Even the women writers generally lived long lives: Margery Kempe lived to be about sixty-five and Julian of Norwich lived to be one hundred. Catherine of Siena, on the other hand, died at the age of thirty-five.

Modern attitudes, approaches, and evaluations of the six fourteenth-century literatures represented here are certainly not uniform. Although modern readers have great admiration for the English and Italian literature of the century, they tend to neglect or even scorn some of the other literatures. In spite of that mixed attitude, the findings of the essays in this volume indicate quite clearly that there has been a pronounced and healthy growth of studies dealing with all six literatures. There have been, for example, many new and improved editions of fourteenth-century works, though Professor Burke cautions that some new editions have been too mechanical with insufficient critical apparatus.

As for critical approaches, on the one hand Professors Bergin and Burke, who both feel scholarship in their fields has been too conservative, welcome the use of formalist criticism for Italian and Spanish literature, while Professor Fisher feels that criticism is too common for English literature and pleads for more scholarship. Fisher also feels that the semiotic and structural approach to medieval literature has not been that helpful, while Burke feels that it has. Professors Knight and Nichols both make a plea for a better understanding of the literature on its own terms and in its own time. Some valuable new areas of study have been in rhetoric, oral literature, and in folklore.

All centuries are times of change and complexity. Whether or not the fourteenth is more so than others is a question beyond the scope of this volume. An overview of the times and its literature, however, seems to suggest that those one hundred years were more than usually complex and contradictory. The terms that scholars apply to the period justify that interpretation. It was a time, as we have seen, of optimism and pessimism, of disasters and discoveries, a century that was the end of a period, the beginning of another, and a bridge between the two.

It is the beginning of some forms of literature, the end of others, and the development of most. Its literary works include unified collections of tales, and collections of tales that also include a little bit of everything else. Its literature is religious and bawdy, realistic and allegorical, medieval and humanistic. The authors of those literary works were commoners and nobles, hermits and world-travellers, educators and soldiers, respected and persecuted, and despite all the dangers and diseases of the times, most lived to uncommonly advanced ages.

Most medieval people of the fourteenth century would be, no doubt, quite baffled if they could have read such an array of judgments and conclusions about their times and literature. If, however, some precocious thinker of the times could have devised something like that twentieth-century device, the opinion poll, and if he had asked the citizenry of the times typical pollster's questions, it is quite possible that the results of those polls would have justified the interpretations of modern scholars. It is interesting to imagine the complex results of such polls, and it is more than likely that they would reveal, once again, how similar are the fourteenth and the twentieth centuries.

A Select List of Works Related to Fourteenth-Century Literature

Coleman, Janet. *Medieval Readers and Writers, 1350–1400*. New York: Columbia University Press, 1981.

Jackson, W. T. H. *Medieval Literature: A History and a Guide*. New York: The Macmillan Company, 1966.

Leff, Gordon. *The Dissolution of the Medieval Outlook: An Essay on Intellectual and Spiritual Change in the Four-*

teenth Century. New York: New York University Press, 1976.

Lerner, Robert E. *The Age of Adversity: The Fourteenth Century.* Ithaca, New York: Cornell University Press, 1968.

Lewis, C. S. *The Discarded Image: An Introduction to Medieval and Renaissance Literature.* Cambridge: Cambridge University Press, 1964.

Reinsma, Luke. "The Middle Ages," in *Historical Rhetoric: An Annotated Bibliography of Selected Sources in English.* Edited by Winifred Bryan Horner. Boston: G. K. Hall & Co., 1980.

Szarmach, Paul E., and Bernard S. Levy, eds., *The Fourteenth Century. Acta,* Vol. 4, 1977. The Center for Medieval and Early Renaissance Studies. Binghamton, New York: The State University of New York at Binghamton, 1978.

Tuchman, Barbara W. *A Distant Mirror: The Calamitous 14th Century.* New York: Alfred A. Knopf, 1978.

Tydeman, William. *The Theatre in the Middle Ages: Western European Stage Conditions, c. 800–1576.* Cambridge: Cambridge University Press, 1978.

Utley, Francis Lee. *The Forward Movement of the Fourteenth Century.* Columbus: Ohio State University Press, 1961.

ENGLISH LITERATURE

John H. Fisher*

There have been efforts in recent years to depict the last half of the fourteenth century in England as a cultural period. Barbara Tuchman's award-winning *A Distant Mirror: The Calamitous 14th Century* (50) suggests parallels between the threats of the Black Death and the Atomic Bomb and between the tensions of the Great Schism and those between the East and West today. These natural disasters and doctrinal schisms produced in the fourteenth century—as in our own—a collage of cold and hot wars, shifting alliances, domestic unrest, and rapid changes in fortune. Ms. Tuchman follows the tribulations of the century largely through the experiences of Enguerrand de Coucy, Comte de Soissons in France and Duke of Bedford in England. Although her book pays most attention to the Continent, it reveals the intellectual and artistic flowering out of the carnage. This first English golden age, like the later Elizabethan and Victorian, was rooted in warfare abroad and revolution at home.

Charles Muscatine in *Poetry and Crisis in the Age of Chaucer* (139) finds a relation between the social unrest and poetic styles. He interprets the formal perfection of

*__John H. Fisher__ is John C. Hodges Professor of English at the University of Tennessee in Knoxville. Among his many publications are the *Medieval Literature of Western Europe: A Review of Research, Mainly 1930–1960* (1966) and the *Complete Poetry and Prose of Geoffrey Chaucer* (1977). He has been editor of *PMLA* (1963–1971), President of the Modern Language Association (1974), and is currently President of the New Chaucer Society. A forthcoming publication will be a study of Chancery English.

1

the *Pearl* poems as a retreat from turmoil. The poet took refuge in complex metrical forms, intricate arrangements of events and characters, and elaborate variations in lexicon and syntax as a way of blotting out the chaos around him. In contrast, *Piers Plowman* conveys the instability of the epoch in its very structure and style, as well as in its argument. Unlike the detachment of the *Pearl* poems and the involvement of *Piers Plowman*, Chaucer's poems reveal an exquisitely controlled irony. This irony does not resolve the contradictions and disparities of late medieval life; rather it embraces and makes capital of them.

In *Ricardian Poetry* (52), John Burrow seeks to interpret the reign of Richard II as a literary period. He finds the origin of "the great English art tradition" that extended from 1350 to 1900 in what he regards as the common style and world view of Chaucer, Gower, Langland, and the *Pearl* poet—the use of the fictional narrator and the dream vision, the view of man as a weak and beseiged creature whose triumph is merely to endure. This interpretation has been extended by Anne Middleton (44), who chronicles the rise of "public poetry," that is, poetry concerned with public affairs, in the Ricardian Period.

Other background studies that have been published since 1960 are less concerned with literary style than Muscatine and Burrow's. There are good social histories by F. R. H. DuBoulay (36), Denys Hay (40), and Edmund King (42), and interesting studies of special topics, like John Barnie's (34) on war in medieval society, Charles Moorman's (45) on the evolution of the knight in literature, and Henry Kelly's (41) and Wilhelm Busse's (53) repudiation of the notion of courtly love. Richard Firth Green's perceptive study, *Poets and Princepleasers* (38), examines the relations between the court poets and their patrons and audiences. Few of us recognize the extent to which patronage influenced the subject matter, structure, and idiom of medieval literature. John Norton-Smith's *Geoffrey Chaucer*

(122) is particularly sensitive to this aspect of Chaucer's dream poems.

One paramount problem with attempting a brief survey of recent scholarship and criticism dealing with the literary culture of the fourteenth century is the explosion in publications. In his chapter in *The Medieval Literature of Western Europe: A Review of Research, Mainly 1930–1960* (8), to which this series is in some sense a continuation, Robert Ackerman mentioned 483 books and articles dealing with the whole spectrum of Middle English literature between 1150 and 1400. In the bibliographies, I found more than 400 books and 1,500 articles dealing with the fourteenth century alone. Obviously some selection had to be made. With considerable reluctance I decided to concentrate on the books. Eventually I settled on the 386 titles listed in the bibliography. I shall not be able to discuss all of these; however, a study of the classifications and titles gives a comprehensive view of the concerns of scholars over the last twenty years.

BIBLIOGRAPHIES AND RESEARCH TOOLS

Our access to the journal publications will come through the annotated bibliographies now being commissioned by publishers such as Garland, G. K. Hall, and others. Elaine Penninger's *English Drama to 1660* (321) and A. J. Colaianne's *Piers Plowman* (256) presage the kind of tools that will make a survey similar to this more comprehensive ten years from now. The summaries of the main points of books and articles in these annotated bibliographies make it possible to follow the trend of scholarship and criticism and to decide which titles one must consult. Volumes of annotated bibliographies on the works of Chaucer, Arthurian studies, and sermons and manuals of instruction are now in preparation. The weakness of the bibliographic volumes is, of course, that even as they are being compiled and published, the river of publication flows on. In an effort to cope, we have begun to prepare an annual annotated bibliography of Chaucer studies (85, 86). Such annotated bibliographies seem to me a more promising format than the venerable *Year's Work in English Studies* because, as lists rather than essays, they are easier to consult and because they are intended to be comprehensive rather than selective. The humanistic disciplines must organize on-going abstracting systems like those that have long been provided in the sciences. Only thus can we hope to master the mass of publication. Recent literary studies appear to be turning back from the extremes of the formalist and structuralist criticism, which cared for nothing but the text. But this laudable return to cultural and intellectual contexts can never be satisfactory until the tools of access are improved. And unless the prices of the annotated bibliographies can be kept below what the commercial publishers are now charging, they can never be consulted in any but a few research libraries.

Prime examples of the limitations of the bibliographical monograph are the five volumes of the revised *Manual of Writings in Middle English* (1–5) published so far. These are exemplary in their coverage, but they are from five to ten years out-of-date by the time they are published, which makes the first two, edited by Burke Severs and published in 1967 and 1970, now more than twenty years old. Niel Ker's *Medieval Manuscripts in British Libraries* (10) proceeds very slowly. Robbins and Cutler's *Supplement to the Index of Middle English Verse* (13) comes near to completing that list, although there have been corrections and amplifications in the journals. The proposed "Index of Middle English Prose" has not really gotten off the ground. It is beset by problems of definition and coverage. How far should it go beyond belletristic and ecclesiastical materials? How can prose pieces, whose incipits are not uniform, and which are subject to infinite abbreviation, rearrangement, and conflation, be accurately and economically identified?

Of the various anthologies of Middle English writings that have been published since 1960, none is likely to rival the books of Kenneth Sisam or Fernand Mossé as a teaching text. Charles Dunn and Edward Byrnes's *Middle English Literature* (21) is most nearly adequate, but its glossary and other apparatus are skimpy. William Matthews's *Later Medieval English Prose* (17) concentrates on the fifteenth century. The other editions and translations listed in the bibliography are most useful for the independent reader.

FACSIMILES

The improved methods of offset printing and the renewed interest in reading literature in context have encouraged the production of some excellent facsimiles of important medieval manuscripts. Derek Brewer and Scolar Press have produced handsome and useful facsimiles of the Auchinleck (22), Findern (23), and Thornton manuscripts (24), and the Corpus manuscript of *Troilus and Criseyde* (27). These facsimiles make it possible to study the hands, arrangement of the text on the page, ordering of fascicles, colophons, marginalia, and other details of *ordinatio* and *compilatio* that Malcolm Parkes (46) has shown are so important to our understanding of the intention and reception of the text. Paul Ruggiers and the University of Oklahoma Press in 1979 published a facsimile of the Hengwrt manuscript of the *Canterbury Tales* (26) as the first volume of a series of facsimiles of the manuscripts upon which the texts of the variorum Chaucer will be based. The Leeds University School of English is sponsoring facsimiles of the important manuscripts of the mystery cycles (28, 29, 31, 32). And there are others (25, 30). These make possible more sophisticated study of scribal practice.

THEMATIC STUDIES

Before turning to individual works and authors, I should mention some of the important studies of themes. There have been three books on pilgrims and pilgrimage. Donald Hall (39) has written a factual history of the English shrines. Bridget Henisch (58) has written an attractive general introduction to medieval travel literature. In *Curiosity and Pilgrimage* (67), Christian Zacher has explored the transition from the medieval ideal of pilgrimage in Chaucer to the Renaissance ideal of exploration in Mandeville and Richard de Bury. Recognition of this seminal transformation throws light on Chaucer's ironic mode. George Economou's *The Goddess Natura* (56) is after the manner of Howard Patch's *The Goddess Fortuna.* Penelope Doob (55) has discussed medieval literary treatments of madness; Michael Means (61) has written about the *consolatio* as a genre; Birgit Moske (69) about the iconography of *caritas* in Gower, Langland, and fifteenth-century writers. Constance Hieatt (59), James Wimsatt (66), and A. C. Spearing (63) have discussed the dream vision and visionary landscapes. James Winny has treated *Chaucer's Dream Poems* (224). Pietro Cali has discussed *Allegory and Vision in Dante and Langland* (268), Elizabeth Kirk has treated *The Dream Thought of "Piers Plowman"* (274), and Morton Bloomfield (266) has set *Piers* in a tradition of medieval apocalyptic poetry. Paul Piehler (62) has subjected the dream landscape to Jungian interpretation, and Derek Pearsall and Elizabeth Salter (70) traced medieval descriptions of landscapes and seasons from their classical origins. Virginia Egbert's volume on *The Medieval Artist at Work* (68) reproduces marvelous illuminations and paintings of writers and painters at work in their studios and annotates them with quotations from contemporary writings. Marcelle Thiébaux (72) traced the iconography of the stag hunt in literature, with interesting discussions of both *Gawain and the Green Knight* and *The Book of the Duchess.* Kenneth Varty (73) has described 290 foxes in medieval sculptures and decorations, with pictures of many of them.

A. C. Spearing's *Criticism and Medieval Poetry* (63), first published in 1964 and revised in 1972, is a pioneering experiment in close reading. Unlike Lowes, Tatlock, and other critics who were also concerned about words and phrases, Spearing does not turn to classical or romance sources or analogues as controls and has little interest in the authors' intentions. Like the formalist critics of modern literature, he is principally interested in the effect of vocabulary, rhythms, and patterns of expression upon the reader. His method has been adopted by many other critics, particularly the Chaucerian. Pamela Gradon's *Form and Style in Early English Literature* (57) is a complex study of the nature of allegory, of figurative language, narrative structure, romance, realism, and much else. It ranges widely over all European literature. Like many other recent studies—and unlike such classics as Northrop Frye's *Anatomy of Criticism* or Wayne Booth's *Rhetoric of Fiction*—Gradon's book has no thesis, no informing cohesiveness. Donald Howard's *The Three Temptations: Medieval Man in Search of the World* (60) does have a thesis. He views the temptations of the world, the flesh, and the devil as tensions, and in his analysis of *Troilus, Piers Plowman,* and *Gawain,* he brings into question D. W. Robertson's view of the Middle Ages as a culture without tension, in which each category in the hierarchy recognized and accepted its place.

Finally among these general discussions there is Thorlac Turville-Petre's *The Alliterative Revival* (65), which summarizes both older and more recent scholarship on the subject. Turville-Petre associates the alliterative poems with the decline of French as a literary language and the emergence of a bourgeois audience that wanted to be entertained in English. Although he remarks on the insulation of the alliterative school from the court school of Chaucer and Gower, he takes no notice of Hulbert's suggestion that the alliterative poems represented an anti-establishment protest against the language and prosody of London and the court.

LANGUAGE, PROSODY, RHETORIC, AND PALEOGRAPHY

The Middle English Dictionary (6) proceeds apace, and there are several monographs on linguistics and rhetoric listed in the bibliography. James J. Murphy's *Rhetoric in the Middle Ages* (80) has no specific reference to the fourteenth century, but it provides a splendid background for understanding the rhetorical principles with which Chaucer, Gower, and their contemporaries were indoctrinated. Norman Blake's *The English Language in Medieval Literature* (74) is more sophisticated than earlier books in its sociolinguistic treatments. He provides an excellent discussion of the effect of translation on syntax and style and makes a useful attempt to distinguish levels of discourse. His treatment of the methods of editing a medieval manuscript can be compared with Charles Moorman's *Editing the Middle English Manuscript* (79). And like the facsimiles mentioned above, the reproductions and transcriptions in Anthony Petti's *English Literary Hands from Chaucer to Dryden* (81) offer a good introduction to fourteenth- and fifteenth-century paleography.

CHAUCER

Bibliographies and Research Tools

I have listed 143 books in the Chaucer portion of the bibliography, and Chaucer articles are being published at the rate of 125 to 150 a year. Keeping up is a full-time job, but the tools for keeping up are good and getting better. Eleanor P. Hammond and Dudley D. Griffith's bibliographies cover the period to 1953. W. R. Crawford's bibliography (82) covers 1954 to 1963, and Lorrayne Baird's (83) surveys 1964 to 1973. My own edition of Chaucer (84) contains a bibliography covering 1974 to 1979, and the annotated Chaucer bibliography in *Studies in the Age of Chaucer* (the publication of the recently formed New Chaucer Society) begins with 1975 (85, 86). But to list or even to annotate the publications is not to read and to assimilate them. The publication thicket has grown so dense that my advice to my students is to write their papers first on the basis of their own reading of the text and afterward to go through the scholarship to see how their insights are enhanced or changed. As I read the books and articles being published, it appears that many other Chaucerians are doing the same thing, except that they are making only the most perfunctory gesture of going through the literature. As with Shakespeare studies, the sheer mass of material has had a stultifying effect on Chaucer scholarship and criticism. Even if one does go through the scholarship conscientiously, there is so much repetition that it is hard to know what to acknowledge. Many of the books in the last twenty years are close readings of the text, often perceptive and ingenious, but strictly provisional, standing as one possibility among many. Martin Crow and Clair C. Olson's *Chaucer Life Records* (89), and the Chaucer dictionaries of Norman Davis, Bert Dillon, and Francis P. Magoun (90, 91, 93) are factual contributions. The most recent attempt to summarize trends in critical opinion is Florence Ridley's "Survey of Chaucer Studies" in the first volume of *Studies in the Age of Chaucer* (94). The valuable *Companion to Chaucer Studies* (95) edited by Beryl Rowland is excellent through 1965. The new edition, which appeared in 1979, adds two new essays and brings the bibliographies up-to-date. In addition, there are many useful collections of essays, some original and some reprints, which I have omitted from this bibliography, but which are listed in all of the specialized Chaucer bibliographies.

The Robinson edition of Chaucer, still the standard for scholarly citation, has begun to be superseded as a classroom text. *Approaches to Teaching Chaucer's "Canterbury Tales"* (92), recently published by the MLA, provides a survey of texts, materials, and methods for teaching Chaucer. Albert Baugh, Talbot Donaldson, Kenneth Kee, Robert Pratt, and others have produced selected editions (98–101). Pratt and Larry Benson are heading a team that is making a thorough revision of the Robinson edition. In 1977, I completed an edition of the *Complete Poetry and Prose of Geoffrey Chaucer* (97), including the "Equatorie of the Planets," reprinted in 1982 with an updated bibliography. Like the selected editions, this one has glossary and annotations at the foot of each page. Its critical and bibliographical apparatus is deliberately muted on the premise that the first task of the student is to grapple with the text. Paul Ruggiers and the University of Oklahoma Press have in hand a variorum edition of Chaucer's works that will summarize all of the scholarship up to the date of publication of each volume. The first volume, containing the short poems, edited by George Pace and Alfred David, is scheduled for publication in 1982.

Background and General Discussion

Among the twenty-four books I have grouped under "Background and General Discussion," I would call attention to Derek Brewer's *Chaucer and His World* (106) as an informed, up-to-date, beautifully illustrated introduction to the poet and his times. George Kane's *The Autobiographical Fallacy in Chaucer and Langland Studies* (116) and Edward Wagenknecht's *The Personality of Chaucer* (124) represent diametrically opposed tendencies that appear in current criticism. Kane, following the tradition of Donaldson's famous "Chaucer the Pilgrim" (*PMLA*, 1954), warns against taking any of the first-person observations in the poems as autobiographical. As in Judith Anderson's *The Growth of a Personal Voice: "Piers Plowman" and "The Faerie Queene"* (265), he views the personal voice strictly as an artistic device. Wagenknecht's book is, in contrast, a frank experiment in psychobiography, drawing upon the episodes, characters, and images in the works for evidence of Chaucer's own ideals and prejudices. We find a bit of this in Brewer's book and even more (and used more rashly) in George Williams's *A New View of Chaucer* (126), from which John Gardner (108) drew so many of his conclusions.

Commentary and Criticism

The most effective general criticism of Chaucer's works in recent years has dealt with their structure and rhetoric. This approach has culminated in Donald Howard's *The Idea of the "Canterbury Tales"* (173), which depicts the collection as complete in conception even though not in execution. This gestalt criticism is the end product of a long evolution beginning with Ralph Baldwin's *The Unity of the "Canterbury Tales"* (1955), D. W. Robertson's *A Preface to Chaucer* (141), Paul Ruggiers's *The Art of the "Canterbury Tales"* (177), Robert Jordan's *Chaucer and the Shape of Creation* (174), and many others. In their various ways, all of these studies argue for a typological, associative conception of unity in the Middle Ages in contrast to a logical conception of unity today. This interpretation has given rise to the conception of an elusive, evasive, ambiguous, ironic Chaucer in Alfred David's *The Strumpet Muse* (131), Charles Muscatine's *Poetry and Crisis* (139), Paul Thurston's *Artistic Ambivalence in Chaucer's Knight's Tale* (197), Sheila Delany's *Chaucer's "House of Fame": The Poetics of Skeptical Fideism* (217),

Sister Barbara Gill's *Paradoxical Patterns in Chaucer's "Troilus"* (206), Donald Rowe's *O Love, O Charite!: Contraries Harmonized in Chaucer's "Troilus"* (212), and others, in contrast to the hearty, straightforward artist of Kittredge, Tatlock, and Walter Clyde Curry.

Robert O. Payne's *The Key of Remembrance* (163) is the basic study of Chaucer's poetics. From the medieval rhetorics he adduced the medieval conceptions of the various genres of poetry and proceeded to demonstrate how these conceptions influenced Chaucer's practice. Fyler (171), Hoffman (172), and others have discussed Chaucer's relation to Ovid and the medieval philosophers and rhetoricians. Talbot Donaldson (132) has exemplified the way in which rhetorical criticism can be combined with philology and close reading to achieve fuller appreciation of Chaucer's humor and irony. Burnley (157), Elliott (159), Ross (165), and others have likewise compared Chaucer's semantics with the semantics of his classical antecedents and his French and English contemporaries. Eliason (158) has been emphatic about the essential Englishness of Chaucer's poetry, as has Ian Robinson (164). Peter Elbow, *Oppositions in Chaucer* (133), managed an almost structuralist reading of *Troilus and Criseyde* in terms of scholastic dialectic. This kind of semantic and formalist commentary is especially common in journal articles.

Consideration of Chaucer's development as an artist has been renewed in Robert Burlin's *Chaucerian Fiction* (130), which shows Chaucer growing from the poetic fictions of the dream visions, through the philosophic fictions of *Troilus* and the *Knight's Tale*, to the psychological fictions of the later *Canterbury Tales*. Robert Frank discusses the stories in the *Legend of Good Women* (219) in a similar evolutionary vein. And there have been studies on special topics—Chaucer and the liturgy and religion (128, 144), his poetical uses of astrology (140, 147), his treatment of mythography (145), mutability (138), chivalry (143), poverty (146), and animal imagery (142).

The reception of Chaucer's poetry in the seventeenth and eighteenth centuries and his influence on later poets have been given increasing attention. Alice Miskimin (152) has shown how the image of the poet was enhanced and transformed in the Renaissance. William Alderson and Arnold Henderson (148) demonstrated how he was converted into a classic by Augustan scholarship. Margaret Greaves, *The Blazon of Honour: A Study of Renaissance Magnanimity* (149); Harriett Hawkins, *Poetic Freedom and Poetic Truth: Chaucer, Shakespeare, Marlowe, and Milton* (150); Kent Hieatt, *Chaucer, Spenser, Milton: Mythopoetic Continuities and Transformations* (151); and Raymond Tripp, *Beyond Canterbury: Chaucer, Humanism, and Literature* (154), have shown how Chaucerian themes were continued and transformed by his successors. Ann Thompson (153) has shown, in particular, how Shakespeare made use of Chaucerian materials in *Midsummer Night's Dream, Troilus and Cressida,* and *Two Noble Kinsmen.*

In contrast to the philosophical and formalist bent of so much recent criticism, Jill Mann developed in *Chaucer and Medieval Estates Satire* (175) the suggestion earlier proposed by myself in *John Gower* (288), that the models for the characters in the General Prologue were the complaints against the estates as they appeared in medieval sermons and penitentials. Also returning to a more historical concern, Charles Owen has reexamined the problem ignored almost since the time of Furnivall, Koch, and Morley, of the number of days envisaged for the Canterbury pilgrimage and the arrangements of the tales on the days. In *Pilgrimage and Storytelling in the "Canterbury Tales": The Dialectic of "Ernest" and "Game"* (176), Owen finds the conception of the *Canterbury Tales* to be an inherent conflict between the *ernest* of a pilgrimage to a martyr's shrine in Canterbury and the *game* of storytelling to be consummated by a feast in Southwark. In contrast to the followers of Baldwin, who see the action developing toward a somber, spiritual conclusion, Owen finds it developing away from Canterbury and toward Southwark. The crucial moment in the evolution of the plot came when Chaucer detached the Wife of Bath's developing confession from the Man of Law's epilogue and moved it into a position on the homeward journey. In the final plan, the *Canterbury Tales* was not intended to end with the *Parson's Tale*, but with the marriage group back at Southwark. Supporting this view of a merrier Chaucer are Helen Corsa's *Chaucer, Poet of Mirth and Morality* (107), and three books on the fabliaux, Thomas Cooke's *The Old French and Chaucerian Fabliaux* (180), Janette Richardson's *Study of Imagery in Chaucer's Fabliaux* (181), and Larry Benson's and Theodore Andersson's *The Literary Context of Chaucer's Fabliaux* (179), which prints more analogues than are found in Bryan and Dempster.

With Bernadette McCoy's *Boccaccio's "Book of Theseus"* (193), we finally have a translation of the *Teseida* into English, but most of the books listed in connection with the individual *Canterbury Tales* are editions. Cambridge University Press has nearly finished a series of useful editions of individual tales by James Winny, A. C. Spearing, and Maurice Hussey. Florence Ridley's *The Prioress and the Critics* (194) provides a useful summary and critique of the conflicting views of the Prioress as a devoted religious and as a silly social climber. A similar study would be useful for the Wife of Bath and perhaps for one or two of the other controversial pilgrims. Other monographs on individual tales have been mentioned above in other connections.

Troilus and Criseyde

Alice R. Kaminsky's *Chaucer's "Troilus and Criseyde" and the Critics* (208) provides a useful analysis of the criticism to 1978. She divides the critics into four groups: historical, philosophical, formalist, and psychological, and she concludes that a comprehensive survey reveals chiefly the diversity in the points of view. Ann Barbara Gill's *Paradoxical Patterns in Chaucer's "Troilus"* (206) and William Provost's *The Structure of "Troilus"* (211) deal largely with the patterns of the action, stressing again the symmetry and the Boethian wheel of fortune. Monica McAlpine (209) analyzes the structure of *Troilus* as a *de casibus* Boethian tragedy. Ida Gordon, *The Double Sorrow of "Troilus"* (207), treats as ironical the fact that what appears to be eroticism in the poem really concerns the perversion of divine love. John Steadman's *Disembodied Laughter* (213) gives a strictly Boethian interpretation to the poem, and Donald Rowe's *O Love, O Charite!* (212) interprets the poem as almost sacramental. Kaminsky evaluates these and many other *Troilus* studies with a tart, but perceptive pen.

Early Poems

The translation of Wolfgang Clemen's *Chaucer's Early Poetry* (216) falls within our period, even though it is an expansion of his 1938 *Der Junge Chaucer*. For an informed introduction to the shorter poems this remains the standard. Ronald Sutherland's parallel-text edition of the *Romaunt of the Rose* (222) has not solved the problem of authorship, but it has provided an edition of the French that would make possible a close study of the language and technique of the English translation that has not yet been made. James Wimsatt in *Chaucer and the French Love Poets* (223) and in a number of articles has made such a study of the parallels between the language of Machaut and Chaucer that has enormously reinforced the impression created long ago by Kittredge and Lowes of Chaucer's direct indebtedness to the French court poets. Wimsatt demonstrates what Clemens asserts—that Chaucer's early poetry was indeed transmutation of the French idiom into English. To his earlier commentary on the *Parliament of Fowls* (1957), J. A. W. Bennett in 1968 added *An Exposition of the "House of Fame"* (214). Sheila Delany, in *Chaucer's "House of Fame"* (217), and B. G. Koonce, in *Chaucer and the Tradition of Fame* (221), have developed the proposition first set forward by R. J. Allen (*JEGP*, 1956) that in the *House of Fame* Chaucer was exploring the nature and substance of poetry, preparing himself for the deeper, more sustained effort to which he was soon to turn.

This has been an inadequate survey of Chaucerian scholarship. But when one considers that Rowland's *Companion to Chaucer Studies* comprises 516 pages, and Kaminsky's *Chaucer's "Troilus and Criseyde"* contains 244 pages summarizing the criticism on that poem alone, it is evident that in Chaucer studies, at least, we now require a third kind of specialists. We still need textual and documentary specialists, and we need specialists in criticism and interpretation. But to these two must now be added specialists in analytical and critical bibliography, whose task will be simply to keep up with the flow of publication.

THE GAWAIN POET

When we turn from Chaucer to other writers of the fourteenth century, the problem is less acute. During the past five years, the first two editions of all four of the poems in MS. Nero A.x have been published: the first by Charles Moorman (235) in 1976 and the second by Malcolm Andrew and Ronald Waldron (227) in 1978. Moorman's edition of the *Pearl* poems is of special value to the scholar because the text is unpunctuated, in nearly diplomatic transcription, and most of his annotations are concerned with the readings. Andrew and Waldron present a more fully edited reader's edition with explanatory notes. There have also been two books containing translations of all of the *Pearl* poems and *St. Erkenwald*, the first by John Gardner (232) and the second by Margaret Williams (240). Both of these have full introductions discussing the authorship, text, and interpretations. None of these editions or translations makes a substantive contribution to the question of common authorship, although all assume it. The question of common vocabulary could be attacked more directly by using Kottler and Markman's concordance to the *Pearl* poems and *St. Erkenwald* (234), as in G. Kjellmer's *Did the "Pearl Poet" Write "Pearl"?* (248). Through the study of lexical frequency, clausal usage, subordination, and alliteration, Kjellmer concludes that *Pearl* differs so much from *Gawain* and the other poems in Nero A.x that "everything goes to indicate that the *Pearl* poet did not write *Pearl*" (248, p. 98). Indeed, the language of *St. Erkenwald* is more like that of the other poems than is that of the *Pearl*.

There has been surprisingly little fresh interpretation of the *Pearl* poems. Most recent studies are close readings and commentaries on the language and structure. John Burrow, *A Reading of "Sir Gawain and the Green Knight"* (245), has interesting things to say about the orality and audience of the poem. He estimates that it would take about two and a half hours to perform. Larry Benson, on the other hand, in *Art and Tradition in "Sir Gawain"* (241), discusses the poem as a consummate example of written literature. He argues that the epic is based upon oral sources and the romance on books, and he goes on to demonstrate the bookishness of *Sir Gawain and the Green Knight*. Elisabeth Brewer in *From Cuchulain to Gawain* (244) prints the sources and analogues from Irish, French, and English (all in English translation) of the sort that the author might have known. A. C. Spearing, in *The Gawain Poet* (252), provides a thoughtful analysis of each of the four poems. In his discussion of *Pearl*, he skillfully interweaves the elegy over the lost child with the dramatic confrontation between human and divine knowledge. In *Gawain*, he notes the similarity between the beheading game, the seduction, and the hunt in testing Sir Gawain. W. A. Davenport (246), acknowledging the influence of Spearing, gives his own reading for each poem, commenting on the various levels of meaning and the vivid descriptions and dramatizations. Hans Schnyder (251) offers an exegetical, allegorical interpretation of *Sir Gawain*. It is interesting to find the title of his chapter on "The Three Temptations" appearing four years later as the title of Donald Howard's book (60). For Schnyder, the three temptations are the attempted seductions; for Howard, they are lust of the flesh (used as the basis for an interpretation of *Troilus and Criseyde*), lust of the eyes (used as a basis for an interpretation of *Piers Plowman*), and the pride of life (used as the basis for an interpretation of *Sir Gawain and the Green Knight*). Marie Borroff's *Sir Gawain and the Green Knight* (243) begins with two interesting chapters on the meaning of style, which she limits strictly to vocabulary and syntax. This is very different from the cultural definition of style that Howard lays out at the beginning of his book and the social interpretation of style (as courtly or bourgeois) found in Charles Muscatine's *Chaucer and the French Tradition* and Per Nykrog's *Les Fabliaux*.

Ian Bishop in *"Pearl" in Its Setting* (242) and Patricia Kean in *The "Pearl": An Interpretation* (247) outline the structure of the argument in the poem. Bishop, like Spearing, concludes that it is fundamentally autobiographical, but he prefers to call it a *consolatio* rather than an elegy. Kean concentrates on the mystical theology of the poem, with extensive reference to Dante and St. Bernard. In *The Pattern of Judgment in the "Queste" and "Cleanness"* (250), Charlotte Morse follows the paradigm of the vessel as an image of man from biblical and exegetical writings, through the Holy Grail in the *Queste del Saint Graal*, to the wedding vessels in *Cleanness*.

PIERS PLOWMAN

A. J. Colaianne's *"Piers Plowman": An Annotated Bibliography of Editions and Criticism, 1550–1977* (256) offers a good way into *Piers Plowman* scholarship. The great event in the last twenty years has been the appearance of the text of the A version edited by George Kane (258) and the B version edited by Kane and E. Talbot Donaldson (259). The C version in the same series, edited by G. H. Russell, is now in press. The appearance of this edition marks a conclusion to a project begun in 1909 by R. W. Chambers and J. H. G. Grattan in response to the lost-leaf, multiple-author theory advanced by J. M. Manly. While the new edition cannot be said to lay to rest finally the question of single or multiple authorship, Kane has independently argued the case for single authorship (272, 273), and the editorial procedures of his and Donaldson's editions proceed on the assumption of a single authorship considerably modified in the process of scribal transmission. One important indirect contribution of the Kane-Donaldson methodology has been to discredit the genealogical process for establishing a text. They have replaced the deterministic method used by Manly and Rickert and earlier scholars with a study of scribal tendencies in substitution. This does not mean that Kane and Donaldson ignored genetic evidence. But even where it was available, they treated it as only one among a number of indications of originality. This procedure will no doubt influence the editing of all medieval manuscripts in the future. The case for multiple authorship has continued to be argued by David C. Fowler in his reviews of the Kane-Donaldson edition and in his earlier *"Piers Plowman": Literary Relations of the A and B Texts* (271), in which he suggested that the B version might be the work of John Trevisa, the translator of Higden's *Polychronicon*. There are several student editions of *Piers Plowman*. Most are very expensive or out of print. The most available is J. A. W. Bennett's (254), which unfortunately includes only Passus I–VII. A. V. C. Schmidt has recently edited the complete B version for Everyman's Library (261).

The theological background to *Piers Plowman* has been studied in monographs by David Aers (263), Ruth Ames (264), Daniel Murtaugh (278), Ben Smith (281), and Edward Vasta (282). These books treat indirectly the prophetic voice, which was discussed more directly by Morton Bloomfield in *"Piers Plowman" as a Fourteenth-Century Apocalypse* (266). The personal voice, the personification, and the allegory have been explored in books by Judith Anderson (265), Hans Bruneder (267), Pietro Cali (268), Elizabeth Kirk (274), and Priscilla Martin (277). Mary Carruthers in *The Search for St. Truth: A Study of Meaning in "Piers Plowman"* (269) dealt with the epistomology of the poem, its concern for what language can and cannot reveal. Jeanne Krochalis and Edward Peters's *The World of "Piers Plowman"* (275) includes Thomas Brinton's Sermon 44 and selections from other works that provided the spiritual and social milieu of the poem. John Yunck in *The Lineage of Lady Mede* (283) examines the roots of *mede* in classical and medieval satire. Yunck's is the only one of the monographs published since 1960 (and that was written as a dissertation before 1955) that places *Piers Plowman* firmly in the realm of social criticism. All of the other books since 1960 have concentrated on its mystical and theological dimensions.

JOHN GOWER

My study *John Gower: Moral Philosopher and Friend of Chaucer* (288) was the first attempt to survey the poet's life and works. At almost the same time, Edwart Weber wrote two studies on Gower. In *John Gower: Dichter Einer Ethisch-Politischen Reformation* (291), he concentrated more heavily than myself on the abstract moral and political theory in Gower's *Mirour de l'Omme* and *Vox Clamantis*, and less on his contemporary political involvement. In *John Gower: Zur literarischen Form seiner Dichtung* (292), Weber explored the relations between subject, structure, and style in all three poems. The compression of Weber's style would make him hard to read in any language, and it is perhaps not surprising to find no reference to him in Russell Peck's *Kingship and Common Profit in Gower's "Confessio Amantis"* (290), which also concentrates largely on abstract theory. Patrick Gallacher, *Love, the Word, and Mercury* (289), uses the *Confessio Amantis* to put forward a theory concerning the human desire for perfect verbal communication. Eric Stockton translated all of Gower's Latin works into English (286), and Terence Tiller has modernized selections of the *Confessio Amantis* (287). J. A. W. Bennett (284) and Russell Peck (285) have edited selections from the *Confessio*.

MINOR AUTHORS AND WORKS

Recent editions of minor authors and works like Sir John Clanvowe (299) and *The Assembly of Ladies* (298), listed in the bibliography, require no particular comment. Michael Sawyer has provided an annotated bibliography of the writings on the English mystics (304). Clifton Walters has provided good translations of Julian of Norwich and *The Cloud of Unknowing* (305, 306), and Eric Colledge (301) edited an excellent edition of representative selections from all of the important medieval English mystical writers. David Knowles's *The English Mystical Tradition* (307) supersedes earlier general studies, and George Tuma (312) has provided a detailed comparison of topics treated by Hilton, Rolle, Julian of Norwich, Margery Kempe, and other fourteenth-century mystical writers. There have been separate monographs on special motifs in, and on the styles of, the various writers (309–311).

Manfred Görloch continues to edit and to sponsor editions of various parts of the South English Legendary (314–316). Saara Nevanlinna (317) has edited the Harley-Cotton Manuscripts of the latest version of the Northern Homily Cycle. Thomas J. Heffernan has in hand an edition of the original version, extant in sixteen manuscripts. Edward Block has written a general introduction on *John Wyclif, Radical Dissenter* (318) and L. J. Daly one on *The Political Thought of John Wyclif* (319), and there have been editions of his Latin writings. Sven Fristedt's exhaustive study of the composition of the Wyclif Bible has resulted in a third volume (320). I noted above that David Fowler proposes John Trevisa as the author of the B version of *Piers Plowman.* Fristedt argues that Trevisa also assisted Purvey in translating the second version of the Wyclif Bible. If during the 1380s, while he was at Oxford working on his translation of the *Polychronicon,* Trevisa also helped on the second translation of the Bible and revised *Piers Plowman,* he was one of the major literary figures of the day and deserves more extensive study than he has received.

DRAMA

Elaine Penninger's annotated bibliography *English Drama to 1660* (321) provides a way into recent writings on medieval English drama. Of all of the genres, developments in the study of the drama have been most exciting during the last twenty years. The older studies by Tucker Brooke, Karl Young, and Hardin Craig were essentially apologetic as to the dramatic and literary quality of the plays and were concerned largely with their supposed evolution from ritual to drama. Arnold Williams's *The Drama of Medieval England* (348) and Eleanor Prosser's *Drama and Religion in English Mystery Plays: A Re-evaluation* (347) were two of the first studies to assert the literary and dramatic value of the plays. These were followed by

Bevington (332), Collier (334), and Kolve (342), who demonstrated the effectiveness of their language and structure, and Fifield (343), who argued their intellectual sophistication. Perhaps the most important contribution is that of O. B. Hardison in *Christian Rite and Christian Drama in the Middle Ages* (339). Hardison demonstrated that the nineteenth-century evolutionary view of the medieval drama was largely created by literary historians on the model of Greek drama, unsupported by medieval documentary evidence. He then proceeded to rearrange the texts of the medieval plays to show that they were not "biological growths." Complex forms preceded simpler ones. The plays are the creations of gifted and creative artists experimenting with various themes and forms. A useful guide through this continuing revival is Stanley Kahrl's *Traditions of Medieval Drama* (340). Rosemary Woolf's *The English Mystery Plays* (349) provides information on the theological ambience of the plays and their reception by the Church authorities.

The effectiveness of the plays as theatrical presentations has been further demonstrated in their revivals at York, Chester, and elsewhere. All of this in turn has led to the publication of the facsimiles mentioned earlier (28–32), to fresh editions of the texts of the plays (324–330), and, finally, to a plan to publish all of the records of early English drama by the University of Toronto. Under the sponsorship of this project, the records of York and Chester have already been published. More than forty-five editors are now at work and more than thirty volumes of records are projected. Both the texts of the plays and the scholarly data are being computerized for future use.

ROMANCE

There is not as yet an annotated bibliography to lead one through the literature on the romances, although Edmund Reiss is at work on such a compilation for the

Arthurian materials. The alliterative and stanzaic versions of *Morte Arthure* have been several times reedited: John Finlayson's (351) and Valeria Krishna's (353) are both excellent for the alliterative, and P. F. Hissiger's (352) is satisfactory for the stanzaic. Larry Benson has edited both together in a useful student's edition (350). *Ywain and Gawain* (355) and *Lybeaus Desconus* (360) have appeared in EETS editions. Louis Hall has translated *The Knightly Tales of Sir Gawain* (356), and there are other editions both for scholars and general readers listed in the bibliography. Of the studies, William Matthews's *The Tragedy of Arthur* (367) is the most interesting. He finds specific commentary on Edward III's wars in France in the *Morte Arthure* and points out its structural dependence on the romances of Alexander. Velma Richmond (369) has traced popular customs in the romances, and Hanspeter Schelp (370) has shown how the non-Arthurian romances, in particular, were pamphlets for popular moral instruction.

THE LYRICS

As with the romances, there has been no comprehensive annotated bibliography of scholarship on the lyrics. The various editions and translations are not confined to lyrics of the fourteenth century. R. T. Davies (373), Theodore Silverstein (376), and Robert D. Stevick (378) have edited miscellaneous collections of medieval English lyrics with translations or normalized spelling and such full glosses that they amount to translations. Maxwell Luria and Richard Hoffman edited a Norton Critical Edition (375) of six poems with elaborate textual and critical commentary. Theodore Stemmler (377) produced an edition of all the medieval English love poems (sixty-eight from before 1400) in normalized spelling but without glossary or notes. Douglas Gray has edited *A Selection of Religious Lyrics* (374) to complement the editions of Carleton Brown.

The most impressive critical discussion is Rosemary

Woolf's *The English Religious Lyric in the Middle Ages* (386). She groups the poems topically and discusses the theological and liturgical tradition behind each group. She distinguishes the genesis of the religious lyrics from that of the secular. The secular lyric was an adjunct to song and dance, erotic, rhythmic, characterized by its stanzaic forms and refrains. The religious lyric was not intended to be sung. It is serious, longer, and characterized by its content rather than by its form. Books by Douglas Gray (380), Stephen Manning (382), and Sarah Weber (385) are likewise devoted to doctrine and expression in the religious lyrics. David Jeffrey, *The Early English Lyric and Franciscan Spirituality* (381), argues that the secular lyrics that have been preserved were all written by Franciscan friars as part of the homiletic efflorescence in the thirteenth and fourteenth centuries. Although an interesting idea, this theory has not met with much critical approval. Frederick Goldin (379) has traced the imagery of Narcissus's mirror through the courtly lyrics. Raymond Oliver (383) and Edmund Reiss (384) have provided close readings, commenting on the language, style, content, and tradition of a number of poems.

Bibliography

Bibliographies and Research Tools

1. *A Manual of Writings in Middle English, 1050–1500. Romances.* Edited by J. Burke Severs, vol. 1. New Haven: Connecticut Academy of Arts and Sciences, 1967.
2. ———. *The "Pearl" Poet, Wyclif, Biblical Materials, Saints' Legends, Religious Instruction.* Edited by J. Burke Severs, vol. 2. New Haven: Connecticut Academy of Arts and Sciences, 1970.
3. ———. *Debates, Hoccleve, Malory, and Caxton.* Edited by Albert E. Hartung, vol. 3. Hamden, Conn.: Shoestring Press, 1975.
4. ———. *Middle Scots Writers, Chaucerian Apocrypha.* Edited by Albert E. Hartung, vol. 4. Hamden, Conn.: Shoestring Press, 1973.
5. ———. *Drama, Poems Dealing with Contemporary Conditions.* Edited by Albert E. Hartung, vol. 5. Hamden, Conn.: Shoestring Press, 1975.
6. *Middle English Dictionary.* Edited by Sherman Kuhn et al. Ann Arbor: University of Michigan Press, 1952–. (To the letter P in 1982).
7. Ferguson, Mary Anne H. *Bibliography of English Translations from Medieval Sources, 1943–1967.* New York: Columbia University Press, 1974. (Annotated; up to 1500; supplements Farrar and Evans up to 1943.)
8. Fisher, John H., ed. *The Medieval Literature of Western Europe: A Review of Research, Mainly 1930–1960.* New York: Modern Language Association and New York University Press, 1966.
9. Jolliffe, P. S. *A Check-List of Middle English Prose Writings of Spiritual Guidance.* Toronto: Pontifical Institute, 1974.
10. Ker, Neil. *Medieval Manuscripts in British Libraries.*

London, vol. 1; *Abbotsford-Keele*, vol. 2. Oxford: Oxford University Press, 1969, 1977. (Intended to cover all libraries except the British Library, Bodleian, Cambridge University, and National Libraries of Wales and Scotland.)

11. Preston, Michael J. *A Concordance to the Middle English Shorter Poems.* 2 vols. Leeds: Maney, 1975. (Concordance to 1,328 poems in anthologies of Brown, Brook, Robbins, Greene, Stevens, Person.)

12. Reel, Jerome V. *Index to Biographies of Englishmen 1000–1485, Found in Dissertations and Theses.* Westport, Conn.: Greenwood, 1975. (Dissertations and theses, 1930–1970.)

13. Robbins, Russell H., and John L. Cutler. *Supplement to the Index of Middle English Verse.* Lexington: University Press of Kentucky, 1965.

See also entry 220.

ANTHOLOGIES AND TRANSLATIONS

14. Burrow, John, ed. *English Verse, 1300–1500.* London: Longmans, 1977.

15. Gardner, John, trans. *The Alliterative "Morte Arthure," "The Owl and the Nightingale," and Five Other Middle English Poems in Modernized Versions.* Carbondale: Southern Illinois University Press, 1971. (The other five are "Winner and Waster," "Parliament of the Three Ages," "Summer Sunday," "Debate of the Body and Soul," "The Thrush and the Nightingale.")

16. Haskell, Ann S., ed. *A Middle English Anthology.* Garden City: Doubleday, 1971.

17. Matthews, William, ed. *Later Medieval English Prose.* New York: Appleton, 1963.

18. Owen, Lewis J., and Nancy H. Owen, *Middle English Poetry.* Indianapolis: Bobbs-Merrill, 1971.

19. Spearing, A. C., ed. *Poetry of the Age of Chaucer.* London: Arnold, 1974.

20. Stone, Brian, ed. and trans. *Medieval English Verse.* Penguin Books, 1964.

21. Dunn, Charles, and Edward T. Byrnes. *Middle English Literature.* New York: Harcourt, 1973.

FACSIMILES

22. *Auchinleck MS. National Library of Scotland. Advocates' MS. 19.2.1.* Introduction by Derek Pearsall and I. C. Cunningham. London: Scolar Press, 1977.

23. *Findern MS. Cambridge University Library MS. Ff.1.6.* Introduction by Richard Beadle and A. E. B. Owen. London: Scolar Press, 1977.

24. *Thornton MS. Lincoln Cathedral MS. 91.* Introduction by Derek Brewer and A. E. B. Owen. London: Scolar Press, 1975.

25. *British Library MS. 2253.* Introduction by N. R. Ker. EETS 255, 1965.

26. *The Canterbury Tales. A Facsimile and Transcription of the Hengwrt Manuscript with Variants from the Ellesmere Manuscript.* Edited by Paul G. Ruggiers. Norman: University of Oklahoma Press, 1979.

27. *Troilus and Criseyde. A Facsimile of Corpus Christi College, Cambridge, MS. 61.* Introduction by M. B. Parkes and Elizabeth Salter. Cambridge: Brewer, 1978.

28. *Chester Mystery Cycle. A Facsimile of MS. Bodley 175.* Introduction by R. M. Lumiansky and David Mills. Leeds: Leeds University School of English, 1973.

29. *Digby Plays. Facsimiles of the Plays of Bodley MSS. Digby 133 and e Museo 160.* Leeds: Leeds University School of English, 1976.

30. *Macro Plays. The Castle of Perseverence, Wisdom, Will, Mankind.* Edited by David Bevington. Washington: Folger Library, 1972.

31. *N-Town Plays. A Facsimile of B. L. MS. Cotton Vespasian D.VIII.* Introduction by Peter Meredith and Stanley J. Kahrl. Leeds: Leeds University School of English, 1977.

32. *Towneley Cycle. A Facsimile of Huntington MS. HM 1.* Introduction by A. C. Cawley and Martin Stevens. Leeds: Leeds University School of English, 1976.

BACKGROUND STUDIES

33. Aston, Margaret. *Thomas Arundel: A Study of Church Life in the Reign of Richard II.* Oxford: Clarendon Press, 1967.

34. Barnie, John. *War in Medieval English Society: Social Values in the Hundred Years War, 1337–1399.* Ithaca: Cornell University Press, 1974.

35. Bryant, Arthur. *The Medieval Foundation.* London: Collins, 1966. (Making of the law, medieval village, travelers and traders, and so on.)

36. DuBoulay, F. R. H. *An Age of Ambition: English Society in the Late Middle Ages.* New York: Viking, 1970. (Economy, class, sex, authority, and so on.)

37. ———. *The Lordship of Canterbury.* New York: Barnes & Noble, 1966. (Analysis of the Canterbury Cathedral archives.)

38. Green, Richard Firth. *Poets and Princepleasers: Literature and the English Court in the Later Middle Ages.* Toronto: University of Toronto Press, 1980.

39. Hall, Donald John. *English Medieval Pilgrimage.* London: Routledge, 1965. (History of the English shrines.)

40. Hay, Denys, ed. *Europe in the Fourteenth and Fifteenth Centuries.* London: Longmans, 1966.

41. Kelly, Henry Ansgar. *Love and Marriage in the Age of Chaucer.* Ithaca: Cornell University Press, 1975.

42. King, Edmund. *England 1175–1425.* London: Routledge, 1979.

43. Metlitzki, Dorothee. *The Matter of Araby in Medieval England.* New Haven: Yale University Press, 1977.

44. Middleton, Anne. "The Idea of Public Poetry in the Reign of Richard II." *Speculum* 53 (1978): 94–114.

45. Moorman, Charles. *A Knight There Was: The Evolution of the Knight in Literature.* Lexington: University Press of Kentucky, 1967.

46. Parkes, Malcolm B. "The Influence of *Ordinatio* and *Compilatio* on the Development of Books." In *Medieval Learning and Literature: Essays Presented to R. W. Hunt,* edited by J. J. Alexander and M. T. Gibbs, pp. 115–44. Oxford: Clarendon Press, 1976.

47. Talbot, C. H. *Medicine in Medieval England.* London: Oldbourne, 1967.

48. Wilkinson, B. *The Later Middle Ages in England, 1216–1485.* New York: McKay, 1969.

49. Young, Charles R. *The Royal Forests of Medieval En-*

gland. Philadelphia: University of Pennsylvania Press, 1979.
50. Tuchman, Barbara. *A Distant Mirror: The Calamitous 14th Century.* New York: Knopf, 1978.
See also entries 125, 139, 192, 198.

LITERARY HISTORY AND CRITICISM

51. Ackerman, Robert. *Backgrounds to Medieval English Literature.* New York: Random House, 1968.
52. Burrow, John. *Ricardian Poetry: Chaucer, Gower, Langland and the "Gawain" Poet.* London: Routledge, 1971.
53. Busse, Wilhelm G. *Courtly Love oder Paramours.* Düsseldorf: Stern, 1975.
54. Crampton, Georgia R. *The Condition of Creatures: Suffering and Action in Chaucer and Spenser.* New Haven: Yale University Press, 1974.
55. Doob, Penelope. *Nebuchadnezzar's Children: Conventions of Madness in Middle English Literature.* New Haven: Yale University Press, 1974.
56. Economou, George. *The Goddess Natura in Medieval Literature.* Cambridge, Mass.: Harvard University Press, 1972.
57. Gradon, P. *Form and Style in Early English Literature.* London: Methuen, 1971.
58. Henisch, Bridget A. *Medieval Armchair Travels.* State College, Pa.: Carnation Press, 1967. (Essays on medieval travel literature.)
59. Hieatt, Constance. *The Realism of Dream Visions: The Poetic Exploitation of the Dream-Experience in Chaucer and His Contemporaries.* The Hague: Mouton, 1967.
60. Howard, Donald. *The Three Temptations: Medieval Man in Search of the World.* Princeton: Princeton University Press, 1966. (Especially *Troilus, Piers Plowman, Gawain.*)
61. Means, Michael H. *The "Consolatio" Genre in Medieval English Literature.* Gainesville: University of Florida Press, 1972.
62. Piehler, Paul. *The Visionary Landscape: A Study of Medieval Allegory.* London: Arnold, 1971.
63. Spearing, A. C. *Criticism and Medieval Poetry.* 2d ed. rev.

New York: Barnes & Noble, 1972. (Pioneer model of close reading.)

64. ———. *Medieval Dream Poetry.* Cambridge: Cambridge University Press, 1976.

65. Turville-Petre, Thorlac. *The Alliterative Revival.* Cambridge: Brewer, 1977.

66. Wimsatt, James. *Allegory and Mirror: Tradition and Structure in Middle English Literature.* New York: Pegasus, 1970.

67. Zacher, Christian. *Curiosity and Pilgrimage.* Baltimore: Johns Hopkins University Press, 1976.

ART, ICONOGRAPHY

68. Egbert, Virginia W. *The Medieval Artist at Work.* Princeton: Princeton University Press, 1967.

69. Moske, Birgit. *Caritas: Ihre figurative Darstellung in der englischen Literatur des 14. bis 16. Jahrhunderts.* Bonn: Bouvier, 1977.

70. Pearsall, Derek A., and Elizabeth Salter. *Landscapes and Seasons in the Medieval World.* London: Elek, 1973.

71. Pritchard, V. *English Medieval Graffiti.* Cambridge: Cambridge University Press, 1967.

72. Thiébaux, Marcelle. *The Stag of Love: The Chase in Medieval Literature.* Ithaca: Cornell University Press, 1974.

73. Varty, Kenneth. *Reynard the Fox: A Study of the Fox in Medieval English Art.* Leicester: Leicester University Press, 1967.

LANGUAGE, PROSODY, RHETORIC, PALEOGRAPHY

74. Blake, Norman. *The English Language in Medieval Literature.* London: Dent, 1977.

75. Conner, Jack. *English Prosody from Chaucer to Wyatt.* The Hague: Mouton, 1974.

76. Kristensson, Gillis. *Studies on Middle English Topographical Terms.* Lund: Gleerup, 1971.

77. McLaughlin, John C. *Aspects of the History of English.* New York: Holt, 1970.

78. ———. *A Graphemic-Phonemic Study of a Middle En-*

glish Manuscript. The Hague: Mouton, 1963. (British Library MS. Cotton A.x.)
79. Moorman, Charles. *Editing the Middle English Manuscript.* Jackson: University Press of Mississippi, 1975.
80. Murphy, James J. *Rhetoric in the Middle Ages.* Berkeley: University of California Press, 1974.
81. Petti, Anthony G. *English Literary Hands from Chaucer to Dryden.* Cambridge, Mass.: Harvard University Press, 1977.

CHAUCER

Bibliographies, Research Tools

82. Crawford, William R. *Bibliography of Chaucer 1954–1963.* Seattle: University of Washington Press, 1967. (Continues Hammond and Griffith.)
83. Baird, Lorrayne Y. *A Bibliography of Chaucer 1964–1973.* Boston: Hall, 1977.
84. Fisher, John H. *The Complete Poetry and Prose of Geoffrey Chaucer.* 1977. Reprint. New York: Holt, 1982. (Updated bibliography, 1974–1979.)
85. Fisher, John H., et al. "An Annotated Chaucer Bibliography 1975–76." *Studies in the Age of Chaucer* 1 (1979): 201–55.
86. ———. "An Annotated Chaucer Bibliography 1977–78." *Studies in the Age of Chaucer* 2 (1980): 221–85.
87. Baugh, Albert. *Chaucer.* Goldentree Bibliographies. New York: Appleton, 1968.
88. Benson, L. D. "Chaucer: A Select Bibliography." In *Geoffrey Chaucer,* edited by Derek Brewer, pp. 352–72. London: Bell, 1974.
89. Crow, Martin, and Clair C. Olson, eds. *Chaucer Life Records.* From material compiled by John M. Manly et al. Oxford: Clarendon Press, 1966.
90. Davis, Norman, et al. *A Chaucer Glossary.* Oxford: Oxford University Press, 1979.
91. Dillon, Bert. *A Chaucer Dictionary: Proper Names and Allusions, Excluding Place Names.* Boston: Hall, 1974.
92. Gibaldi, Joseph, ed. *Approaches to Teaching Chaucer's "Canterbury Tales."* New York: MLA, 1980.

93. Magoun, Francis P. *A Chaucer Gazeteer.* Chicago: University of Chicago Press, 1961.
94. Ridley, Florence. "The State of Chaucer Studies: A Brief Survey." *Studies in the Age of Chaucer* 1 (1979): 3–16.
95. Rowland, Beryl, ed. *Companion to Chaucer Studies.* 2d ed. Toronto: Oxford University Press, 1978. (Bibliographical essays with select bibliographies: "Chaucer the Man," A. C. Baugh; "Chaucer, the Church and Religion," R. W. Ackerman; "Chaucer and the Art of Rhetoric," R. O. Payne; "Chaucer's Prosody," T. F. Mustanoja; "Chaucerian Narrative," R. M. Jordan; "Chaucer's Imagery," B. Rowland; "The French Influence on Chaucer," H. Braddy; "The Italian Influence on Chaucer," P. G. Ruggiers; "The Influence of the Classics on Chaucer," R. L. Hoffman; "Chaucer and Astrology," C. Wood; "The Design of the Canterbury Tales," C. A. Owen, Jr.; "The General Prologue," T. A. Kirby; "The Tales of Romance," J. B. Severs; "The Fabliaux," D. S. Brewer; "Allegory in the Canterbury Tales," R. P. Miller; "Modes of Irony in the Canterbury Tales," V. Ramsey; "The Lyrics," R. H. Robbins; "The Book of the Duchess," D. W. Robertson, Jr.; "The House of Fame," L. K. Shook; "The Parliament of Fowls," D. C. Baker; "Troilus and Criseyde," J. P. McCall; "The Legend of Good Women," J. H. Fisher.)
96. Scott, A. F. *Who's Who in Chaucer.* London: Elm Tree, 1974.

Editions and Selections of the Complete Works

97. Fisher, John H., ed. *The Complete Poetry and Prose of Geoffrey Chaucer.* New York: Holt, 1977.
98. Baugh, Albert C., ed. *Chaucer's Major Poetry.* New York: Appleton, 1963.
99. Donaldson, E. Talbot, ed. *Chaucer's Poetry: An Anthology for the Modern Reader.* 2d ed. New York: Ronald, 1975.
100. Kee, Kenneth, ed. *Geoffrey Chaucer: A Selection of His Works.* New York: Odyssey, 1966.
101. Pratt, Robert A., ed. *Geoffrey Chaucer: Selections from "The Tales of Canterbury" and Short Poems.* Boston: Houghton Mifflin, 1966.

34 / Fourteenth-Century Literature

Background and General Discussion

102. Bennett, J. A. W. *Chaucer at Oxford and Cambridge.* Oxford: Clarendon Press, 1974.
103. Bowden, Muriel. *A Reader's Guide to Geoffrey Chaucer.* New York: Farrar Straus, 1964.
104. Boyd, Beverly. *Chaucer and the Medieval Book.* San Marino: Huntington Library, 1973.
105. Brewer, Derek. *Chaucer in His Time.* London: Longmans, 1973.
106. ———. *Chaucer and His World.* New York: Dodd, Mead, 1978.
107. Corsa, Helen Storm. *Chaucer, Poet of Mirth and Morality.* Notre Dame: Notre Dame University Press, 1964.
108. Gardner, John C. *The Life and Times of Chaucer.* New York: Knopf, 1977.
109. ———. *The Poetry of Chaucer.* Carbondale: Southern Illinois University Press, 1977.
110. Grose, M. W. *Chaucer.* London: Evans, 1967.
111. Halliday, Frank E. *Chaucer and His World.* London: Thames, 1969.
112. Howard, Edwin J. *Geoffrey Chaucer.* New York: Twayne, 1964.
113. Hussey, Maurice, A. C. Spearing, and James Winny. *An Introduction to Chaucer.* Cambridge: Cambridge University Press, 1965.
114. Hussey, Maurice. *Chaucer's World: A Pictorial Companion.* Cambridge: Cambridge University Press, 1967.
115. ———. *Chaucer: An Introduction.* London: Methuen, 1971.
116. Kane, George. *The Autobiographical Fallacy in Chaucer and Langland Studies.* London: University College, 1965.
117. Lawlor, John. *Chaucer.* New York: Harper, 1969.
118. Loomis, Roger S. *A Mirror of Chaucer's World.* Princeton: Princeton University Press, 1965.
119. Mehl, Dieter. *Geoffrey Chaucer: Eine Einfuhrung in seine erzahlenden Dichtungen.* Berlin: Schmidt, 1973.
120. Miller, Robert P., ed. *Chaucer: Sources and Backgrounds.* New York: Oxford University Press, 1977.
121. Myers, A. R. *London in the Age of Chaucer.* Norman: University of Oklahoma Press, 1972.

122. Norton-Smith, John. *Geoffrey Chaucer.* London: Routledge, 1974.
123. Robinson, Ian. *Chaucer and the English Tradition.* Cambridge: Cambridge University Press, 1972.
124. Wagenknecht, Edward C. *The Personality of Chaucer.* Norman: University of Oklahoma Press, 1969.
125. Wilkins, Nigel. *Music in the Age of Chaucer.* Cambridge: Brewer, 1979.
126. Williams, George. *A New View of Chaucer.* Durham: Duke University Press, 1965.
See also entries 37, 39, 41, 43, 45, 49, 52, 54, 56, 59, 67, 73.

Commentary and Criticism

127. Bartholomew, Barbara. *Fortuna and Natura: A Reading of Three Chaucer Narratives.* The Hague: Mouton, 1968. (The tales are *The Physician's Tale, The Clerk's Tale,* and *The Knight's Tale.*)
128. Boyd, Beverly. *Chaucer and the Liturgy.* Philadelphia: Dorrance, 1967.
129. Bronson, Bertrand H. *In Search of Chaucer.* Toronto: University of Toronto Press, 1960.
130. Burlin, Robert B. *Chaucerian Fiction.* Princeton: Princeton University Press, 1977.
131. David, Alfred. *The Strumpet Muse: Art and Morals in Chaucer's Poetry.* Bloomington: Indiana University Press, 1976.
132. Donaldson, E. Talbot. *Speaking of Chaucer.* London: Athlone, 1970.
133. Elbow, Peter. *Oppositions in Chaucer.* Middletown, Conn.: Wesleyan University Press, 1975.
134. Haskell, Ann S. *Essays on Chaucer's Saints.* The Hague: Mouton, 1976.
135. Huppé, Bernard F., and D. W. Robertson, Jr. *Fruyt and Chaf: Studies in Chaucer's Allegories.* Princeton: Princeton University Press, 1963.
136. Kean, Patricia. *Chaucer and the Making of English Poetry.* 2 vols. London: Routledge, 1972.
137. Knight, Stephen. *The Poetry of the "Canterbury Tales."* Sydney: Angus, 1973.

138. Morgan, Joseph J. *Chaucer and the Theme of Mutability.* The Hague: Mouton, 1969.

139. Muscatine, Charles. *Poetry and Crisis in the Age of Chaucer.* Notre Dame: University of Notre Dame Press, 1972.

140. North, J. D. "Kalenderes Enlumyned Ben They: Some Astronomical Themes in Chaucer." *RES* 20 (1969): 129–54, 257–83, 418–44.

141. Robertson, D. W., Jr. *A Preface to Chaucer: Studies in Medieval Perspectives.* Princeton: Princeton University Press, 1962.

142. Rowland, Beryl. *Blind Beasts: Chaucer's Animal World.* Kent, Ohio: Kent State University Press, 1971.

143. Schaefer, Ursula. *Höfisch-ritterliche Dichtung und sozialhistorische Realität: Literatursoziologische Studien zum Verhältnis von Adelsstruktur, Ritterideal und Dichtung bei Geoffrey Chaucer.* Frankfurt: Lang, 1977.

144. Taitt, Peter S. *Incubus and Ideal: Ecclesiastical Figures in Chaucer and Langland.* Salzburg: University of Salzburg, 1975.

145. Twycross, Meg. *The Medieval Anadyomene: A Study in Chaucer's Mythography.* Oxford: Blackwell, 1972.

146. Uhliz, Claus. *Chaucer und die Armut: Zum Prinzip der Kontextuellen Wahrheit in der "Canterbury Tales."* Wiesbaden: Steiner, 1974.

147. Wood, Chauncey. *Chaucer and the Country of the Stars: Poetic Uses of Astrological Imagery.* Princeton: Princeton University Press, 1970.

Chaucer's Influence

148. Alderson, William L., and Arnold C. Henderson. *Chaucer and Augustan Scholarship.* Berkeley: University of California Press, 1970.

149. Greaves, Margaret. *The Blazon of Honour: A Study in Renaissance Magnanimity.* London: Methuen, 1964.

150. Hawkins, Harriett. *Poetic Freedom and Poetic Truth: Chaucer, Shakespeare, Marlowe, and Milton.* Oxford: Clarendon, 1976.

151. Hieatt, A. Kent. *Chaucer, Spenser, Milton: Mythopoetic*

Continuities and Transformations. Montreal: McGill University Press, 1975.

152. Miskimin, Alice. *The Renaissance Chaucer.* New Haven: Yale University Press, 1975.

153. Thompson, Ann. *Shakespeare's Chaucer: A Study in Literary Origins.* New York: Barnes & Noble, 1978.

154. Tripp, Raymond P. J. *Beyond Canterbury: Chaucer, Humanism, and Literature.* Denver: Society for New Language Study, 1977.

Language, Prosody, Rhetoric

155. Baum, Paull F. *Chaucer's Verse.* Durham: Duke University Press, 1961.

156. Bauer, Gero. *Studien zum System und Gebrauch der "Tempora" in der Sprache Chaucers und Gowers.* Vienna: Braumuller, 1970.

157. Burnley, J. D. *Chaucer's Language and the Philosopher's Tradition.* Ipswich: Brewer, 1979.

158. Eliason, Norman. *The Language of Chaucer's Poetry: An Appraisal of the Verse, Style, and Structure.* Copenhagen: Rosenkilde, 1972.

159. Elliott, Ralph W. V. *Chaucer's English.* London: Deutsch, 1974.

160. Fifield, Merle. *Theoretical Techniques for the Analysis of Variety in Chaucer's Metrical Stress.* Muncie, Ind.: Ball State University, 1973.

161. Fisiak, Jacek. *Morphemic Structure of Chaucer's English.* University: University of Alabama Press, 1965.

162. Knight, Stephen. *Ryming Craftily: Meaning in Chaucer's Poetry.* Atlantic Highlands, N.J.: Humanities, 1973.

163. Payne, Robert O. *The Key of Remembrance: A Study of Chaucer's Poetics.* New Haven: Yale University Press, 1963.

164. Robinson, Ian. *Chaucer's Prosody: A Study in Middle English Verse Tradition.* Cambridge: Cambridge University Press, 1971.

165. Ross, Thomas W. *Chaucer's Bawdy.* New York: Dutton, 1972.
See also entry 75.

Editions, Selections, Translations

166. Halverson, John, ed. *Geoffrey Chaucer, "The Canterbury Tales."* Indianapolis: Bobbs-Merrill, 1971.
167. Howard, Donald and James Dean, eds. *"The Canterbury Tales": A Selection.* New York: New American, 1969.
168. Pratt, Robert A. *The Tales of Canterbury.* Boston: Houghton Mifflin, 1974.
169. Wright, David, trans. *The Canterbury Tales.* New York: Random House, 1965.

See also entry 26.

Commentary and Criticism

170. Craik, T. W. *The Comic Tales of Chaucer.* London: Methuen, 1964.
171. Fyler, John M. *Chaucer and Ovid.* New Haven: Yale University Press, 1979.
172. Hoffman, Richard L. *Ovid and the "Canterbury Tales."* Philadelphia: University of Pennsylvania Press, 1966.
173. Howard, Donald. *The Idea of the "Canterbury Tales."* Berkeley: University of California Press, 1976.
174. Jordan, Robert M. *Chaucer and the Shape of Creation: The Aesthetic Possibilities of Inorganic Structure.* Cambridge, Mass.: Harvard University Press, 1967.
175. Mann, Jill. *Chaucer and Medieval Estates Satire: The Literature of Social Classes and the General Prologue.* Cambridge: Cambridge University Press, 1973.
176. Owen, Charles A., Jr. *Pilgrimage and Storytelling in the "Canterbury Tales": The Dialectic of "Ernest" and "Game."* Norman: University of Oklahoma Press, 1977.
177. Ruggiers, Paul G. *The Art of the "Canterbury Tales."* Madison: University of Wisconsin Press, 1965.
178. Whittock, Trevor. *A Reading of the "Canterbury Tales."* Cambridge: Cambridge University Press, 1968.

The Fabliaux

179. Benson, Larry D., and Theodore M. Andersson. *The Literary Context of Chaucer's Fabliaux.* Indianapolis: Bobbs-Merrill, 1971.

180. Cooke, Thomas D. *The Old French and Chaucerian Fabliaux: A Study of Their Comic Climax.* Columbia: University of Missouri Press, 1978.
181. Richardson, Janette. *"Blameth Nat Me": A Study of Imagery in Chaucer's Fabliaux.* The Hague: Mouton, 1970.

The Prologue and Individual Tales

182. Bethurum, Dorothy, ed. *The Squire's Tale.* Oxford: Clarendon, 1965.
183. Blanch, Robert J., ed. *Geoffrey Chaucer, Merchant's Tale.* Columbus, Ohio: Merrill Casebooks, 1970.
184. Brooks, Harold F. *Chaucer's Pilgrims: The Artistic Order of the Portraits in the Prologue.* London: Methuen, 1962.
185. Cigman, Gloria, ed. *The Wife of Bath's Prologue and Tale and the Clerk's Prologue and Tale from the "Canterbury Tales."* London: University of London Press, 1975.
186. Havely, N. R., ed. *The Friar's Summoner's and Pardoner's Tales from the "Canterbury Tales."* New York: Holmes, 1976.
187. Hieatt, Constance B., ed. *The Miller's Tale.* New York: Odyssey, 1970.
188. Hodgson, Phyllis, ed. *The Franklin's Tale.* London: Athlone, 1960.
189. ———. *General Prologue to the "Canterbury Tales."* London: Athlone, 1969.
190. Hussey, Maurice, ed. *The Canon's Yeoman's Prologue and Tale from the "Canterbury Tales."* Cambridge: Cambridge University Press, 1965.
191. ———. *The Merchant's Prologue and Tale.* Cambridge: Cambridge University Press, 1966.
192. Kohl, Stephan. *Wissenschaft und Dichtung bei Chaucer: dargestellt hauptsächlich am Beispiel der Medizin.* Frankfurt: Akademische, 1973.
193. McCoy, Bernadette Marie, trans. *Boccaccio's "Book of Theseus": Teseida delle Nozze d'Emilia.* New York: Medieval Text Association, 1974.
194. Ridley, Florence. *The Prioress and the Critics.* Berkeley: University of California Press, 1965.

195. Spearing, A. C., ed. *The Franklin's Prologue and Tale.* London: Cambridge University Press, 1966.
196. ———. *The Knight's Tale.* London: Cambridge University Press, 1966.
197. Thurston, Paul T. *Artistic Ambivalence in Chaucer's "Knight's Tale."* Gainesville: University of Florida Press, 1968.
198. Ussery, Huling F. *Chaucer's Physician: Medicine and Literature in Fourteenth-Century England.* New Orleans: Tulane University Press, 1971.
199. Winny, James, ed. *The Clerk's Prologue and Tale.* London: Cambridge University Press, 1966.
200. ———. *The Miller's Prologue and Tale from the "Canterbury Tales."* Cambridge: Cambridge University Press, 1971.
201. ———. *The Prioress's Prologue and Tale.* Cambridge: Cambridge University Press, 1975.
202. ———. *The Wife of Bath's Prologue and Tale.* Cambridge: Cambridge University Press, 1965.
See also entry 127.

TROILUS AND CRISEYDE

Editions and Translations

203. Cook, Daniel S., ed. *Troilus and Criseyde.* Anchor Books. Garden City: Doubleday, 1966.
204. Donohue, James J., trans. *"Troilus and Criseyde": Five Books in Present-Day English.* Dubuque: Loras College, 1975.
205. Howard, Donald, and James Dean, eds. *Troilus and Criseyde.* New York: New American, 1976.
See also entry 27.

Commentary and Criticism

206. Gill, Sister Ann Barbara. *Paradoxical Patterns in Chaucer's "Troilus": An Explanation of the Palinode.* Washington, D.C.: Catholic University of America, 1960.
207. Gordon, Ida L. *The Double Sorrow of Troilus: A Study of*

Ambiguities in "Troilus and Criseyde." Oxford: Clarendon Press, 1970.

208. Kaminsky, Alice R. *Chaucer's "Troilus and Criseyde" and the Critics.* Athens: Ohio University Press, 1980.

209. McAlpine, Monica E. *The Genre of "Troilus and Criseyde."* Ithaca: Cornell University Press, 1978.

210. Neumann, Fritz-Wilhelm. *Symbole der Initiation im "Troilus."* Nonn: Bouvier, 1979.

211. Provost, William. *The Structure of Chaucer's "Troilus and Criseyde."* Copenhagen: Rosenkilde, 1974.

212. Rowe, Donald. *O Love, O Charite!: Contraries Harmonized in Chaucer's "Troilus."* Carbondale: Southern Illinois University Press, 1976.

213. Steadman, John M. *Disembodied Laughter: "Troilus" and the Apotheosis Tradition: A Re-examination of Narrative and Thematic Contexts.* Berkeley: University of California Press, 1972.

See also entry 60.

Other Works

214. Bennett, J. A. W. *Chaucer's Book of Fame: An Exposition of the "House of Fame."* Oxford: Clarendon, 1968.

215. Brewer, Derek S., ed. *The Parlement of Foulys.* London: Nelson, 1960.

216. Clemen, Wolfgang. *Chaucer's Early Poetry.* Translated by C. A. M. Sym. New York: Barnes & Noble, 1964.

217. Delany, Sheila. *Chaucer's "House of Fame": The Poetics of Skeptical Fideism.* Chicago: University of Chicago Press, 1972.

218. Donohue, James J., trans. *Chaucer's Lesser Poems Complete in Present-Day English.* Dubuque: Loras College, 1974.

219. Frank, Robert W., Jr. *Chaucer and the "Legend of Good Women."* Cambridge, Mass.: Harvard University Press, 1972.

220. Knedlik, Will Roger. "Chaucer's 'Book of the Duchess': A Bibliographical Compendium of the First 600 Years." Ph.D. diss., University of Washington, 1978. (Annotated bibliography through 1969.)

221. Koonce, B. G. *Chaucer and the Tradition of Fame.* Princeton: Princeton University Press, 1966.
222. Sutherland, Ronald, ed. *The "Romaunt of the Rose": A Parallel-text Edition.* Oxford: Blackwell, 1968.
223. Wimsatt, James. *Chaucer and the French Love Poets: The Literary Background of the "Book of the Duchess."* Chapel Hill: University of North Carolina Press, 1968.
224. Winny, James. *Chaucer's Dream Poems.* London: Chatto, 1973.

WORKS OF THE GAWAIN POET

Concordance, Editions, and Translations

225. Anderson, J. J., ed. *Patience.* Manchester: Manchester University Press, 1969.
226. ———. *Cleanness.* Manchester: Manchester University Press, 1977.
227. Andrew, Malcolm, and Ronald Waldron, eds. *The Poems of the "Pearl" Manuscript.* London: Arnold, 1978.
228. Barron, William, ed. and trans. *Sir Gawain and the Green Knight.* Manchester: Manchester University Press, 1974.
229. Borroff, Marie, trans. *"Sir Gawain and the Green Knight": A New Verse Translation.* New York: Norton, 1967.
230. Burrow, John A., ed. *Sir Gawain and the Green Knight.* New York: Penguin Books, 1972. (Modernized)
231. de Ford, Sara, ed. and trans. *The Pearl.* New York: Appleton, 1967.
232. Gardner, John, trans. *The Complete Works of the "Gawain" Poet.* Chicago: University of Chicago Press, 1965.
233. Hieatt, Constance, trans. *"Sir Gawain and the Green Knight" Retold.* Illustrated by Walter Lorraine. New York: Crowell, 1967.
234. Kottler, Barnet, and Alan M. Markman. *A Concordance to Five Middle English Poems.* Pittsburgh: University of Pittsburgh Press, 1966. (The *Gawain* poems and *St. Erkenwald.*)
235. Moorman, Charles, ed. *The Works of the "Gawain" Poet.* Jackson: University Press of Mississippi, 1976.

236. Silverstein, Theodore, trans. *"Sir Gawain and the Green Knight": A Comedy for Christmas.* Chicago: University of Chicago Press, 1974.

237. Tolkien, J. R. R., and E. V. Gordon, eds. *Sir Gawain and the Green Knight.* 2d ed., rev. by Norman Davis. Oxford: Clarendon, 1967.

238. Tolkien, J. R. R., trans. *"Sir Gawain and the Green Knight" and "Sir Orfeo."* London: Allen & Unwin, 1975.

239. Waldron, R. A., ed. *Sir Gawain and the Green Knight.* London: Arnold, 1970.

240. Williams, Margaret, trans. *The "Pearl" Poet: His Complete Works.* New York: Random House, 1967.

Commentary and Criticism

241. Benson, Larry D. *Art and Tradition in "Sir Gawain and the Green Knight."* New Brunswick: Rutgers University Press, 1965.

242. Bishop, Ian. *"Pearl" in Its Setting.* Oxford: Blackwell, 1968.

243. Borroff, Marie. *"Sir Gawain and the Green Knight": A Stylistic and Metrical Study.* New Haven: Yale University Press, 1962.

244. Brewer, Elisabeth. *From Cuchulain to Gawain.* Cambridge: Brewer, 1973.

245. Burrow, J. A. *A Reading of "Sir Gawain and the Green Knight."* London: Routledge, 1965.

246. Davenport, W. A. *The Art of the Gawain-Poet.* London: Athlone, 1978.

247. Kean, P. M. *"The Pearl": An Interpretation.* New York: Barnes & Noble, 1967.

248. Kjellmer, Göran. *Did the "Pearl Poet" Write the "Pearl"?* Göteborg: University of Göteborg, 1975.

249. Moorman, Charles. *The Pearl-Poet.* New York: Twayne, 1968.

250. Morse, Charlotte. *The Pattern of Judgment in the "Queste" and "Cleanness."* Columbia: University of Missouri Press, 1978.

251. Schnyder, Hans. *"Sir Gawain and the Green Knight": An Essay in Interpretation.* Bern: Francke, 1962.

252. Spearing, A. C. *The Gawain-Poet: A Critical Study.* Cambridge: Cambridge University Press, 1970.
253. Wilson, Edward. *The Gawain Poet.* Leiden: Brill, 1976.
See also entries 60, 61, 62, 72.

PIERS PLOWMAN

Bibliography and Editions

254. Bennett, J. A. W., ed. *"Piers Plowman": The Prologue and Passus I–VII of the B Text as found in Bodleian MS. Laud Misc. 581.* Oxford: Clarendon, 1972.
255. Brook, Stella, ed. *Piers Plowman.* New York: Barnes & Noble, 1975. (Selections from Laud Misc. 581.)
256. Colaianne, A. J. *"Piers Plowman": An Annotated Bibliography of Editions and Criticism, 1550–1977.* New York: Garland, 1978.
257. Hussey, S. S., ed. *Piers Plowman.* London: Methuen, 1969.
258. Kane, George, ed. *"Piers Plowman": The A Version.* London: Athlone, 1960.
259. Kane, George, and E. Talbot Donaldson, eds. *"Piers Plowman": The B Version.* London: Athlone, 1975.
260. Salter, Elizabeth, and Derek Pearsall, eds. *Piers Plowman.* London: Arnold, 1967. (Selections from C Text.)
261. Schmidt, A. V. C., ed. *"Piers Plowman": The B Version.* London: Dent, 1980. (Everyman)
262. Williams, Margaret, trans. *"Piers Plowman" by William Langland.* New York: Random House, 1971.

Commentary and Criticism

263. Aers, David. *"Piers Plowman" and Christian Allegory.* London: Arnold, 1975.
264. Ames, Ruth. *The Fulfillment of the Scriptures, Abraham, Moses, and Piers.* Evanston: Northwestern University Press, 1970.
265. Anderson, Judith H. *The Growth of a Personal Voice: "Piers Plowman" and "The Faerie Queene."* New Haven: Yale University Press, 1976.
266. Bloomfield, Morton. *"Piers Plowman" as a Fourteenth-*

Century Apocalypse. New Brunswick: Rutgers University Press, 1961.

267. Bruneder, Hans. *Personifikation und Symbol in William Langland's "Piers Plowman."* Vienna: Bruneder, 1963.

268. Cali, Pietro. *Allegory and Vision in Dante and Langland.* Cork: Cork University Press, 1971.

269. Carruthers, Mary. *The Search for St. Truth: A Study of Meaning in "Piers Plowman."* Evanston: Northwestern University Press, 1973.

270. Coghill, Nevill. *Langland: "Piers Plowman."* New York: Longmans, 1965.

271. Fowler, David C. *"Piers Plowman": Literary Relations of the A and B Texts.* Seattle: University of Washington Press, 1961.

272. Kane, George. *The Autobiographical Fallacy in Chaucer and Langland Studies.* London: University College, 1965.

273. ———. *"Piers Plowman": The Evidence for Authorship.* London: Athlone, 1965.

274. Kirk, Elizabeth. *The Dream Thought of "Piers Plowman."* New Haven: Yale University Press, 1972.

275. Krochalis, Jeanne, and Edward Peters, eds. and trans. *The World of "Piers Plowman."* Philadelphia: University of Pennsylvania Press, 1975.

276. Lawlor, John. *"Piers Plowman": An Essay in Criticism.* London: Arnold, 1962.

277. Martin, Priscilla. *"Piers Plowman": The Field and the Tower.* London: Macmillan, 1979.

278. Murtaugh, Daniel Maher. *"Piers Plowman" and the Image of God.* Gainesville: University of Florida Press, 1978.

279. Ryan, William M. *William Langland.* New York: Twayne, 1968.

280. Salter, Elizabeth. *"Piers Plowman": An Introduction.* Cambridge, Mass.: Harvard University Press, 1962.

281. Smith, Ben H., Jr. *The Traditional Imagery of Charity in "Piers Plowman."* The Hague: Mouton, 1966.

282. Vasta, Edward. *The Spiritual Basis of "Piers Plowman."* The Hague: Mouton, 1965.

283. Yunck, John. *The Lineage of Lady Mede.* Notre Dame: Notre Dame University Press, 1963.

See also entries 60, 65.

JOHN GOWER

Editions and Translations

284. Bennett, J. A. W., ed. *Selections from John Gower.* Oxford: Clarendon, 1968.
285. Peck, Russell, ed. *Confessio Amantis.* New York: Holt, 1968. (Rinehart edition, selections based on Macaulay.)
286. Stockton, Eric W., trans. *The Major Latin Works of John Gower: "The Voice of One Crying in the Wilderness" and "The Tripartite Chronicle."* Seattle: University of Washington Press, 1962.
287. Tiller, Terence, trans. *Confessio Amantis.* New York: Penguin, 1963. ("The Lover's Shift.")

Commentary and Criticism

288. Fisher, John H. *John Gower: Moral Philosopher and Friend of Chaucer.* New York: New York University Press, 1964.
289. Gallacher, Patrick J. *Love, the Word, and Mercury: A Reading of John Gower's "Confessio Amantis."* Albuquerque: University of New Mexico Press, 1975.
290. Peck, Russell. *Kingship and Common Profit in Gower's "Confessio Amantis."* Carbondale: Southern Illinois University Press, 1978.
291. Weber, Edwart. *John Gower: Dichter Einer Ethischpolitischen Reformation.* Bad Homburg, 1965.
292. ———. *John Gower: Zur literarischen Form seiner Dichtung.* Bad Homburg, 1966.

See also entries 61, 156.

MINOR AUTHORS AND WORKS

293. Bestul, Thomas H. *Satire and Allegory in "Wynnere and Wastoure."* Lincoln: University of Nebraska Press, 1974.
294. Boyd, Beverly, ed. *The Middle English Miracles of the Virgin.* San Marino: Huntington Library, 1964.
295. Manzalaoui, M. A., ed. *"Secretum Secretorum": Nine English Versions.* Text EETS 276, 1977.
296. Miskimin, Alice, ed. *"Susannah": An Alliterative Poem*

of the Fourteenth Century. New Haven: Yale University Press, 1969.

297. Offord, M. Y., ed. *The Parlement of the Three Ages.* EETS 246, 1959.

298. Pearsall, Derek A., ed. *"The Floure and the Leafe" and "The Assembly of Ladies."* London: Nelson, 1962.

299. Scattergood, V., ed. *The Works of Sir John Clanvowe.* Cambridge: Brewer, 1975.

300. Seymour, M. C., ed. *Mandeville's Travels.* Oxford: Clarendon, 1967. (Based on British Library MS. Cotton Titus C.xvi; this is now the standard edition.)

MYSTICAL WRITERS

Editions, Translations, Bibliography

301. Colledge, Eric, ed. *The Mediaeval Mystics of England.* New York: Scribner's, 1961. (Selections from St. Aelred of Rievaulx, St. Edmund Rich, Rolle, *Book of Privy Counsel,* Hilton, Julian of Norwich, Margery Kempe.)

302. Kuriyagawa, Fumio, ed. *Walter Hilton's "Eight Chapters on Perfection."* Tokyo: Keio Institute, 1967. (Replaces his 1958 edition.)

303. Moon, Helen M. *"ðe Lyfe of Soule": An Edition with Commentary.* Salzburg: University of Salzburg, Institute für englische Sprache & Literatur, 1978.

304. Sawyer, Michael E., comp. *A Bibliographical Index of Five English Mystics.* Pittsburgh: Barbour Library, Pittsburgh Theological Seminary, 1978. (Annotated.)

305. Walters, Clifton, trans. *The Cloud of Unknowing.* New York: Penguin, 1961.

306. ———. *Julian of Norwich: Revelations of Divine Love.* New York: Penguin, 1966.

Commentary

307. Knowles, David. *The English Mystical Tradition.* London: Burns & Oates, 1961.

308. Knowlton, Sister Mary A. *The Influence of Richard Rolle and of Julian of Norwich on Middle English Lyrics.* The Hague: Mouton, 1973.

309. Madigan, Mary F. *The "Passio Domini" Theme in the Works of Richard Rolle.* Salzburg: University of Salzburg, Institut für englische Sprache & Literatur, 1978.
310. Milosh, Joseph E. *"The Scale of Perfection" and the English Mystical Tradition.* Madison: University of Wisconsin Press, 1966.
311. Stone, R. K. *Middle English Prose Style: Margery Kempe and Julian of Norwich.* The Hague: Mouton, 1970.
312. Tuma, George Wood. *The Fourteenth-Century English Mystics: A Comparative Analysis.* 2 vols. Salzburg: University of Salzburg, Institut für englische Sprache & Literatur, 1977.

SERMONS AND MANUALS OF RELIGIOUS INSTRUCTION

313. Kristensson, Gillis, ed. *John Mirk's "Instructions for Parish Priests": Edited from MS. Cotton Claudius A.ii and Six Other Manuscripts.* Lund: Gleerup, 1974.

SOUTH ENGLISH LEGENDARY

314. Görlach, Manfred. *The South English Legendary, Gilte Legende and Golden Legend.* Braunschweig: Technische Universität Carolo-Wilhelmina, Institut für Anglistik und Amerikanistik, 1972.
315. ———. *The Textual Tradition of the South English Legendary.* Leeds: Leeds University School of English, 1974.
316. Pickering, O. S., ed. *The South English Nativity of Mary and Christ.* Heidelberg: Winter, 1975. (Edited from British Library MS. Stowe 949.)

NORTHERN HOMILY CYCLE

317. Nevanlinna, Saara, ed. *The Northern Homily Cycle: The Expanded Version in MSS. Harley 4196 and Cotton Tiberius E.vii.ii, from Septuagesima to the Fifth Sunday After Trinity.* Helsinki: Société Néophilologique, 1973.

JOHN WYCLIF

318. Block, Edward A. *John Wyclif, Radical Dissenter.* San Diego: San Diego College Press, 1962.
319. Daly, L. J., S. J. *The Political Theory of John Wyclif.* Chicago: Loyola University Press, 1962.
320. Fristedt, Sven L. *The Wycliffe Bible: Part III, Relationships of Trevisa and the Spanish Medieval Bibles.* Stockholm: Almqvist, 1973.

See also entry 271.

DRAMA

Bibliographies and Finding Lists

321. Penninger, Frieda Elaine. *English Drama to 1660 (Excluding Shakespeare): A Guide to Information Sources.* Detroit: Gale, 1976. (Annotated bibliography.)
322. Davidson, Clifford. *Drama and Art: An Introduction to the Use of Evidence from the Visual Arts for the Study of Early Drama.* Kalamazoo, Mich.: Medieval Institute, 1977.
323. Davidson, Clifford, and David E. O'Connor. *York Art: A Subject List of Extant and Lost Art Including Items Relevant to Early Drama.* Kalamazoo, Mich.: Medieval Institute, 1978.

Editions

324. Bevington, David, ed. *Medieval Drama.* Boston: Houghton-Mifflin, 1975.
325. Davies, Reginald T., ed. *The Corpus Christi Play of the English Middle Ages.* London: Faber, 1972. (Selections from *Ludus Coventriae* and all extant versions of the play of *Abraham and Isaac.*)
326. Davis, Norman, ed. *Non-Cycle Plays and Fragments.* EETS Supplementary Texts 1, 1970.
327. Franklin, Alexander, ed. *Seven Miracle Plays.* Oxford:

Oxford University Press, 1963. *(Cain, Noah's Flood, Abraham and Isaac, The Shepherds, The Three Kings, Herod, and Adam and Eve.)*

328. Lumiansky, Robert M., and David Mills, eds. *The Chester Mystery Cycle.* EETS Supplementary Texts 3, 1974.
329. Rose, Martial, ed. *The Wakefield Mystery Plays.* London: Evans, 1961.
330. Thomas, R. George, ed. *Ten Miracle Plays.* London: Arnold, 1966.

See also entries 28, 29, 30, 31, 32.

History, Commentary, and Criticism

331. Anderson, M. D. *Drama and Imagery in English Medieval Churches.* Cambridge: Cambridge University Press, 1963.
332. Bevington, David. *From Mankind to Marlowe.* Cambridge, Mass.: Harvard University Press, 1962.
333. Clarke, Sidney W. *The Miracle Play in England: An Account of the Early Religious Drama.* New York: Haskell House, 1964.
334. Collier, Richard. *Poetry and Drama in the York Corpus Christi Play.* Hamden, Conn.: Archon, 1978.
335. Diller, Hans-Jürgen. *Redeformen des englischen Minsterienspiels.* Munich: Fink, 1973.
336. Forrester, Jean. *Wakefield Mystery Plays and the Burgess Court Records: A New Discovery.* Ossett, Yorkshire: H. Speak, 1974.
337. Gardner, John. *The Construction of the Wakefield Cycle.* Carbondale: Southern Illinois University Press, 1974.
338. Halevy, Miriam. *The Evolution of Medieval Drama: From the Life to Come to Recorded Time.* London: Jewish Literary Publishers, 1974.
339. Hardison, O. B. *Christian Rite and Christian Drama in the Middle Ages: Essays in the Origins and Early History of the Modern Drama.* Baltimore: Johns Hopkins University Press, 1965.
340. Kahrl, Stanley. *Traditions of Medieval Drama.* London: Hutchinson, 1974.

341. Kinghorn, A. M. *Literature in Perspective: Medieval Drama.* London: Evans, 1968.
342. Kolve, V. A. *The Play Called Corpus Christi.* Stanford: Stanford University Press, 1966.
343. Fifield, Merle. *The Rhetoric of Free Will.* Leeds: University of Leeds, School of English, 1974.
344. Meyers, Walter E. *A Figure Given: Typology in the Wakefield Plays.* Pittsburgh: Duquesne University Press, 1970.
345. Miyajima, Sumiko. *The Theatre of Man: Dramatic Technique and Stagecraft in the English Medieval Moral Plays.* Clevedon, Avon: Clevedon Printing, 1977.
346. Nelson, Alan H. *The Medieval Stage: Corpus Christi Pageants and Plays.* Chicago: University of Chicago Press, 1974.
347. Prosser, Eleanor A. *Drama and Religion in English Mystery Plays: A Re-evaluation.* Stanford: Stanford University Press, 1961.
348. Williams, Arnold. *The Drama of Medieval England.* East Lansing: Michigan State University Press, 1961.
349. Woolf, Rosemary. *The English Mystery Plays.* Berkeley: University of California Press, 1973.

ROMANCES

Editions and Anthologies

350. Benson, Larry, ed. *King Arthur's Death: The Middle English Stanzaic "Morte Arthur" and Alliterative "Morte Arthure."* Indianapolis: Bobbs-Merrill, 1974.
351. Finlayson, John, ed. *Morte Arthure.* London: Arnold, 1967.
352. Hissiger, P. F., ed. *"Le Morte Arthur": A Critical Edition.* The Hague: Mouton, 1975.
353. Krishna, Valeria S., ed. *The Alliterative "Morte Arthure": A Critical Edition.* New York: Franklin, 1976.
354. Hanna, Ralph, ed. *"The Awntyrs off Arthure at the Terne Wathelyn": An Edition Based on the Bodleian MS. Douce 324.* Manchester: Manchester University Press, 1974.
355. Friedman, Albert B., and Norman T. Harrington, eds. *Ywain and Gawain.* EETS 254, 1964.

356. Hall, Louis B., trans. *The Knightly Tales of Sir Gawain.* Chicago: Nelson Hall, 1976.

357. Bliss, A. J., ed. *Sir Launfal.* London: Nelson, 1960.

358. ———. *Sir Orfeo.* 2d ed. Oxford: Clarendon, 1966.

359. Broughton, Bradford B., trans. *"Richard the Lion-Hearted" and Other Medieval English Romances.* New York: Dutton, 1966.

360. Mills, Maldwyn, ed. *Lybeaus Desconus.* EETS 261, 1969.

361. ———. *Six Middle English Romances.* London: Dent, 1973.

362. Gibbs, A. C., ed. *Middle English Romances.* London: Arnold, 1966.

363. Rumble, Thomas C., ed. *The Breton Lays in Middle English.* Detroit: Wayne State University Press, 1965.

364. Sands, Donald B., ed. *Middle English Verse Romances.* New York: Holt, 1966.

365. Stevick, Robert D., ed. *Five Middle English Narratives.* Indianapolis: Bobbs-Merrill, 1967.

See also entries 22, 23, 24.

Commentaries

366. Broughton, Bradford. *The Legends of King Richard I, Coeur de Lion: A Study of Sources and Variations to the Year 1600.* The Hague: Mouton, 1966.

367. Matthews, William. *The Tragedy of Arthur.* Berkeley: University of California Press, 1960.

368. Mehl, Dieter. *The Middle English Romances of the Thirteenth and Fourteenth Centuries.* London: Routledge, 1969.

369. Richmond, Velma. *The Popularity of the Middle English Romance.* Bowling Green, Ohio: Bowling Green University, Popular Press, 1975.

370. Schelp, Hanspeter. *Exemplarische Romanzen im Mittelenglischen.* Göttingen: Vandenhoeck, 1967.

371. Stevens, John. *Medieval Romance: Themes and Approaches.* New York: Norton, 1973.

372. Wittig, Susan. *Stylistic and Narrative Structures in the Middle English Romances.* Austin: University of Texas Press, 1978.

LYRICS

Editions

373. Davies, R. T., ed. and trans. *Medieval English Lyrics: A Critical Anthology.* Evanston: Northwestern University Press, 1964.
374. Gray, Douglas, ed. *A Selection of Religious Lyrics.* Oxford: Clarendon, 1975.
375. Luria, Maxwell, and Richard L. Hoffman, eds. *Middle English Lyrics: Authoritative Texts; Critical and Historical Background; Perspectives on Six Poems.* New York: Norton, 1975.
376. Silverstein, Theodore, ed. *English Lyrics Before 1500.* Evanston: Northwestern University Press, 1971.
377. Stemmler, Theodore, ed. *Medieval English Love Lyrics.* Tübingen: Niemeyer, 1970.
378. Stevick, Robert D., ed. *One Hundred Middle English Lyrics.* Indianapolis: Bobbs-Merrill, 1964.

See also entries 25, 306.

Commentary and Criticism

379. Goldin, Frederick. *The Mirror of Narcissus in the Courtly Love Lyric.* Ithaca: Cornell University Press, 1967.
380. Gray, Douglas. *Themes and Images in the Medieval English Religious Lyric.* London: Routledge, 1972.
381. Jeffrey, David L. *The Early English Lyric and Franciscan Spirituality.* Lincoln: University of Nebraska Press, 1975.
382. Manning, Stephen. *Wisdom and Number: Toward a Critical Appraisal of the Middle English Religious Lyric.* Lincoln: University of Nebraska Press, 1962.
383. Oliver, Raymond. *Poems without Names: The English Lyric 1200–1500.* Berkeley: University of California Press, 1970.
384. Reiss, Edmund. *The Art of the Middle English Lyric: Essays in Criticism.* Athens: University of Georgia Press, 1972.

385. Weber, Sarah A. *Theology and Poetry in the Middle English Lyric: A Study of Sacred History and Aesthetic Form.* Columbus: Ohio State University Press, 1969.
386. Woolf, Rosemary. *The English Religious Lyric in the Middle Ages.* Oxford: Clarendon, 1968.

FRENCH LITERATURE

Alan E. Knight*

The fourteenth century has always been the *parent pauvre* of French literary studies. Boasting neither a Chaucer nor a Petrarch, it has traditionally been viewed by French historians of literature as an age of embarrassing sterility. Indeed, anyone seeking reasons to condemn the artificial periodization of the past need look no farther than our stereotyped views of the fourteenth century in France. At the end of the last century, when Gustave Lanson wrote his widely used history of French literature, the fourteenth century was perceived as a period of winter desolation between the fruitfulness of the high Middle Ages and the renewal of the Renaissance. Lanson, for whom the advent of the Valois dynasty in 1328 marked the end of the Middle Ages, describes it thus: "Le XIVe et le XVe siècle forment entre le moyen âge et la Renaissance une longue époque de transition, pendant laquelle tout l'édifice intellectuel et social du moyen âge tombe lentement, tristement en ruines." And though the seeds of the Renaissance may be scattered here and there, "le XVe siècle se clôt, en laissant l'impression d'un monde qui finit, d'un avortement irrémédiable et désastreux." The literature of the period, according to Lanson, shares the same fate. "Elle se dissout ou se dessèche; l'âme et la sève s'en reti-

---

***Alan E. Knight** is Associate Professor of French at the Pennsylvania State University. He has worked principally in the history and criticism of medieval drama, particularly on various aspects of the medieval farce. A recent study, *Aspects of Genre in Late Medieval French Drama*, is scheduled for publication in the near future.

55

rent. Ce n'est que bois mort ou végétation stérile." Finally, shifting metaphors, he sees the fourteenth and fifteenth centuries as nothing but "un trou entre les richesses du moyen âge et les splendeurs de la Renaissance."[1]

A generation later Henri Chamard, feeling this almost universal disdain of the fourteenth century to be unwarranted, compared the period to a valley between two impressive peaks.[2] This metaphor is still somewhat condescending, since it invites us to place ourselves on the mountain tops and, like Montesquieu's fortunate Troglodytes, gaze impassively on the disasters below. Yet there is less open hostility and undisguised revulsion than exhibited by Lanson.

Such attitudes die hard, however, and one finds as late as 1959 that the *Guide de la littérature française du Moyen Age* (3) designates the fourteenth century as a "siècle d'infortune et de décadence." In such a fetid critical atmosphere one can well understand that Grace Frank's essay on fourteenth-century French literature (11) came as a breath of fresh air on the very threshold of our period of bibliographic enquiry. Published in 1960 in a collection of essays entitled *The Forward Movement of the Fourteenth Century*, the essay reappraises the literary production of France in that "calamitous fourteenth century," to use Barbara Tuchman's phrase (14). Frank sees the century, not as a disaster, but as a turning point—a period that witnessed the rise of "citizen authors" and a literature that exhibits "an interested awareness of the common man and his problems" (11, p. 63). She finds the latter trait particularly in the drama. Yet even Grace Frank was unable to break completely free of so heavy a critical tra-

---

1. Gustave Lanson and Paul Tuffrau, *Histoire de la littérature française* (Paris: Hachette, 1955), pp. 141–45.

2. Henri Chamard, *Les Origines de la poésie française de la Renaissance* (Paris: E. de Boccard, 1920), p. 43.

dition. Referring to the prolonged interest in old epics and romances, she says that "the patina of the past remained, a kind of rust that failed to cover a rotting core" (11, p. 70). As we review the works of the past twenty years dealing with the fourteenth century, we shall see the beginning of a significant shift of attitude toward this period in France. Indeed, the more we learn about the fourteenth century, the more we realize that what was perceived as a "rotting core" was only a distortion in the lens of our own understanding.

BIBLIOGRAPHIES

There is no general bibliography of the fourteenth century alone, and the medieval bibliographies of Robert Bossuat and Urban T. Holmes[3] have not been updated since Charles A. Knudson and Jean Misrahi (2) made their bibliographic survey of medieval French literature in the early 1960s. The best sources of bibliographic information for the period are the standard annual bibliographies such as the *MLA International Bibliography* (4), Otto Klapp's *Bibliographie der französischen Literaturwissenschaft* (1), *The Year's Work in Modern Language Studies* (7), and René Rancoeur's *Bibliographie de la littérature française* (5). Among more specialized bibliographies is Brian Woledge's supplement to his *Bibliographie des romans et nouvelles en prose française antérieurs à 1500* (6), which updates the entries to 1973.

GENERAL STUDIES

There are numerous general works on medieval literature that touch upon the fourteenth century or that throw

---

3. Robert Bossuat, *Manuel bibliographique de la littérature française médiévale* (Melun: Librairie d'Argences, 1951), supplements published in 1955 and 1961; David C. Cabeen, ed., *A Critical Bibliography of French Literature*, vol. 1, *The Medieval Period*, edited by Urban T. Holmes, 2d ed. (Syracuse: Syracuse University Press, 1952).

light on some of its literary aspects. From among these I have selected three studies for mention because they are particularly important in providing contexts for understanding the literature of the fourteenth century. The first is Paul Zumthor's *Essai de poétique médiévale* (15), a monumental work providing a theoretical background for all of medieval French literature. Writing from the perspective of the newer critics, Zumthor brings into high relief the formalist and rhetorical underpinnings of medieval literature. Ironically, one of the most important effects of this type of criticism is that we can now see originality in works that were previously condemned for lacking literary value. In addition, we have become more sensitive to the originality even of translations and adaptations.

The second general work is Douglas Kelly's *Medieval Imagination: Rhetoric and the Poetry of Courtly Love* (12), an important study that defines the concept and function of the imagination in medieval literature. Kelly examines the "tendency of romance to move from history towards Imaginary dream worlds, replacing historical veracity with allegorical truth" (12, p. 24). This will become an important characteristic of fourteenth-century literary works. Moreover, as we come to understand the role of rhetoric in medieval writing, we see that "the formality and conventionality of the literature are not marks against it" (12, p. xiii). Kelly considers many fourteenth-century works, pointing out, for example, that "Machaut is a cornerstone in the adaptation of Imagination to courtly literature" (12, p. 96).

The third general work is Jean Alter's *Les Origines de la satire anti-bourgeoise en France* (8), the medieval section of which provides ample treatment of the fourteenth century. Alter delineates two clearly defined periods in the development of the bourgeoisie. In the twelfth and thirteenth centuries, the bourgeoisie established itself as a social presence, and in the fourteenth and fifteenth centuries, it made a political consolidation of its economic advantages. This study provides an essential background to the many satirical works of the fourteenth century and makes us particularly aware of how literature reflects political, economic, and moral conditions.

Among the several histories of medieval French literature that have appeared in the last twenty years, one is particularly noteworthy: Daniel Poirion's study of the fourteenth and fifteenth centuries (13) published in the *Littérature française* series. Poirion, more than anyone else, is responsible for rehabilitating the literature of the late Middle Ages by teaching us how to read it. In his literary history, he shows how the notion of decline or waning has been inappropriately applied to the late Middle Ages. He demonstrates that the shift in mentality that characterizes the fourteenth century should in no sense be equated with a cultural debasement. He even calls into question the very idea of a *middle* age as denying an identity to an entire epoch. The present essay is, in part, an attempt to assess the progress made in addressing some of the problems of attitude toward the fourteenth century that Poirion has articulated.

EPIC

As we consider the various genres of fourteenth-century literature, it is important to bear in mind that the thirteenth-century genres of epic and romance never lost their popularity. In fact, they were read in even greater numbers after the introduction of printing in the fifteenth century. Jean Miquet, in an article entitled "A propos de la fixité thématique de l'épopée aux XIVe et XVe siècles" (27), shows that the conventional themes of honor and heroism persist in the epic but that there is no admixture of the new. Fourteenth-century epics do not reflect the radical changes in warfare, feudalism, religion, and other institutions that were so prominent a part of the real world.

Miquet sees the epic world as an immutable, archaic domain, where the old ideals of feudal and religious service remained a reality. There have been several new editions of fourteenth-century epics. Robert Cook edited the *Bâtard de Bouillon* (17), and he and Larry Crist edited *Le Deuxième Cycle de la croisade* (18). William W. Kibler, Jean-Louis Picherit, and Thelma S. Fenster undertook the ambitious project of editing *Lion de Bourges* (24), an epic poem of more than thirty-four thousand lines. Keith Sinclair edited *Tristan de Nanteuil* (29), a mid-fourteenth-century epic from Hainaut. David Dougherty and E. B. Barnes edited a version of the *Geste de Monglane* (21). Giuseppe Di Stefano (20), in an attempt to correct one line of this last edition, made a study of epic versification in middle French. *Baudouin de Sebourc* has received some attention recently. William Kibler, in "The Unity of *Baudouin de Sebourc*" (23), claims that the work was written by one poet rather than two as had previously been thought. Robert Cook (16) provides a detailed description of the two manuscripts of this work in the Bibliothèque Nationale. Jean-Louis Picherit (28) examines the "merveilleux chrétien" of *Lion de Bourges* in the context of the mentality of the fourteenth century. The north Italian-French epic, *L'Entrée d'Espagne*, has also attracted a certain amount of critical attention. Alberto Limentani, in an article entitled "L'Art de la comparaison dans *L'Entrée d'Espagne*" (25), suggests that the author, who was an Italian from Padua, was influenced by Dante. The author's use of simile is adduced as evidence. Nancy Cromey, in a study of the same work entitled "Roland as 'Baron Révolté' " (19), states that the north Italian public of the fourteenth century may have been less interested in feudal conflict than in the balance of power between the citizens and their leaders. Finally, the epic figure, Ogier le Danois, has been the object of studies by André Goosse (22) and François Suard (30).

ROMANCE

Even more popular than the epic in the fourteenth century was the romance, which was also a continuation of
a thirteenth-century genre. The longest and most intricate of the fourteenth-century romances was the *Roman
de Perceforest*, which has received the most critical attention in the last few years. This is indeed a welcome development in the light of Poirion's claim that "il faut lire
Perceforest pour comprendre Froissart et les autres chro-
niqueurs de l'époque" (13, p. 15). Louis-Fernand Flutre
(36, 37) concluded his long series of articles summarizing
the romance and also provided us with a compilation of
proverbs from the work. Jane Taylor (46–48) recently completed an edition of the first part of *Perceforest*, as well
as an article on "Aroes the Enchanter" and another on
"Reason and Faith in the *Roman de Perceforest*." The
fourteenth-century Alexander romances have also been
objects of study. David J. A. Ross compiled *Alexander
Historiatus: A Guide to Medieval Illustrated Alexander
Literature* (45), which includes several important versions belonging to the fourteenth century. André Giacchetti analyzes one of these romance heroes in "Le
Personnage d'Alexandre dans *Les Voeux du paon*" (38). He
finds in this early fourteenth-century romance, previously thought to lack unity, both a gradual growth in the
character of Alexander and a literary aesthetic that set
the tone of narrative genres for the rest of the century.
The hero becomes a *miroir* or moral example both for the
other characters of the romance and for the readers or
listeners. Richard Carey (32, 33) completed new editions
of the two sequels to this work of Jacques de Longuyon:
first *Le Restor du paon* by Jean Brisbare and then *Le Parfait du paon* by Jean de La Motte. Enid Donkin (35) studies the borrowings of Jean Brisbare from the work of his
predecessor. There has been relatively little work done on

the important romance of *Bérinus*. Douglas Kelly, in an illuminating study of Fortune in *Bérinus* (40), warns that "our understanding of medieval romance . . . is jeopardized without more serious detailed study of that great mass of adventure romances that sprang up around Chrétien and continued to thrive for several centuries after him" (40, p. 6). In a linguistic study of *Bérinus* (43), Malcolm Offord adduces evidence that three persons were involved in writing it. Work on other romances includes Lynette Muir's reappraisal of the prose *Yvain* (42), in which she assesses its place in the development of Arthurian romance, and Marcello Cocco's analysis of the unedited *Roman de Cardenois* (34), in which nine poems of Machaut are embedded. Jacques Le Goff (41) made a sociological study of the myth of Mélusine, which he attempts to understand from the point of view of late fourteenth-century society. C. E. Pickford's fascinating study, *L'Evolution du roman arthurien en prose vers la fin du Moyen Age* (44), though based on a fifteenth-century manuscript, treats the fourteenth century to some extent in its examination of the influence of the Arthurian romance on late medieval life and culture.

Lyric Poetry

Turning now to the courtly lyrics of the fourteenth century, one should mention Ulrich Mölk's *Répertoire métrique de la poésie lyrique française des origines à 1350* (50). Though it covers only the first half of our period, it treats that half thoroughly. The most detailed and influential study of the fourteenth-century courtly lyric is Daniel Poirion's *Le Poète et le prince* (51). The author reveals the meaning behind the fixed forms and the conventional themes by analyzing the function of lyricism in the princely courts. In tracing the evolution of lyric forms from Guillaume de Machaut to Charles d'Orléans, Poirion reconstitutes the ideological vision of the world that the poems expressed and makes us feel the magic power in which they held their original listeners. This evolution of late medieval lyricism was closely connected to social changes, for, to quote Poirion, "Entre les mystères de la poésie et les arcanes de la politique, il n'y a pas de séparation naturelle: dans les ténèbres de l'action et du langage ce sont les mêmes énigmes de la situation humaine qui sont en jeu. Mais les secrets que la politique cherche à dissimuler, la poésie, même hermétique, tend à les révéler" (51, p. 11). Since the publication of Poirion's study, our reading of the fourteenth-century courtly lyric can, happily, never be the same. Henrik Heger (49) studies the theme of melancholy in the poetry of the late Middle Ages. Deschamps and Froissart are among the poets he considers. James Wimsatt (52), in a study of French poetic influence on Chaucer, treats Machaut and, to a lesser extent, Froissart and other poets of the period.

In his literary history, Poirion asserts that the *Roman de la Rose* is the doctrinal text to which all poets of the late Middle Ages refer. There has just appeared a superb study that examines this proposition in depth. Pierre-Yves Badel's *Le Roman de la rose au XIVe siècle* (152) makes a detailed and stimulating analysis of the profound influence of this work on the French writers of the fourteenth century. Cited continually throughout the period, the *Roman de la Rose* was an example for writers to follow. Moreover, just as Jean de Meung enlarged the narrative framework of Guillaume de Lorris, so the writers of the fourteenth century endeavored to enlarge their works to encompass all human and institutional relationships. The forms of the *Roman de la Rose* were imitated as well: the dream narrative, the dramatic dialogue, and the debate. Badel's book is a major contribution to our understanding of both the poetic and the allegorical traditions of the fourteenth century.

Guillaume de Machaut

The poetry of Guillaume de Machaut has stimulated a fair amount of critical interest in the last two decades. Madeleine Cosman and Bruce Chandler recently edited a collection of essays entitled *Machaut's World: Science and Art in the Fourteenth Century* (57). The cultural context in which Machaut wrote is evoked by articles on philosophy, science, technology, medicine, music, and art. In addition, several of the essays examine various aspects of the poetry of Machaut. Kevin Brownlee (53) suggests that Machaut's work presents a new concept of poetic identity derived from the *Roman de la Rose.* He argues that Machaut's self-presentation as *poeta* approaches our modern notion of poet. In the same collection Poirion treats the personal perspective of the poet in "The Imaginary Universe of Guillaume de Machaut" (62). Nigel Wilkins edited *La Louange des dames* (63), a collection of poems to which Machaut made additions throughout his creative life. William Calin's book, *A Poet at the Fountain* (55), is the first detailed study of the narrative poems of Guillaume de Machaut. One of these narrative works, the *Judgement dou Roy de Navarre,* is examined by Margaret Ehrhart (58) in an article that is important for studying the development of the allegorized virtues in the fourteenth century. Sarah Williams (64) examines Machaut's role in the production of the physical book of his *Voir Dit.* G. B. Gybbon-Monypenny (59) compares the *Voir Dit* with the *Frauendienst,* the *Vita Nuova,* and the *Libro de buen amor* in an effort to define the "erotic pseudo-autobiography" as a genre. Constance Hieatt (60) tries to establish the dream vision as a genre by examining works of Machaut and Chaucer. In this regard, the increasing interest of Chaucer scholars in Machaut and other French poets is worth noting. Marc Pelen, in "Machaut's Court of Love Narratives and Chaucer's *Book of the Duchess*" (61), discusses the English poet's French and Latin models.

James Wimsatt (66, 67) also explores Chaucer's indebtedness to Machaut. In his book, *The Marguerite Poetry of Guillaume de Machaut* (68), Wimsatt brings to light a previously unpublished poem of Machaut and studies two other Machaut poems connected with the name Marguerite.

Eustache Deschamps

The critical work on Machaut's poetry seems quite voluminous when compared to that devoted to Eustache Deschamps. Here, Chaucerians are almost more numerous than French scholars. Gretchen Mieszkowski (71) has reinterpreted Deschamps's ballade for Chaucer, and Glending Olson (72) sees similarities between the attitudes toward poetry of Chaucer and Deschamps, especially as expressed in the *Art de Dictier*. This work of Deschamps was the first *art poétique* written in French and, as such, has been the object of some critical interest. Roger Dragonetti (69) made a penetrating analysis of Deschamps's concept of poetry as a *musique naturelle*. Deschamps viewed the poet as the only authentic musician because poetry is a natural rather than an artificial music. Dragonetti sees this position as marking a clear break with the prevailing lyric tradition. I. S. Laurie (70) compares Deschamps's poetic theory to his practice and suggests that he developed his concept of poetry as a *musique naturelle* in order to justify the fact that he was not a musician. Outside of Poirion's monumental study of the courtly lyric, there has been virtually no critical interest in Deschamps's poetry. Except for a few ballades, his lyrics have seemed daunting to most modern readers. Grace Frank found him "dour" and "embittered" (11, p. 68). John Fox calls him "a fertile versifier, a mediocre poet" (10, p. 298). One critic even suggested that his *Art de Dictier* is misunderstood because he wrote so badly. Clearly Deschamps needs a friend and defender in the court of literary criticism. Poirion views him as a poet who was conformist in his ideas, but daring in his words (51, p. 621). Surely this daring poetry needs to be better understood.

Jean Froissart

The poetry of Jean Froissart has benefited from a number of new editions. Anthime Fourrier alone has provided us with excellent editions of *L'Espinette amoureuse, La Prison amoureuse, Le Joli Buisson de jonece,* and *Les Dits et les débats* (81–84). Rae Baudouin edited the *Ballades et rondeaux* (73), and Rob Roy McGregor edited *The Lyric Poems of Jean Froissart* (89). As for critical studies of Froissart's poetry, Nigel Wilkins (92) analyzes the structure of the fixed forms in the work of both Froissart and Christine de Pisan. Audrey Graham (86) looks at Froissart's use of classical allusion and concludes that the myths "are often told at such length that the reader loses sight of the main theme" (86, p. 29). Jean-Louis Picherit (90) disagrees, however, and states that "les éléments mythologiques . . . jouent un rôle fonctionnel original, en reflétant . . . les modalités et les circonstances de l'aventure onirique du poète" (90, p. 507). Picherit's insight represents a significant advance in understanding Froissart's poems over the much earlier article of Graham. As for the individual poems, Michelle Freeman (85) sees the *Joli Buisson de jonece* as a poetic testament, and Peter Dembowski (77), in his analysis of *Li Orloge amoureus,* provides a fascinating essay on the intersection of technology and poetry. William Kibler, studying "Self-Delusion in Froissart's *Espinette Amoureuse*" (88), finds a suggestion of cynicism in this poem, a trait that will become significant in the lyric poetry of the fifteenth century. Claude Thiry, in his "Allégorie et histoire dans la *Prison amoureuse*" (91), notes that Froissart, even in his narrative love poems, remained sensitive to the historical world around him. A similar notion is proposed by A. H. Diverres in

"Froissart's *Meliador* and Edward III's Policy Towards Scotland" (78). The author speculates that Froissart favored Edward's policy of placing a Plantagenet prince on the throne of Scotland and that he wrote *Meliador* (in which the Duke of Cornwall's son marries the King of Scotland's daughter) to encourage the idea. Diverres also made other studies of Froissart's relationship to the British Isles (79, 80). Normand Cartier (74, 75) analyzes *Le Bleu Chevalier*, seeing it as a source of Chaucer's *Book of the Duchess*. James Wimsatt (93), however, regards the *Bleu Chevalier* as Froissart's imitation of Chaucer.

Other Poets

A few of the less well known poets of the fourteenth century have been the objects of critical studies, though our knowledge in this area remains sketchy. One of the most significant contributions is Jacques Ribard's *Un Ménestrel du XIVe siècle: Jean de Condé* (99). This excellent study of the poet-minstrel at the court of Jean de Beaumont in Hainaut fills a notable lacuna and can well serve as a model for the investigation of other poets of the period. Ribard (97, 98) also produced shorter pieces on Jean de Condé and edited *La Messe des oiseaux* (100) of the same poet. Concerning other poets, Normand Cartier (94) asserts that the princesse of Oton de Grandson's love poetry was a fiction despite efforts to identify her. Watriquet de Couvin has also stimulated some interest among critics (95, 96). An important article by Nigel Wilkins (101) focuses attention on the many poet-musicians who continued the old tradition of setting their poems to music.

CHRONICLES

Froissart, the chronicler, has consistently received a certain amount of critical attention, but there is much room for further study. George Diller (107, 108) edited from the *Chroniques*, the *Dernière rédaction du premier livre*. Paul Archambault places the *Chroniques* in the broad context of fourteenth-century thought in his stimulating study, "Froissart and the Ockhamist Movement" (103). Archambault's essay on Froissart in his book, *Seven French Chroniclers* (104), allows us to see Froissart's position in the whole spectrum of medieval French historiography. Kenneth McRobbie's article, "Woman and Love: Some Aspects of Competition in Late Medieval Society" (113), is an interesting attempt to articulate the value system surrounding women, love, and marriage as reflected in Froissart's *Chroniques*. He shows that Froissart was fully aware of the great distance between poetic ideals and the position of women in the real world. Froissart's style has been studied by Stephen Nichols (114), who examines the use of discourse as an artistic device to convey a sense of the real, and by Peter Ainsworth (102), who suggests that Froissart was more concerned with literary style than with historical objectivity. Jacqueline Picoche wrote a book entitled *Le Vocabulaire psychologique dans les chroniques de Froissart* (115), and Granville Price (116) made a study of fourteenth-century syntax based on the *Chroniques*. Concerning other chronicles of the period, David Jacoby (111) examines the *Chronique de Morée* and Robert Bossuat (105) describes the late fourteenth-century rhymed chronicle, *Le Dit des roys*, which traces royal genealogy from its Trojan origins to Charles V. André Goosse (109, 110) made a study of the influence of Mandeville on Jean d'Outremeuse and edited a fragment of his *Myreur des histors*. Related to the chronicle is Jean de Mandeville's *Voyages d'outremer*, a work widely known in the fourteenth century, having been translated into ten other languages. Rita Lejeune (112) reviews the theories on the identity of Mandeville and discusses his relations with the city of Liège.

Drama

It is regrettable that relatively few plays have survived from the fourteenth century because the drama was an area of significant development and originality during that period. We are fortunate, however, in having new editions of several of the plays that did survive. The collection of plays in Manuscript 1131 of the Bibliothèque Sainte Geneviève, some of which belong to the fourteenth century, has received much attention. No less than two editions of the passion play from that collection have appeared in the last few years, one by Graham Runnalls (132) and one by Edward Gallagher (121). Gallagher also studied the sources of one of the characters of the Sainte Geneviève passion (120). The *Geu Saint Denis* (133) was edited by Bernard Seubert and the *Vie Monseigneur Saint Fiacre* (118) by James F. Burks, Barbara M. Craig, and M. E. Porter; both are plays from the same Sainte Geneviève manuscript. No general study of fourteenth-century theater has been written, but Jean Frappier's *Le Théâtre profane en France au Moyen Age* (119) treats briefly the Griseldis play and several of the dialogued poems of Deschamps. One of the most important studies of medieval drama published in recent years is Elie Konigson's *L'Espace théâtral médiéval* (123). While this work deals mainly with the theater of the fifteenth and sixteenth centuries, a few fourteenth-century works are included and some of the general conclusions are applicable to the fourteenth century as well.

The majority of the plays surviving from the fourteenth century are found in the Cangé manuscript of the *Miracles de Nostre Dame.* The forty plays of this collection have been the object of two important studies by Graham Runnalls (128, 129). "Medieval Trade Guilds and the *Miracles de Nostre Dame*" is a significant contribution to our understanding of the social background and institutional context of the production of the miracle plays. It is important also for its implications about the extent of dramatic activity in the fourteenth century. Runnalls also made a close study of the Cangé manuscript with its problematic erasures and ascertained dates for a number of the miracles. Other scholars have also provided insights into the *Miracles de Nostre Dame*. Elie Konigson (124) analyzes the relationships between social roles and dramatic roles in four of the plays, and Willem Noomen (127) studies the typology of the characters. Nigel Wilkins (134) wrote a significant article on the music in these plays, and Pierre Gallais (122) made a study of their structure. Graham Runnalls has given us a new edition of one of the plays, the *Miracle de l'enfant ressuscité* (131). In a study of *Le Mystère de Saint Christofle* (130), Runnalls provides sound linguistic evidence for attributing the original version of this sixteenth-century printed play to the fourteenth century. In a substantial article entitled "Lectures du *Palatinus*" (117) Jean-Pierre Bordier makes an excellent analysis of this passion play from a structuralist point of view. Donald Maddox, in "The Hunting Scenes in *L'Estoire de Griseldis*" (126), demonstrates that these scenes reveal the character of the Marquis and foreshadow his subsequent behavior toward Griseldis. Moshé Lazar (125) analyses the conventional and popular scenario of the confrontation between Satan and Notre Dame in the miracle plays and in the *Advocacie Nostre Dame*.

HUMANISM

An extremely important aspect of French literature of the fourteenth century is the humanist movement or, to be more precise, the beginnings of humanism in France. Franco Simone in his book, *The French Renaissance* (150), notes a significant change in French attitudes toward the ancients between the first and second halves of the century. He attributes this to the influence of the papal court at Avignon and of Petrarch. Albert-Marie Schmidt (149) devotes a monograph to the sources of humanism in the fourteenth and fifteenth centuries, and Alexander Saccaro provides a survey of the period in his book, *Französischer Humanismus des 14. und 15. Jahrhunderts* (147). Georges Gougenheim (141), in a brief summary of humanist activities, identifies three major areas of humanist endeavor. First are the translations of the classics made in the fourteenth century. Second is what he terms the Cenacle of 1390–1420, which included such figures as Gerson, Muret, Nicolas de Clamanges, and Jean de Montreuil. Third, but outside our area of interest, are the fifteenth-century translators of the court of Burgundy. Jacques Monfrin (142, 143) treats the question of fourteenth-century translation in general terms in two articles in the *Journal des Savants*. Charles Brucker (137, 138) considers the enrichment of the French language by neologisms derived from Latin in two articles on Denis Foulechat, a translator for Charles V. Charles Samaran and Jacques Monfrin (148) made an exhaustive study of the life and works of Pierre Bersuire, which appeared in volume 39 of the *Histoire littéraire de la France*. Jean Rychner (146), in a study of Bersuire as translator, stresses the fact that the history of French prose has not yet been written. Giuseppe Di Stefano in his book, *La Découverte de Plutarque en Occident* (140), provides much information on the background of humanism in the fourteenth century, particularly in regard to the intellectual life of Avignon.

I have not included the humanists of the end of the century in this bibliographical survey because the major part of their activity belongs to the fifteenth century. I would, however, like to mention examples of what is currently being done in this area. In 1969 Ezio Ornato published an excellent study entitled *Jean Muret es ses amis Nicolas de Clamanges et Jean de Montreuil* (144). Ornato was, at the time, a member of a team of scholars pursuing research on French humanism of the fourteenth and fifteenth centuries. The team is a subdivision of the Centre National de Recherche Scientifique (CNRS), and its members are devoting themselves both to editing humanist texts and to writing historical studies of the period. A new dimension of the project is the use of a computer for processing biographical data relevant to the humanists. This is described by Gian Piero Zarri, also of the CNRS, in his paper, "An Artificial Intelligence Approach to the Study of the Humanist Literary Movement in 14th and 15th Century France" (151). The use of the computer as a research tool in the humanities will become common in the next decade, and the CNRS is one of the leaders in this trend.

ALLEGORICAL, DIDACTIC, AND DREAM LITERATURE

We have now reviewed the major genres, writers, and movements of fourteenth-century French literature and have found that in virtually all cases we are still far from a real understanding of their character and function in the society that gave them birth.

Other writers and literary aspects of the period are less well known and less often studied. As one might expect, the level of genuine understanding falls sharply, despite the existence of a few excellent critical studies. One of the most important of the neglected aspects of fourteenth-century literature is the widespread use of allegory as a mode of expression. The question of allegory is sometimes touched upon in studies of the major poets, but it has never been treated in terms of the fourteenth-century world view that it was. We have already noted Badel's (152) study of the *Roman de la Rose* in the fourteenth century; in addition, Karl Uitti (181) investigates the relevance of this thirteenth-century allegory to Machaut's world. At the same time, some of the most important fourteenth-century works in the allegorical mode are virtually unread. There have been, for example, discouragingly few studies in the last two decades of the important and influential works of Guillaume de Digulleville (or Deguilleville), the best known of which is the *Pèlerinage de la Vie Humaine.* Rosemond Tuve (180) discusses Digulleville among others in her book on allegorical imagery, as does D. D. R. Owen (177) in his descriptive catalogue of medieval French accounts of hell and its visitors. Joan Blythe completed an important study of fourteenth-century allegorical techniques in "The Influence of Latin Manuals on Medieval Allegory: Deguilleville's Presentation of Wrath" (155). Siegfried Wenzel (182), using Digulleville's work as an example, defines the pilgrimage of life as a genre distinct from other pilgrimage works such as the morality play. He is apparently unaware that a fifteenth-century playwright transformed Digulleville's *Pèlerinage* into a morality play called *L'Homme Juste et l'Homme Mondain.* Related to this kind of literature is an important study in intellectual history by Françoise Joukovsky-Micha (172) tracing the notion of *vaine-gloire* from the thirteenth to the fifteenth century.

Concerning other allegorical works, Paule Demats (161) made a study of the *Ovide moralisé,* in which she traces the evolution of the medieval understanding of Ovid's *Metamorphoses* from the twelfth to the mid-fourteenth century. Sister Marie Brisson (157, 158) identified the author of the *Chastel périlleux* and edited the same work. George Keith (174) briefly describes a prose *Voie de Paradis,* a work that may be of some significance for the study of fourteenth-century allegory. Geneviève Hasenohr (169) made a biographical study of Gace de La Bigne, author of the *Roman des Desduis,* an allegorical hunting treatise. She also edited Jean Le Fèvre's *Respit de la mort* (171), a didactic work in which the author, asking the court for a "lettre de répit" against the judgment of death, reviews the commonly accepted knowledge about man's nature and his place in the world.

Aside from Froissart, the prose writers of the fourteenth

century have received scant attention. Janet Ferrier's book, *French Prose Writers of the Fourteenth and Fifteenth Centuries* (162), provides brief introductions to the major prose works of the period, which tend to be didactic in nature. Ferrier (163, 165) wrote two brief studies of *Le Menagier de Paris* and recently completed a new edition of this work begun by the late Georgine Brereton (156). John Grigsby (166) found the *Miroir des Bonnes Femmes* to be a significant source of the *Livre du Chevalier de La Tour Landry*. Under the rubric of didactic prose, one must note the great need for further study of the medieval sermon. Sermon rhetoric is important for understanding medieval literature in general. Moreover, sermon *exempla* have a bearing on the history of the *nouvelle*, and sermon topics are significant in the history of the drama. In this area, E. Beltran (154) edited a late-fourteenth-century sermon attributed to Jacques Legrand.

Dream literature constituted an important dimension of writing in the fourteenth century, as it had in earlier periods. It is a category related to allegory because many of the dream visions are meant to be understood allegorically. The dream work that has received the most attention in the last two decades is the *Songe du Vergier,* a compilation of legal and juridical texts concerning relations between Church and State. Jeannine Quillet (178) completed a book on the political philosophy of the *Songe.* Briefer studies of the same work were made by Francis Bar (153), F. Chatillon (159), and Marion Lièvre (175). Quillet also wrote an article entitled "Songes et songeries dans l'art de la politique au XIVe siècle" (179), in which she treats not only the *Songe du Vergier* but also the *Songe du vieil pèlerin* of Philippe de Mézières. The latter work, which is essential for understanding certain aspects of fourteenth-century political and religious life, was recently edited by George Coopland (160). Another new edition of a dream vision is Jean Dupin's *Les Mélancolies* (176), which is the eighth book of his *Livre de Mandevie.*

Marc-René Jung (173), in a review of Lindgren's edition, further enhances our knowledge of the work. John Grigsby (167) edited the *Liber Fortunae,* another of the dream visions so well liked in the fourteenth century.

ANGLO-NORMAN LITERATURE

One domain of literature in French not yet mentioned is Anglo-Norman literature. Mary Dominica Legge made a complete survey of these works in her *Anglo-Norman Literature and Its Background* (185). We find there a number of fourteenth-century writers such as Henry of Lancaster, Nicole Bozon, and John Gower. Anyone interested in Gower must, of course, consult John Fisher's thorough study of this poet (183). More recently Kurt Olsson (186) made an important study of the cardinal virtues in Gower's *Mirour de l'omme,* providing a deeper insight into allegorical modes of writing. Two new editions of fourteenth-century works have been published by the Anglo-Norman Text Society: the ancestral romance *Fouke le Fitz Waryn* (184) and the *Holkham Bible Picture Book* (187).

DICTIONARIES AND LANGUAGE STUDIES

Two new dictionaries of medieval French language appeared during the past two decades. A. J. Greimas's *Dictionnaire de l'ancien français* (194) covers the period up to 1350, and the new *Dictionnaire étymologique de l'ancien français* (189) covers Old French to the mid-fourteenth century. Studies of the language of the fourteenth century include a work by A. Dees (191) on the evolution of demonstratives in Old and Middle French, as well as an analysis by T. G. Fennell (192) of the morphology of the future tense in Middle French. A new work by Christiane Marchello-Nizia, *Histoire de la langue française aux XIVe et XVe siècles* (196), throws light on many aspects of this language that until now were poorly understood. The author considers the French of this period not as a transition between two more highly developed forms of French but as a language in its own right, and thus rejects the term *Middle French*. Other studies of fourteenth-century language tend to be narrowly focused and particularized. Marguerite Gonon (193), for example, studies the vocabulary of family life in the fourteenth century based on wills and testaments from Forez. Malcolm Offord (198) analyzes negation in medieval French based on the *Roman de Bérinus*. Raymond Arveiller (188) edited passages from a fourteenth-century medical treatise that were chosen for their linguistic interest. The language of the French writers of northern Italy has been studied by Robert Massart (197) and Lorenzo Renzi (199). Leena Löfstedt (195) and Robert Taylor (200) analyze linguistic aspects of two translators, and Nina Catach and Gilbert Ouy (190) study the written language at the end of the fourteenth century.

Conclusion

Now that we have reviewed most of the studies of fourteenth-century French literature that have appeared in the last two decades, let us analyze briefly the state in which we find ourselves. First, we are gradually emerging from the mentality in which one condemns literary works as boring or worse because one does not know how to read them as they were intended. Second, there is an increasing flow of good editions of works previously unavailable. Third, there is a small but growing number of excellent monographs and studies on various fourteenth-century writers and anonymous works. All of these are gradually changing the way in which we approach and therefore understand the literature of the fourteenth century.

Encouraging as these trends are, they still fall far short

of what is needed for a complete rehabilitation of the period. In order to accomplish this, several things are required. First, we must cultivate a desire to understand the writers of the fourteenth century on their terms rather than ours. Nothing is more fruitless than to condemn the past for not anticipating the tastes of the present. Second, we must acquire a thorough knowledge of the fourteenth-century prerequisites of literary expression and the context of literary activities. This includes a systematic study of language and rhetoric, of the ideals and myths of the various social levels, and of the enormous changes that were taking place both in the real world and in the mentalities interpreting that world. Finally, we must make fundamental and thoroughgoing studies of the works, their authors, and their audiences in order to understand how literature functioned in that society. I am not suggesting that we should ultimately find everything perfect, nor that we should be insensitive to qualitative differences in fourteenth-century literature. After all, even Homer may have nodded from time to time. But such moments of authorial inattention, once we learn to judge them properly, will turn out to be nothing compared to the slumber of our ignorance.

Bibliography

Bibliographies

1. Klapp, Otto. *Bibliographie des französischen Literatur-wissenschaft.* Frankfurt: V. Klostermann. Published annually.
2. Knudson, Charles A., and Jean Misrahi. "French Medieval Literature." In *The Medieval Literature of Western Europe: A Review of Research, Mainly 1930–1960,* edited by John H. Fisher. New York: New York University Press, 1966.
3. Kukenheim, Louis, and Henri Roussel. *Guide de la littérature française du Moyen Age.* 2d ed. Leiden: Universitaire Pers Leiden, 1959.
4. *MLA International Bibliography.* Published annually as a supplement to *PMLA.*
5. Rancoeur, René. *Bibliographie de la littérature française du Moyen Age à nos jours.* Paris: Armand Colin. Published annually.
6. Woledge, Brian. *Bibliographie des romans et nouvelles en prose française antérieurs à 1500: Supplément, 1954–1973.* Geneva: Droz, 1975.
7. *The Year's Work in Modern Language Studies.* Published annually by the Modern Humanities Research Association.

General Studies

8. Alter, Jean V. *Les Origines de la satire anti-bourgeoise en France.* 2 vols. Geneva: Droz, 1966.
9. Faral, Edmond, Mario Roques, Alfred Jeanroy, and Charles Samaran. *Histoire littéraire de la France.* Vol. 39. *Suite du XIVe siècle.* Paris: Klincksieck, 1964.
10. Fox, John H. *A Literary History of France: The Middle Ages.* New York: Barnes & Noble, 1974.

11. Frank, Grace. "French Literature in the Fourteenth Century." In *The Forward Movement of the Fourteenth Century*, edited by Francis Lee Utley. Columbus: Ohio State University Press, 1961.

12. Kelly, Douglas. *Medieval Imagination: Rhetoric and the Poetry of Courtly Love.* Madison: University of Wisconsin Press, 1978.

13. Poirion, Daniel. *Littérature française: Le Moyen Age, 1300–1480.* Paris: Arthaud, 1971.

14. Tuchman, Barbara W. *A Distant Mirror: The Calamitous 14th Century.* New York: Knopf, 1978.

15. Zumthor, Paul. *Essai de poétique médiévale.* Paris: Seuil, 1972.

EPIC

16. Cook, Robert F. "Note sur les manuscrits de *Baudouin de Sebourc* et du deuxième Cycle de la Croisade." *Romania* 91 (1970): 83–97.

17. Cook, Robert F., ed. *Le Bâtard de Bouillon: Chanson de geste.* Geneva: Droz, 1972.

18. Cook, Robert F., and Larry S. Crist. *Le deuxième Cycle de la Croisade.* Geneva: Droz, 1972.

19. Cromey, Nancy B. "Roland as 'Baron Révolté': The Problem of Authority and Autonomy in *L'Entrée d'Espagne.*" *Olifant* 5 (1978): 285–97.

20. Di Stefano, Giuseppe. "Flexion et versification en moyen français." In *Etudes de langue et de littérature du Moyen Age offerts à Félix Lecoy*, pp. 67–72. Paris: H. Champion, 1973.

21. Dougherty, David M., and E. B. Barnes, eds. *La Geste de Monglane.* Eugene: University of Oregon Press, 1966.

22. Goosse, André. "*Ogier le Danois*, chanson de geste de Jean d'Outremeuse." *Romania* 86 (1965): 145–98.

23. Kibler, William W. "The Unity of *Baudouin de Sebourc.*" *Studies in Philology* 67 (1970): 461–71.

24. Kibler, William W., Jean-Louis Picherit, and Thelma S. Fenster, eds. *Lion de Bourges: Poème épique du XIVe siècle.* 2 vols. Geneva: Droz, 1980.

25. Limentani, Alberto. "L'Art de la comparaison dans l'*En-

trée d'Espagne." In *Société Rencesvals: Actes du VIe Congrès International*, pp. 351–71. Université de Provence: Imprimerie du Centre d'Aix, 1975.

26. ———. "Epica e racconto: Osservazioni su alcune struture e sull'incompiutezza dell'*Entrée d'Espagne*." *Atti del R. Instituto Veneto di Scienze, Lettere ed Arti* 133 (1974–1975): 393–433.

27. Miquet, Jean. "A propos de la fixité thématique de l'épopée aux XIVe et XVe siècles." In *Charlemagne et l'épopée romane: Actes du VIIe Congrès International de la Société Rencesvals*, pp. 433–42. 2 vols. Paris: Belles Lettres, 1978.

28. Picherit, Jean-Louis. "Le Merveilleux Chrétien et le motif du Mort reconnaissant dans la chanson de *Lion de Bourges*." *Annuale Medievale* 16 (1975): 41–51.

29. Sinclair, Keith V., ed. *Tristan de Nanteuil, chanson de geste inédite*. Assen: Van Gorcum, 1971.

30. Suard, François. "*Ogier le Danois* aux XIVe et XVe siècles." In *Société Rencesvals IVe Congrès International: Actes et Mémoires*, pp. 54–62. Heidelberg: Winter, 1969.

31. Zezula, Jindrich. "L'Elément historique et la datation d'*Anseÿs de Mes* (MS. N)." *Romania* 97 (1976): 1–22.

See also entry 199.

ROMANCE

32. Carey, Richard J., ed. *Le Restor du paon*. Geneva: Droz, 1966. (Jean Brisbare)

33. ———. *Jean de Le Mote: Le Parfait du paon*. Chapel Hill: University of North Carolina Press, 1972.

34. Cocco, Marcello. "L'Inedito *Roman de Cardenois* et la fortuna di Guillaume de Machaut." *Cultura Neolatina* 31 (1971): 125–53.

35. Donkin, Enid. "Le 'plagiat' de Jean Brisbare." *Romania* 86 (1965): 395–404.

36. Flutre, Louis-Fernand. "Etudes sur le roman de *Perceforest*." *Romania* 88(1967): 475–508; 90(1969): 341–70; 91(1970): 189–226.

37. ———. "Les Proverbes du roman de *Perceforest*." *Revue de Linguistique Romane* 31 (1967): 89–104.

38. Giacchetti, André. "Le personnage d'Alexandre dans *Les Voeux du paon.*" In *Mélanges de langue et de littérature du Moyen Age et de la Renaissance offerts à Jean Frappier*, pp. 351–64. 2 vols. Geneva: Droz, 1970.

39. ———. "Une nouvelle forme du *lai* apparue à la fin du XIVe siècle." In *Etudes de langue et de littérature du Moyen Age offertes à Félix Lecoy*, pp. 147–55. Paris: H. Champion, 1973.

40. Kelly, Douglas. "Fortune and Narrative Proliferation in *Berinus.*" *Speculum* 51 (1976): 6–22.

41. Le Goff, Jacques, and E. Le Roy Ladurie. "Mélusine maternelle et défricheuse." *Annales: Economies, Sociétés, Civilisations* 26 (1971): 587–622.

42. Muir, Lynette R. "A Reappraisal of the Prose *Yvain.*" *Romania* 85 (1964): 355–65.

43. Offord, Malcolm Y. "A Textual Problem of *Bérinus.*" *Studia Neophilologica* 41 (1969): 13–24.

44. Pickford, Cedric E. *L'Evolution du roman arthurien en prose vers la fin du Moyen Age, d'après le manuscrit 112 du fonds français de la Bibliothèque Nationale.* Paris: Nizet, 1960.

45. Ross, David J. A. *Alexander Historiatus: A Guide to Medieval Illustrated Alexander Literature.* London: Warburg Institute, 1963.

46. Taylor, Jane H. M. "Aroes the Enchanter: An Episode in the *Roman de Perceforest* and Its Sources." *Medium Aevum* 47 (1978): 30–39.

47. ———. "Reason and Faith in the *Roman de Perceforest.*" In *Studies in Medieval Literature and Languages in Memory of Frederick Whitehead*, pp. 303–22. Manchester: Manchester University Press, 1973.

48. Taylor, Jane H. M., ed. *Le Roman de Perceforest: Première partie.* Geneva: Droz, 1979.

See also entry 198.

LYRIC POETRY

49. Heger, Henrik. *Die Melancholie bei den französischen Lyrikern des Spätmittelalters.* Bonn: Romanisches Seminar der Univerität, 1967.

50. Mölk, Ulrich. *Répertoire métrique de la poésie lyrique française des origines à 1350.* Munich: Fink, 1972.
51. Poirion, Daniel. *Le poète et le prince: L'Evolution du lyrisme courtois de Guillaume de Machaut à Charles d'Orléans.* Paris: Presses Universitaires de France, 1965.
52. Wimsatt, James I. *Chaucer and the French Love Poets: The Literary Background of the "Book of the Duchess."* Chapel Hill: University of North Carolina Press, 1968.

See also entries 12, 152.

Guillaume de Machaut

53. Brownlee, Kevin. "The Poetic *Oeuvre* of Guillaume de Machaut: The Identity of Discourse and the Discourse of Identity." In *Machaut's World: Science and Art in the Fourteenth Century,* edited by M. P. Cosman and B. Chandler, pp. 219–33. New York: New York Academy of Sciences, 1978.
54. ———. "Transformations of the Lyric 'Je': The Example of Guillaume de Machaut." *L'Esprit Créateur* 18 (1978): 5–18.
55. Calin, William. *A Poet at the Fountain: Essays in the Narrative Verse of Guillaume de Machaut.* Lexington: University Press of Kentucky, 1974.
56. ———. "The Poet at the Fountain: Machaut as Narrative Poet." In *Machaut's World: Science and Art in the Fourteenth Century,* edited by M. P. Cosman and B. Chandler, pp. 177–87. New York: New York Academy of Sciences, 1978.
57. Cosman, Madeleine P., and Bruce Chandler, eds. *Machaut's World: Science and Art in the Fourteenth Century.* New York: New York Academy of Sciences, 1978.
58. Ehrhart, Margaret J. "Guillaume de Machaut's *Jugement dou Roy de Navarre* and Medieval Treatments of the Virtues." *Annuale Mediaevale* 19 (1979): 46–67.
59. Gybbon-Monypenny, G. B. "Guillaume de Machaut's Erotic 'Autobiography': Precedents for the Form of the *Voir-Dit.*" In *Studies in Medieval Literature and Languages in Memory of Frederick Whitehead,* pp. 133–52. Manchester: Manchester University Press, 1973.

60. Hieatt, Constance. "*Une Autre Fourme:* Guillaume de Machaut and the Dream Vision Form." *The Chaucer Review* 14 (1979): 97–115.

61. Pelen, Marc M. "Machaut's Court of Love Narratives and Chaucer's *Book of the Duchess.*" *The Chaucer Review* 11 (1976): 128–55.

62. Poirion, Daniel. "The Imaginary Universe of Guillaume de Machaut." In *Machaut's World: Science and Art in the Fourteenth Century,* edited by M. P. Cosman and B. Chandler, pp. 199–206. New York: New York Academy of Sciences, 1978.

63. Wilkins, Nigel, ed. *La Louange des dames.* New York: Barnes & Noble, 1973.

64. Williams, Sarah J. "An Author's Role in Fourteenth-Century Book Production: Guillaume de Machaut's 'Livre ou je met toutes mes choses.' " *Romania* 90 (1969): 433–54.

65. ———. "Machaut's Self-Awareness as Author and Producer." In *Machaut's World: Science and Art in the Fourteenth Century,* edited by M. P. Cosman and B. Chandler, pp. 189–97. New York: New York Academy of Sciences, 1978.

66. Wimsatt, James I. "Guillaume de Machaut and Chaucer's Love Lyrics." *Medium Aevum* 47 (1978): 66–87.

67. ———. "Guillaume de Machaut and Chaucer's *Troilus and Criseyde.*" *Medium Aevum* 45 (1976): 277–93.

68. ———. *The Marguerite Poetry of Guillaume de Machaut.* Chapel Hill: University of North Carolina Press, 1970.

See also entry 181.

Eustache Deschamps

69. Dragonetti, Roger. " 'La poesie . . . ceste musique naturelle': Essai d'exégèse d'un passage de l'*Art de Dictier* d'Eustache Deschamps." In *Fin du Moyen Age et Renaissance: Mélanges offerts à Robert Guiette,* pp. 49–64. Antwerp: De Nederlandsche Boekhandel, 1961.

70. Laurie, I. S. "Deschamps and the Lyric as Natural Music." *Modern Language Review* 59 (1964): 561–70.

71. Mieszkowski, Gretchen. " 'Pandras' in Deschamps' Ballade for Chaucer." *The Chaucer Review* 9 (1974): 327–36.

72. Olson, Glending. "Deschamps' *Art de dictier* and Chaucer's Literary Environment." *Speculum* 48 (1973): 714–23.

Jean Froissart

73. Baudouin, Rae S., ed. *Ballades et rondeaux*. Geneva: Droz, 1978.
74. Cartier, Normand R. "*Le Bleu Chevalier.*" *Romania* 87 (1966): 289–314.
75. ———. "*Le Bleu Chevalier* de Froissart et le *Livre de la Duchesse* de Chaucer." *Romania* 88 (1967): 232–52.
76. ———. "Froissart, Chaucer, and Enclimpostair." *Revue de Littérature Comparée* 38 (1964): 18–34.
77. Dembowski, Peter F. "*Li Orloge amoureus* de Froissart." *L'Esprit Créateur* 18 (1978): 19–31.
78. Diverres, A. H. "Froissart's *Meliador* and Edward III's Policy Towards Scotland." In *Mélanges offerts à Rita Lejeune*, pp. 1399–1409. 2 vols. Gembloux: J. Duculot, 1969.
79. ———. "The Geography of Britain in Froissart's *Meliador.*" In *Medieval Miscellany Presented to Eugene Vinaver by Pupils, Colleagues, and Friends*, pp. 97–112. Manchester: Manchester University Press, 1965.
80. ———. "The Irish Adventures in Froissart's *Meliador.*" In *Mélanges de langue et de littérature du Moyen Age et de la Renaissance offerts à Jean Frappier*, pp. 235–51. 2 vols. Geneva: Droz, 1970.
81. Fourrier, Anthime, ed. *Le joli buisson de Jonece*. Geneva: Droz, 1975.
82. ———. *Les Dits et les débats*. Geneva: Droz, 1979.
83. ———. *L'espinette amoureuse*. Paris: Klincksieck, 1963.
84. ———. *La prison amoureuse*. Paris: Klincksieck, 1974.
85. Freeman, Michelle A. "Froissart's *Le Joli Buisson de Jonece*: A Farewell to Poetry?" In *Machaut's World: Science and Art in the Fourteenth Century*, edited by M. P. Cosman and B. Chandler, pp. 235–47. New York: New York Academy of Sciences, 1978.
86. Graham, Audrey. "Froissart's Use of Classical Allusion in His Poems." *Medium Aevum* 32 (1963): 24–33.
87. Kibler, William W. "Poet and Patron: Froissart's *Prison amoureuse.*" *L'Esprit Créateur* 18 (1978): 32–46.

88. ———. "Self-Delusion in Froissart's *Espinette amou-reuse.*" *Romania* 97 (1976): 77–98.

89. McGregor, Rob Roy, ed. *The Lyric Poems of Jean Froissart: A Critical Edition.* Chapel Hill: University of North Carolina Press, 1975.

90. Picherit, Jean-Louis. "Le rôle des éléments mythologiques dans le *Joli Buisson de Jonece* de Jean Froissart." *Neophilologus* 63 (1979): 498–508.

91. Thiry, Claude. "Allégorie et histoire dans la *Prison amou-reuse* de Froissart." *Studi Francesi,* nos. 61–62 (1977): 15–29.

92. Wilkins, Nigel. "The Structure of Ballades, Rondeaux, and Virelais in Froissart and in Christine de Pisan." *French Studies* 23 (1969): 337–48.

93. Wimsatt, James I. "The *Dit dou Bleu Chevalier:* Froissart's Imitation of Chaucer." *Medieval Studies* 34 (1972): 388–400.

Other Poets

94. Cartier, Normand R. "Oton de Grandson et sa Princesse." *Romania* 85 (1964): 1–16.

95. Livingston, Charles H. "Manuscrit retrouvé d'oeuvres de Watriquet de Couvin." In *Mélanges de linguistique romane et de philologie médiévale offerts à Maurice Delbouille,* vol. 2, 439–46. 2 vols. Gembloux: J. Duculot, 1964.

96. Payen, Jean-Charles. "Le *Dit des .VII. vertus* de Watriquet de Couvin et le *Livre de philosophie* d'Alard de Cambrai." *Romania* 86 (1965): 386–93.

97. Ribard, Jacques. "Contribution à la conaissance de la tradition manuscrite de l'oeuvre de Jean de Condé." *Romania* 89 (1968): 125–29.

98. ———. "Des Lais au XIVe siècle? Jean de Condé." In *Mélanges de langue et de littérature du Moyen Age et de la Renaissance offerts à Jean Frappier,* pp. 945–55. 2 vols. Geneva: Droz, 1970.

99. ———. *Un ménestrel du XIVe siècle: Jean de Condé.* Geneva: Droz, 1969.

100. Ribard, Jacques, ed. *La Messe des oiseaux et le Dit des*

jacobins et des fremeneurs. Geneva: Droz, 1970. (Jean de Condé)

101. Wilkins, Nigel. "The Post-Machaut Generation of Poet-Musicians." *Nottingham Medieval Studies* 12 (1968): 40–84.

CHRONICLES

102. Ainsworth, Peter F. "Style direct et peinture des personnages chez Froissart." *Romania* 93 (1972): 498–522.

103. Archambault, Paul J. "Froissart and the Ockhamist Movement: Philosophy and Its Impact on Historiography." *Symposium* 28 (1974): 197–211.

104. ———. *Seven French Chroniclers: Witnesses to History.* Syracuse: Syracuse University Press, 1974.

105. Bossuat, Robert. "Le *Dit des roys:* Chronique rimée du XIVe siècle." In *Mélanges de linguistique romane et de philologie médiévale offerts à Maurice Delbouille,* vol. 2, pp. 49–58. 2 vols. Gembloux: J. Duculot, 1964.

106. Cartier, Normand R. "The Lost Chronicle." *Speculum* 36 (1961): 424–34.

107. Diller, George T. "La Dernière rédaction du premier livre des *Chroniques* de Froissart: Une étude du Reg. lat. 869." *Le Moyen Age* 76 (1970): 91–125.

108. Diller, George T., ed. *Chroniques: Dernière rédaction du premier livre. Edition du manuscrit de Rome Reg. lat. 869.* Geneva: Droz, 1972. (Froissart)

109. Goosse, André. "Jean d'Outremeuse et Jean de Mandeville." In *Festschrift Walther von Wartburg zum 80. Geburtstag,* vol. 1, pp. 235–50. 2 vols. Tübingen: Max Niemeyer, 1968.

110. Goosse, André, ed. *Ly myreur des histors: Fragment du Second Livre (Années 794–826).* Brussels: Académie Royale de Belgique, 1965. (Jean d'Outremeuse.)

111. Jacoby, David. "Quelques considérations sur les versions de la *Chronique de Morée.*" *Journal des Savants* (1968): 133–89.

112. Lejeune, Rita. "Jean de Mandeville et les Liégeois." In *Mélanges de linguistique romane et de philologie mé-*

diévale offerts à Maurice Delbouille, vol. 2, pp. 409–37. 2 vols. Gembloux: J. Duculot, 1964.

113. McRobbie, Kenneth. "Woman and Love: Some Aspects of Competition in Late Medieval Society." *Mosaic* 5 (1972): 139–68. (Froissart.)

114. Nichols, Stephen G., Jr. "Discourse in Froissart's *Chroniques*." *Speculum* 39 (1964): 279–87.

115. Picoche, Jacqueline. *Le Vocabulaire psychologique dans les chroniques de Froissart*. Paris: Klincksieck, 1976.

116. Price, Granville. "Aspects de l'ordre des mots dans les *Chroniques* de Froissart." *Zeitschrift für Romanische Philologie* 77 (1961): 15–48.

DRAMA

117. Bordier, Jean-Pierre. "Lectures du *Palatinus*." *Le Moyen Age* 80 (1974): 429–82.

118. Burks, James F., Barbara M. Craig, and M. E. Porter, eds. *La Vie Monseigneur Saint Fiacre*. Lawrence: University of Kansas Press, 1960.

119. Frappier, Jean. *Le Théâtre profane en France au Moyen Age*. Paris: Centre de Documentation Universitaire, 1960.

120. Gallagher, Edward J. "Sources and Secondary Characterization in the Sainte-Geneviève *Passion Nostre Seigneur*." *Neuphilologische Mitteilungen* 79 (1978): 173–79.

121. Gallagher, Edward J., ed. *A Critical Edition of La Passion nostre seigneur from Ms. 1131 from the Bibliothèque Sainte-Geneviève*. Chapel Hill: University of North Carolina Press, 1976.

122. Gallais, Pierre. "Remarques sur la structure des *Miracles de Notre Dame*." In *Epopées, légendes et miracles*, pp. 117–34. Paris: Vrin, 1974.

123. Konigson, Élie. *L'Espace théâtral médiéval*. Paris: Centre National de Recherche Scientifique, 1975.

124. ———. "Structures élémentaires de quelques fictions dramatiques dans les miracles par personnages du ms. Cangé." *Revue d'Histoire du Théâtre* 29 (1977): 105–27.

125. Lazar, Moshé. "Satan and Notre Dame: Characters in a

Popular Scenario." In *A Medieval French Miscellany,* edited by Norris J. Lacy, pp. 1–14. Lawrence: University of Kansas Press, 1972.

126. Maddox, Donald. "The Hunting Scenes in *L'Estoire de Griseldis.*" In *Voices of Conscience: Essays on Medieval and Modern French Literature in Memory of James D. Powell and Rosemary Hodgins,* pp. 78–94. Philadelphia: Temple University Press, 1977.

127. Noomen, Willem. "Pour une typologie des personnages des *Miracles de Nostre Dame.*" In *Mélanges de linguistique et de littérature offerts à Lein Geschiere,* pp. 71–89. Amsterdam: Rodopi, 1975.

128. Runnalls, Graham A. "Medieval Trade Guilds and the *Miracles de Nostre Dame par personnages.*" *Medium Aevum* 39 (1970): 257–87.

129. ———. "The *Miracles de Nostre Dame par personnages:* Erasures in the MS. and the Dates of the Plays and the 'Serventois'." *Philological Quarterly* 49 (1970): 19–29.

130. ———. "A Newly Discovered Fourteenth-Century Play? *Le Mystère de saint Christofle.*" *Romance Philology* 24 (1971): 464–77.

131. Runnalls, Graham A., ed. *Le Miracle de l'enfant ressuscité.* Paris: Minard; Geneva: Droz, 1972.

132. ———. *Mystère de la Passion Nostre Seigneur.* Geneva: Droz, 1974.

133. Seubert, Bernard J., ed. *Le Geu Saint Denis.* Geneva: Droz, 1974.

134. Wilkins, Nigel. "Music in the Fourteenth-Century *Miracles de Nostre Dame.*" *Musica Disciplina* 28 (1974): 39–75.

HUMANISM

135. Arcaini, Enrico. "Pierre Bersuire, primo traduttore de Tito Livio." *Convivium* 35 (1967): 732–45.

136. Avril, François. *La Librairie de Charles V.* Catalogue de l'Exposition à la Bibliothèque Nationale. Paris: Bibliothèque Nationale, 1968.

137. Brucker, Charles. "Les Néologismes de Denis Foulechat, traducteur de Charles V, d'après les trois premiers livres

du *Policratique.*" *Revue de Linguistique Romane* 33 (1969): 317–24.

138. ———. "Quelques aspects du style de Denis Foulechat, traducteur de Charles V." *Zeitschrift für Französische Sprache und Literatur* 80 (1970): 97–106.

139. Callu, Florence and François Avril. *Boccace en France.* Catalogue de l'Exposition à la Bibliothèque Nationale. Paris: Bibliothèque Nationale, 1975.

140. Di Stefano, Guiseppe. *La Découverte de Plutarque en Occident.* Turin: Accademia delle Scienze, 1968.

141. Gougenheim, Georges. "L'Humanisme en France aux XIVe et XVe siècles." *Bulletin de l'Association Guillaume Budé* (1974): 413–20.

142. Monfrin, Jacques. "Humanisme et traductions au Moyen Age." *Journal des Savants* (1963): 161–90.

143. ———. "Les traducteurs et leur public au Moyen Age." *Journal des Savants* (1964): 5–20.

144. Ornato, Ezio. *Jean Muret et ses amis Nicolas de Clamanges et Jean de Montreuil: Contribution à l'étude des rapports entre les humanistes de Paris et ceux d'Avignon, 1394–1420.* Geneva: Droz, 1969.

145. Ouy, Gilbert. "L'humanisme et les mutations politiques et sociales en France aux XIVe et XVe siècles." In *L'Humanisme français au début de la Renaissance: Colloque International de Tours*, pp. 27–44. Paris: J. Vrin, 1973.

146. Rychner, Jean. "Observations sur la traduction de Tite-Live par Pierre Bersuire (1354–1356)." *Journal des Savants* (1963): 242–67.

147. Saccaro, Alexander P. *Französischer Humanismus des 14. und 15. Jahrhunderts.* Munich: Wilhelm Fink, 1975.

148. Samaran, Charles and Jacques Monfrin. *Pierre Bersuire: Prieur de Saint-Eloi de Paris.* Paris: Imprimerie Nationale, 1962.

149. Schmidt, Albert-Marie. *XIVe-XVe siècles, les sources de l'humanisme.* Paris: Seghers, 1964.

150. Simone, Franco. *The French Renaissance.* Translated by H. Gaston Hall. London: Macmillan, 1969.

151. Zarri, Gian Piero. "An Artificial Intelligence Approach to the Study of the Humanist Literary Movement in XIVth

and XVth Century France." *Computers and the Humanities* 11 (1977): 289–97.
See also 190, 195, 200.

ALLEGORICAL, DIDACTIC, AND DREAM LITERATURE

152. Badel, Pierre-Yves. *Le Roman de la Rose au XIVe siècle.* Geneva: Droz, 1980.
153. Bar, Francis. "Langage familier et proverbes dans la première partie du *Songe du Vergier.*" In *Etudes de langue et de littérature du Moyen Age offertes à Félix Lecoy,* pp. 7–17. Paris: H. Champion, 1973.
154. Beltran, E. "Un sermon français inédit attribuable à Jacques Legrand." *Romania* 93 (1972): 460–78.
155. Blythe, Joan H. "The Influence of Latin Manuals on Medieval Allegory: Deguileville's Presentation of Wrath." *Romania* 95 (1974): 256–83.
156. Brereton, Georgine E., and Janet M. Ferrier, eds. *Le Menagier de Paris.* Oxford: Clarendon Press, 1981.
157. Brisson, Sister Marie. "Frère Robert, chartreux du XIVe siècle." *Romania* 87 (1966): 543–50.
158. Brisson, Sister Marie, ed. *A Critical Edition and Study of Frère Robert (Chartreux), Le chastel perilleux.* 2 vols. Salzburg: Institut für Englische Sprache und Literatur, 1974.
159. Chatillon, F. "Ecriture et décret dans le *Songe du Vergier.*" *Cahiers d'Histoire* 17 (1972): 217–36.
160. Coopland, George W., ed. *Le Songe du vieil pèlerin.* 2 vols. New York: Cambridge University Press, 1969. (Philippe de Mézières)
161. Demats, Paule. *Fabula: Trois études de mythographie antique et médiévale.* Geneva: Droz, 1973. (*Ovide moralisé*)
162. Ferrier, Janet M. *French Prose Writers of the Fourteenth and Fifteenth Centuries.* Oxford: Pergamon, 1966.
163. ———. "A Husband's Asides: The Use of the Second Person Singular in *Le Ménagier de Paris.*" *French Studies* 31 (1977): 257–67.

164. ———. "The Old Pilgrim's Catch-Words: Notes on *parlant moralment* and *quel merveille* in *Le Songe du vieil pelerin.*" In *History and Structure of French: Essays in Honour of Professor T. B. W. Reid*, pp. 99–116. Oxford: Blackwell, 1972. (Philippe de Mézières)

165. ———. "*Seulement pour vous endoctriner:* The Author's Use of *Exempla* in *Le Ménagier de Paris.*" *Medium Aevum* 48 (1979): 77–89.

166. Grigsby, John L. "A New Source of the *Livre du Chevalier de La Tour Landry.*" *Romania* 84 (1963): 171–208.

167. Grigsby, John L., ed. *The Middle French "Liber Fortunae:" A Critical Edition.* Berkeley: University of California Press, 1967.

168. Guillemain, Alice. "Le *Testament* de Philippe de Mézières (1392)." In *Mélanges de littérature du Moyen Age au XXe siècle offertes à Mlle Jeanne Lods*, pp. 297–322. 2 vols. Paris: Ecole Normale Supérieure de Jeunes Filles, 1978.

169. Hasenohr, Geneviève. "Gace de La Bigne, maître chapelain de trois rois de France." In *Etudes de langue et de littérature du Moyen Age offertes à Félix Lecoy*, pp. 181–92. Paris: H. Champion, 1973.

170. ———. "Un Recueil de *distinctiones* bilingue du début du XIVe siècle: Le Manuscrit 99 de la bibliothèque municipale de Charleville." *Romania* 99 (1978): 47–96, 183–206.

171. Hasenohr-Esnos, Geneviève, ed. *Le Respit de la mort, par Jean Le Fèvre.* Paris: Picard, 1969.

172. Joukovsky-Micha, Françoise. "La Notion de 'vaine gloire' de Simund de Freine à Martin le Franc." *Romania* 89 (1968): 1–30, 210–39.

173. Jung, Marc-René. "Jean Dupin: Le *Livre de Mandevie* et les *Mélancolies.*" *Zeitschrift für Romanische Philologie* 84 (1968): 30–48.

174. Keith, George H. "A Medieval Prose *Voie de Paradis.*" *Romanic Review* 58 (1967): 166–72.

175. Lièvre, Marion. "Note sur les sources du *Somnium Viridarii* et du *Songe du Vergier.*" *Romania* 81 (1960): 483–91.

176. Lindgren, Lauri, ed. *Les Mélancolies de Jean Dupin.* Turku: Yliopisto, 1965.
177. Owen, D. D. R. *The Vision of Hell, Infernal Journeys in Medieval French Literature.* Edinburgh: Scottish Academy Press, 1970.
178. Quillet, Jeannine. *La Philosophie politique du "Songe du Vergier."* Paris: J. Vrin, 1977.
179. ———. "Songes et songeries dans l'art de la politique au XIVe siècle." *Les Etudes Philosophiques* (1975): 327–49.
180. Tuve, Rosemond. *Allegorical Imagery: Some Medieval Books and Their Posterity.* Princeton: Princeton University Press, 1966.
181. Uitti, Karl D. "From *Clerc* to *Poète:* The Relevance of the *Romance of the Rose* to Machaut's World." In *Machaut's World: Science and Art in the Fourteenth Century,* edited by M. P. Cosman and B. Chandler, pp. 209–16. New York: New York Academy of Sciences, 1978.
182. Wenzel, Siegfried. "The Pilgrimage of Life as a Late Medieval Genre." *Medieval Studies* 35 (1973): 370–88.
See also entries 58, 186.

ANGLO-NORMAN LITERATURE

183. Fisher, John H. *John Gower, Moral Philosopher and Friend of Chaucer.* New York: New York University Press, 1964.
184. Hathaway, E. J., P. T. Ricketts, C. A. Robson, and A. D. Wilshere, eds. *Fouke le Fitz Waryn.* Oxford: Blackwell, 1975.
185. Legge, Mary Dominica. *Anglo-Norman Literature and Its Background.* Oxford: Clarendon Press, 1963.
186. Olsson, Kurt. "The Cardinal Virtues and the Structure of John Gower's *Speculum Meditantis.*" *Journal of Medieval and Renaissance Studies* 7 (1977): 113–48.
187. Pickering, F. P., ed. *The Anglo-Norman Text of the Holkham Bible Picture Book.* Oxford: Blackwell, 1971.

DICTIONARIES AND LANGUAGE STUDIES

188. Arveiller, Raymond. "Textes médicaux français d'environ 1350." *Romania* 94 (1973): 157–77.

189. Baldinger, Kurt, Jean-Denis Gendron, and Georges Straka, eds. *Dictionnaire étymologique de l'ancien français.* 5 vols. Paris: Klincksieck, 1974.

190. Catach, Nina, and Gilbert Ouy. "De Pierre d'Ailly à Jean Antoine de Baïf: Un Exemple de double orthographe à la fin du XIVe siècle." *Romania* 97 (1976): 218–48.

191. Dees, A. *Étude sur l'évolution des démonstratifs en ancien et en moyen français.* Groningen: Wolters-Noordhoff, 1971.

192. Fennell, T. G. *La Morphologie du futur en moyen français.* Geneva: Droz, 1975.

193. Gonon, Marguerite. *La vie familiale en Forez au XIVe siècle et son vocabulaire d'après les testaments.* Paris: Belle Lettres, 1961.

194. Greimas, A. J. *Dictionnaire de l'ancien français jusqu'au milieu du XIVe siècle.* Paris: Larousse, 1968.

195. Löfstedt, Leena. "*Res* et *causa:* Étude lexicographique sur la base de trois traductions." *Archiv für das Studium der neueren Sprachen und Literaturen* 209 (1972): 310–26. (Jean de Vignay)

196. Marchello-Nizia, Christiane. *Histoire de la langue française aux XIVe et XVe siècles.* Paris: Bordas, 1979.

197. Massart, Robert. "Contribution à l'étude du vocabulaire de Nicolas de Vérone." *Mélanges de linguistique romane et de philologie médiévale offertes à Maurice Delbouille.* 2 vols. Gembloux: J. Duculot, 1964, 1: 421–50.

198. Offord, Malcolm Y. "Negation in *Bérinus:* A Contribution to the Study of Negation in Fourteenth-Century French." *Zeitschrift für Romanische Philologie* 92 (1976): 313–85.

199. Renzi, Lorenzo. "Per la lingua del l'*Entrée d'Espagne.*" *Cultura Neolatina* 30 (1970): 59–87.

200. Taylor, Robert. "Les néologismes chez Nicole Oresme, traducteur du XIVe siècle." In *Actes du Xe Congrès International de Linquistique et Philologie Romanes,* pp. 727–36. Paris: Klincksieck, 1965.

See also entries 116, 137, 138, 146, 170.

GERMAN LITERATURE

Ingeborg Glier*

For a long time, German literature of the fourteenth century was regarded by scholars like an unloved step-child. Two of the main reasons were that there was so terrifyingly much of it and that it seemed unglamorous. Earlier centuries in which considerably fewer texts were transmitted attracted much more scholarly attention, especially the years between 1170 and 1230. This great period of medieval German literature tended to overshadow the following centuries. Although the literature of the twelfth and thirteenth centuries will always rank high in scholarly interest, considerable progress has been achieved within the last twenty-five years in research on the fourteenth and fifteenth centuries.

When we remain within the fourteenth century and look beyond language boundaries, German literature also presents a rather bewildering picture, and the Germanist is bound to feel some envy when contemplating how other European literatures flourished and how many great names abound: Dante, Petrarch, and Boccaccio in Italy; Guillaume de Machaut, Jean Froissart, and Christine de Pisan in France; and Langland, Gower, and Chaucer in England. The names that a Germanist might offer have a different

*Ingeborg Glier received a Doctor of Philosophy in English and a *Habilitation* in German from the University of Munich, where she taught from 1958 to 1972. Since 1973 she has been Professor of Germanic Languages and Literature at Yale University. Her research has been far-ranging and has included Jacobean Drama, German metrics, Minnereden, and Shrovetide plays. She currently is at work on Minnesang and allegory in medieval literature.

and less familiar ring: Meister Eckhart, Heinrich der Teichner, and Oswald von Wolkenstein, although some may not even agree on these names. The first of them, Meister Eckhart (ca. 1260–1328), is considered one of the most profound mystical thinkers in the Middle Ages. The second, Heinrich der Teichner (ca. 1300–before 1377), was a most prolific writer, who composed a huge number of short didactic poems on almost every conceivable topic and who was widely renowned until the end of the Middle Ages but not much beyond. The third, Oswald von Wolkenstein (1377–1445), was an exuberant lyrical poet, whose songs often relate the vicissitudes of his life and who has lately gained considerable popularity within and beyond the community of scholars. These three names, however, compose a disparate group. Although the degree to which we can regard them as representative for the literature of the period remains limited, their incompatibility is an indication of how fourteenth-century German literature is diversified, enervating, and challenging.

Another problem in interdisciplinary discussion concerns the semantic range of the term *literature* itself. Scholars of medieval German literature in general and of fourteenth-century literature in particular tend to use it in an inclusive rather than an exclusive way. In this case, what is meant by *literature* is not just *belles lettres* or *schöne/hohe Literatur* but the sum total of *Schriftkultur* in the vernacular, every German text that to our knowledge reached the written page (15). This broad understanding of literature enormously complicates the tasks of literary historians, editors, lexicographers, and other scholars, yet it also provides a firmer grasp on the various roles of literature in the narrower sense, and, more importantly, it allows for valuable insights into the ever changing, at times dramatic, interplay of Latin and vernacular culture. It can also function as a healthy antidote against overestimating the importance of works (*we* find most attractive) within their medieval contexts, or against underestimating what seems to *us* less appealing.

Furthermore, my colleagues in other disciplines view the fourteenth century as a period. The majority of scholars of German medieval literature would not agree. Their starting point is a late medieval period that begins between 1230 and 1250 and ends around 1500; further subdivision of these centuries is a much debated question involving various approaches and criteria. If one is not too orthodox about it, however, I think a good case could be made for a turning point around 1300, when *Minnesang* (love poetry and related genres) as well as romances were coming to an end of sorts. Likewise, I would argue that subtle yet decisive shifts occurred around 1400 when humanist tendencies were gradually rising and when the inhabitants of cities and towns became increasingly interested and productive in literary matters. I would, however, also maintain that the literature originating between these two turning points is far from presenting a unified picture.

GENERAL WORKS

General works on late medieval German literature are predominantly organized generically. Studies primarily concentrate on literary genres or comparable groupings of texts and then follow chronological developments within the genre. This pattern dominates the only complete, comprehensive, and detailed literary history of the late Middle Ages so far: the last volume of Gustav Ehrismann's *Geschichte der deutschen Literatur bis zum Ausgang des Mittelalters* (7), which contains stupendous amounts of material, rather haphazardly organized, and by now very much dated. One of the main problems with this approach is that since late medieval literature differs in generic organization so much from that in the preceding centuries, as well as from literature in more modern times, no two literary histories or general surveys of the period agree in generic subdivision. Striking differences surface when one compares Ehrismann's volume to more recent efforts, such as Max Wehrli's *Geschichte der deutschen Literatur vom frühen Mittelalter bis zum Ende des 16. Jahrhunderts* (19), and also when one compares more recent efforts with one another, such as Wehrli's book and the forthcoming volume by myself and others (10). This may indicate that we are still far from agreement on the generic subdivison or *Feinstruktur* in those centuries.

The generic approach also has provided the structure for two excellent critical reviews of research on late medieval German literature, "Neue Forschungen zur deutschen Dichtung des Spätmittelalters (1230–1500)," the first by Hanns Fischer (2) and the second covering more recent research by Johannes Janota (5). They concentrate on *Dichtung*, which means that they exclude all research on late medieval prose. Together they survey research published between 1945 and 1968. For research after 1968 one has to consult the *Spätmittelalter* section in the biographical quarterly *Germanistik* (4). Incidentally, W. T. H. Jackson's review on research on all of medieval German literature in the volume *The Medieval Literature of Western Europe* (3) scarcely touches the late Middle Ages in general and the fourteenth century in particular, which leaves me in a quandary concerning the starting point of my survey on recent trends in scholarship.

Another excellent tool has to be mentioned here, although it covers far more than late medieval or fourteenth-century literature. Since 1978, a thoroughly revised and updated second edition of the venerable *Verfasserlexikon* (1) has been published in installments and has reached the letter H. It is an indispensable handbook that concentrates on German writers and anonymous works but also includes a great deal of medieval Latin literature. Leading experts in every period are contributors, and the quality of the individual articles is consistently high.

A combination of generic and national approaches is the guiding principle of a different kind of handbook, which is also much larger in scale and therefore less thorough on individual figures and works. *Europäisches Spätmittelalter* (8) is the eighth volume of an ambitious, multi-volumed survey of world literatures. Volume eight explores the European literatures in the late Middle Ages and includes some historical background. Most of the essays were contributed by German experts in the various fields, and some are interdisciplinary in approach. Although the quality of individual essays does vary, a few of them introduce their subjects admirably.

All of these general works cover late medieval literature between 1230 and 1500. None of them singles out the fourteenth century as a particular unit, rather the reader is left to extract the information he requires. There will be a volume devoted almost entirely to fourteenth-century German literature: *Die deutsche Literatur im späten Mittelalter* (10), edited by myself and written by a team of experts in various areas. This volume will close the medieval gap in an overall history of German literature. Even though sharing the effort is a great help, we will not be able to deliver the final and authentic version of literary history for that century but only a preliminary one. Despite all the efforts and energy that have gone into research of fourteenth-century literature recently and despite many achievements, much remains to be done.

EDITING OF TEXTS

In some areas of fourteenth-century literature, more advanced research continues to be severely limited by the lack of reliable editions. Quite a few texts are only available in manuscripts and/or early printed books. Others were published in the nineteenth and early twentieth

centuries, often without sufficient knowledge of all extant manuscripts and according to editorial standards that
seem rather questionable today.

Fourteenth-century texts frequently present editorial
problems that differ from those in texts of earlier centuries. In some areas, as in short rhymed narratives, discourses, or sermons, the manuscript transmission often
yields several equally valid versions rather than a single
authentic text. In other cases, writers used a particular
kind of fiendishly complicated style (*geblümter Stil*), which
was especially prone to being garbled in transmission. Or,
as often happened in drama, texts survived in abbreviated
versions because they were meant to have been performed by people who were thoroughly familiar with the
tradition, and such texts were not meant to be read as
whole works (22). Accordingly, editors had to find a variety of solutions if they either could not follow established
Lachmannian principles or did not want to settle for a
mere transcription. The following are examples.

(a) The monumental and critical edition of Meister Eckhart's Latin and German works is one of the editorial
landmarks of the period (165). Including a critical apparatus, substantial notes, and full translations, it is the standard edition and an achievement, especially considering
the vast editorial problems. Of all the editors to be mentioned in this context, Josef Quint is the one most indebted to Lachmannian principles because he has
reconstructed authentic texts based on manuscript affili-
ations and presented them in a normalized Middle High
German. Since most of the sermons in the vernacular
survived in listeners' notes rather than authentic texts,
this method of editing has also met with some controversy.

(b) There has been an increasing skepticism concerning
the applicability of Lachmann's principles to fourteenth-
century texts. When Karl Stackmann decided to edit the
short poems of Heinrich von Mügeln, he chose a different

approach. Mügeln's texts were written in a highly complicated style. Stackmann provides the reader with parallel texts that include a transcription of the manuscript and his own cautious critical text on facing pages (184).

(c) The problems that Heinrich Niewöhner faced were of a different nature. He set out to edit the roughly 67,000 lines of approximately 720 didactic poems attributed to Heinrich der Teichner. Niewöhner followed the manuscripts closely; starting with the earliest Teichner collections and correcting only obvious mistakes, he refrained from normalizing and kept the critical apparatus to a minimum. Versions are printed in appendixes (28). K. O. Seidel recently reproduced versions of selected Teichner poems directly from the manuscripts (31).

(d) Some of my final examples transcend our time limit, but since we are dealing with solutions to representative problems, this seems justified. Hanns Fischer in his *Deutsche Märendichtung des 15. Jahrhunderts* (26) followed roughly the same principles as Niewöhner concerning the evaluation of manuscripts and the constitution of his texts. Where the need arose, however, he did not banish versions into the apparatus or an appendix but presented them on facing pages. Similarly, F. Heinzle took versions seriously in her edition of a fourteenth-century narrative (36) by discussing each version individually and comparing them.

(e) In recent years, a wide variety of facsimile editions has enjoyed an increasing popularity (31, 146, 203, 204, 205). Facsimiles have been oriented toward works of the twelfth and thirteenth centuries, but gradually texts or manuscripts of the fourteenth century are being reproduced. There is also a new type of edition, in which later texts seem to prosper more; they are minimally edited transcriptions of entire manuscripts, usually with notes and useful introductions. One example is U. Schmid's *Codex Karlsruhe 408* (30). Apart from the fact that such editions make available large numbers of works, most of which are anonymous, they are helpful for studies examining how certain text collections were assembled and, possibly, how they were used.

The approaches to presenting editions, particularly by scholars in the late 1960s, are documented in a volume *Kolloquium über Probleme altgermanistischer Editionen* (23), which came out of a lively conference of the younger editors of the time. Discussions such as this one or methods developed in numerous new editions have not been confined to specialists in late medieval literature. They have challenged and changed many established notions about editing in other areas as well (20–25).

AREAS OF RESEARCH

As I mentioned earlier, most general works on late medieval German literature tend to be organized according to literary genres or groups of genres. This area of literary genres has recently seen quite a few scholarly battles—it has not been scholar against scholar, although that also happened, but rather it has been scholar against terrifying amounts of material—and despite all those many and productive battles, we are still far from having won the entire war. The particular need for the investigation of literary genres in the fourteenth century follows from literary developments in the thirteenth century that decisively changed the structure of German literature. Somewhat similar changes can, incidentally, be observed in France at about the same time. Whereas literature that originated in Germany in the decades between 1170 and 1220 can almost be subsumed under the two generic headings, lyrical songs (*Minnesang*, love songs; and *Sangspruch*, didactic and political poetry) and narrative poems (Arthurian romance and heroic epic), the picture rapidly changed. The thirteenth century saw a quantitative and generic explosion of German literature. Almost all of these genres and additional ones continued into the fourteenth century.

By the time we reach the fourteenth century, *Minnesang* and *Sangspruch* have gone underground (but we do not know enough about that as yet), and Arthurian romance and heroic epic have virtually disappeared. Instead we find religious and secular drama, large amounts of religious and some pragmatic prose, and a vast array of short and long rhymed poems, which for a long time resisted any of the usual generic classifications (some of the more dubious but popular ones were didactics, satire, parody, and allegory).

SHORT POEMS IN RHYMED COUPLETS AND RELATED FORMS

This large group of poems in rhymed couplets (*kleine Reimpaargedichte*) is rather prominent in fourteenth-century German literature. That it was conceived of as something of a unity is borne out by the manuscript transmissions in which these texts either form entire collections or are preserved as distinctive groups within codices. Their common denominators are their shortness (fifty to several hundred lines long) and the use of the rhymed couplet as their basic metrical unit. For a long time, the problem of how to structure this huge bulk of texts was either ignored, extemporized, or excited controversy. In 1968, Hanns Fischer finally devised an explicitly tentative system of subdivisions for that group. He suggested a main division into basically narrative and basically discoursive texts, *maeren* and *reden.* He was aware that he was describing tendencies and that there are many borderline cases. Fischer also proceeded cautiously when he further subdivided those two main groups. He suggested seven subgroups for the narratives and sixteen for the discourses, largely based on subject matter and explicit authorial intentions (33, pp. 35–55). Even though everyone familiar with this material will disagree with Fischer here and there, his suggestions have remained valid and proved very helpful indeed. The numbers of his subgroups—seven for narratives and sixteen for discourses—adequately reflect the stark asymmetries in the field, for example, the fact that discourses outnumber narratives by far. Accordingly, we have gained an incomplete but recognizable picture of the fourteenth-century short narrative texts, whereas discourses, with a few exceptions, remain a jungle.

Fischer himself provided an exemplary study of the *maeren* (short secular narratives) in his groundbreaking *Studien zur deutschen Märendichtung* (33). He investigated this body of more than two-hundred texts from a variety of perspectives, for instance, themes and main characters, authors and audience, the making, reciting, and transmission of texts. Fischer only needed to touch upon the subject of transmission because a comprehensive investigation by Arend Mihm (38) already existed, yet he included an extensive, systematic bibliography. Fischer curiously, though for good reasons, shied away from outlining the history of the genre, and that, by the way, is still a *desideratum*. Karl-Heinz Schirmer (41) studied style and motifs in a group of earlier short narratives concentrating on courtly elements, thereby contributing aspects absent from Fischer's work. In the wake of Fischer's book, articles by T. Andersson (32), Kurt Ruh (40), Stephen Wailes (46, 47), Werner Schröder (42–44), and others have shed more light on individual texts, and studies by F. Frosch-Freiburg (34), H. Hoven (37), H. Mundschau (39), and J. Suchomski (45) clarified a variety of aspects. The short secular narrative is a genre that is unusually well edited; quite a few of these editions were completed or instigated by Fischer himself, for instance, P. Sappler's fine edition of Heinrich Kaufringer's works (29).

The fable is the second narrative genre that has been comprehensively investigated. Klaus Grubmüller chose a primarily historical approach to this genre, which was part of that generic explosion in the thirteenth century

(35). He followed it well into the fifteenth century, yet he also devoted attention to unraveling the complicated Latin traditions of the genre beginning with classical antiquity. Likewise, he provides many interesting insights into the possible social contexts of various fable collections.

Zeitgedichte, poems dealing in one way or another with historical and political topics, events, or figures, cuts across the areas of narrative and discourse. They are partially covered by Ulrich Müller's *Untersuchungen* (159) and a text collection under the somewhat misleading title *Politische Lyrik des deutschen Mittelalters* (145). It is misleading because neither "political" nor "lyrical" sufficiently characterizes what Müller is after. Even though a good case could be made for going beyond poems in rhymed couplets and including some of the historical and political songs, the whole problem of the relationships between these poems and the earlier *Sangspruch* tradition could bear investigation.

Recent trends in research about the second and larger area short poems in rhymed couplets—discourses (*reden*)—leaves us with a bleak vista. However, a decisive gain for the whole area—and indeed a landmark—was Eberhard Lämmert's *Reimsprecherkunst im Spätmittelalter* (49), which illuminatingly investigates the 720 short poems transmitted under the name *der Teichner*. Lämmert's book is clearly a borderline case between a monograph on a literary genre and one on an individual author, yet this is particularly suited to the topic. For, on the one hand, we know that Heinrich der Teichner was a historically documented figure and a prolific author, and on the other hand, *ein Teichner*, a Teichner, later also denoted a genre of a short moral or didactic poem in rhymed couplets on almost any conceivable subject usually ending with the line *Also sprach der Teichner (Thus spoke the Teichner)*. When looking for some kind of guiding principles behind the making of these Teichner discourses, Lämmert found the closest parallels in the arts of preaching, the *sermo humilis* in particular. This assiduous self-effacement of the author or authors for the sake of the self-improvement of the audience is an important aspect of this oeuvre and indeed relativizes the question of authenticity much more than in other cases.

Of all the various kinds of discourses, *reden*, only one has recently received a lot of scholarly attention and is well researched. Those are *Minnereden*, discourses on all kinds of love, but mostly courtly love. In this genre, we have Tilo Brandis's exemplary repertoire *Mittelhochdeutsche, mittelniederdeutsche und mittelniederländische Minnereden* (52), which gives a detailed and most reliable bibliography, including the complete manuscript transmission of more than 500 texts. There is also my investigation, *Artes amandi* (54). Both were followed by dissertations by R. Leiderer (27), M. Rheinheimer (57), and M. Schierling (58), which investigated texts or groups of texts in more detail and also contributed desirable new editions.

I have attempted to outline the history of the genre from the early thirteenth to the beginning of the sixteenth century and supplement such information with discussions of manuscript transmissions and typology. As the numbers demonstrate, discourses on love seem to have been a popular literary genre, especially in the fourteenth century, but their subject matter may have favored their having been better preserved than other kinds of discourses. Unlike Fischer, Grubmüller, and Lämmert, I also had to go beyond the short form and had to include a few longer ones, mostly allegories of love from the fourteenth century. A more detailed study on German allegories of love was written by W. Blank (51).

It is interesting to note that all these monographs on literary genres are quite different in approach, although they are dealing with similar material that originated and was transmitted in the same kind of literary environment. These differences reflect the individuality of the investigators, and, to a larger extent, the particular problems that each had to face.

DRAMA

When a younger generation of scholars decided in the late fifties that something had to be done for late medieval literature, short poems in rhymed couplets profited a great deal, and yet much remains to be done. Turning to late medieval German drama, we find a state of affairs not all that much different. Here a comprehensive and reliable monograph, which would be highly desirable, is nowhere in sight. Two recent attempts, W. Michael's *Das deutsche Drama des Mittelalters* (62) and D. Brett-Evans's *Von Hrotsvit bis Folz und Gegenbach* (61), have been severely criticized by reviewers for their inaccuracies and misrepresentations. One of the two most formidable obstacles for such a monograph is about to be overcome. A team at the University of Cologne under H. Linke's competent guidance is preparing the first complete bibliography on medieval German drama. The other obstacle is the lack of reliable editions, which is a more serious problem in this area than in others and will not be remedied quickly. Earlier editions suffer from too many undocumented editorial additions or changes of the texts. Besides, performance scripts of plays were much more vulnerable in manuscript transmission than other late medieval texts. Our knowledge of late medieval dramatic and theatrical activities is, therefore, bound to be spotty. It is difficult to anticipate how long it will take to edit what remains in dependable and helpful ways, but among the promising beginnings are K. Schneider's edition of the *Eisenacher Zehnjungfrauenspiel* (77), F. Christ-Kutter's edition of *Frühe Schweizerspiele* (66), and the combined efforts of R. Schützeichel and others for the *mittelrheinisches St. Galler Passionsspiel* (78).

Important information on performances of plays is about

to be available in B. Neumann's *Geistliches Schauspiel im Zeugnis der Zeit* (87). For the first time, Neumann has systematically gathered related references and documents. These materials outnumber extant texts by far (there are twice as many for secular plays and five times as many for religious ones, according to H. Linke; 8, p. 736), and they contain much information on the social and economic aspects of producing plays and on the regional distribution of these theatrical activities.

Research on medieval drama is so behind in Germany, in addition to the reasons mentioned, because research activities were sluggish for thirty years and did not seriously resume until the early sixties. Surprising as this may seem on an international level, within Germany this renewed interest in medieval drama coincides with a growing interest in the late Middle Ages. For the plays in particular, lingering prejudices against their reputed aesthetic unattractiveness, their occasional moral offensiveness, and their pragmatic and didactic purposes gradually disappeared as obstacles. Certain comfortable Darwinistic notions that simpler dramatic forms were always earlier or older than more complicated ones also had to be unlearned. In this respect, O. B. Hardison's book, *Christian Rite and Christian Drama in the Middle Ages* published in 1965, has had an impact on rethinking established notions. German medieval drama is generally divided into religious and secular plays. The religious group contains the European staples: Easter, Passion, Corpus Christi, and Christmas plays, in addition to plays on the lives of the saints, and on the end of the world involving the Antichrist and the Last Judgment. The secular group consists almost exclusively of *Fastnachtspiele* (Shrovetide plays), which seem to be a German specialty. Even though both groups flourished in the fifteenth and early sixteenth centuries, we find religious drama in German, or in Latin and German, beginning in the thirteenth century, and secular drama appearing in the fourteenth century.

For the Shrovetide plays, the books of E. Catholy, *Das Fastnachtspiel des Spätmittelalters* (64) and *Fastnachspiel* (65), and the work of W. Lenk, *Das Nürnberger Fastnachtspiel des 15. Jahrhunderts* (68), heralded new approaches. From 1961, Shrovetide plays were reclaimed for the history of literature from the playground of folklorists and mythologists. Although Catholy went a bit too far along the lines of New Criticism for the tastes of many reviewers, he has developed a useful typology for the entire secular drama *(Reihenspiel/Revue—Handlungsspiel—Mischformen)*. The main focus of Catholy's books, as well as of most recent research on Shrovetide plays, has been on the fifteenth century in general and the especially rich Nürnberg tradition (73). Some of the intriguing early secular plays of the fourteenth century, especially *St. Pauler Neidhartspiel, Streit zwischen Mai und Herbst*, have been thoroughly investigated in articles by E. Simon (69–72), with regard to their literary backgrounds and to the season when they were performed. Simon suggested elimination of the unjustified subdivisions like Neidhart plays or *Jahreszeitenspiele* (seasonal plays) and consideration of them as Shrovetide plays. Simon has also announced a book-length study on the beginnings of secular drama in Germany.

Among the various types of religious drama in the fourteenth century, Passion plays have attracted much scholarly interest in recent years. R. Bergmann thoroughly investigated the origin and history of Passion plays in the thirteenth and fourteenth centuries (79). He arrived at quite a few more precise datings and localizations for some texts and has stressed that they are much less interdependent than had been previously assumed. Rolf Steinbach, on the other hand, included fourteenth-century Easter and Passion plays in a comprehensive study of all extant German Easter and Passion plays (91). Steinbach emphasized aspects in which each play markedly differs from other, similar ones, and he also assembled a very useful and detailed bibliography of more than sixty pages (91, pp. 225–91) on the topic. Easter plays and their dependencies on one another were also studied by B. Thoran (92), whereas E. Ukena dedicated a comprehensive investigation to miracle plays (93). Recurring elements in many plays, as the presentation and criticism of the various estates were addressed within larger contexts by W. Heinemann (13) or W. Michael (62) and also in specific studies by R. Kulli (85) and S. Grosse (81). Likewise, the fundamental question of how Latin and vernacular language are related to each other was approached on a broader scale by W. Werner (94) and on a more specific one by R. Wimmer (96). Studies of particular episodes or individual plays have further prepared the ground for a future comprehensive monograph on German medieval drama.

RELIGIOUS PROSE

Besides drama and short poems in rhymed couplets, there is a third area in German literature of the fourteenth and fifteenth centuries that has received considerable attention in recent years. This is the vast area of religious prose, which, except for the star mystics Eckhart, Tauler, and Seuse, was neglected for a long time. Kurt Ruh, who is the expert in the field, once estimated (8, p. 565) that religious prose accounts for no less than 70 to 80 percent of the vernacular manuscripts produced in fourteenth and fifteenth century Germany. What swells it to such an extent, however, is not so much the number of individual works but rather the larger numbers of parallel transmissions that dwarf those of secular texts in the narrower sense. A small part of this huge field, of course, has been claiming the intensive attention of scholars for a long time, namely the writings of the three best-known mystics of the age: Meister Eckhart, Johannes Tauler, and Heinrich Seuse. Quantitatively speaking, they are just the tip of the iceberg, and as much as they deserve this attention, it is also important to rediscover the larger contexts in which they belong. Ruh and his special research institute on late medieval prose in Würzburg are at present, and have been for some time, the leading force in mapping out this territory. They have been collecting data, editing texts (some of them in the series *Kleine deutsche Prosadenkmäler des Mittelalters*), and publishing many studies venturing into *terra incognita*. In this area, it is even more difficult than in the others discussed to do justice to what has been achieved, since that is part of so much still underway, and many new vistas are about to open up.

The best introduction to this complicated field is the highly compact and illuminating overview that K. Ruh recently completed on European religious prose in the late Middle Ages (8, pp. 565–605). Ruh has decisively contributed to research on this area ever since his dissertation on Heinrich von St. Gallen. Beginning with his influential study *Bonaventura deutsch* (122), an investigation of Bonaventura's Latin works in German, the writings of the Franciscans have been close to Ruh's heart and mind. He edited a first volume of *Franziskanische Schriften* (109) and is about to follow it up with a second one. He also edited a representative collection of articles on *Altdeutsche und altniederländische Mystik* (123) and advised and instigated numerous studies by others.

Editions in this area are perhaps even more needed than in other fields, yet editors are often faced with formidable tasks in locating parallel transmission and in coping with its quantity and quality. Of better-known authors, Heinrich von St. Gallen (97), Heinrich von Langenstein (98), Konrad von Megenberg (99), and especially Marquard von Lindau (100–102) have profited by recent editions. Many of these new German prose texts are translations and/or adaptations of Latin works, ranging from biblical and liturgical texts (106) over St. Benedict's rule (105, 112) and prayer books (108) to legends (104) and sermons (110).

By the fourteenth century, almost any kind of Latin religious prose seemed to be fit for reception into the vernacular, and reception included a range of activities from translating to adapting to freely re-creating. Modern investigations of individual texts or groups of texts are, for this reason, often combined with editions and commentaries. It is impossible to mention more than a few of them. K. Berg investigated how certain works of Thomas Aquinas were assimilated into German prose (114) and is now preparing an edition. G. Steer studied the reception of scholasticism in German (124, 125). A variety of catechistic treatises that originated after 1370 mainly in southern Germany and are preserved in Munich manuscripts are the core of E. Weidenhiller's book (130), and B. Adam edited and investigated catechistic explanations of the Lord's Prayer in the vernacular (113). There has also been a steady and recently increasing interest in the lives and revelations of thirteenth- and fourteenth-century nuns (115, 118, 119, 121). And to give yet another example of the variety of research being pursued, K. Morvay and D. Grube compiled an extensive and useful bibliography on German sermons throughout the Middle Ages containing several chapters on the fourteenth century (120; yet not including the well-documented works of Meister Eckhart and Tauler). Given the dimensions of the field of religious prose and the amounts of material still to be covered or even found, it will take some time until our grasp of it will be reasonably adequate.

PROSE TEXTS ON THE ARTES (FACHPROSA)

It will also take time before scholars have thoroughly investigated texts on the various *artes liberales et mechanicae*. Over the last two decades, it has prospered considerably from detailed research. Yet for reasons of space, it can only get shorter shrift than some of the other fields. Almost every new issue of *Germanistik* (4) in its sections on *Fachprosa* attests to the diversity of work in this area. Like religious prose, *artes* prose is a territory once dominated by Latin but now being infiltrated by the vernacular language. Again, most of it is translated and/or adapted from Latin sources. Its scope is wide and includes a detailed and ambitious history of Nature, such as Konrad von Megenberg's *Buch der Natur,* as well as vocabularies, cookbooks, and all kinds of practical how-to manuals.

Research in the field is indebted to G. Eis, its pioneering spririt, who wrote many articles, a selection of which appeared in 1971 (137). Previously, Eis also had written the first general introduction to the field (136). Among the leading younger scholars of the following generation are P. Assion and G. Keil. Assion presented a more recent and comprehensive survey of prose on the *artes* (134) in a different format than G. Eis used, and he and G. Keil also edited a series of lectures contributed to by specialists in various subfields and reflecting aptly on achievements and goals (140). Although the boundaries of the field have become much clearer over the past two decades, they still contain much uncharted territory.

LYRICS

When we talk about lyrics in the fourteenth century— or for that matter in the preceding and following centuries—we actually mean stanzaic poetry that was sung. In Germany, the two basic types were *Lied* and *Spruch.* A *Lied,* or song, usually contained a definite number of stanzas and was sung to an individual melody. A *Spruch* could consist of one stanza only, or several stanzas of the same metrical pattern could combine to form larger, more or less loose units, and by using the same tune repeatedly, a *Spruchton* could consist of an indefinite number of stanzas.

For German lyrics, the fourteenth century is even more of a transitional period than for other genres. In its beginning, *Minnesang* proper came to an end of sorts, emphasized by the harvesting of the rich tradition in the three main *Minnesang* collections. Organized *Meistersang*, on the other hand, which was practiced mainly in the cities, did not become visible until well into the fifteenth century. In between stretches a gray zone that is flanked by two rather colorful transitional figures: around 1300 by Heinrich Frauenlob, whom some consider to be the first *Meistersinger*, and around 1400 by Oswald von Wolkenstein, whom many regard as the last *Minnesinger*. I have here excluded the former because he seems to belong more closely to the thirteenth century. I have, however, included the latter, since he appears closer in spirit to the fourteenth century.

The lyric is another of those areas that recently has profited from detailed research. There are a few anthologies that contain many fourteenth-century lyrics (143–145). Curiously enough, the editors, T. Cramer, E. and H. Kiepe, and U. Müller, decided to include texts in rhymed couplets along with lyrics proper, and, although the dividing line between the two is admittedly fine, this seems unnecessarily confusing. D. Boueke (142) has shed light on the intricacies of the Neidhart transmission and reception. Both *Bruder Hansens Marienlieder* (147) and the religious songs of the so-called Mönch von Salzburg (148) have been published in new editions. The famous *Kolmarer Liederhandschrift* (146), though a manuscript of the fifteenth century, contains many texts from preceding centuries and is for the first time accessible in a facsimile-type edition compiled by U. Müller, F. V. Spechtler, and H. Brunner. C. Petzsch (162) has investigated its origins and history in detail.

B. Nagel wrote an introduction to *Meistersang* (160) and edited a collection of research articles on the same topic (161), both of which touch the fourteenth century. Two areas of major interest in recent research are religious songs and their reception, and they have been doc-

umented by J. Janota (156), V. Mertens (157), P. Appelhans
(150), H. Brunner (152, 153), and W. Röll (163). The lectures of the *Würzburger Colloquium* (164) throw light on
both religious and secular texts or groups of texts. T. Brandis edited and investigated Harder's work, except for his
discourse on love (151). G. Moczygemba wrote a comprehensive monograph on Hugo von Montfort (158), and
J. M. Clifton-Everest studied the origins of the Tannhäuser legend (154), which, like the even more popular Neidhart legend, raises interesting problems of reception.

INDIVIDUAL AUTHORS

The works of many individual authors are covered
in the previous sections. I have selected a few of long-
standing or of recent interest for mention here.

Meister Eckhart, Johannes Tauler, and Heinrich Seuse

The large edition of Meister Eckhart's works (165) has
made considerable progress in the last two decades. Unfortunately, J. Quint died in 1976 before he could complete the German section. Eckhart and Tauler had
anniversaries that instigated *Gedenkschriften* (169, 179)
to which numerous specialists in mysticism contributed.
V. Lossky (176) wrote an influential study on Eckhart's
negative theology, and I. Degenhardt (168) investigated
the decisive changes in Eckhart's image. Studies on Meister Eckhart vary quite a bit in scope; S. Ueda (183), for
instance, compared Eckhart's mystical anthropology to
that of Zen Buddhism, and T. Beckmann (167) took a closer
look at Eckhart's biographical data and at his trial (including a detailed bibliography). In the past decade, three introductions into Meister Eckhart's life and teaching were
written from different points of view by E. Soudek (182),
H. Fischer (170), and A. Haas (173), whose book is particularly well written and informative. To this list should be

added K. Ruh's excellent general article (1). In recent research, there has developed an openness for the paradoxes in Meister Eckhart's teaching as illustrated by C. F. Kelly's fine study on divine knowledge (174) and A. Haas's books (171–173). We also find a stronger emphasis on the problems of mysticism, theology, and language (177, 172, 181). Comparative studies of all three great mystics, Eckhart, Tauler, and Seuse, center on the concept of self-knowledge (171) and on stylistics (181). In Haas, research on mysticism has attracted one of those rare scholars who is as knowledgeable about problems of literature and language as he is about theology.

Heinrich von Mügeln

Increasing interest in late medieval literature over the past two decades has greatly benefited Heinrich von Mügeln. A groundbreaking event was the publication of K. Stackmann's edition of Mügeln's *Spruchdichtung* (184), which made the work available in its entirety for the first time. Soon after, two investigations by Stackmann (190) and J. Kibelka (189) focused attention on vernacular traditions and Latin backgrounds respectively. In their wake, J. Hennig (186) rigorously reexamined Mügeln's biographical data and the chronology of his works and raised some provocative questions. H. Hilgers's substantial study (187) is dedicated to the transmission of Mügeln's commentary to Valerius Maximus and serves as a decisive step toward a needed critical edition. A number of articles (not all listed in this bibliography) helped to clarify details and to broaden insights. Heinrich von Mügeln should continue to emerge as a complex, transitional figure.

Johannes von Tepl, *Der Ackermann aus Böhmen*

Like the works of Meister Eckhart, Tauler, Seuse, and Wittenwiler, the *Ackermann* has been a staple for research on late medieval German literature. It is in need of research efforts that differ from those demanded by less well-known works. Welcome contributions were R. Anderson's and J. Thomas's *Index verborum* to the various editions (191), G. Sichel's overview of previous research (198), and the collection of representative articles by various scholars, edited by E. Schwarz (197). Three fundamental aspects of the *Ackermann*, namely rhetorical devices, the problem of composition, and the question of sources, were reexamined by F. Bäuml (192), G. Hahn (193, 194), and A. Hrubý (195) respectively.

Heinrich Wittenwiler

Wittenwiler's *Ring*, a unique and puzzling blend of narrative, satire, didactics, and black humor, has continued to attract scholarly interest. An incomplete bibliography and an overview of research is to be found in B. Plate's recent study (202). More recently, R. Mueller (201) illuminatingly investigated the topics of marriage, folly, and play, and K. Jürgens-Lochthove (200) examined the work in relation to much earlier courtly romances. A little earlier, J. Bismark (199) offered a fresh look at the author and the bent of his social and satirical messages.

Oswald von Wolkenstein

No other poet or writer of the time can match Oswald von Wolkenstein in the amount of recent interest within the scholarly community and well beyond it. The renaissance in Oswald studies was ushered in when K. K. Klein and his collaborators presented a new and complete edition of Oswald's songs, which has been revised since then (206). Reproductions of all the major manuscripts (203–205) and a verse concordance (207) followed. The proceedings of two major conferences on Oswald in 1973 and 1977 (211, 214) were published and contain contributions by notable scholars. Recently, U. Müller edited a volume of representative articles on Oswald (216) that have been written in the past two decades. It also contains a useful and detailed bibliography by H. Mück.

N. Mayr's book (213) on Oswald's extensive traveling and his songs about it opened a long line of studies concentrating on the autobiographical elements in Oswald's poetry. New historical documents on his life were unearthed and familiar ones reevaluated; several biographies resulted: the first one in English by G. F. Jones (209), followed by A. Schwob's (218) and Dieter Kühn's (211) books. Kühn's *Ich Wolkenstein* is noteworthy because it blends research, fact, and fiction (without confusing them) with a fresh approach and a broad appeal rarely found in German books of this kind.

Although the details of Oswald's life have attracted attention, his songs have also been extensively investigated within a variety of historical, critical, and aesthetic contexts. This bibliographical selection can only suggest the liveliness of research that Oswald's work has sparked in the past twenty years.

CONCLUSION

I would like to conclude by mentioning a treasure of a work, which does not strictly fall within the domain of German literature, but which would be a loss for anyone interested in the fourteenth century to overlook, *Die Parler und der schöne Stil 1350–1400* (221), a three-volume catalogue of a recent exhibition in Cologne. It is lavishly illustrated and contains a vast amount of diversified background information contributed by many scholars from various countries. It includes an interesting section on literature as well as numerous reproductions from manuscripts of the period. It may serve as a reminder that the art of the fourteenth century transcended national boundaries.

Bibliography

Bibliography, Reference, Reviews of Research

1. *Die deutsche Literatur des Mittelalters: Verfasserlexikon.* Edited by Kurt Ruh et al. 2d ed. Vol. 1. Berlin and New York: de Gruyter, 1978–.
2. Fischer, Hanns. "Neue Forschungen zur deutschen Dichtung des Spätmittelalters (1230–1500)." *Deutsche Vierteljahrsschrift* 31 (1957): 303–45.
3. Fisher, John H., ed. *The Medieval Literature of Western Europe: A Review of Research, Mainly 1930–1960.* New York: MLA and New York University Press, 1966.
4. *Germanistik: Internationales Referatenorgan mit bibliographischen Hinweisen.* Vol 1. Tübingen: Niemeyer, 1960–.
5. Janota, Johannes. "Neue Forschungen zur deutschen Dichtung des Spätmittelalters (1230–1500), 1957–1968." *Deutsche Vierteljahrsschrift* 45 (1971): Sonderheft pp. 1–242*.
6. Jones, George F. *Spätes Mittelalter (1300–1450).* Bern: Francke, 1971.

Commentary and Criticism

7. Ehrismann, Gustav. *Geschichte der deutschen Literatur bis zum Ausgang des Mittelalters.* Zweiter Teil: Die mittelhochdeutsche Literatur. Schlussband. Reprint. Munich: Beck, 1959.
8. Erzgräber, Willi, ed. *Europäisches Spätmittelalter.* Neues Handbuch der Literaturwissenschaft, edited by Klaus von See, vol. 8. Wiesbaden: Akademische Verlagsgesellschaft Athenaion, 1978.

---

*An asterisk by page numbers designates a specially numbered issue.

9. Fleckenstein, Josef, and Karl Stackmann, eds. *Über Bürger, Stadt und städtische Literatur im Spätmittelalter.* Bericht über Kolloquien der Kommission zur Erforschung der Kultur des Spätmittelalters 1975–1977. Göttingen: Vandenhoeck & Ruprecht, 1980.

10. Glier, Ingeborg, ed. *Die deutsche Literatur im späten Mittelalter.* Zweiter Teil: 1300–1400. Geschichte der deutschen Literatur von den Anfängen bis zur Gegenwart von Helmut de Boor und Richard Newald, vol. 3, part 2. Munich: Beck, forthcoming.

11. Harms, Wolfgang, and L. Peter Johnson, eds. *Deutsche Literatur des späten Mittelalters: Hamburger Colloquium 1973.* Berlin: E. Schmidt, 1975.

12. Haug, Walter, ed. *Formen und Funktionen der Allegorie: Symposion 1978.* Stuttgart: Metzler, 1979.

13. Heinemann, Wolfgang. "Zur Ständedidaxe in der deutschen Literatur des 13.–15. Jahrhunderts." *Beiträge zur Geschichte der deutschen Sprache und Literatur* (Halle) 88 (1966): 1–90; 89 (1967): 290–403; 92 (1970): 388–437.

14. Keyser, Peter. *Michael de Leone (†1355) und seine literarische Sammlung.* Würzburg: Schöningh, 1966.

15. Kuhn, Hugo. "Versuch einer Literaturtypologie des deutschen 14. Jahrhunderts." In *Typologia litterarum* (Festschrift Max Wehrli), edited by Stefan Sonderegger et al, pp. 261–80. Zürich: Atlantis, 1969. Reprinted in *Liebe und Gesellschaft*, pp. 121–34, 193–95. Stuttgart: Metzler, 1980.

16. Nyholm, Kurt. *Studien zum sogenannten geblümten Stil.* Åbo: Åbo Akademi, 1971.

17. Rosenfeld, Hans Friedrich, and Hellmut Rosenfeld, *Deutsche Kultur im Spätmittelalter: 1250–1500.* Wiesbaden: Akademische Verlagsgesellschaft Athenaion, 1978.

18. Schützeichel, Rudolf, ed. *Studien zur deutschen Literatur des Mittelalters.* In Verbindung mit Ulrich Fellman. Bonn: Bouvier, 1979.

19. Wehrli, Max. *Geschichte der deutschen Literatur vom frühen Mittelalter bis zum Ende des 16. Jahrhunderts.* Stuttgart: Reclam, 1980.

PROBLEMS OF EDITING

20. Bäuml, Franz. "Some Aspects of Editing the Unique Manuscript. A Criticism of Method." *Orbis Litterarum* 16 (1961): 27–33.
21. Ganz, Peter. "Editionen spätmittelhochdeutscher Texte. Ein Bericht." *Zeitschrift für deutsche Philologie* 92 (1973): 65–87.
22. Janota, Johannes. "Auf der Suche nach gattungsadäquaten Editionsformen bei der Herausgabe mittelalterlicher Spiele." In *Tiroler Volksschauspiel*, edited by Egon Kühebacher, pp. 74–78. Bozen: Athesia, 1976.
23. Kuhn, Hugo et al., eds. *Kolloquium über Probleme altgermanistischer Editionen.* Wiesbaden: Steiner, 1968.
24. Spechtler, Franz V. "Zur Methode der Edition mittelalterlicher Texte." *Studia Musicologica Academiae Scientiarum Hungaricae* 15 (Budapest 1973): 225–45.
25. Stackmann, Karl. "Mittelalterliche Texte als Aufgabe." In *Festschrift Jost Trier*, edited by William Foerste und Karl Heinz Borck, pp. 240–67. Köln: Böhlau, 1965.

SHORT POEMS IN RHYMED COUPLETS
(KLEINE REIMPAARGEDICHTE)

Editions

26. Fischer, Hanns, ed. *Die deutsche Märendichtung des 15. Jahrhunderts.* Munich: Beck, 1966.
27. Leiderer, Rosemarie, ed. *Zwölf Minnereden des Cgm 270.* Berlin: E. Schmidt, 1972.
28. Niewöhner, Heinrich, ed. *Die Gedichte Heinrichs des Teichners.* 3 vols. Berlin: Akademie-Verlag, 1953–1956.
29. Sappler, Paul, ed. *Heinrich Kaufringer: Werke.* 2 vols. Tübingen: Niemeyer, 1972–1974.
30. Schmid, Ursula, ed. *Codex Karlsruhe 408.* Bern and Munich: Francke, 1974.
31. Seidel, Kurt Otto, ed. *Teichner-Reden.* Ausgewählte Abbildungen zur handschriftlichen Überlieferung. Göppingen: Kümmerle, 1978.

(Many of the studies below also contain text editions)

Narrative Genres

32. Andersson, Theodore M. "Rüdiger von Munre's *Irregang und Girregar:* A Courtly Parody?" *Beiträge zur Geschichte der deutschen Sprache und Literatur* (Tübingen) 93 (1971): 311–50.

33. Fischer, Hanns. *Studien zur deutschen Märendichtung.* Tübingen: Niemeyer, 1968.

34. Frosch-Freiburg, Frauke. *Schwankmären und Fabliaux: Ein Stoff- und Motivvergleich.* Göppingen: Kümmerle, 1971.

35. Grubmüller, Klaus. *Meister Esopus: Untersuchungen zu Geschichte und Funktion der Fabel im Mittelalter.* Munich: Artemis, 1977.

36. Heinzle, Franziska. *Der Württemberger: Untersuchung, Texte, Kommentar.* Göppingen: Kümmerle, 1974.

37. Hoven, Heribert. *Studien zur Erotik in der deutschen Märendichtung.* Göppingen: Kümmerle, 1978.

38. Mihm, Arend. *Überlieferung und Verbreitung der Mären- dichtung im Spätmittelalter.* Heidelberg: Winter, 1967.

39. Mundschau, Heinz. *Sprecher als Träger der tradition vi- vante in der Gattung Märe.* Göppingen: Kümmerle, 1972.

40. Ruh, Kurt. "Zur Motivik und Interpretation der *Frauen- treue.*" In *Festschrift für Ingeborg Schröbler,* edited by Dietrich Schmidtke and Helga Schüppert, pp. 258–272. Tübingen: Niemeyer, 1973.

41. Schirmer, Karl-Heinz. *Stil- und Motivuntersuchungen zur mittelhochdeutschen Versnovelle.* Tübingen: Niemeyer, 1969.

42. Schröder, Werner. "Niewöhners Text des *bîhtmaere* und seine überlieferten Fassungen." *Beiträge zur Geschichte der deutschen Sprache und Literatur* (Tübingen) 91 (1969): 260–301; Korrekturnote: 92 (1970): 180.

43. ———. *"Von dem Rosen Dorn ein gut red."* In *Mediaeva- lia litteraria* (Festschrift für Helmut de Boor), edited by Ursula Hennig and Herbert Kolb, pp. 541–564. Munich: Beck, 1971.

44. ———. "Additives Erzählen in der Mären-Überlieferung." In *Zeiten und Formen in Sprache und Dichtung* (Fest-

schrift für Fritz Tschirch), edited by Karl-Heinz Schirmer and Bernhard Sowinski, pp. 187–202. Köln: Böhlau, 1972.

45. Suchomski, Joachim. *"Delectatio" und "utilitas." Ein Beitrag zum Verständnis mittelalterlicher komischer Literatur.* Bern and Munich: Francke, 1975.

46. Wailes, Stephen. "Konrad von Würzburg and Pseudo-Konrad: Varieties of Humour in the *Märe.*" *Modern Language Review* 69 (1974): 98–114.

47. ———. "Social Humor in Middle High German Mären." *Amsterdamer Beiträge zur älteren Germanistik* 10 (1976): 119–48.

Heinrich der Teichner

48. Bögl, Heribert. *Soziale Anschauungen bei Heinrich dem Teichner.* Göppingen: Kümmerle, 1975.

49. Lämmert, Eberhard. *Reimsprecherkunst im Spätmittelalter: Eine Untersuchung der Teichnerreden.* Stuttgart: Metzler, 1970.

50. Seidel, Kurt Otto. *"Wandel" als Welterfahrung des Spätmittelalters im didaktischen Werk Heinrichs des Teichners.* Göppingen: Kümmerle, 1973.

Discoursive Genres

51. Blank, Walter. *Die deutsche Minneallegorie: Gestaltung und Funktion einer spätmittelalterlichen Dichtungsform.* Stuttgart: Metzler, 1970.

52. Brandis, Tilo. *Mittelhochdeutsche, mittelniederdeutsche und mittelniederländische Minnereden: Verzeichnis der Handschriften und Drucke.* Munich: Beck, 1968.

53. Bührer, Wolfgang. "*Der Kleine Renner.* Untersuchungen zur spätmittelalterlichen Ständesatire." *Bericht des Historischen Vereins Bamberg* 105 (1969): 1–201.

54. Glier, Ingeborg. *Artes amandi: Untersuchung zu Geschichte, Überlieferung und Typologie der deutschen Minnereden.* Munich: Beck, 1971.

55. Kasten, Ingrid. *Studien zu Thematik und Form des mittelhochdeutschen Streitgedichts.* Hamburg: Ph.D. diss., 1973.

56. Mihm, Arend. "Aus der Frühzeit der weltlichen Rede:

Inedita des Cod. Vindob.2705." *Beiträge zur Geschichte der deutschen Sprache und Literatur* (Tübingen) 87 (1965): 406–33.

57. Rheinheimer, Melitta. *Rheinische Minnereden: Untersuchungen und Edition.* Göppingen: Kümmerle, 1975.

58. Schierling, Maria. *"Das Kloster der Minne." Edition und Untersuchung.* (Anhang: Vier weitere Minnereden der Donaueschinger Liedersaal-Handschrift.) Göppingen: Kümmerle, 1980.

59. Van D'Elden, Stéphanie Cain. "The *Ehrenreden* of Peter Suchenwirt and Gelre." *Beiträge zur Geschichte der deutschen Sprache und Literatur* (Tübingen) 97 (1975): 88–101.

60. ———. *Peter Suchenwirt and Heraldic Poetry.* Wien: Halosar, 1976.

DRAMA

61. Brett-Evans, David. *Von Hrotsvit bis Folz und Gengenbach: Eine Geschichte des mittelalterlichen deutschen Dramas.* 2 vols. Berlin: E. Schmidt, 1975.

62. Michael, Wolfgang F. *Das deutsche Drama des Mittelalters.* Berlin: de Gruyter, 1971.

63. ———. "Das deutsche Drama und Theater vor der Reformation. Ein Forschungsbericht." *Deutsche Vierteljahrsschrift* 47 (1973), Sonderheft pp. 1–47*.

Shrovetide Plays

64. Catholy, Eckehard. *Das Fastnachtspiel des Spätmittelalters: Gestalt und Funktion.* Tübingen: Niemeyer, 1961.

65. ———. *Fastnachtspiel.* Stuttgart: Metzler, 1966.

66. Christ-Kutter, Friederike, ed. *Frühe Schweizerspiele.* Bern: Francke, 1963.

67. Glier, Ingeborg. "Personifikationen im deutschen Fastnachtspiel des Spätmittelalters." *Deutsche Vierteljahrsschrift* 39 (1965): 542–87.

68. Lenk, Werner. *Das Nürnberger Fastnachtspiel des 15. Jahrhunderts: Ein Beitrag zur Theorie und zur Interpre-

tation des Fastnachtspiels als Dichtung. Berlin: Akademie-Verlag, 1966.

69. Simon, Eckehard. "The Origin of Neidhart Plays." *Journal of English and Germanic Philology* 67 (1968): 458–74.

70. ———. "The Staging of Neidhart Plays: With Notes on Six Documented Performances." *Germanic Review* 44 (1969): 5–20.

71. ———. "The Alemannic *Herbst und Mai* Play and Its Literary Background." *Monatshefte* 62 (1970): 217–30.

72. ———. "Neidhart Plays as Shrovetide Plays: Twelve Additional Documented Performances." *Germanic Review* 52 (1977): 87–98.

73. Simon, Gerd. *Die erste deutsche Fastnachtspieltradition: Zur Überlieferung, Textkritik und Chronologie der Nürnberger Fastnachtspiele des 15. Jahrhunderts.* (mit kurzen Einführungen in Verfahren der quantitativen Linguistik). Lübeck: Matthiesen, 1970.

Religious Drama

Editions

74. Bätschmann, Emilia, ed. *Das St. Galler Weihnachtsspiel.* Bern: Francke, 1977.

75. Pausch, Oskar, ed. "Das Kremsmünsterer Osterspiel. Ein Fragment aus dem 14. Jahrhundert." *Zeitschrift für deutsches Altertum* 108 (1979): 51–57.

76. Schmidtke, Dietrich, Ursula Hennig, Walther Lipphardt, eds. "Füssener Osterspiel und Füssener Marienklage." *Beiträge zur Geschichte der deutschen Sprache und Literatur* (Tübingen) 98 (1976): 231–88, 395–423.

77. Schneider, Karin, ed. *Das Eisenacher Zehnjungfrauenspiel.* Berlin: E. Schmidt, 1964.

78. Schützeichel, Rudolf et al., eds. *Das mittelrheinische Passionsspiel der St. Galler Handschrift 919.* Tübingen: Niemeyer, 1978.

Studies

79. Bergmann, Rolf. *Studien zur Entstehung und Geschichte der deutschen Passionsspiele des 13. und 14. Jahrhunderts.* Munich: Fink, 1972.

80. ———. "Die Prophetenszene der Frankfurter Dirigier-rolle." *Zeitschrift für deutsche Philologie* 94 (1975): Sonderheft 22–29.

81. Grosse, Siegfried. "Zur Ständekritik in den geistlichen Spielen des späten Mittelalters." *Zeitschrift für deutsche Philologie* 86 (1967): Sonderheft 63–79.

82. Hennig, Ursula. "Die Ereignisse des Ostermorgens in der *Erlösung*. Ein Beitrag zu den Beziehungen zwischen geistlichem Spiel und erzählender Dichtung im Mittelalter." In *Mediaevalia litteraria* (Festschrift für Helmut de Boor), edited by Hennig and Herbert Kolb, pp. 507–29. Munich: Beck, 1971.

83. ———. "Die Klage der Maria Magdalena in den deutschen Osterspielen. Ein Beitrag zur Textgeschichte der Spiele." *Zeitschrift für deutsche Philologie* 94 (1975): Sonderheft 108–138.

84. King, Norbert. *Mittelalterliche Dreikönigsspiele: Eine Grundlagenarbeit zu den lateinischen, deutschen und französischen Dreikönigsspielen und—spielszenen bis zum Ende des 16. Jahrhunderts.* Freiburg and Schweiz: Universitätsverlag, 1979.

85. Kulli, Rolf Max. *Die Ständesatire in den deutschen geistlichen Spielen des ausgehenden Mittelalters.* Bern: Francke, 1966.

86. Kuné, Jacoba Hendrica. *Die Auferstehung Christi im deutschen religiösen Drama des Mittelalters.* Amsterdam: Rodopi, 1979.

87. Neumann, Bernd. *Geistliches Schauspiel im Zeugnis der Zeit: Zur Aufführung mittelalterlicher religiöser Dramen im deutschen Sprachgebiet.* Munich and Zürich: Artemis, 1981.

88. Pflanz, Hermann Manfred. *Die lateinischen Texgrundlagen des St. Galler Passionsspieles in der mittelalterlichen Liturgie.* Frankfurt, Bern, and Las Vegas: Lang, 1977.

89. Roeder, Anke. *Die Gebärde im Drama des Mittelalters: Osterfeiern, Osterspiele.* Munich: Beck, 1974.

90. Schmid, Rainer. *Raum, Zeit und Publikum des geistlichen Spiels: Aussage und Absicht eines mittelalterlichen Massenmediums.* Munich: Tuduv, 1975.

91. Steinbach, Rolf. *Die deutschen Oster- und Passionsspiele*

des Mittelalters: Versuch einer Darstellung und Wesens-
bestimmung (nebst einer Bibliographie zum deutschen
geistlichen Schauspiel des Mittelalters). Köln and Wien:
Böhlau, 1970.

92. Thoran, Barbara. *Studien zu den österlichen Spielen des*
deutschen Mittelalters: Ein Beitrag zur Klärung ihrer Ab-
hängigkeit voneinander. Göppingen:Kümmerle, 1976.

93. Ukena, Elke. *Die deutschen Mirakelspiele des Spätmit-*
telalters. 2 vols. Bern, Frankfurt: Lang, 1975.

94. Werner, Wilfried. *Studien zu den Passions- und Oster-*
spielen des deutschen Mittelalters in ihrem Übergang vom
Latein zur Volkssprache. Berlin: E. Schmidt, 1963.

95. Wildenberg-deKroon, Cornelia. *Das Weltleben und die*
Bekehrung der Maria Magdalena im deutschen religiösen
Drama und in der bildenden Kunst des Mittelalters. Am-
sterdam: Rodopi, 1979.

96. Wimmer, Ruprecht. *Deutsch und Latein im Osterspiel:*
Untersuchungen zu den volkssprachlichen Entspre-
chungstexten der lateinischen Strophenlieder. Munich:
Beck, 1974.

RELIGIOUS PROSE

Editions

97. Legner, Wolfram, ed. *Heinrich von St. Gallen: Die Mag-*
nifikat-Auslegung. Munich: Fink, 1973.

98. Rudolf, Rainer, ed. *Heinrich von Langenstein: "Erchant-*
nuzz der sund." Berlin: E. Schmidt, 1969.

99. Steer, Georg, ed. *Konrad von Megenberg: "Von der sel."*
Eine Übertragung aus dem "Liber de proprietatibus re-
rum" des Bartholomäus Anglicus. Munich: Fink, 1966.

100. Hofmann, Annelies Julia, ed. *Der Eucharistie-Traktat*
Marquards von Lindau. Tübingen: Niemeyer, 1960.

101. Greifenstein, Eckart, ed. *Der Hiobtraktat des Marquard*
von Lindau: Überlieferung, Untersuchung und kritische
Textausgabe. Munich and Zürich : Artemis, 1979.

102. Van Maren, Jacobus Willem, ed. *Marquard von Lindau:*
"Die zehen gebot." Ein katechetischer Traktat. (Textaus-
gabe mit Einleitung und sprachlichen Beobachtungen.)
Amsterdam: Rodopi, 1980.

103. Schmidt, Margot, ed. *Rudolf von Biberach: "Die siben strassen zu got." Die hochalemannische Übertragung nach der Hs. Einsiedeln 278.* Florentiae: Collegium Sancti Bonaventurae, 1969.

104. Brett-Evans, David, ed. *Bonaventuras "Legenda sancti Francisci" in der Übersetzung der Sibilla von Bondorf.* Berlin: E. Schmidt, 1960.

105. Coun, Theo, ed. *De oudste middelnederlandse vertaling van de "Regula S. Benedicti."* With a general introduction in English. Mit einer allgemeinen Einleitung in Deutsch. Hildesheim: Gerstenberg, 1980.

106. Eggers, Hans, ed. *Zwei Psalter aus dem 14. Jahrhundert (Dresden Ms. M 287 und Hamburg in scr. 142) und drei verwandte Bruchstücke aus Schleiz, Breslau und Düsseldorf.* Berlin: Akademie-Verlag, 1962.

107. Kamber, Urs, ed. *"Arbor amoris." Der Minnebaum: Ein Pseudo-Bonaventura-Traktat.* Berlin: E. Schmidt, 1964.

108. Rooth, Erik, ed. *Niederdeutsche Breviertexte des 14. Jahrhunderts aus Westfalen.* Stockholm: Almqvist & Wiksell, 1969.

109. Ruh, Kurt, ed. *Franziskanisches Schrifttum im deutschen Mittelalter I.* Munich: Beck, 1965.

110. Schmidtke, Dietrich, ed. "Die *Feigenbaumpredigt* eines Straßburger Augustinereremiten. Mit einer Vorbemerkung zum deutschsprachigen Schrifttum der Straßburger Augustinereremiten im 14. Jahrhundert." *Zeitschrift für deutsches Altertum* 108 (1979): 137–57.

111. Schmitt, Margarete, ed. *"Der große Seelentrost." Ein niederdeutsches Erbauungsbuch des 14. Jahrhunderts.* Köln and Graz: Böhlau, 1959.

112. Sullivan, Mary C., ed. *A Middle High German Benedictine Rule: Ms. 4486a Germanisches Nationalmuseum Nürnberg.* Hildesheim: Gerstenberg, 1976.

Studies

113. Adam, Bernd. *Katechetische Vaterunserauslegungen: Texte und Untersuchungen zu deutschsprachigen Auslegungen des 14. und 15. Jahrhunderts.* Zürich and Munich: Artemis, 1976.

114. Berg, Klaus. *"Der tugenden bûch."* *Untersuchungen zu mittelhochdeutschen Prosatexten nach Werken des Thomas von Aquin.* Munich: Beck, 1964.

115. Blank, Walter. *Die Nonnenviten des 14. Jahrhunderts: Eine Studie zur hagiographischen Literatur des Mittelalters* (unter besonderer Berücksichtigung der Visionen und ihrer Lichtphänomene). Freiburg i. Br.: Ph.D. diss., 1962.

116. Dusch, Marieluise. *"De veer utersten." Das "Cordiale de quatuor novissimis" von Gerhard von Vliederhoven in mittelniederdeutscher Überlieferung.* Köln, Wien: Böhlau, 1975.

117. Eis, Gerhard. *Altgermanistische Beiträge zur geistlichen Gebrauchsliteratur: Aufsätze—Fragmentfunde—Miszellen.* Bern and Frankfurt: Lang, 1974.

118. Grubmüller, Klaus. "Die Viten der Schwestern von Töss und Elsbeth Stagel." *Zeitschrift für deutsches Altertum* 98 (1969): 171–204.

119. Montag, Ulrich. *Das Werk der heiligen Birgitta von Schweden in oberdeutscher Überlieferung: Texte und Untersuchungen.* Munich: Beck, 1968.

120. Morvay, Karin and Dagmar Grube. *Bibliographie der deutschen Predigt des Mittelalters: Veröffentlichte Predigten.* Munich: Beck, 1974.

121. Ringler, Siegfried. *Viten- und Offenbarungsliteratur in Frauenklöstern des Mittelalters: Quellen und Studien.* Zürich and Munich: Artemis, 1980.

122. Ruh, Kurt. *Bonaventura deutsch: Ein Beitrag zur deutschen Franziskaner mystik und -scholastik.* Bern: Francke, 1956.

123. Ruh, Kurt, ed. *Altdeutsche und altniederländische Mystik.* Darmstadt: Wissenschaftliche Buchgesellschaft, 1964.

124. Steer, Georg. *Scholastische Gnadenlehre in mittelhochdeutscher Sprache.* Munich: Beck, 1966.

125. ———. "Germanistische Scholastikforschung. Ein Bericht." *Theologie und Philosophie* 45 (1970): 204–26; 46 (1971): 195–222; 48 (1973): 65–106.

126. Völker, Paul-Gerhard. *Die deutschen Schriften des Franziskaners Konrad Bömlin I: Überlieferung und Untersuchung.* Munich: Beck, 1964.

127. ———. "Die Überlieferungsformen mittelalterlicher deutscher Predigten." *Zeitschrift für deutsches Altertum* 92 (1963): 212–27.
128. Wallach-Faller, Marianne. "Die erste deutsche Bibel? Zur Bibelübersetzung des Zürcher Dominikaners Marchwart Biberli." *Zeitschrift für deutsches Altertum* 110 (1981): 35–57.
129. Warnock, Robert G., und Adolar Zumkeller. *Der Traktat Heinrichs von Friemer über die Unterscheidung der Geister: Lateinisch-mittelhochdeutsche Textausgabe mit Untersuchungen.* Würzburg: Augustinus, 1977.
130. Weidenhiller, Egino. *Untersuchungen zur deutschsprachigen katechetischen Literatur des späten Mittelalters: Nach Handschriften der Bayerischen Staatsbibliothek.* Munich: Beck, 1965.
131. Williams-Krapp, Werner. "Die deutschen Übersetzungen der *Legenda aurea* des Jacobus de Voragine." *Beiträge zur Geschichte der deutschen Sprache und Literatur* (Tübingen) 101 (1979): 252–76.
132. *Würzburger Prosastudien I: Wort-, begriffs- und textkundliche Untersuchungen,* edited by Forschungsstelle für deutsche Prosa des Mittelalters, Würzburg. Munich: Fink, 1968.
133. *Würzburger Prosastudien II: Untersuchungen zur Sprache und Literatur des Mittelalters,* edited by Peter Kesting. Festschrift für Kurt Ruh. Munich: Fink, 1975.

PROSE LITERATURE ON THE ARTES

134. Assion, Peter. *Altdeutsche Fachliteratur.* Berlin: E. Schmidt, 1973.
135. Cossar, Clive Douglas. *The German Translations of the Pseudo-Bernhardine "Epistola de cura rei familiaris."* Göppingen: Kümmerle, 1975.
136. Eis, Gerhard. *Mittelalterliche Fachliteratur,* 2d ed. Stuttgart: Metzler, 1967.
137. ———. *Forschungen zur Fachprosa: Ausgewählte Beiträge.* Bern, Munich: Francke, 1971.
138. Grubmüller, Klaus. *"Vocabularius ex quo." Untersuchungen zu lateinisch-deutschen Vokabularien des Spätmittelalters.* Munich: Beck, 1967.

139. Keil, Gundolf. "Der deutsche Branntweintraktat des Mittelalters: Texte und Quellenuntersuchungen." *Centaurus* 7 (1960): 53–100.
140. Keil, Gundolf, and Peter Assion, eds. *Fachprosaforschung: Acht Vorträge zur mittelalterlichen Artesliteratur.* Berlin: E. Schmidt, 1974.
141. Ploss, Emil. *Ein Buch von alten Farben.* Heidelberg: Impuls, 1962.

Lyrics

Editions and Anthologies

142. Boueke, Dietrich, ed. *Materialien zur Neidhart-Überlieferung.* Munich: Beck, 1967.
143. Cramer, Thomas, ed. *Die kleineren Liederdichter des 14. und 15. Jahrhunderts.* 3 vols. Munich: Fink, 1977–.
144. Kiepe, Eva, and Hansjürgen Kiepe, eds. *Gedichte 1300–1500: Nach Handschriften und Frühdrucken in zeitlicher Folge.* (Epochen der deutschen Lyrik, edited by Walther Killy, vol. 2). Munich: Deutscher Taschenbuch-Verlag, 1972.
145. Müller, Ulrich, ed. *Politische Lyrik des deutschen Mittelalters: Texte.* 2 vols. Göppingen: Kümmerle, 1972–1974.
146. Müller, Ulrich, Franz V. Spechtler, Horst Brunner, eds. *Die Kolmarer Liederhandschrift der Bayerischen Staatsbibliothek München (cgm 4997). In Abbildungen.* 2 vols. Göppingen: Kümmerle, 1976.
147. Batts, Michael S., ed. *Bruder Hansens Marienlieder.* Tübingen: Niemeyer, 1963.
148. Spechtler, Franz V., ed. *Die geistlichen Lieder des Mönchs von Salzburg.* Berlin, New York: de Gruyter, 1972.
See also 184, 203–6, 208.

Studies

149. Adam, Wolfgang. *Die "wandelunge." Studien zum Jahreszeitentopos in der mittelhochdeutschen Literatur.* Heidelberg: Winter, 1979.
150. Appelhans, Peter. *Untersuchungen zur spätmittelalter-*

*lichen Mariendichtung: Die rhythmischen mittelhoch-
deutschen Mariengrüße.* Heidelberg: Winter, 1970.

151. Brandis, Tilo. *Der Harder: Texte und Studien I.* Berlin:
de Gruyter, 1964.

152. Brunner, Horst. "Überlieferung und Rezeption der mittelhochdeutschen Lyriker im Spätmittelalter und in der
frühen Neuzeit. Probleme und Methoden der Erforschung." In *Historizität in Sprach- und Literaturwissenschaft*, edited by Walter Müller-Seidel et al, pp. 133–41.
Munich: 1974.

153. ————. *Die alten Meister: Studien zu Überlieferung und
Rezeption der mittelhochdeutschen Sangspruchdichter
im Spätmittelalter und in der frühen Neuzeit.* Munich:
Beck, 1975.

154. Clifton-Everest, J. M. *The Tragedy of Knighthood: Origins
of the Tannhäuser Legend.* Oxford: Society for the Studies of Mediaeval Languages and Literature, 1979.

155. Holtorf, Arne. *Neujahrswünsche im Liebesliede des
ausgehenden Mittelalters.* Göppingen: Kümmerle, 1973.

156. Janota, Johannes. *Studien zu Funktion und Typus des
deutschen geistlichen Liedes im Mittelalter.* Munich:
Beck, 1968.

157. Mertens, Volker. "Der Ruf—eine Gattung des deutschen
geistlichen Liedes im Mittelalter?" *Zeitschrift für
deutsches Altertum* 104 (1975): 68–89.

158. Moczygemba, Gustav. *Hugo von Montfort.* Fürstenfeld:
Selbstverlag, 1967.

159. Müller, Ulrich. *Untersuchungen zur politischen Lyrik
des deutschen Mittelalters.* Göppingen: Kümmerle, 1974.

160. Nagel, Bert. *Meistersang.* Stuttgart: Metzler, 1962. 2d
ed., 1971.

161. ————, ed. *Der deutsche Meistersang.* Darmstadt: Wissenschaftliche Buchgesellschaft, 1967.

162. Petzsch, Christoph. *Die Kolmarer Liederhandschrift:
Entstehung und Geschichte.* Munich: Fink, 1978.

163. Röll, Walther. *Vom Hof zur Singschule: Überlieferung
und Rezeption eines Tones im 14. bis 17. Jahrhundert.*
Heidelberg: Winter, 1976.

164. Ruh, Kurt and Werner Schröder, eds. *Beiträge zur weltlichen und geistlichen Lyrik des 13. bis 15. Jahrhun-*

derts: Würzburger Colloquium 1970. Berlin: E. Schmidt,
1973.
See also 185–90, 209–20.

MEISTER ECKHART AND OTHERS

Edition, Translation

165. *Meister Eckhart: Die deutschen und lateinischen Werke.*
1. *Abteilung: Die deutschen Werke,* edited by Josef Quint.
Stuttgart: Kohlhammer, 1936–. Completed: vol. 1 (1958),
2 (1971), 3 (1976), 5 (1963). 2. *Abteilung: Die lateinischen Werke,* edited by various editors. Stuttgart: Kohlhammer, 1936–. Completed: vol. 1 (by K. Weiß, 1964), 4
(by E. Benz, B. Decker, J. Koch, 1956). Installments of
vols. 2, 3, 5.
166. Quint, Josef, ed. and trans. *Meister Eckhart: Deutsche
Predigten und Traktate,* 2d. ed. Munich: Hanser, 1978.

Studies

167. Beckmann, Till. *Daten und Anmerkungen zur Biographie Meister Eckharts und zum Verlauf des gegen ihn
angestrengten Inquisitionsprozesses.* Mit einer Bibliographie von Texten, Übersetzungen, und Interpretati-
onen. Frankfurt: R. G. Fischer, 1978.
168. Degenhardt, Ingeborg. *Studien zum Wandel des Eck-
hartbildes.* Leiden: Brill, 1967.
169. Filthaut, Ephrem, ed. *Johannes Tauler: Ein deutscher
Mystiker.* Gedenkschrift zum 600. Todestag. Essen:
Driewer, 1961.
170. Fischer, Heribert. *Meister Eckhart: Einführung in sein
philosophisches Denken.* Freiburg: Alber, 1974.
171. Haas, Alois M. *"Nim din selbes war." Studien zur Lehre
der Selbsterkenntnis bei Meister Eckhart, Johannes Tauler und Heinrich Seuse.* Freiburg and Schweiz: Universitätsverlag, 1971.
172. ———. *"Sermo mysticus." Studien zur Theologie und
Sprache der deutschen Mystik.* Freiburg and Schweiz:
Universitätsverlag, 1979.

173. ———. *Meister Eckhart als normative Gestalt geistlichen Lebens.* Einsiedeln: Johannes Verlag, 1979.
174. Kelley, C. F. *Meister Eckhart on Divine Knowledge.* New Haven: Yale University Press, 1977.
175. Kern, Udo, ed. *Freiheit und Gelassenheit: Meister Eckhart heute.* In Verbindung mit Heino Falcke und Fritz Hoffmann. München: Kaiser, 1980.
176. Lossky, Vladimir. *Théologie négative et connaissance de Dieu chez Maître Eckhart.* Paris: J. Vrin, 1960.
177. Margetts, John. *Die Satzstruktur bei Meister Eckhart.* Stuttgart: Kohlhammer, 1969.
178. Mieth, Dietmar. *Die Einheit von "vita activa" und "vita contemplativa" in den deutschen Predigten und Traktaten Meister Eckharts und bei Johannes Tauler: Untersuchungen zur Struktur des christlichen Lebens.* Regensburg: Pustet, 1969.
179. Nix, Udo, und Raphael Öchslin, eds. *Meister Eckhart, der Prediger* (Festschrift zum Eckhart-Gedenkjahr). Freiburg i. Br.: Herder, 1960.
180. Schaller, Toni. "Die Meister Eckhart-Forschung von der Jahrhundertwende bis zur Gegenwart." *Freiburger Zeitschrift für Philosophie und Theologie* 15 (1968): 262–316, 403–26.
181. Siegroth-Nellesen, Gabriele von. *Versuch einer exakten Stiluntersuchung für Meister Eckhart, Johannes Tauler und Heinrich Seuse.* München: Fink, 1979.
182. Soudek, Ernst. *Meister Eckhart.* Stuttgart: Metzler, 1973.
183. Ueda, Shizuteru. *Die Gottesgeburt in der Seele und der Durchbruch zur Gottheit: Die mystische Anthropologie Meister Eckharts und ihre Konfrontation mit der Mystik des Zen-Buddhismus.* Gütersloh: G. Mohn, 1965.
See also entry 123.

Heinrich von Mügeln

Edition

184. Stackmann, Karl, ed. *Heinrich von Mügeln: Kleinere Dichtungen.* 3 vols. Berlin: Akademie-Verlag, 1959.

Studies

185. Behr, Hans-Joachim. "Der *ware meister* und der *schlechte lay.* Textlinguistische Beobachtungen zur Spruchdichtung Heinrichs von Mügeln und Heinrichs des Teichners." *Zeitschrift für Literaturwissenschaft und Linguistik* 10 (1980): 70–85.

186. Hennig, Jörg. *Chronologie der Werke Heinrichs von Mügeln.* Hamburg: Buske, 1972.

187. Hilgers, Heribert. *Die Überlieferung der Valerius-Maximus-Auslegung Heinrichs von Mügeln: Vorstudien zu einer kritischen Ausgabe.* Köln, Wien: Böhlau, 1973.

188. Huber, Christoph. "Karl IV. im Instanzensystem von Heinrichs von Mügeln *Der meide kranz.*" *Beiträge zur Geschichte der deutschen Sprache und Literatur* (Tübingen) 103 (1981): 63–91.

189. Kibelka, Johannes. *"Der ware meister."* Denkstile und Bauformen in der Dichtung Heinrichs von Mügeln. Berlin: E. Schmidt, 1963.

190. Stackmann, Karl. *Der Spruchdichter Heinrich von Mügeln: Vorstudien zur Erkenntnis seiner Individualität.* Heidelberg: Winter, 1958.

JOHANNES VON TEPL, DER ACKERMANN AUS BÖHMEN

191. Anderson, Robert R., and James C. Thomas. *Index verborum zum "Ackermann aus Böhmen." Ein alphabetisch angeordnetes Wortregister zu Textgestaltungen des "Ackermann aus Böhmen" von Knieschek bis Jungbluth.* 2 vols. Amsterdam: Rodopi, 1973–1974.

192. Bäuml, Franz. *Rhetorical Devices and Structure in the "Ackermann aus Böhmen."* Berkeley and Los Angeles: University of California Press, 1960.

193. Hahn, Gerhard. *Die Einheit des "Ackermann aus Böhmen": Studien zur Komposition.* Munich: Beck, 1963.

194. ———. *Johannes von Saaz: "Der Ackermann aus Böhmen." Interpretation.* Munich: Oldenbourg, 1964.

195. Hrubý, Antonín. *Der Ackermann und seine Vorlage.* Munich: Beck, 1971.

196. Natt, Rosemarie. *"Der Ackerman aus Böhmen" des Jo-*

hannes von Tepl: Ein Beitrag zur Interpretation. Göppingen: Kümmerle, 1978.

197. Schwarz, Ernst, ed. *"Der Ackermann aus Böhmen" des Johannes von Tepl und seine Zeit.* Darmstadt: Wissenschaftliche Buchgesellschaft, 1968.

198. Sichel, Giorgio. *"Der Ackermann aus Böhmen." Storia della critica.* Firenze: Olschki, 1971.

HEINRICH WITTENWILER

199. Bismark, Jörg. *Adlige Lebensformen in Wittenwilers "Ring." Untersuchung über die Person des Dichters und die ständische Orientierung seiner Lehren und seiner Satire.* Freiburg, 1976.

200. Jürgens-Lochthove, Kristina. *Heinrich Wittenwilers "Ring" im Kontext hochhöfischer Epik.* Göppingen: Kümmerle, 1980.

201. Müller, Rolf R. *Festival and Fiction in Heinrich Wittenwiler's "Ring." A Study of the Narrative in Its Relation to the Traditional Topoi of Marriage, Folly, and Play.* Amsterdam: Benjamins, 1977.

202. Plate, Bernward. *Heinrich Wittenwiler.* Darmstadt: Wissenschaftliche Buchgesellschaft, 1977. (Review of research with bibliography.)

OSWALD VON WOLKENSTEIN

Facsimiles, Edition, Concordance

203. *Oswald von Wolkenstein: Handschrift A.* Vollständige Faksimile-Ausgabe im Original format des Codex Vindobonensis 2777 der Österreichischen Nationalbibliothek. Kommentar Francesco Delbono. Graz: Akademische Druck- und Verlagsanstalt, 1977.

204. Moser, Hans, and Ulrich Müller, eds. *Oswald von Wolkenstein: Abbildungen zur Überlieferung I: Die Innsbrucker Wolkenstein-Handschrift B.* Göppingen: Kümmerle, 1972.

205. Moser, Hans, Ulrich Müller, and Franz V. Spechtler, eds. *Oswald von Wolkenstein: Abbildungen zur Überliefer-*

ung II: Die Innsbrucker Wolkenstein-Handschrift C. Göppingen: Kümmerle, 1973.

206. Klein, Karl Kurt, ed. *Die Lieder Oswalds von Wolkenstein.* Unter Mitwirkung von Walter Weiss und Notburga Wolf. Mit einem Musikanhang von Walter Salmen. Tübingen: Niemeyer, 1962. 2. neubearbeitete und erweiterte Auflage von Hans Moser, Norbert Richard Wolf und Notburga Wolf. Tübingen: Niemeyer, 1975.

207. Jones, George Fenwick, Hans-Dieter Mück, and Ulrich Müller, eds. *Verskonkordanz zu den Liedern Oswalds von Wolkenstein. (Hss. A und B.).* 2 vols. Göppingen: Kümmerle, 1973.

Melodies

208. Ganser, Hans, and Rainer Herpichböhm, eds. *Oswald von Wolkenstein-Liederbuch.* Eine Auswahl von Melodien. Göppingen: Kümmerle, 1978.

Studies

209. Jones, George F. *Oswald von Wolkenstein.* New York: Twayne, 1973.

210. Kersken, Wolfgang. *"Genner beschnaid." Die Kalendergedichte und der Neumondkalender des Oswald von Wolkenstein. Überlieferung—Text—Deutung.* Göppingen: Kümmerle, 1975.

211. Kühebacher, Egon, ed. *Oswald von Wolkenstein: Beiträge der philologisch-musik wissenschaftlichen Tagung in Neustift bei Brixen 1973.* Im Auftrag des Südtiroler Kulturinstituts. Innsbruck: Institut für deutsche Philologie, 1974.

212. Kühn, Dieter. *Ich Wolkenstein: Eine Biographie.* Frankfurt: Insel, 1977. (Neue, erweiterte Ausgabe 1980.)

213. Mayr, Norbert. *Die Reiselieder und Reisen Oswalds von Wolkenstein.* Innsbruck: Wagner, 1961.

214. Mück, Hans-Dieter, and Ulrich Müller, eds. *Gesammelte Vorträge der 600-Jahrfeier Oswalds von Wolkenstein, Seis am Schlern 1977.* Göppingen: Kümmerle, 1978.

215. Mück, Hans-Dieter. *Untersuchungen zur Überlieferung und Rezeption spätmittelalterlicher Lieder und Spruch-*

*gedichte im 15. und 16. Jahrhundert: Die "Streuüberlie-
ferung" von Liedern und Reimpaarrede Oswalds von
Wolkenstein.* 2 vols. Göppingen: Kümmerle, 1980.

216. Müller, Ulrich, ed. *Oswald von Wolkenstein.* Darmstadt: Wissenschaftliche Buchgesellschaft, 1980. (Detailed bibliography by Hans-Dieter Mück.)

217. Robertshaw, Alan T. *Oswald von Wolkenstein: The Myth
and the Man.* Göppingen: Kümmerle, 1977.

218. Schwob, Anton. *Oswald von Wolkenstein: Eine Biographie.* Bozen: Althesia, 1977.

219. ———. *Historische Realität und literarische Umset-
zung: Beobachtungen zur Stilisierung der Gefangen-
schaft in den Liedern Oswalds von Wolkenstein.*
Innsbruck: Institut für deutsche Philologie, 1979.

220. Wachinger, Burkhart. "Sprachmischung bei Oswald von
Wolkenstein." *Zeitschrift für deutsches Altertum* 106
(1977): 277–96.

CONCLUSION

221. Legner, Anton, ed. *Die Parler und der schöne Stil 1350–
1400.* Europäische Kunst unter den Luxemburgern. Ein
Handbuch zur Ausstellung des Schnütgen-Museums in
der Kuntshalle Köln. 3 vols. Köln, 1978.

ITALIAN LITERATURE

Thomas Goddard Bergin[*]

In Italian letters, the fourteenth century is the period in which the language attained its maturity and established the country's contributions to world literature. If the history of Italian literature ended with the death of Boccaccio, the collective prestige of the *Divine Comedy*, the *Canzoniere*, and the *Decameron* is of such magnitude that the century would maintain its preeminence. The Trecento presents contradictory aspects to the student and to the bibliographer because the century is rich in the quality of its writers and is meager in quantity. Aside from the great trio, few figures of importance used the vernacular, and paradoxically, two of the three creators, Petrarch and Boccaccio, composed a large portion of their works in Latin. Fifteen of seventeen principal works in the Petrarchan canon are written in Latin, and Boccaccio's later years were dedicated to his massive *Genealogies* and other Latin exercises. As a result, the humanism inspired by both writers nearly suffocated the vernacular they had shared in creating. For the purpose of our census, many of the writings of both masters must be categorized as medieval Latin literature, excluding them from this

[*]**Thomas Goddard Bergin** is Sterling Professor of Romance Languages Emeritus at Yale University. He has published numerous books and studies on Dante, Petrarch, and Boccaccio, and he has translated the *Divine Comedy* and various works of Petrarch. Professor Bergin has received many awards and honors, including both the Dante and Petrarch Medals. He currently is at work on a *History of the Harvard-Yale Game (1875–1983)*.

chapter's concern with Italian works. We shall also exclude Dante from our survey because he is, in preparation at least, a figure of the Duecento and because a survey of Dante scholarship would exhaust the space allotted to the entire century.

We may properly begin by noting a few works of comprehensive range. In this area, Natalino Sapegno's *Il Trecento* (12), sound, lucid, and representative of a critical consensus among Italian scholars, is an excellent point of departure. Volume 2 of the *Storia della letteratura italiana* (3) is another valuable panoramic survey; it contains chapters on Dante and Petrarch by Sapegno, on Boccaccio and the other *novellieri* by Carlo Muscetta, and one on the poetry and literary currents of the time is contributed by Giorgio Petrocchi. Salvatore Battaglia's *Medioevo e umanesimo* (2) is an illuminating introduction to this age of transition. Rocco Montano's approach (8) stresses the moral and social context of the fourteenth century, its decadence and its ready acceptance of middle-class standards. T. K. Seung, in his *Cultural Thematics* (14), proposes the provocative theory that the century witnessed the formation of "the Faustian ethic," which came to its fulfillment in the individualism of the *Decameron.* A clear and unprejudiced report on the writers of the Trecento is offered by E. H. Wilkins in his *History of Italian Literature* (15).

In the past decades, the harvest in the field of specialized studies has been abundant. The cult of Petrarch and Boccaccio has never lacked devotees, but aside from the population explosion among scholars (and scholarly journals) in our time, a fact of history has intensified interest in the two masters. During the last decade the six-hundredth anniversaries of the deaths of both of the great Trecento figures occurred and were universally memorialized. Congresses of scholars were held in Europe and the United States and were followed by publication of the papers read at the meetings (75, 98, 142, 325, 351, 451).

Other commemorative miscellanies were also published. Reading their tables of contents, one cannot fail to note how perceptively—in the case of both authors but particularly in that of Petrarch—scholars are recognizing that their works in Latin and the vernacular cannot be compartmentalized as was often the practice in the past; "the *Secretum* is the indispensable gloss to the *Rime*," as Morris Bishop aphoristically wrote.[1]

The anniversaries do not entirely explain the lively interest of our century in the authors of the *Rhymes* and the *Decameron*. They have also been brought into prominence by the vigorous current of medieval studies that has characterized our age and the all but obsessional cult of Dante among the intellectuals of today. Perhaps as a result of this closer scrutiny, the introspective, restless, and sometimes even morbid personality revealed in the *Canzoniere* and the emancipated, skeptical world portrayed in the *Decameron* have come to seem strikingly modern. The ambiguities latent in both authors, manifest in their artifacts, and the multiple meanings of the *Divine Comedy* appeal to twentieth-century critics, who are eager for subtleties and impatient with simplicities. The subtitle of Barbara Tuchman's study of the century —"a century of disaster"—implies an affinity between the troubled Trecento and our own age of tension and conflict.[2]

Stars of the first magnitude as they are, Petrarch and Boccaccio have different authorial personas. Each will be considered in his own right, and to give precedence to seniority, we shall begin with Petrarch and move from editions, translations, and general studies to a survey of critical items on the *Canzoniere* and the *Trionfi*. We have already mentioned the miscellanies that attempt, with

---

1. Morris Bishop, *Petrarch and His World* (entry 52), p. 213.
2. Barbara Tuchman, *A Distant Mirror: The Calamitous 14th Century* (New York: Alfred A. Knopf, 1978).

varying degrees of completeness, to present the different facets of the man and his labors. A number of new biographies of the sage of Vaucluse have been written in recent years, addressed to divers levels of readers. The authoritative survey of Umberto Bosco (55) focuses on the works rather than on purely biographical data, and the meticulous *Life* (186) written by E. H. Wilkins is scrupulous in chronological and factual reportage; both presuppose a public of scholars. The engaging monograph by G. Frasso (99) and Morris Bishop's lively *Petrarch and His World* (52), which contains the author's admirable translations from the *Rhymes*, are addressed to a more general audience.

Of Petrarch's "vulgar fragments" themselves, it may be said that the centuries have not diminished their appeal to readers or critics. A number of new and excellent editions of the *Rhymes* have been published in recent years. The two most frequently used as reference texts are those edited by Ferdinando Neri (16) and Gianfranco Contini (18). Those of Giovanni Ponte (19) and Giosuè Carducci and S. Ferrari (17, reprinted with an introduction by Contini) are also valuable. Two concordances of the *Canzoniere* are now available; one was compiled by Kenneth McKenzie (27), and a new two-volume work containing a *rimario* was prepared for the Accademia della Crusca in 1971 (28). In this connection, we may mention the updating of the *Catalogue of the Collection* at Cornell (31) by Morris Bishop and others. The catalogue is now the most exhaustive bibliography of the works of Petrarch in print; however, an even more comprehensive census (at least for the years it covers), compiled by the late J. G. Fucilla, is in course of publication (33). An English prose translation of the *Canzoniere* (25) by Robert Durling was published in 1975 and is a useful tool for scholars not at home in Italian. There have also been sporadic attempts at translations in verse.

The *selva* of studies of the *Canzoniere* is so vast and

thick as to intimidate the explorer. Our summary follows, however tentatively, a few well-defined trailways: discussions of the work as a whole, essays on particular aspects of it, and consideration of the legacy of Petrarch, under which we may place the related and sometimes merging lines of *petrarchismo* and *fortuna*, as the Italians denominate them. Natalino Sapegno's *La personalità e la poesia del Petrarca* (158) is a good example of the first category, reinforced by his *Commento alle Rime* (159). To these may be added the perceptive contribution of Adelia Noferi, *L'esperienza poetica del Petrarca* (135), and the interesting interpretation of Nicolae Iliescu, the nature of which is revealed by its title, *Il "Canzoniere" petrarchesco e Sant'Agostino* (120). Many articles follow the same quest; for examples one need look no further than the memorial miscellany *Francis Petrarch, Six Centuries Later* (162), edited by Aldo Scaglione, which includes Sara Sturm's "The Poetic Persona in the *Canzoniere*" (172) and the ingenious interpretation of the *Rhymes* by Oscar Büdel in "Illusion Disabused: A Novel Mode in Petrarch" (61).

The probing into Petrarch's self-conscious or subconscious motivations leads to consideration of the object of his attention, and Laura has been no less attractive than her devoted swain to the Petrarch enthusiasts of our day. It seems to be generally accepted that there are two Lauras in the *Canzoniere*, and the title of Kenelm Foster's erudite exercise, "Beatrice or Medusa; The Penitential Element in Petrarch's *Canzoniere*" (96) defines this dichotomy. A fuller development of the theme, through a commentary on the successive versions of the *Rhymes*, appears in Aldo Bernardo's *Petrarch, Laura and the "Triumphs"* (46). Laura's mythological genesis, with consequent allegorical interpretations, has been the subject of the investigation of Ugo Dotti's "Petrarca: Il mito dafneo" (82), Marga Cottino-Jones's "The Myth of Apollo and Daphne in Petrarch's *Canzoniere*" (78), and the more spacious and far-reaching monograph, José Basile's *Forma Simbolica ed allegorica nei "Rerum Vulgarium" Fragmenta ed altre cose* (41).

On such themes as poetics and structure, symbiotic topics that are appealing to the critical tendencies of our times, a number of valuable and provocative studies have been made. Marguerite Waller's recent book, *Petrarch's Poetics and Literary History* (183), contains a chapter on the *Canzoniere* in which the author implements Morris Bishop's suggestion, calling on the *Secretum* for enlightenment. *Structure* is an elastic term when used in connection with the *Rhymes*, but it primarily signifies speculation on the order and sequence Petrarch gave to his *fragmenta*. Among a number of illuminating contributions to this major concern of students of the *Rhymes*, G. Herczeg's "Struttura e antitesi nel *Canzoniere* petrarchesco" (118) and A. Jenni's "Un sistema del Petrarca nell'ordinamento del *Canzoniere*" (121) may illustrate contemporary efforts to find reason or purpose in the disposition of these fragments. Of course, all biographies of the poet deal with the problem, which also has its chronological aspect, investigated in a previous generation by E. H. Wilkins and Ruth Shepard Phelps. A special kind of pattern is discussed by Thomas P. Roche, Jr., in "The Calendrical Structure of Petrarch's *Canzoniere*" (153), and a hitherto all but neglected aspect of structure is exhaustively and shrewdly surveyed by Maria Picchio Simonelli in "Strutture foniche nei *Rerum vulgarium fragmenta*" (168). Within the *Canzoniere*, the sonnet's structure and architecture have been analyzed by Fernando Figurelli (93) and tangentially by Christopher Kleinhenz (123) and others. If much has been written about the legacy of the *Rhymes*, little has been said about Petrarch's indebtedness to his predecessors, although all good commentaries touch on it. In this sector, Maria Teresa Cattaneo's book *Francesco Petrarca e la lirica d'arte del 200* (65) is a notable contribution. Ladislas Galdi's brief article (104) assaying the Provençal influence on the metrics of the *canzoni* and, more extensively, the essay by Helga Grübitzsch-Rodewald on "Petrarca und Arnaud Daniel. Petrarcas Imitations-technik in der canzone 'Verdi panni' " (110), with reference to Daniel's presence in *Rime* 29, are tokens of what such investigations can reveal.

A number of individual items of the *Canzoniere* seem to have had a special attraction for the mentality of our times. The sestine particularly exercise a notable fascination. Mario Fubini dedicates a substantial chapter to a discussion of the form (5), and Marianne Goldner Shapiro has recently published a full-scale, sophisticated analysis of the sestine of the *Canzoniere* (167). Robert Durling's sensitive analysis of "Giovene donna" (85) reveals the richness of significance and artistry contained within this example of the highly disciplined pattern. Perhaps not surprisingly, both for the resonance it has called forth in other lands and its own haunting charm, the "canzone delle visioni" ("Standomi un giorno," *Rhymes* 323) has attracted a number of critics. Fredi Chiappelli has dedicated a monograph (68) to it, and, more recently, Julia Bondanella has published a one-hundred-page study of the poem and its Renaissance analogues, which includes a sizable bibliography indicative of the growing critical interest in this tiny sibling of the *Trionfi* (53).

On other components of the *Canzoniere*, we may cite the meticulous linguistic-stylistic essay of Dennis Dutschke on *Rhymes* 23 (87). He follows the successive versions of the poem and notes (as had Durling) its connection with the "canzoni delle visioni." The significant role of the introductory sonnet has not been overlooked; it has been the subject of an interesting essay by Francisco Rico (150), and suggestive readings of this confessional exordium have been contributed by Adelia Noferi (136) and Bruce Merry (132). Other individual *Rhymes* that have attracted critical attention are 71 (Enza Biagini, 47), 52 (William Paden, Jr., 140), and the introspective "Di pensier in pensier," *Rhymes* 129 (Pierre Antonetti, 36).

If scholars and readers today find the *Canzoniere* as magnetic as have previous generations, they also follow their predecessors (beginning in the sixteenth century) in displaying a certain indifference to Petrarch's only other vernacular work, the *Triumphs*. Morris Bishop spoke for our times when he affirmed "the endless parade of classical figures bores us . . . their ox drawn floats pass all too slow."[3] Umberto Bosco, too, although his chapter on the work is a sympathetic exegesis, speaks of its "long files of prosaically arid figures."[4] Critics of our time find the *Trionfi* interesting principally for its impact on the Renaissance and the association of its classical catalogues with the author's Latin works. This is not to say that the poem has been neglected. New editions have been published in the Ricciardi collection (16) and that of Giovanni Ponte (19). A new, presumably definitive text is now in preparation under the aegis of the Accademia della Crusca (142, pp. 199–240). Two English translations of the *Trionfi* have been published in recent years, one by E. H. Wilkins in unrhymed iambic pentameter (21); the other, of peculiar interest, is a new edition of Lord Morley's sixteenth-century version in rhymed couplets (24). The editor, D. D. Carnicelli, supplies an enlightening introduction commenting on the appreciation of the poem in Tudor times, its notable effect on Renaissance iconography, and its influence on Shelley. Aldo Bernardo's *Petrarch, Laura and the "Triumphs"* (46) analyzes the work in relationship to the *Canzoniere* and to its author's motivations. In her exercise on Petrarch's poetics, Marguerite Waller (183) defends the structure and artistic integrity of the poem against

---

3. Bishop, *Petrarch and His World* (entry 52), p. 299.
4. Umberto Bosco, *Francesco Petrarca* (entry 56), p. 202.

the charges of inconsistency and prolixity leveled at it by earlier scholars.

All biographies and general studies deal in some degree with *petrarchismo* in its narrower sense or with the broader aspects of the poet's impact on successive generations. *Petrarca e il petrarchismo* go hand in hand not only on the title page of volume seven of *Studi petrarcheschi* (143). In addition to such collaborative enterprises, special studies are numerous. John H. Whitfield (185), Robert M. Durling (84), and Charles Trinkaus (175) have assessed the impact of Petrarch's poetic and humanistic persona on the mentality and sentiments of the Renaissance. Leonard Forster's *The Icy Fire* (95) is a notable contribution that suggests a pervasive influence of the master in such intriguing areas as Renaissance Latin poetry, Tudor politics, and the diction of Shakespeare. Dámaso Alonso (34) has attempted to define the essence of *petrarchismo,* and Michele Feo (91) has discussed the resonance of a theme dear to the master's heart: "Pallida no, ma più che neve bianca." These examples may serve to indicate the varied attractions of the spectral Petrarch.

Humanism itself is a kind of *petrarchismo,* but the study of the movement, intense in recent years, centers on the poet's Latin works and is not our concern here. We shall merely note that in addition to critical studies of historical and interpretative nature the last twenty years have been uncommonly rich in the production of bibliographical substance, catalogues of manuscripts, textual studies, and the like. In this area, the work of such outstanding scholars as P. O. Kristeller, Nicholas Mann, and Berthold Ullman has been notable.[5]

The posthumous changes in the critical attitudes toward

---

5. Since the work of these outstanding scholars centers on the Latin Petrarch, we have not included their contributions in our bibliography.

the bard of Vaucluse through Europe have received due attention. The main lines of his European *fortuna* have been carefully traced by a number of scholars. A concise account is provided by Ettore Bonora in Walter Binni's *I classici italiani nella storia della critica* (51, vol. 1, pp. 97–167); B. T. Sozzi's book-length survey (170) offers more extensive and up-to-date coverage. For the poet's presence in England, George Watson's *The English Petrarchans: A Critical Bibliography of the "Canzoniere"* (184) presents an excellent summary with percipient commentary. Of interest too is the specialized study of Donald L. Guss, *John Donne, Petrarchist* (113). On the poet's French incarnation, Gianfranco Contini's "Pétrarque et la France" (73) is compact and authoritative. Some of the many other articles on the subject focus on particular figures in French letters who have felt the influence of Petrarch's poetics or personality, such as Maurice Scève (76), Du Bartas (37), and Montaigne (173).

Spanish petrarchism has been scrupulously catalogued by J. G. Fucilla (103). For the master's sojourn across the Rhine, we may cite Horst Rüdiger's "Petrarca e il petrarchismo nella letteratura germanica" (155). Marvin Schindler (164) uses *Rhymes* 132 as a point of departure for his study of the cult of the poet in Germany. To bring the topic down to our own times, Cynthia G. Tucker (178) offers an essay comparing the Rilkean Orpheus poems and the Petrarchan sonnet tradition. The abiding presence of the singer of Vaucluse in his own country has not passed undetected, as witnessed by Guido Di Pino's "La presenza del Petrarca nella poesia del Novecento" (81), and, at greater length, the volume edited by Marziano Guglielminetti and Mariarosa Masoero (112) deals with contemporary *petrarchismo*. At least as firmly as its predecessors, the criticism of our age reaffirms the permanence of Petrarch.

Every generation and to some degree every decade has its own angle of vision. We may note here that Aldo S. Scaglione's comments on recent publications concerning

Petrarch (32) and his own "Petrarch 1974: A Sketch for a Portrait" (160) illuminate the modern image of the poet.

Moving to a consideration of Boccaccian studies, the first thing that stands out is the almost equal division between editorial (a designation that may cover translation, which is in some measure an editorial exercise) and critical labors. Editors of Boccaccio's works have been unusually productive in recent decades, much more so than in the case of Petrarch, not only because the vernacular Boccaccio presents a larger number of titles than his master but also because, for the minor works especially, new editions were sorely needed. Between 1964 and 1977, all of Boccaccio's vernacular works (save for the *Elegy of Madonna Fiammetta* and the *Corbaccio*) were published in the series *Tutte le opere* (192), under the direction of Vittore Branca. All of these editions contain informative introductions, copious notes, and comprehensive bibliographies. The two volumes of the Riccardo Ricciardi omnibus (190) contain annotated texts of *Ameto, Fiammetta, Ninfale fiesolano, The Life of Dante*, and the *Decameron*, as well as generous excerpts from the other works, including some selections from the *Rime*. Nor do these enterprises exhaust the list of recent editions. Since 1960, a considerable number of new translations both of the *Decameron* and of the minor works have been published.

In our survey, we shall combine the account of editorial labors with comment on the critical contributions, taking the minor works in chronological sequence and concluding with the *Decameron*. We may begin, however, with some mention of works that deal with Boccaccio in toto, and among these, two contributions of Vittore Branca merit special attention. His *Boccaccio medievale* (304), first published in 1956 and revised in 1970, is a milestone in Boccaccio studies. Branca's work is to some degree polemical, intended to revise the opinion, springing from old anticlerical and more recent nineteenth-century misreading, that Boccaccio (particularly in the *Decameron*) represents or incarnates "the negation or even the mockery of the Middle Ages."[6] Branca does not deny Boccaccio's innovations; indeed, his definition of the *Decameron* as "the epic of the merchant class" implies a departure from medieval standards that would hardly have considered merchants as worthy of an epic, but he prefers to stress Boccaccio's indebtedness to the culture of an earlier generation and his identification with the world of his times—the autumn of the Middle Ages. Rich in erudition and compellingly written, *Boccaccio medievale* redirected and undeniably invigorated the field of Boccaccian studies.

Another work of this tireless and brilliant scholar that must stand on an easily accessible shelf for the student of Certaldo's first citizen is *Giovanni Boccaccio: Profilo biografico* (302). In these pages, Branca traces his subject year by year through his vicissitudes and comments on the sources, inspiration, and significance of the successive products of his pen. The *Profilo* draws, necessarily, on the findings of earlier scholars, but they are assayed, scrutinized, and validated by Branca's own authoritative judgment. Although Branca's method is somewhat similar to that of Wilkins in his *Life of Petrarch*, the *Profilo* is richer in critical commentary. Branca rejects the French mother of whom Boccaccio obliquely speaks in his youthful works and whose existence had been recognized by earlier critics. He is also skeptical of Maria d'Aquino, the Fiammetta of the Neapolitan romances. The *Profilo* is the most authoritative account of Boccaccio's life and works that has yet appeared. Another comprehensive study of biographical-critical nature is that of Carlo Muscetta (392), a section of *Il Trecento*, published by Laterza. Muscetta's *Boccaccio* is somewhat more expansive than the *Profilo* in critical assessments and includes many excerpts from the works he discusses.

Coming to the individual works, we shall consider, first

---

6. Vittore Branca, *Boccaccio medievale* (entry 304), p. 28.

of all, those conventionally assigned to the Neapolitan period of Boccaccio's life: the *Caccia di Diana*, the *Filocolo*, the *Filostrato*, and the *Teseida*. Although the dating of these items is still controversial, Branca would put the *Filostrato* before the *Filocolo*, and P. G. Ricci would include the *Ninfale* among the earliest of Boccaccio's compositions. Beyond Branca's comments in his edition of the *Caccia* (201), this modest *primizia* has had scant critical attention; the *Filocolo*, edited by E. A. Quaglio (241), has attracted some interest. A number of scholars have pried into the sources of the Byzantine romance, notably, but not solely, Quaglio himself. The genesis of the story has been reexamined by Virginio Berrolini (294), and N. J. Perrella has contributed a cogent essay on "The World of Boccaccio's *Filocolo*" (409). Critical assessments may be found in the inclusive studies of Sapegno (12), Branca (304), and Muscetta (392), but compared to other minor works of Boccaccio, the *Filocolo* has not yet had the critical attention it deserves.

The case of the *Filostrato* is quite different. Its Chaucerian association—and its own artistry—has given it a prominent position among the minor works, and it has continued to attract scholars over the past two decades. In the introduction to his edition (243), Vittore Branca remarks on the popular character of the poem, particularly with regard to the use of the octave, and the author's experience of love (fact or fiction as it may be) that gives the narrative its strength. The sources of the poem have been scrutinized anew by Maria Gozzi (353), and Robert apRoberts has written an analysis of "Love in the *Filostrato*" (423). The *Teseida*, edited by Alberto Limentani (260), has also been for the first time translated into English by Bernadette Marie McCoy (263), who defines the epic as a "morality play" that "celebrates the triumph of harmonious mastery more than it memorializes the deeds of warriors or lovers."[7] Limentani comments on the poet's

---

7. *The Book of Theseus* (entry 263), p. 17.

uses of his sources (371), and a study by E. H. Branch (308) explores the theme of the individual versus society in the *Teseida* and in *The Knight's Tale* of Chaucer. On the Neapolitan productions of Boccaccio's pen, taken collectively, Carmela Merola (386) has written a dissertation dealing with the three love romances. In this connection, we may cite two other studies that examine in some detail the substance and intention of all the so-called minor works of Boccaccio: Bernhard König's *Boccaccio vor dem "Decameron"* (367) and Robert Hollander's *Boccaccio's Two Venuses* (360). The latter is particularly interesting since the author, detecting an ethical current pervading all the lesser works, offers illuminating and provocative comment.

To return to our chronological census, *L'Ameto* and *L'Amorosa visione* might by their nature be expected to appeal to our allegory-loving generation. In fact, aside from Hollander, they have tempted very few scholars or critics. Both works have been edited in the Mondadori series: the former under the title of *Comedia delle ninfe fiorentine* by A. E. Quaglio (205), who finds that the work's significance lies in its stylistic intransigence, the latter by Vittore Branca himself (198). His definition of the poem as a "mediocrissimo poemetto" (198, p. 20) expresses the general verdict of readers; he does not fail, however, to note its influence on both Petrarch and Ariosto. For the *Comedia*, Giuseppe Velli's article (453) provides a sympathetic gloss.

The portraits of the heroines of the *Elegy of Madonna Fiammetta* and the *Corbaccio* have been subjected to scrutiny as critics debate to what degree they are drawn from life and how clearly they reveal their classical origins—Ovid and Seneca for the former, Juvenal for the latter. On the structure of the *Fiammetta*, an original essay has been published by Cesare Segre (436). The *Corbaccio* has received quite a lot of attention. Marga Cottino-Jones examines (322) the work's ethical implications, Mario

Marti sees the tale as a repudiation of *Fiammetta* (381), and Jean-Pierre Barricelli (289) argues that Boccaccio was satirizing not womankind but misogyny. A good presentation of the work may be found in Anthony K. Cassell's introduction to his lively translation (211) of the subversive little fable. The *Fiammetta* and the *Corbaccio* have both been published in the Riccardo Ricciardi anthology (190, 193), the former edited by Carlo Salinari and Natalino Sapegno, the latter by P. G. Ricci. Tauno Nurmela's scrupulous and scholarly edition of the *Corbaccio* works appeared early in 1968 (209). The dating of the *Corbaccio* (a work that, incidentally, Marga Cottino-Jones sees as marking "a dramatic change" in the author's "way of thinking and writing")[8] is still controversial. New translations of the *Fiammetta* into German and Russian were published in 1968.

The *Ninfale fiesolano* has enjoyed two recent editions, one at the hands of P. G. Ricci (252), who believes that, aside from a few lyrics, it is the first work of the young Boccaccio, and another by Armando Balduino (250), who dates its composition just before that of the *Decameron.* The idyll has twice been translated into English: in prose by Daniel Donno (253), in modified *ottava rima* by Joseph Tusiani (254), and in Russian (256) and Hungarian (255) as well. The freshness and simple style of the *Ninfale* continue to appeal to critics such as Sapegno, Muscetta, and Wilkins. A study of its diction has led Armando Balduino (284) to a wide-ranging essay on the public Boccaccio had in mind for his works. The *Rhymes* have been relatively neglected; there has been no edition since Branca's revised version, which he himself does not regard as definitive; he has, however, contributed an illuminating chapter on the lyrics in *Boccaccio medievale* (304), and Rosario Ferreri, in a trio of articles (337–39), has discussed their

---

8. Marga Cottino-Jones, "The *Corbaccio:* Notes for a Mythical Perspective of Moral Alternatives" (entry 322), p. 506.

style, critical history, and indebtedness to Ovid. Boccaccio's *Vita di Dante*, as it is commonly called, and his *Esposizioni* on the *Divine Comedy* have not been overlooked. P. G. Ricci's edition of *Trattatello* (265) presents the texts of all three versions in a convenient fashion; his crisp introduction defines the relationship between the versions, and his notes provide ample commentary on the sources and dependability of the *Life*. Giorgio Padoan's edition of the *Esposizioni sopra la Comedia di Dante* (239), abundantly annotated, stresses their significance not only for the history of Dante studies but also for that of humanism. In the course of the last twenty years, new translations of the *Life* have been made into Czechoslovakian, German, English, and Japanese.[9]

Confronting the accumulation of works of all categories on the *Decameron*, one is tempted to say that perhaps never in its long career has the masterpiece enjoyed wider appreciation than in our times. Several editions have achieved special distinction. The Hamiltonian manuscript, "autografo," in the general opinion of scholars, has been edited by Charles S. Singleton (222) and again by Vittore Branca, who also brought out the edition of the work that forms a part of the Mondadori series (214, 215). Published in 1976, this volume will probably remain the edition of reference for years to come; six hundred compact pages of informational and interpretative notes facilitate the reader's appreciation of the substance of the tales, and the extensive introduction defines and elucidates the legend of Everyman, as the editor perceives it. Nor is Branca's the only edition of the hundred tales in recent years; scholars such as Marti (217), Salinari (221), and Quaglio (219) have completed their own editions, and, at the hands of Edoardo Sanguineti (218), the old school text of Momigliano has been republished. Translations abound.

---

9. Enzo Esposito, *Boccacciana: Bibliographia delle edizioni e degli scritti critici (1939–1974)* (entry 276), pp. 23–43.

Within the last twenty years alone, new versions of the *Decameron* have appeared in more than twenty languages, including Bulgarian, Korean, and Albanian; all are duly noted in Enzo Esposito's *Boccacciana* (276). In English, the version of G. H. McWilliam (223) has been widely acclaimed; the selections translated and edited by Mark Musa and Peter Bondanella (224) are faithful and readable and are accompanied by useful critical and informative commentary.

In the area of criticism, a number of notable, full-length studies of the *Decameron* have been published during the last two decades. Branca's *Boccaccio medievale* (304), as already cited, centers principally on the masterpiece, although it covers a broader area. Aldo Scaglione's indispensable *Nature and Love in the Late Middle Ages* (434) surveys the sources, the uses, and the innovations in Boccaccio's naturalism. Giovanni Getto in *Vita di forme e forme di vita nel "Decameron"* (350) finds in the work a celebration of the art of living as exemplified by the Decameronians, an art in which appetite, discretion, resourcefulness, and a kind of social awareness are blended. Critics such as Guido Almansi (280) and Millicent Marcus (379) focus attention on the storytelling persona of the author, his manipulation of his readers, and the underlying irony of his approach. Marga Cottino-Jones (320) studies the style of the *Decameron,* a subject handled also in a chapter of Branca's *Boccaccio medievale* (304, vol. 3), and Tsvetan Todorov probes for a kind of metaphysical structure of the work in *La Grammaire du Décaméron* (450), an approach that has some affinity to that of Cesare Segre (435).

Such themes are proposed and developed in the vast outpouring of specialized articles. The examples of critical essays in Mark Musa and Peter Bondanella's *The Decameron* (224) provide useful guidelines illustrating the various approaches or methods of contemporary criticism: historical, philosophical, formalist, structural or archetypal, and, perhaps more specifically, allegorical. The frame, the frame characters, and the villas and gardens of the background have been combed for symbolism (310, 335, 363). A number of critics too see a Dantesque type of allegory in the pattern of the work.[10]

Within the extensive *Decameron* realm, certain provinces have been singled out for special scrutiny. The Sixth Day, for instance, has been repeatedly analyzed for what it tells us about the author's concept of the art of story-telling (299, 340, 342, 447). Because of their distinctive place in the series, days one and ten also draw a good deal of critical attention. The tales of Ciappelletto and Griselda in particular, encouraging multiple interpretation, have inevitably tempted the critical mentality of our times; a complete bibliography of either would run to several pages. Such characters as the luckless Ghismonda, the vengeful Rinieri, and the resourceful Fra Cipolla might also claim a kind of bibliographical autonomy.[11] Many such essays, classifiable under the categories outlined by Musa and Bondanella, are subtle and original. It is sometimes difficult to cling to Wilkins's unabashed affirmation that the *Decameron* is primarily "a book of laughter,"[12] or to heed Bosco's admonition that "Boccaccio isn't trying to teach anyone anything."[13] In general, Boccaccian criti-

---

10. Notably Ferdinando Neri's "Il disegno ideale del *Decameron*" in *Poesia e storia* (entry 395) and Charles Trinkaus's *The Poet as Philosopher* (entry 175), p. 128.

11. Examples of such sharply focused studies may be found in this bibliography. For Ciappelletto, see entry 379, pp. 11–26; entry 14, pp. 193–99; entry 304, pp. 34–100. For Griselda, see entries 278, 288, and 323. For Ghismonda and Rinieri, see entry 280, pp. 133–39; pp. 147–52 for the former and pp. 92–99 for the latter. For Fra Cipolla, see entry 331, pp. 140 ff. In addition, all full-scale studies of Boccaccio give substantial treatment to these characters. Branca's edition of the *Decameron* (entry 214) provides an exhaustive bibliography for each of the hundred tales.

12. Ernest Hatch Wilkins, *A History of Italian Letters* (entry 15), p. 109.

13. *Saggi sul rinascimento italiano* (Florence: Le Monnier, 1970), p. 80.

cism today is highly sophisticated and, save for Almansi's contribution, somewhat austere. The search for a design, a message, some kind of *sovrasenso* in the hundred tales, motivates many students of Boccaccio nowadays.

The endurance of Boccaccio's attraction and prestige through the centuries, in Italy and elsewhere, has been the subject of intense investigation, covering the varying estimates of his contribution, the inspiration provided by his example, and specific derivations or imitations of his sundry artifacts in poetry and prose. If there is no *boccaccismo* of manner, the genres he originated, summed up by Wilkins (15, p. 102), remain a unique legacy. For the fortune of his work through the years, particularly the *Decameron*, the account of Giuseppe Petronio (51, pp. 169–232) is still useful; Achille Tartaro's *Boccaccio* (449) is a more recent and more detailed survey of the response of Italian critics from Leonardo Bruni to the present. Boccaccio's influence on other national literatures has been extensively studied. G. H. Wright's *Boccaccio in England from Chaucer to Tennyson* (458) is exhaustive in its coverage. A more recent collaborative volume, edited by Giuseppe Galigani (344), extending the topic chronologically and geographically, takes in America as well as England. Carlo Pellegrini (407) has edited a similar collection of essays dealing with the Boccaccian presence in France, a zone also explored by Patricia May Gathercole (348, 349) and Franco Simone (438, 439), among others. The trail of the poet-scholar in both his Latin and vernacular aspects has been followed through Europe from Portugal to Rumania (382).

In what might be called the service area, two items call for special notice. A two-volume concordance of the *Decameron* was published in 1969 (272); it is the first of its kind. In 1975 Enzo Esposito and Christopher Kleinhenz (276) compiled a useful bibliography of contemporary Boccacciana, covering the years 1939 to 1974. Finally, the founding of *Studi sul Boccaccio*, under the direction of Vittore Branca, was at once a token of the prestige of

Boccaccian studies in our times and a stimulus to their growth.

Petrarch and Boccaccio are not, of course, the only vernacular writers of the Trecento. Their preeminence and their appeal through the years, however, have cast a shadow that eclipses their contemporaries. This is not to say that the minor figures of the century have been ignored by scholars. Cino da Pistoia, who served as a personal link between his friends Dante and Petrarch and his student, Boccaccio, was duly memorialized in 1975 by a *colloquio* (489) with notable contributions from Aurelio Roncaglia, Armando Balduino, and Emilio Pasquini, whose essay embraces the production of other minor poets of the period. Cino has been the subject of a few other studies as well (488, 490). St. Catherine of Siena, the centenary of whose canonization was celebrated in 1981, has appeared frequently in annual bibliographies. Her *epistolario*, devotional, practical, and at times polemical in content and uniquely personal in manner, can hardly be ignored; her affinity with St. Teresa of Avila has not escaped the attention of her readers (480, 485).

Most of the noteworthy publications dealing with other lesser figures of the century have been of an editorial rather than a critical nature. In support of this impression, we may cite the edition of the poems of the eccentric Antonio da Ferrara by Laura Bellucci (469), the useful glossary of Bonvesin de la Riva's sturdy Milanese by Fabio Marri (472), and sundry textual studies of Passavanti (496), Sacchetti (499), and Cecco d'Ascoli (487). In the same general sector of investigation, the case for Antonio Pucci as author of *Il fiore* has been reviewed (498). Apart from such special studies, the minor writers of the century have been perceptively if somewhat briefly presented and analyzed in such inclusive volumes as Sapegno's *Il Trecento* (12) and the collaborative venture of like title published by Garzanti (3), which includes individual chapters on the novellieri, the poets, and the Franco Venetian epic. For

Sacchetti, Peter Brockmeier's discussion in *Lust und Herrschaft* (309) is of interest.

A number of studies in recent years have focused on specific genres. The *cantari* and their propagators, the *giullari*, have been objects of critical and historical reassessment, notably by Franca Ageno (473). The Viterbo *convegno* of 1977 (461) emphasized the contribution of the minstrels to the early Italian theater. On this topic, the work of Emilio Faccioli (463) provides the most thorough exposition available. Giovanni Getto's two-volume treatise on religious literature (465) is rich and authoritative.

Although the lesser writers of the century have not been forgotten, the harvest is scanty. Such authors as Sacchetti, Pucci, and Sercambi, for example, deserve fuller treatment than they have received.

References in the foregoing survey are of course selective and by no means exhaustive. To a lesser degree the same may be said of the Bibliography that follows, although I believe it provides tolerably ample coverage of the areas explored and includes the principal explorers. I should like to add here a few titles of publications too recent for inclusion in the Bibliography. Mark Musa and Peter Bondanella have now brought out their translation of the entire *Decameron* (New York and Scarborough, Ontario: The New American Library, 1982); Howard C. Cole has contributed *The All's Well Story from Boccaccio to Shakespeare* (Urbana, Chicago, London, University of Illinois Press, 1981); and Charles Franco's *Arte e poesia nel Reggimento e costumi di donna di Francesco da Barberino* (Ravenna: Longo, 1982) is a substantial monograph on a minor but not insignificant writer.

Bibliography

General and Comprehensive Studies

1. Amaturo, Raffaele, et al. *Dalla crisi dell'età comunale all'umanesimo*. Naples: Liguori, 1965; Bari: Laterza, 1971.
2. Battaglia, Salvatore. *Medioevo e umanesimo*. Florence: Sansoni; Milan: Accademia, 1971.
3. Cecchi, Emilio, and Natalino Sapegno, eds. *Storia della Letteratura Italiana*. Vol. 2. *Il Trecento*. 1965. Reprint. Milan: Garzanti, 1976. Includes chapters on Dante and Petrarch by Natalino Sapegno, Boccaccio and the storytellers by Carlo Muscetta, culture and poetry by Giorgio Petrocchi, and Franco-Venetian literature by Aurelio Roncaglia.
4. Dotti, Ugo. *L'età dell' umanesimo*. Palermo: Palumbo, 1978.
5. Fubini, Mario. *Metrica e poesia. Lezioni sulle forme metriche italiane*. Vol. 1. *Da Dante al Petrarca*. Milan: Feltrinelli, 1962.
6. Lanza, Antonio. *Studi sulla lirica del Trecento*. Rome: Bulzoni, 1978.
7. Larner, John. *Culture and Society in Italy, 1290–1420*. New York: Scribner's, 1971.
8. Montano, Rocco. *Lo spirito e le lettere: Disegno storico della letteratura italiana*. Vol. 1. Milan: Marzorati, 1970. Parts 3, 4, and 5 deal with the Trecento.
9. Muscetta, Carlo, ed. *Il Trecento*. Section 2. *Letteratura Italiana Laterza*. 4 vols.: *Petrarca, Forme poetiche del Trecento, Boccaccio*, and *La letteratura civile e religiosa del Trecento*. Bari: La Terza, 1971–.
10. Palanza, Ugo. *La letteratura italiana. Storia e pagine rappresentative*. 3 vols. Milan: Società editrice Dante Alighieri, 1968. Vols. 1 and 2 deal with the Trecento.
11. Petrocchi, Giorgio. *La prosa del Trecento*. Messina: editrice universitaria, 1961.

12. Sapegno, Natalino. *Il Trecento.* 3d ed. with updated bibliography. Milan: Vallardi, 1973.
13. Savona, Eugenio. *Cultura e ideologia nell'età comunale. Ricerche sulla letteratura italiana dell'età comunale.* Ravenna: Longo, 1975.
14. Seung, Thomas K. *Cultural Thematics.* New Haven, Conn.: Yale University Press, 1976.
15. Wilkins, Ernest Hatch. *A History of Italian Literature.* 2d ed. Revised by Thomas G. Bergin. Cambridge, Mass.: Harvard University Press, 1975.

Most of the volumes cited contain substantial bibliographies. For current compilations, see the annual exhaustive bibliographies of the MLA and the selective ones published in *The Year's Work in Modern Languages.* For most of the years of this survey, publications are summarized with some assessment in the *Rassegna della Letteratura Italiana.*

PETRARCH

Editions

(Listed chronologically)

16. *Francesco Petrarca, "Rime," "Trionfi" e Poesie Latine. Rime* and *Trionfi* edited by Ferdinando Neri; *Appendice ai "Trionfi"* edited by Guido Martellotti; *Frammenti* and *Rime disperse* edited by Natalino Sapegno. La Letteratura Maliana. Storia e Testi, vol. 6. Milan and Naples: Ricciardi, 1951.
17. *Le Rime di Francesco Petrarca.* Edited by Giosuè Carducci and S. Ferrari. Florence: Sansoni, 1899. Reprinted with an introduction by Gianfranco Contini, 1956.
18. *Francesco Petrarca: Il "Canzoniere."* Edited by Gianfranco Contini. Notes by Daniele Ponchiroli. Turin: Einaudi, 1966.
19. *Opere.* Edited by Giovanni Ponte. Milan: Mursia, 1968. Includes *Rerum vulgarium fragmenta, Triumphi,* and *Appendice ai Trionfi.*
20. *Selected Poems of Petrarch.* Edited by T. Gwynfor Griffith

and P. R. J. Hainsworth. Manchester: Manchester University Press, 1971.

English Translations

(Listed Chronologically)

21. *Triumphs.* Translated by Ernest Hatch Wilkins. Chicago: University of Chicago Press, 1962.
22. *Petrarch: Selected Sonnets, Odes and Letters.* Edited by Thomas G. Bergin. New York: Appleton-Century-Crofts, 1966.
23. *Italian Poets of the Renaissance.* Translated by Joseph Tusiani. Long Island City, N.Y.: The Baroque Press, 1971.
24. *Lord Morley's Tryumphes of Fraunces Petrarcke.* Edited by D. D. Carnicelli. Cambridge, Mass.: Harvard University Press, 1971.
25. *Petrarch's Lyric Poems: The Rime Sparse and Other Lyrics.* Translated and edited by Robert M. Durling. Cambridge, Mass.: Harvard University Press, 1976.
26. *Petrarch: Selected Poems.* Translated by Anthony Mortimer, Jr. University: University of Alabama Press, 1977.

Concordances and Bibliographies

27. *Concordanza delle Rime di Francesco Petrarca.* Edited by Kenneth McKenzie. 2 vols. 1912. Reprint. Turin, 1969.
28. *Concordanze del "Canzoniere" di Francesco Petrarca.* Edited by Aldo Duro. 2 vols. Florence: Accademia della Crusca, 1971.
29. *The English Petrarchans: A Critical Bibliography of the Canzoniere.* Compiled by George Watson. Warburg Institute Surveys, no. 3. London: Warburg Institute, University of London, 1967.
30. "The Present Status of Petrarchan Studies." J. G. Fucilla. In *Six Centuries Later* (entry 162), pp. 25–55.
31. *Catalogue of the Petrarch Collection in Cornell University Library.* Introduction by Morris Bishop. Millwood, N.Y.: Krause-Thompson Organization, 1974.
32. "Rassegna di studi petrarcheschi" Aldo S. Scaglione. *Romance Philology* 28, no. 1 (1974): 61–75; 29, no. 1 (1977): 111–27.

33. "Oltre un cinquantennio di scritti sul Petrarca (1916–1973)." Compiled by J. G. Fucilla. *Studi sul Petrarca,* forthcoming.

Criticism

(Listed alphabetically by author)

34. Alonso, Dámaso. "La poesia del Petrarca e il Petrarchismo." *Lettere italiane* 11 (1959): 277–319.
35. Amaturo, Raffaele. *Petrarca.* Bari: Laterza, 1971.
36. Antonetti, Pierre. "Poésie et littérature dans la canzone 'Di pensier in pensier . . .' (Pétrarque: *Canzoniere* CXXIX)." *Annales de la faculté des lettres d'Aix* 38 (1964): 195–204.
37. Arthos, John. "Du Bartas, Petrarch, and the Poetry of Deism." In *Renaissance Studies in Honor of Carroll Camden,* edited by J. A. Ward, pp. 1–17. Houston: Rice University Press, 1974.
38. Bacchelli, Riccardo. "Chiose petrarchesche." *Approdo* 7, no. 16 (1961): 45–98.
39. Baggio, Serenella. "L'immagine di Laura." *Giornale Storico della Letteratura Italiana* 156 (1979): 321–24.
40. Barber, Joseph A. "Rhyme Scheme Patterns in Petrarch's *Canzoniere.*" *Modern Language Notes* 92 (1976): 139–46.
41. Basile, José. *Forma simbolica ed allegorica nei "Rerum Vulgarium" Fragmenta ed altre cose.* Assisi-Rome: Carucci, 1971.
42. Battisti, Eugenio. "Non chiare acque." In *Six Centuries Later* (entry 162), pp. 303–59.
43. Bergin, Thomas G. *Petrarch.* New York: Twayne, 1970.
44. Bernardo, Aldo S. "Laura as a *nova figura.*" In *Francesco Petrarca: Citizen of the World* (entry 98), pp. 179–92. Padua: Antenora, 1980.
45. ———. "Petrarch and the Art of Literature." In *Petrarch to Pirandello: Studies in Italian Literature in Honor of Beatrice Corrigan,* edited by Julius Molinaro, pp. 19–43. Toronto: University of Toronto Press, 1973.
46. ———. *Petrarch, Laura and the "Triumphs."* Albany: State University of New York Press, 1974.

47. Biagini, Enza. "Le prime due stanza della Canzone 71." *Paragone* 296 (1973): 24–37.

48. Bigi, Emilio. "Le ballate del Petrarca." *Giornale Storico della Letteratura Italiana* 151 (1974): 481–93.

49. Billanovich, Giuseppe. "Dalle prime alle ultime letture del Petrarca." In *Il Petrarca ad Arquà* (entry 142), pp. 13–50.

50. ———. "Petrarca e gli storici romani." In *Citizen of the World* (entry 98), pp. 13–50.

51. Binni, Walter. *I classici italiani nella storia della critica.* Florence: La Nuova Italia, 1970.

52. Bishop, Morris. *Petrarch and His World.* Bloomington: Indiana University Press, 1963.

53. Bondanella, Julia Conway. *Petrarch's Visions and Their Renaissance Analogues.* Madrid: Jose Porrúa Turanzas, 1978.

54. Borchardt, Frank L. "Petrarch: The German Connection." In *Six Centuries Later* (entry 162), pp. 418–31.

55. Bosco, Umberto. "Cittadino del mondo." In *Citizen of the World* (entry 98), pp. 7–15.

56. ———. *Francesco Petrarca.* Edizione aggiornata e ampliata. Bari: Laterza, 1961.

57. Branca, Vittore. "Implicazioni strutturali ed expressive fra Petrarca e Boccaccio e l'idea dei Trionfi." In *Convegno internazionale Francesco Petrarca* (entry 75), pp. 141–61.

58. ———. "Petrarch and Boccaccio." In *Citizen of the World* (entry 98), pp. 193–221.

59. Brenkman, John. "Writing, Desire, Dialectic in Petrarch's *Rime* 23." *Pacific Coast Philology* 9 (1974): 12–19.

60. Brianza, Sophie. "Quomodo F. Petrarcha rerum naturam senserit atque in carminibus italico sermone compositis effinxerit." *Latinitas* 13 (1965): 44–53.

61. Büdel, Oscar. "Illusion Disabused: A Novel Mode in Petrarch's *Canzoniere*." In *Six Centuries Later* (entry 162), pp. 128–51.

62. Caione, Giuseppe. *Il sentimento del tempo nel "Canzoniere" del Petrarca.* Lecce: I.T.E.S., 1969.

63. Cale, Frano. "La canzone conclusiva delle 'Rime sparse' e la sua secolare fortuna nella letteratura croata." In *Il Petrarca ad Arquà* (entry 142), pp. 51–60.

64. Capovilla, Guido. "Le ballate del Petrarca e il codice metrico due-trecentesco." *Giornale Storico della Letteratura Italiana* 154 (1977): 238–60.

65. Cattaneo, Maria Teresa. *Francesco Petrarca e la lirica d'arte del 200.* Turin: Loescher, 1964.

66. Ceruti-Berengo, Anna. "Strutture simmetriche e amplificazione circolare nella sestina XXX del *Canzoniere.*" *Italianistica* 3(1974): 351–56.

67. Chiappelli, Fredi. "An Analysis of Structuration in Petrarch's Poetry." In *Six Centuries Later* (entry 162), pp. 105–16.

68. ———. *Studi sul linguaggio del Petrarca: "La canzone delle visioni."* Florence: Olschki, 1971.

69. Chirilli, Emilia. "Studi sulle concordanze nel *Canzoniere* di Francesco Petrarca." *Studi e Problemi di Critica Testuale* 16 (1978): 137–91.

70. Cippola, Gaetano. "Labyrinthine Imagery in Petrarch." *Italica* 54(1976): 263–89.

71. Constable, Giles. "Petrarch and Monasticism." In *Citizen of the World* (entry 98), pp. 53–99.

72. Contini, Gianfranco. "Petrarca e le arti figurative." In *Citizen of the World* (entry 98), pp. 115–31.

73. ———. "Pétrarque et la France." *Notiziario culturale italiano* 2(1974): 4–18.

74. ———. *Varianti e altra linguistica.* Turin: Einaudi, 1971.

75. *Convegno internazionale Francesco Petrarca.* Atti dei Convegni Lincei 10 (1974). Rome: Accademia Nazionale dei Lincei, 1976.

76. Cool, Kenneth E. "Scève's Agony of Expression and Petrarchan Discourse." *Stanford French Review* 3(1979): 193–210.

77. Corrigan, Beatrice. "Petrarch in English." *Italica* 50(1973): 400–407.

78. Cottino-Jones, Marga. "The Myth of Apollo and Daphne in Petrarch's *Canzoniere.*" In *Six Centuries Later* (entry 162), pp. 152–76.

79. Davis, Charles R. "Petrarch's *Rime* 323 and Its Tradition Through Spenser." Ph.D. diss., 1973.

80. Diani, Dominique. "Pétrarque: *Canzoniere* 132." *Revue des Études Italiennes* 18(1972): 111–67.

81. Di Pino, Guido. "La presenza del Petrarca nella poesia italiana del Novecento." *Italianistica* 3(1973): 241–59.
82. Dotti, Ugo. "Petrarca: Il mito dafneo." *Convivium* 37(1969): 9–23.
83. ———. *Petrarca a Milano.* Milan: Ceschina, 1972.
84. Durling, Robert M. *The Figure of the Poet in the Renaissance Epic.* Cambridge, Mass.: Harvard University Press, 1965.
85. ———. "Petrarch's 'Giovene donna sotto un verde lauro.' " *Modern Language Notes* 86(1971): 1–20.
86. ———. "Il Petrarca, il Ventoso e la possibilità dell'allegoria." *Revue des études augustiniennes* 23(1977): 304–23.
87. Dutschke, Dennis. *Francesco Petrarca: "Canzone" XXIII from First to Final Version.* Ravenna: Longo, 1977.
88. Engler, Winfried. "Der Symbolwert einzelner Motive zur Idealisierung Lauras in Petrarcas *Canzionere.*" *Die neuren Sprachen* 14(1965): 559–67.
89. Fedi, Roberto. *Francesco Petrarca.* Florence: La Nuova Italia, 1975.
90. Fenzi, Enrico. "Per un sonetto del Petrarca: R.V.F. xciii." *Giornale Storico della Letteratura Italiana* 151(1974): 494–519.
91. Feo, Michele. " 'Pallida no, ma più che neve bianca.' " *Giornale Storico della Letteratura Italiana* 152(1975): 321–61.
92. Fernow, Karl. *Francesco Petrarca.* Amsterdam: Ludwig Hain, 1972.
93. Figurelli, Fernando. "L'architettura del sonetto in Francesco Petrarca." In *Petrarca e il petrarchismo* (entry 143), pp. 179–86.
94. Fisher, John H. "The Myth of Petrarch." *Jean Misrahi Memorial Volume: Studies in Medieval Literature,* edited by Hans Runte et al., pp. 359–73. Columbia, S. C.: French Literature Publications, 1977.
95. Forster, Leonard. *The Icy Fire.* Cambridge: Cambridge University Press, 1969.
96. Foster, Kenelm, "Beatrice or Medusa; the Penitential Element in Petrarch's *Canzoniere.*" *Delta* 3, no. 1 (1963): 31–46.

97. Franceschetti, Antonio. "Il Petrarca nel pensiero critico di Scipione Maffei." In *Venzia e il Veneto* (entry 144), pp. 347–66.

98. *Francesco Petrarca: Citizen of the World.* Proceedings of the World Petrarch Congress, 1974. Studi sul Petrarca, 8. Padua: Editrice Antenore; Albany: State University of New York Press, 1980.

99. Frasso, Giuseppe. *Travels with Francesco Petrarca.* Preface by Giuseppe Billanovich, translated from Italian by Nicholas Mann, and photographs by Lorenzo Capellini. Padua: Antenore, 1974. German version, *Unterwegs mit Francesco Petrarca,* was published in 1975.

100. Freccero, John. "The Fig Tree and the Laurel: Petrarch's Poetics." *Diacritics* 5, no. 1 (1975): 34–40.

101. Fubini, Mario. *Metrica e poesia. Lezioni sulle forme metriche italiane.* Vol. 1. *Dal Duecento al Petrarca.* Milan: Feltrinelli, 1962.

102. ———. "La Sestina." In *Metrica e Poesia* (entry 101), pp. 328–46.

103. Fucilla, J. G. *Estudios sobre el petrarquismo en España.* Madrid: Consejo Superior de Investigaciones Científicas. Patronato "Menéndez y Pelayo." Instituto Miguel de Cervantes, 1960.

104. Galdi, Ladislas. "Les origines provençales de la métrique des 'canzoni' de Pétrarque." *Actes Romanes* 74 (1966): 783–90.

105. Garin, Eugenio. "Francesco Petrarca e le origini del Rinascimento." In *Convegno internazionale Francesco Petrarca* (entry 75), pp. 11–21.

106. Gaye, Vera M. "Il Petrarca, precursore del barocco." *Forum Italicum* 9(1975): 385–408.

107. Gianturco, Elio. "The Double Gift: Inner Vision and Pictorial Sense in Petrarch." *Renaissance and Reformation* 8 (1972): 100–111.

108. Ghertman, Sharon. *Petrarch and Garcilaso: A Linguistic Approach to Style.* London: Tamesis, 1975.

109. Greenfield, Concetta Carestia. "The Poetics of Francis Petrarch." In *Six Centuries Later* (entry 162), pp. 213–22.

110. Grübitzsch-Rodewald, Helga. "Petrarca und Arnaud

Daniel. Petrarcas Imitations-technik in der canzone 'Verdi panni.'" *Arcadia* 8(1972): 135–57.

111. Guglielminetti, Marziano, ed. *Petrarca e il petrarchismo: Un'ideologia della letteratura.* Turin: Paravia, 1977.

112. Guglielminetti, Marziano, and Mariarosa Masoero, eds. *Petrarca e il petrarchismo contemporaneo: Documenti.* Turin: Giappichelli, 1975.

113. Guss, Donald L. *John Donne, Petrarchist: Italianate Conceits and Love Theory in the Songs and Sonnets.* Detroit: Wayne State University Press, 1966.

114. ———. "Petrarchism and the End of the Renaissance." In *Six Centuries Later* (entry 162), pp. 384–401.

115. Hamilton, R. W. "John Donne's Petrarchist Poems." *Renaissance and Modern Studies* 23 (1979): 45–62.

116. Hardison, O. B., Jr. "Petrarch and Modern Lyric Poetry." In *Studies in the Continental Background of Renaissance English Literature: Essays Presented to John L. Lievsay,* edited by Dale B. J. Randall and George W. Williams, pp. 29–41. Durham, N.C.: Duke University Press, 1977.

117. Heitman, Klaus. *Fortuna und Virtus. Eine Studie zu Petrarcas Lebensweisheit.* Studi italiani, 1. Köln and Graz: Böhlau, 1958.

118. Herczeg, G. "Struttura e antitesi nel *Canzoniere* petrarchesco." In *Il Petrarca ad Arquà* (entry 142), pp. 195–208.

119. Hoffmeister, Gerhardt. *Petrarkistiche Lyrik.* Stuttgart: Metzler, 1973.

120. Iliescu, Nicolae. *Il "Canzoniere" petrarchesco e Sant'Agostino.* Rome: Società accademica romena, 1962.

121. Jenni, Adolfo. "Un sistema del Petrarca nell'ordinamento del *Canzoniere.*" In *Studi in onore di Alberto Chiari,* pp. 721–32. Brescia: Paideia, 1973.

122. Keller, Luzius, ed. *Übersetzung und Nachahmung im europäischen Petrarkismus: Studien und Texte.* Stuttgart: Metzler, 1974.

123. Kleinhenz, Christopher. "Petrarch and the Art of the Sonnet." In *Six Centuries Later* (entry 162), pp. 177–91.

124. Klopp, Charles. "Alliterazione e rima nel sonetto proe-

miale ai Rerum vulgarium fragmenta." *Lingua e stile* 12 (1977): 331–42.

125. Kohl, Benjamin. "Mourners of Petrarch." In *Six Centuries Later* (entry 162), pp. 340–52.

126. von Koppenfels, W. "Dantes 'Al poco giorno' und Petrarcas 'Giovene donna': ein Interpretationsvergleich zweier Sestinen." *Deutsches Dante-Jahrbuch* 44–45 (1967): 150–89.

127. Maier, Bruno. "Francesco Petrarca e il *Canzoniere.*" *Cristallo*, 17, no. 1 (1975): 15–36.

128. Mann, Nicholas. "Petrarch and Humanism: The Paradox of Posterity." In *Citizen of the World* (entry 98), pp. 284–99.

129. ———. "La prima fortuna del Petrarca in Inghilterra." In *Petrarca ad Arquà* (entry 142), pp. 279–89.

130. Martinelli, Bortolo. "Feria sexta aprilis: La data sacra del *Canzoniere.*" *Revista di Storia e Letteratura Religiosa* 8 (1972): 449–84.

131. Mazzotta, Giuseppe. "The *Canzoniere* and the Language of Self." *Studies in Philology* 75, no. 3 (1978): 271–96.

132. Merry, Bruce. "Il primo sonetto del Petrarca come modello di lettura." *Paragone* 296 (1974): 73–79.

133. Montanari, Fausto. *Studi sul "Canzoniere" del Petrarca.* 2d ed. Rome: Studium, 1972.

134. Murphy, Francis X. "Petrarch and the Christian Philosophy." In *Citizen of the World* (entry 98), pp. 223–47.

135. Noferi, Adelia. *L'esperienza poetica del Petrarca.* Florence: Le Monnier, 1962.

136. ———. "Da un commento al *Canzoniere:* Lettura del sonetto introduttivo." *Lettere Italiane* 26 (1974): 165–79.

137. ———. "Il *Canzoniere* del Petrarca: scrittura del desiderio o desiderio della scrittura?" *Paragone* 296 (1973): 3–23.

138. ———. "*Sonetto* 151, 198." *Forum Italicum* 8 (1974): 495–512.

139. Noyer-Weidner, Alfred. "Zur Mythologieverwendung in Petrarcas *Canzoniere* (mit einem Ausblick auf die petrarkistische Lyrik)." In *Beiträge zu Werk und Wirkung* (entry 163), pp. 221–42.

140. Paden, William D., Jr. "Aesthetic Distance in Petrarch's Response to the Pastourelle: *Rime* III." *Romance Notes* 16 (1974–1975): 702–7.

141. *Per il VI° centenario della morte di Francesco Petrarca (1304–1374). Italia Medievale e Umanistica* 18 (1975).

142. *Il Petrarca ad Arquà.* Atti del Convegno di studi nel VI° centenario (1370–1374), 1970. Studi sul Petrarca, 2. Padua: Antenore, 1975.

143. *Petrarca e il petrarchismo.* Atti del terzo congresso dell'associazione internazionale per gli studi di lingua e letteratura italiana, 1959. *Studi petrarcheschi* 7 (1961).

144. *Petrarca, Venezia e il Veneto.* Edited by Giorgio Padoan. Florence: Olschki, 1976.

145. Petronio, Giuseppe. "Storicità della lirica politica del Petrarca." In *Petrarca e il petrarchismo* (entry 143), pp. 247–64.

146. Quaglio, Antonio Enzo. *Francesco Petrarca.* Milan: Garzanti, 1967.

147. Rabuse, Georg. "Petrarcas Marienkanzone im Lichte der *Santa Orazione* Dantes." In *Beiträge zu Werk und Wirkung* (entry 163), pp. 243–54.

148. Radcliff-Umstead, Douglas. "Petrarch and the Freedom to Be Alone." In *Six Centuries Later* (entry 162), pp. 236–48.

149. Renucci, Paul. "Nature et histoire dans le *Canzoniere* de Pétrarque." In *Citizen of the World* (entry 98), pp. 17–51.

150. Rico, Francisco. " 'Rime sparse,' 'Rerum vulgarium fragmenta' para el título y el primer soneto del *Canzoniere*." *Medioevo romanzo* 3 (1967): 101–38.

151. Riesz, János. "Petrarcas Sestine im *Canzoniere*." In *Die Sestine, Ihre Stellung in der literarischen Kritik und ihre Geschichte als lyrisches Genus*, pp. 69–71. Munich: Fink, 1971.

152. Rivero, Albert J. "Petrarch's 'Nel dolce tempo de la prima etade.' " *Modern Language Notes* 94 (1979): 92–112.

153. Roche, Thomas P., Jr. "The Calendrical Structure of Petrarch's *Canzoniere*." *Studies in Philology* 71 (1974): 152–72.

154. Rossi, Giuseppe Carlo. "La tradizione del petrarchismo

nella letteratura portoghese." In *Convegno internazionale Francesco Petrarca* (entry 75), pp. 71–102.

155. Rüdiger, Horst. "Petrarca e il petrarchismo nella letteratura germanica." *Cristallo* 17, no. 2 (1975): 23–43.

156. Ruffo-Fiore, Silvia. "Donne's Transformation of Petrarchan Imagery in *The Canonization.*" *Italian Quarterly* 73 (1975): 53–62.

157. Santagata, Marco. "Connessioni intertestuali nel *Canzoniere* del Petrarca." *Strumenti critici* 26 (1975): 80–112.

158. Sapegno, Natalino. *La personalità e la poesia del Petrarca.* Rome: Ricerche, 1965.

159. ———. *La poesia del Petrarca.* Section 2. *Commento alle Rime.* Rome: Bulzoni, 1964.

160. Scaglione, Aldo. "Petrarch 1974: A Sketch for a Portrait." In *Six Centuries Later* (entry 162), pp. 1–24.

161. ———. "La struttura del *Canzoniere* e il metodo di composizione del Petrarca." *Lettere Italiane* 27 (1974): 129–39.

162. Scaglione, Aldo, ed. *Francis Petrarch, Six Centuries Later.* Chapel Hill: University of North Carolina Press; Chicago: Newberry Library, 1975.

163. Schalk, Fritz, ed. *Petrarca 1304–1374: Beiträge zu Werk und Wirkung.* Frankfurt: Vittorio Klostermann, 1975.

164. Schindler, Marvin S. "Petrarch's Sonnet No. 132 to Laura and the German Petrarchists: Mastery of Form or Formal Mastery?" *Semosia* 2 (1975): 271–94.

165. Seung, Thomas K. *Cultural Thematics: The Formation of the Faustian Ethos.* New Haven and London: Yale University Press, 1976.

166. Seznec, Jean. "Petrarch and Renaissance Art." In *Citizen of the World* (entry 98), pp. 133–50.

167. Shapiro, Marianne Goldner. *Hieroglyph of Time: The Petrarchan Sestina.* Minneapolis: University of Minnesota Press, 1982.

168. Simonelli, Maria Picchio. "Strutture foniche nei *Rerum vulgarium fragmenta.*" In *Six Centuries Later* (entry 162), pp. 66–104.

169. Sottili, Agostino. "Il Petrarca autore universitario." In *Venezia e il Veneto* (entry 144), pp. 223–41.

170. Sozzi, B. T., ed. *Petrarca*. Storia della critica, 5. Palermo: Palumbo, 1963.

171. Stevens, Dennis. "Petrarch and Renaissance Music." In *Citizen of the World* (entry 98), pp. 151–78.

172. Sturm, Sara. "The Poet-Persona in the *Canzoniere*." In *Six Centuries Later* (entry 162), pp. 192–212.

173. Tetel, Marcel. "Montaigne et Pétrarque: Irrésolution et Solitude." *Journal of Medieval and Renaissance Studies* 4 (1973): 203–20.

174. Tilden, Jill. "Spiritual Conflict in Petrarch's *Canzoniere*." In *Beiträge zu Werk and Wirkung* (entry 163), pp. 287–319.

175. Trinkaus, Charles. *The Poet as Philosopher: Petrarch and the Formation of Renaissance Consciousness*. New Haven: Yale University Press, 1979.

176. Tripet, Arnaud. *Pétrarque; ou, la connaissance de soi.* Geneva: Droz, 1967.

177. ———. "Pétrarque et le langage." In *Six Centuries Later* (entry 162), pp. 223–35.

178. Tucker, Cynthia G. "The Rilkean Lover and his Laurel: The Orpheus Poems and Petrarchan Sonnet Tradition." *Philological Quarterly* 53 (1974): 256–74.

179. Turchi, Marcello. "Il centenario del Petrarca e la critica." *Italianistica: Rivista di Letteratura Italiana* 7 (1978): 378–99; 8 (1979): 139–55.

180. Ullman, Berthold L. *Petrarch Manuscripts in the United States*. Padua: Antenore, 1964.

181. Velli, Giuseppe. "La memoria poetica del Petrarca." *Italia Medioevale e Umanistica* 19 (1976): 171–207.

182. Viscardi, Antonio. *Petrarca e petrarchismo*. Milan: Goliardica, 1965.

183. Waller, Marguerite. *Petrarch's Poetics and Literary History*. Amherst: University of Massachusetts Press, 1980.

184. Watson, George. *The English Petrarchans: A Critical Bibliography of the "Canzoniere."* London: Warburg Institute, 1967.

185. Whitfield, John H. *Petrarch and the Renascence*. Oxford: Blackwell, 1943.

186. Wilkins, Ernest Hatch. *Life of Petrarch.* Chicago: University of Chicago Press, 1961.
187. ———. *Studies on Petrarch and Boccaccio.* Edited by Aldo S. Bernardo. Studi sul Petrarca, 6. Padua: Antenore, 1978.
188. Wirth, Genevieve Duval. "La Symbolique de Pétrarque jusqu'au seuil de l'âge baroque." *Studi secenteschi* 19(1978): 23–47.
189. Zon, Stephen. "Imitations Petrarch: Opitz, Fleming." *Daphnis* 7 (1978): 497–512.

BOCCACCIO

Editions and Translations: Collections of Works

(Listed chronologically with editions preceding translations)

190. *"Decameron," "Filocolo," "Ameto," "Fiammetta."* Edited by Enrico Bianchi, Carlo Salinari, and Natalino Sapegno. 2 vols. 1952. Reprint. Milan and Naples: Ricciardi, 1962.
191. *Opere di Giovanni Boccaccio.* Edited by Cesare Segre. Notes by Maria Consigli Segre. Milan: Mursia, 1963.
192. *Tutte le opere.* Edited by Vittore Branca. Milan: Mondadori, 1964–1977.
193. *Opere in versi,* etc. Edited by Pier Giorgio Ricci. Milan and Naples: Ricciardi, 1965.
194. *Opere.* Edited by Bruno Maier. Bologna: Zanichelli, 1967.
195. *Opere minori in volgare.* Edited by Mario Marti. 4 vols. Milan: Rizzoli, 1969–1972.
196. *Tutte le opere.* Edited by Vittore Branca. Brescia: La Scuola, 1969.
197. *Boccaccio müvei.* Edited by Zoltán Rózsa. Budapest: Magyar Helikon, 1964. Contains introductions, notes, and translations of these works: *Fiammetta,* Z. Jékely; *Ninfale fiesolano,* G. Végh; *Decameron,* J. Révay and D. Zoltán; *Corbaccio,* Z. Jékely; *Rhymes,* Z. Majtényi, I. Molnár, and G. Végh; *Life of Dante,* J. Fusi. (Hungarian.)

Editions and Translations: Individual Works

(Listed alphabetically by work and by editors for each individual work)

Ameto. See *Comedia delle Ninfe fiorentine.*

198. *Amorosa visione.* Edited by Vittore Branca. In *Tutte le opere* (entry 192), vol. 3 (1974).
199. ———. In *Opere minori in volgare* (entry 195), vol. 3 (1971).
200. ———. (Selections.) In *Opere in versi* (entry 193).

201. *Caccia di Diana.* Edited by Vittore Branca. In *Tutte le opere* (entry 192), vol. 1 (1967).
202. ———. In *Opere minori in volgare* (entry 195), vol. 4 (1972).
203. ———. (Selections.) In *Opere in versi* (entry 193).

204. *Comedia delle ninfe fiorentine.* In *Opere minori in volgare* (entry 195), vol. 3 (1971).
205. ———. Critical edition by Antonio Enzo Quaglio. Florence: Sansoni, 1964.
206. ———. Edited by Antonio Enzo Quaglio. In *Tutte le opere* (entry 192), vol. 2 (1964).

207. *Il Corbaccio.* In *Opere minori in volgare* (entry 195), vol. 4 (1972).
208. ———. In *Opere in versi* (entry 193).
209. ———. Edited with an introduction by Tauno Nurmela. Helsinki: Suomalaisen tiedeakatemian toimituksia, 1968.
210. ———. In *Elegia di Madonna Fiammetta. Corbaccio o Laberinto d'amore.* Introduction by Riccardo Scrivano. Rome: Avanzini e Torraca, 1967.
211. *Corbaccio.* Translated with an introduction by Anthony Kimber Cassell. Urbana: University of Illinois Press, 1975. (English.)
212. *Corbaccio avagy a szerelem útvesztöje.* Translation by Zoltán Jékely. Budapest: Magyar Helikon Kiado, 1968. (Hungarian.)

The following list of editions and translations of the *Deca-meron*, arranged alphabetically by names of editors, is selective. Some thirty new editions of the *Decameron* have been published in the last two decades. See the bibliography of Enzo Esposito (entry 276), pp. 15–18.

213. *Decameron*. Edited by Enrico Bianchi. In *"Decameron," "Filocolo," "Ameto," "Fiammetta"* (entry 190).
214. ———. Edited by Vittore Branca. In *Tutte le opere* (entry 192).
215. ———. Edizione critica secondo l'autografo hamiltoniano edited by Vittore Branca. Firenze: presso l'Accademia della Crusca, 1976.
216. ———. Edited by Bruno Maier. Bologna: Zanichelli, 1967.
217. ———. Edited with an introduction by Mario Marti; notes by Elena Ceva Valla. 2 vols. Milan: Rizzoli, 1974.
218. ———. 49 novelle commentate da Attilio Momigliano. Edited by Edoardo Sanguineti. Turin: Petrini, 1972.
219. ———. Introduction, comments, and notes by Antonio Enzo Quaglio. Milan: Garzanti, 1974.
220. *Il Decameron*. Critical edition by Aldo Rossi. Bologna: Cappelli, 1977.
221. ———. Edizione integrale edited by Carlo Salinari. Rev. ed. Bari: Laterza, 1975.
222. ———. Diplomatic interpretative edition of the Hamilton 90 manuscript by Charles S. Singleton. Baltimore: Johns Hopkins University Press, 1974.

In the last score of years, translations of the *Decameron* in many other languages have been published in addition to the following, which are listed alphabetically by language. See *Boccacciana* (entry 276), pp. 25–43.

223. *Boccaccio, The Decameron*. Translated with an introduction by G. H. McWilliam. Harmondsworth: Penguin Books, 1972. (English.)
224. *The Decameron*. Selected, translated, and edited by Mark Musa and Peter E. Bondanella. New York: Norton, 1977. (Contains twenty-one novelle in addition to a number of critical essays.) (English.)

225. *Le Décaméron.* Translated by Francisque Reynard. Introduction and notes by Vittore Branca; notes translated by André Gisselbrecht. 1953. 2d ed. Paris: Club français du livre, 1962. (French.)

226. *Das Dekameron.* Translated by Albert Wesselski. Frankfurt: Insel Verlag, 1967. (German.)

227. *Decamerão.* Translated by Torrieri Guimarães. São Paulo: Abril Cultural, 1971. (Portuguese.)

228. *Dekameron.* Translated by Nikolaj Ljubimov and J. Korneev. Introduction by R. Chlodovskij; notes by N. Tomaševskij. Moscow: Hudož, 1970. (Russian.)

229. *El Decamerón.* Translated by José Pérez Asensio. 35th ed. Madrid: Pérez del Hoyo, 1973. (Spanish.)

230. *Elegia di Madonna Fiammetta.* Edited by Pia Piccoli Addoli. Milan: Rizzoli, 1962.

231. ———. In *"Decameron," "Filocolo," "Ameto," "Fiammetta"* (entry 190).

232. ———. Edited by Riccardo Scrivano. In *Elegia di Madonna Fiammetta* (entry 230).

233. ———. Edited by Nereo Vianello. Rome: Curcio, 1966.

234. *Amorous Fiammetta.* Translated by Bartholomew Young. Reprint. Westport, Conn.: Greenwood Press, 1970. (English.)

235. *Fiammetta.* Edited by K. Kippenberg. Translated by Sophie Brentano. Frankfurt: Insel Verlag, 1964. (German.)

236. *Die Elegie der Dame Fiammetta. Corbaccio. Das Leben Dantes. Urbano.* Edited by C. Wentzlaff-Eggebert. Translated by Else von Hollander. Munich: Heyne, 1963. (German.)

237. *Fiammetta.* In *Boccaccio müvei* (entry 197). (Hungarian.)

238. *F'jammetta. F'ezolanskie nimfy.* Translated by A. D. Mirhailov. Moscow: Hayka, 1968. (Russian.)

239. *Esposizioni sopra la Comedi di Dante.* Edited by Giorgio Padoan. In *Tutte le opere* (entry 192), vol. 6 (1965).

240. ———. Edited by Mario Marti. In *Opere minori in volgare* (entry 195), vol. 1 (1969).

241. *Filocolo.* Edited by Antonio Enzo Quaglio. In *Tutte le opere* (entry 192), vol. 1 (1967).

242. ———. Edited by Carlo Salinari and Natalino Sapegno. In *"Decameron," "Filocolo," "Ameto," "Fiammetta"* (entry 190).

243. *Filostrato.* Edited by Vittore Branca. In *Tutte le opere* (entry 192), vol. 2 (1964).
244. ———. Edited by Mario Marti. In *Opere minori in volgare* (entry 195), vol. 2 (1970).
245. ———. (Selections.) Edited by Giorgio Ricci. In *Opere in versi* (entry 193).
246. *Il Filostrato.* Translated by R. K. Gordon. In *The Story of Troilus.* 1934. Reprint. Toronto, Buffalo, and London: University of Toronto Press in association with the Medieval Academy of America, 1978. (English.)
247. *The Filostrato.* Translated by Nathaniel Edward Griffin and Arthur Beckwith Myrick. Philadelphia: University of Pennsylvania Press, 1929. Reprint. New York: Octagon, 1978. (English.)

248. *Lettere.* Edited by Mario Marti. In *Opere minori in volgare* (entry 195), vol. 4 (1972).
249. *Epistole.* (Selections.) Edited by Pier Giorgio Ricci. In *Opere in versi* (entry 193).

250. *Ninfale fiesolano.* Edited by Armando Balduino. In *Tutte le opere* (entry 192), vol. 3 (1974).
251. ———. Edited by Mario Marti. In *Opere minore in volgare* (entry 195), vol. 3 (1971).
252. ———. Edited by Pier Giorgio Ricci. In *Opere in versi* (entry 193).
253. *The Nymph of Fiesole.* Translated by Daniel Donno. 1960. Reprint. Westport, Conn.: Greenwood Press, 1974. (English.)
254. *Giovanni Boccaccio's Nymphs of Fiesole.* Translated into verse with an introduction by Joseph Tusiani. Rutherford, Madison, and Teaneck, N.J.: Fairleigh Dickinson University Press, 1971. (English.)

255. ———. Edited by Zoltán Rózsa. In *Boccaccio müvei* (entry 197). (Hungarian.)
256. *E'ezolanskie nimfy.* In *F'jammetta* (entry 238). (Russian.)

257. *Rime.* Edited by Mario Marti. In *Opere minori in volgare* (entry 195), vol. 4 (1972).
258. ———. (Selections.) Edited by Pier Giorgio Ricci. In *Opere in versi* (entry 193).
259. ———. Translated by Zoltán Rózsa. In *Boccaccio Müvei* (entry 197). (Hungarian.)

260. *Teseida delle Nozze di Emilia.* Edited by Alberto Limentani. In *Tutte le opere* (entry 192), vol. 2 (1970).
261. ———. Edited by Mario Marti. In *Opere minori in volgare* (entry 195), vol. 2.
262. *Dal Teseida.* (Selections.) Edited by Pier Giorgio Ricci. In *Opere in versi* (entry 193).
263. *The Book of Theseus.* Translated by Bernadette Marie McCoy. New York: Medieval Text Association, 1974. (English.)

264. *Trattatello in laude di Dante.* Edited by Mario Marti. In *Opere minori in volgare* (entry 195), vol. 4.
265. ———. Edited by Pier Giorgio Ricci. In *Tutte le opere* (entry 192), vol. 3 (1974).
266. *Nejstarši životopisy Dantovy.* Edited by O. F. Babler and Z. Kalista. Prague: SNKLU, 1965. (Czechoslovakian.)
267. *The Life of Dante.* Translated by James Robinson Smith in *The Earliest Lives of Dante*, pp. 9–78. New York: Ungar, 1963. Reprint. New York: Russell & Russell, 1968. (English.)
268. *Das Leben Dantes.* Translated by Else von Hollander. In *Die Elegie der Dame Fiammetta. Corbaccio. Das Leben Dantes* (entry 236). (German.)
269. *Viata lui Dante.* Edited by Zoltán Rózsa. In *Boccaccio müvei* (entry 192). (Hungarian.)
270. *Vita di Dante.* Translated by Kiyushi Ikeda. *Studi Italici* 11(1962): 80–103; 12(1963): 78–100; *31(1964): 104–15. (Japanese.)

271. *Viata lui Dante.* Translated by Stefan Crudu. Bucharest: Editura pentru Literatura universala, 1965. (Rumanian.)

Concordance and Bibliographies

272. Barbina, Alfredo, ed. *Concordanze del "Decameron."* 2 vols. Florence: Giunti G. Barbèra, 1969.
273. Branca, Vittore. *Linee di una storia della critica al "Decameron."* Con bibliografia boccaccesca completamente aggiornata. Milan, Genoa, Rome, and Naples: Dante Alighieri, 1939.
274. Branca, Vittore, and Giorgio Padoan. *Bollettino bibliografia.* In *Studi sul Boccaccio* beginning with volume 1 (1963). Covers publications beginning with 1938.
275. Traversari, Guido. *Bibliografia boccaccesca.* Vol. 1.ˈScritti intorno al Boccaccio e alla fortuna delle sue opere.* 1907. Reprint. New York: Burt Franklin, 1973.
276. Esposito, Enzo. *Boccacciana: Bibliografia delle edizioni e degli scritti critici (1939–1974).* In collaboration with Christopher Kleinhenz. Ravenna: Longo, 1976.

Criticism

277. Aldridge, Alfred Owen. "The First American Interpretation of Boccaccio." In *Il Boccaccio nelle culture e letterature nazionale* (entry 382), pp. 219–30.
278. Allen, Shirley S. "The Griselda Tale and the Portrayal of Women in the *Decameron.*" *Philological Quarterly* 56 (1977): 1–13.
279. Almansi, Guido. *Il ciclo della scommessa dal "Decameron" al "Cymbeline" di Shakespeare.* Rome: Bulzoni, 1975.
280. ———. *The Writer As Liar: Narrative Technique in the "Decameron."* London and Boston: Routledge and Kegan Paul, 1975.
281. Arce, Joaquin. "Boccaccio nella letteratura castigliana: Panorama generale e rassegna bibliografica-critica." In *Il Boccaccio nelle culture e letterature nazionale* (entry 382), pp. 63–104.

282. Artom-Treves, Giuliana. "Landor ed il suo Boccaccio immaginario." In *Il Boccaccio nelle cultura inglese e anglo-americana* (entry 344), pp. 231–43.

283. Bailet, Michel-Henri. *L'homme de verre. Essai d'inter-prétation thématique de l'échec de la maîtrise dans le "Décaméron."* Nice: L'Imprimerie Universelle, 1972.

284. Balduino, Armando. "Tradizione canterina e tonalità po-polareggianti nel *Ninfale fiesolano." Studi sul Boccaccio* 2 (1964): 25–80.

285. Ballerini, Carlo. "Il recupero della letizia dalla tragedia dalla peste alla libera vita di Bruno e di Buffalmacco." In *Atti del convegno di Nimega sul Boccaccio* (entry 286), pp. 51–203.

286. Ballerini, Carlo, ed. *Atti del convegno di Nimega sul Boccaccio.* Bologna: Patron, 1976.

287. Baratto, Mario. *Realta e stile nel "Decameron."* Vicenza: Neri Pozza, 1970.

288. Barberi-Squarotti, Giorgio. "L'ambigua sociologia di Griselda." *Annali della Facoltà di Magistero della Università di Palermo* (1970): 32–75.

289. Barricelli, Jean-Pierre. "Satire of Satire: Boccaccio's *Corbaccio." Italian Quarterly* 72 (1975): 96–111.

290. Battaglia, Salvatore. *Giovanni Boccaccio e la riforma della narrativa.* Naples: Liguori, 1969.

291. Bec, Christian. "Sur le message du *Décameron." Revue des Études Italiennes* 21 (1975): 284–303.

292. Bellosi, Luciano. *Buffalmacco e il Trionfo della morte.* Turin: Einaudi, 1974.

293. Bergin, Thomas G. *Boccaccio.* New York: Viking, Penguin Books, 1981.

294. Bertolini, Virginio. "Alcune ipotesi su possibili fonti del *Filocolo." Annali della Facoltà di Economia e Commercio di Verona. Corso di lingue e letterature straniere* 1 (1965–1966): 39–54.

295. Bettridge, William Edwin, and Francis Lee Utley. "New Light on the Origin of the Griselda Story." *Texas Studies in Literature and Language* 13, no. 2 (1971): 153–208.

296. Bevilacqua, Mirko. "L'amore come 'sublimazione' e 'de-gradazione': Il denudamento della donna angelicata nel

Decameron." *Rassegna della Letteratura Italiana* 79 (1975): 415–32.

297. ——. *L'ideologia letteraria del "Decameron."* Rome: Bulzoni, 1978.

298. Bonadeo, Alfredo. "Some Aspects of Love and Nobility in the Society of the *Decameron.*" *Philological Quarterly* 47 (1968): 513–25.

299. Bosetti, Gilbert. "Analyse structurale de la sixième journée du *Décameron.*" *Studi sul Boccaccio* 7 (1973): 141–58.

300. Boshart, Jon D. "Giovanni Boccaccio's *Amorosa Visione:* A New Appraisal." Ph.D. diss., 1974.

301. Bramanti, Vanni. "Il 'Purgatorio' di Ferrando (*Decameron* III:8)." *Studi sul Boccaccio* 7 (1973): 178–87.

302. Branca, Vittore. *Giovanni Boccaccio: Profilo biografico.* 1967. Rev. ed. Florence: Sansoni, 1977.

303. ——. *Boccaccio: The Man and His Works,* edited by Dennis J. McAuliffe. Translated by Richard Monges and D. J. McAuliffe. Foreword by Robert C. Clements. New York: New York University Press, 1976.

304. ——. *Boccaccio medievale.* Nuova ed. accresciuta. Florence: Sansoni, 1970.

305. ——. "Coerenza dell'introduzione al 'Decameron': Rispondenze strutturali e stilistiche." *Romance Philology* 13, no. 4 (1960): 351–60.

306. ——. "Boccaccio illustratore del suo *Decameron* e la tradizione figurale del suo capolavoro." *Italian Quarterly* 21, no. 79 (Winter 1980): 5–10.

307. Branca, Vittore, and Mariarosa Giacon, "Temi e stilemi fra Petrarca e Boccaccio." *Studi sul Boccaccio* 8 (1974): 215–49.

308. Branch, Eren Hostetter. "Man Alone and Man in Society." Ph.D. diss., 1975.

309. Brockmeier, Peter. *Lust und Herrschaft. Studien über gesellschäftliche Aspekte der Novellistik: Boccaccio, Sacchetti, Margarete von Navarra, Cervantes.* Stuttgart: Metzler, 1972.

310. Brown, Marshall. "In the Valley of the Ladies." *Italian Quarterly* 72 (1975): 33–52.

311. Cartier, Normand R. "Boccaccio's Old Crow." *Romania* 98 (1977): 331–48.

312. Cassell, Anthony Kimber. "An Abandoned Canvas: Structural and Moral Conflict in the Corbaccio." *Modern Language Notes* 89 (1974): 60–70.

313. Cavallini, Giorgio. "Coerenza di struttura e stile nella novella della marchesana di Monferrato del Boccaccio." In *Brevi studi stilistici letterari*, pp. 23–9. Genoa: De-Stefano, 1968.

314. Cerisola, Pier Luigi. "La questione della cornice del *Decameron*." *Aevum* 19 (1975): 137–56.

315. Chandler, S. Bernard. "Man, Emotion and Intellect in the *Decameron*." *Philological Quarterly* 39 (1960): 400–412.

316. Cherchi, Paolo. *Andrea Cappellano, i trovatori e altri temi romanzi*. Rome: Bulzoni, 1979.

317. Chiecchi, Giuseppe. "Sentenze e proverbi nel *Decameron*." *Studi sul Boccaccio* 9 (1975–1976): 119–68.

318. Clements, Robert J. "Anatomy of the Novella in the *Decameron*." In *The Decameron* (entry 224), pp. 258–69.

319. Cole, Howard C. "Dramatic Interplay in the *Decameron*: Boccaccio Neifile and Giletta di Nerbona." *Modern Language Notes* 90 (1975): 38–57.

320. Cottino-Jones, Marga. *An Anatomy of Boccaccio's Style*. Naples: Cymba, 1968.

321. ———. "The City/Country Conflict in the 'Decameron.'" *Studi sul Boccaccio* 8 (1974): 147–84.

322. ———. "The *Corbaccio*. Notes for a Mythical Perspective of Moral Alternatives." *Forum Italicum* 4, no. 4 (1970): 490–509.

323. ———. "Fabula versus Figura: Another Interpretation of the Griselda Story." *Italica* 50 (1973): 38–52. Reprinted in *The Decameron* (entry 224), pp. 295–305.

324. ———. "The Mode and Structure of Tragedy in Boccaccio's *Decameron*." *Italian Quarterly* 11, no. 43 (1967): 63–88.

325. Cottino-Jones, Marga, and Edward F. Tuttle, eds. *Boccaccio: Secoli di vita*. Atti del congresso internazionale Boccaccio 1975. Ravenna: Longo, 1977.

326. D'Andrea, Antonio. "Le rubriche del *Decameron*." *Yale Italian Studies* (1973–1975): 41–67.

327. Deligiorgis, Stauros. "Boccaccio and the Greek Romances." *Comparative Literature* 19, no. 2 (1967): 97–113.

328. ———. *Narrative Intellection in the "Decameron."* Iowa City: University of Iowa Press, 1975.

329. Della Terza, Dante. "La Fontaine, lettore del Boccaccio." In *Il Boccaccio nella cultura francese* (entry 407), pp. 239–64.

330. Di Pino, Guido. "Una estate barocca per *Fiammetta.*" *Italianistica: Rivista di Letteratura Italiana* 5 (1976): 1–19.

331. Dombroski, Robert S., ed. *Critical Perspectives on the Decameron.* New York: Barnes & Noble, 1977.

332. Doni, R. "I piaceri terrestri e il sentimento religioso nel *Decameron.*" In *Atti del convegno di Nimega sul Boccaccio* (entry 286), pp. 237–46.

333. Dutschke, Dennis. "Boccaccio: A Question of Love. (A Comparative Study of *Filocolo* IV:13 and *Decameron* X:4)." *The Humanities Association Review* 26 (1925): 300–312.

334. Falassi, Alessandro. "Il Boccaccio e il folklore di Certaldo." In *Boccaccio: Secoli di vito* (entry 325), pp. 265–92.

335. Ferrante, Joan. "The Frame Characters of the *Decameron:* A Progression of Virtues." *Romance Philology* 19, no. 2 (1965): 212–26.

336. ———. "Narrative Patterns in the *Decameron.*" *Romance Philology* 31 (1978): 585–604.

337. Ferreri, Rosario. "Ovidio e le 'Rime' di Giovanni Boccaccio." *Forum Italicum* 7/8 (1973–1974): 46–55.

338. ———. "Studi sulle Rime." *Studi sul Boccaccio* 7 (1973): 213–37.

339. ———. "Sulle *Rime* del Boccaccio." *Studi sul Boccaccio* 8 (1974): 185–96.

340. Fido, Franco. "Boccaccio's ars narrandi in the sixth day of the *Decameron.*" In *Italian Literature: Roots and Branches,* edited by Giose Rimanelli and Kenneth J. Atchity, pp. 225–42. New Haven, Conn.: Yale University Press, 1976.

341. ———. "Il sorriso di Messer Torello (*Decameron* X:9)." *Romance Philology* 23, no. 2 (1969): 154–71.

342. Freedman, Alan. "Il cavallo del Boccaccio: Fonte, struttura e funzione della metanovella di Madonna Oretta." *Studi sul Boccaccio* 9 (1975–1976): 225–41.

343. Galigani, Giuseppe. "Il Boccaccio nel Cinquecento inglese." In *Il Boccaccio nella cultura inglese e angloamericana* (entry 344), pp. 27–57.

344. Galigani, Giuseppe, ed. *Il Boccaccio nella cultura inglese e anglo-americana.* Florence: Olschki, 1974.

345. Galletti, Salvatore. *Patologia al "Decameron."* Palermo: Flaccovio, 1969.

346. Gathercole, Patricia May. "Boccaccio in English." *Studi sul Boccaccio* 7 (1973): 353–68.

347. ———. *Tension in Boccaccio; Boccaccio and the Fine Arts.* University, Miss.: Mediaeval Studies, Romance Monographs, 1975.

348. ———. "Boccaccio in French." *Studi sul Boccaccio* 5 (1968): 275, 316.

349. ———. "The French Translations of Boccaccio." *Italica* 40, no. 3 (1969): 123–209.

350. Getto, Giovanni. *Vita di forme e forme di vita nel "Decameron."* Turin: G. Petrini, 1958.

351. *Giovanni Boccaccio, 1375–1975.* Homenage en el sexto centenario de su muerte. La Plata: Centro de Estudios Italianos, Facultad de Humanidades, Universidad Nacional de La Plata, 1975.

352. Givens, Azzurra B. *La dottrina d'amore nel Boccaccio.* Messina and Florence: D'Anna, 1968.

353. Gozzi, Maria. "Sulle fonti del *Filostrato.* Le narrazioni di argomento troiano." *Studi sul Boccaccio* 5 (1968): 123, 210.

354. Greene, Thomas M. "Forms of Accommodation in the *Decameron.*" *Italica* 45, no. 3 (1968): 297–313. Reprinted in *Critical Perspectives* (entry 331), pp. 113–28.

355. Griffin, Robert. "Boccaccio's *Fiammetta;* Pictures at an Exhibition." *Italian Quarterly* 18, no. 62 (1975): 75–94.

356. Hastings, Robert. *Nature and Reason in the "Decameron."* Manchester: Manchester University Press, 1975.

357. Heintze, Horst. "Das *Decamerone* und die Welt der Novelle." In *Realismus in der Renaissance: Aneignung der Welt in der Novelle,* edited by Robert Weimann, pp. 297–358. Berlin: Aufbau, 1977.

358. ———. "La fortuna del Boccaccio nella Repubblica Democratica Tedesca." In *Il Boccaccio nelle culture e letterature nazionali* (entry 382), pp. 53–60.

359. Hirdt, Willi. "Boccaccio in Germania." In *Il Boccaccio nelle culture e letterature nazionali* (entry 382), pp. 27–51.

360. Hollander, Robert. *Boccaccio's Two Venuses.* New York: Columbia University Press, 1977.

361. Jannace, Florinda M. *La religione di Boccaccio.* Rome: Trevi, 1977.

362. Kahane, H., and R. Kahane. "Akritas and Arcita: A Byzantine Source of Boccaccio's *Teseida.*" *Speculum* 20 (1945): 415–25.

363. Kern, Edith G. "The Gardens in the *Decameron.*" *PMLA* 66 (1951): 505–23.

364. Kirkham, Victoria. "Numerology and Allegory in Boccaccio's *Caccia di Diana.*" *Traditio* 34 (1978): 303–29.

365. ———. "Reckoning with Boccaccio's Questioni d'amore." *Modern Language Notes* 89 (1974): 45–59.

366. Kleinhenz, Christopher. "Stylistic Gravity: Language and Prose Rhythms in *Decameron* I, 4." *Humanities Association Review* 26 (1975): 289–99.

367. König, Bernhard. *Die Begegnung im Tempel. Abwandlungen eines literarischen Motivs in den Werken Boccaccios.* Hamburg: De Gruyter, 1960.

368. ———. "Boccaccio vor dem 'Decameron' Ein Forschungsbericht." *Romanistisches Jahrbuch* 9 (1960): 108–42.

369. Layman, Beverly Joseph. "Boccaccio's Paradigm of the Artist and His Art." *Italian Quarterly* 13, no. 51 (1970): 19–36.

370. ———. "Eloquence of Pattern in Boccaccio's *Tale of the Falcon.*" *Italica* 46, no. 1 (1969): 3–16.

371. Limentani, Alberto. "Boccaccio traduttore di Stazio." *Rassegna della letteratura italiana* 64 (1960): 231–42.

372. ———. "Storia e Struttura dell'ottava rima." *Lettere italiane* 13, no. 1 (1961): 20–77.

373. Macaluso, Giuseppe. "Il Dante di Giovanni Boccaccio." In *Veggenti e teosofi*, pp. 118–62. Rome: Pensiero e Azione, 1972.

374. Maier, Bruno. "Il Boccaccio e il *Decameron.*" *Cristallo* 18, no. 1 (1976): 15–36.

375. Malagoli, Luigi. *"Decameron" e primo Boccaccio.* Pisa: Libreria goliardica, 1961.

376. Mancuso, Antonio O. *Il Decameron.* Torino: SEI, 1973.

377. Marani, Alma Novella. "La décima jornada del *Decameron.*" In *Giovanni Boccaccio, 1375–1975* (entry 351), pp. 97–121.

378. Marchi, Cesare. *Boccaccio.* Milan: Rizzoli, 1975.

379. Marcus, Millicent. *An Allegory of Form.* Saratoga, Calif.: Anma Libri, 1979.

380. Marino, Lucia. *The Decameron "Cornice": Allusion, Allegory and Iconography.* Ravenna: Longo, 1979.

381. Marti, Mario. "Per una metalettura del *Corbaccio:* Il ripudio di *Fiammetta.*" *Giornale Storico della Letteratura Italiana* 153 (1976): 60–86.

382. Mazzoni, Francesco, ed. *Il Boccaccio nelle culture e letterature nazionali.* Atti del Congresso Internazionale: La Fortune del Boccaccio nelle culture e letterature nazionali. Florence: Olschki, 1978.

383. Mazzotta, Giuseppe. "The Decameron: The Literal and the Allegorical." *Italian Quarterly* 18, no. 72 (1975): 53–73.

384. ———. *"The Decameron:* The Marginality of Literature." *The University of Toronto Quarterly* 18, no. 72 (1975): 53–73. Reprinted in *Critical Perspectives* (entry 331), pp. 129–43.

385. McAlpine, Monica. *The Genre of Troilus and Criseyde.* Ithaca: Cornell University Press, 1978.

386. Merola, Carmela. "Boccaccio's Neapolitan Period: An Analysis of the *Filocolo, Filostrato,* and *Teseida.*" Ph.D. diss., 1975.

387. Miglio, Massimo. "Boccaccio biografo." In *Boccaccio in Europe* (entry 451), pp. 149–63.

388. Montano, Rocco. "Appunti sul *Decameron.*" In *Saggi di cultura umanistica,* pp. 39–57. Naples: Quaderni di Delta, 1962.

389. Moravia, Alberto. *Man As an End: A Defense of Humanism.* Translated by Bernard Wall. New York: Farrar, Straus & Giroux, 1965.

390. ———. "Boccaccio." Adapted from *Man As an End* (entry 389), pp. 134–55, for *Critical Perspectives* (entry 331), pp. 93–112.

391. Musa, Mark, and Peter E. Bondanella. "The Meaning of the *Decameron.*" In *The Decameron* (entry 224), pp. 322–31.

392. Muscetta, Carlo. *Giovanni Boccaccio.* Bari: Laterza, 1972.

393. de' Negri, Enrico. "The Legendary Style of the *Decameron.*" *Romantic Review* 43 (1952): 166–89. Abridged and reprinted in *Critical Perspectives* (entry 331), pp. 82–98.

394. Nelson, John Charles. "Love and Sex in the Decameron." In *Philosophy and Humanism: Renaissance Essays in Honor of Paul Oskar Kristeller*, pp. 339–51. New York: Columbia University Press, 1976.

395. Neri, Ferdinando. *Poesia e storia.* Turin: Gambino, 1976.

396. Neuschäfer, Hans-Jörg. *Boccaccio und die erzählenden Literaturen des Mittelalters.* Munich: Wilhelm Fink Verlag, 1968.

397. ———. *Boccaccio und der Beginn der Novelle; Strukturen der Kurzerzählung auf der Schwelle zwischen Mittelalter und Neuzeit.* Munich: Wilhelm Fink Verlag, 1969.

398. Nicolas, Jean. "Le *Décameron;* oeuvre gaie?" *Revue des Études Italiennes* 21 (1975): 190–208.

399. Olson, Glending. "Petrarch's Views of the Decameron." *Modern Language Notes* 91 (1976): 69–79.

400. Padoan, Giorgio. *Il Boccaccio, le Muse, il Parnaso e l'Arno.* Florence: Olschki, 1978.

401. ———. "Sulla datazione del *Corbaccio.*" *Lettere italiane* 15 (1963): 1–27.

402. ———. "Ancora sulla datazione e sul titolo del *Corbaccio.*" *Lettere italiane* 15 (1963): 191–202.

403. ———. "Sulla genesi del *Decameron.*" In *Boccaccio: Secoli di vita* (entry 325), pp. 143–76.

404. ———. "Mondo aristocratico e mondo comunale nell'ideologia e nell'arte di Giovanni Boccaccio." *Studi sul Boccaccio* 6 (1968): 81–129.

405. Paparelli, Gioacchino. "Note sulla fortuna del Boccaccio a Napoli nel periodo aragonese." In *Il Boccaccio nelle culture e letterature nazionali* (entry 382), pp. 547–561.

188 / Fourteenth-Century Literature

406. Pazitka, Mikulas. "La fortuna del Boccaccio in Ceccoslovacchia." In *Boccaccio nelle culture e letterature nazionali* (entry 382), pp. 415–23.
407. Pellegrini, Carlo, ed. *Il Boccaccio nella cultura francese.* Firenze: Olschki, 1971.
408. Pennington, Kenneth. "A Note to *Decameron* 6:7: The Wit of Madonna Filippa." *Speculum* 52, no. 4 (1977): 902–5.
409. Perella, Nicolas J. "The World of Boccaccio's *Filocolo.*" *PMLA* 76 (1961): 330–9.
410. Perrus, Claude. "La Nouvelle V, 8 du *Décaméron:* Deux expériences de lecture." *Revue des Études Italiennes* 21 (1975): 249–83.
411. Pertusi, Agostino. "Venezia, la cultura greca e il Boccaccio." *Studi sul Boccaccio* 10 (1977–1978): 217–34.
412. Petrocchi, Giorgio. *Stile e critica.* Bari: Adriatica, 1968.
413. Petronio, Giuseppe. "I volti del *Decameron.*" In *Boccaccio: Secoli di vita* (entry 325), pp. 107–24.
414. Potopova, Zlata. "La fortuna del Boccaccio nella cultura russa e sovietica." In *Il Boccaccio nelle culture e letterature nazionali* (entry 382), pp. 293–315.
415. Radcliff-Umstead, Douglas. "Le donne di Boccaccio." *Alla bottega* 13, no. 4 (1975): 45–56.
416. Ramat, Raffaello. "Boccaccio 1340–1344." *Belfagor* 19, no. 1 (1964): 17–30; 154–74.
417. ———. "Girolamo e la Silvestra (*Decameron* IV, VIII)." In *Studi di varia umanità in onore di Francesco Flora.* Milan: Mondadori, 1963. Reprinted in *Saggi sul Rinascimento* (entry 419), pp. 50–69.
418. ———. "L'introduzione alla quarta giornata." *Miscellanea storica della Valdelsa* 69, no. 2–3 (1963): 203—97. Reprinted in *Saggi sul Rinascimento* (entry 419), pp. 93–107.
419. ———. *Saggi sul Rinascimento.* Florence: La Nuova Italia, 1969.
420. Ramat, Raffaello, et al. *Scritti su Giovanni Boccaccio.* Florence: L. S. Olschki, 1964.
421. Ricapito, Joseph V. "Boccaccio and the Picaresque Tradition." In *The Two Hesperias: Literary Studies in Honor of Joseph G. Fucilla on the Occasion of his 80th Birth-

day, edited by Americo Bugliani, pp. 309–328. Madrid: Porrúa, 1977.

422. Ricci, P. G. "Per la cronologia delle opere." *Studi sul Boccaccio* 6 (1971): 109–30.

423. apRoberts, Robert Piggott. "Love in the *Filostrato*." *The Chaucer Review* 7 (1972): 1–26.

424. Rømhild, Lars Peter. "Osservazioni sul concetto e sul significato della cornice nel *Decameron*." *Analecta Romana Instituti Danici* 7 (1974): 157–204.

425. Rossi, Aldo. "La combinatoria decameroniana: Andreuccio." *Strumenti critici* 7 (1973): 3–51.

426. ———. "Dante nella prospettiva del Boccaccio." *Studi danteschi* 37 (1960): 63–140.

427. Rossi, Giuseppe Carlo. "Il Boccaccio nelle letterature in portoghese." *Studi sul Boccaccio* 8 (1974): 273–309.

428. Rossi, Luciano. "Sercambi e Boccaccio." *Studi sul Boccaccio* 6 (1971): 145–78.

429. Rózsa, Zoltán. "La presenza del Boccaccio nella vita letteraria ungherese." In *Il Boccaccio nelle culture e letterature nazionali* (entry 382), pp. 427–35.

430. Ruggieri, Ruggiero M. "Medioevo e umanesimo: materia e stile in Giovanni Boccaccio." In *L'umanesimo cavalleresco italiano: Da Dante a Pulci*. Rome: Edizione dell Ateneo, 1962.

431. Russo, Vittorio. "Il senso tragico del *Decameron*." *Filologia e Letteratura* 11, no. 1 (1965): 29–84.

432. Sapegno, Natalino. "Boccaccio, Giovanni." In *Dizionario biografico degli italiani*, vol. 10, pp. 838–56. Rome: Istituto dell'Enciclopedia Italiana, 1968.

433. Scaglione, Aldo. "Giovanni Boccaccio or the Narrative Vocation." In *Boccaccio: Secoli di vita* (entry 325), pp. 81–104.

434. ———. *Nature and Love in the Late Middle Ages*. Berkeley and Los Angeles: University of California Press, 1963.

435. Segre, Cesare. "Boccaccio: narrazione e realtà." In *Lingua, stile e società*, pp. 301–14. Milan: Feltrinelli, 1974.

436. ———. "Estructuras y registros en la Fiammetta." In *Giovanni Boccaccio, 1375–1975* (entry 351), pp. 23–52.

437. ———. *Le strutture e il tempo*. Turin: Einaudi, 1974.

438. Simone, Franco. "Giovanni Boccaccio, fabbro della sua

prima fortuna francese." In *Il Boccaccio nella cultura francese* (entry 407), pp. 49–80.

439. ———. "La présence de Boccace dans la culture française du xve siècle." *Journal of Medieval and Renaissance Studies* 1 (1971): 17–32.

440. Simonelli, Maria Picchio. "Prima diffusione e tradizione manoscritta del *Decameron*." In *Boccaccio: Secoli di vita* (entry 325), pp. 125–42.

441. Sinicropi, Giovanni. "Il segno linguistico del *Decameron*." *Studi sul Boccaccio* 9 (1975–1976): 169–224.

442. Sklowskij, Viktor. *Lettura del "Decameron." Dal romanzo d'avventura al romanzo di carattere.* Translated by Alessandro Ivanov. Bologna: Il Mulino, 1969.

443. ———. "Riflessioni sui dieci giorni e sui seicento anni." In *Il Boccaccio nelle culture e letterature nazionali* (entry 382), pp. 263–91.

444. Smarr, Janet L. "Symmetry and Balance in the *Decameron*." *Mediaevalia* 2 (1976): 159–87.

445. ———. "Boccaccio and His *Decameron*." Ph.D. diss., 1975.

446. Stäuble, Antonio. "La brigata del *Decameron* come pubblico teatrale." *Studi sul Boccaccio* 9 (1975–1976): 103–17.

447. Stewart, Pamela D. "La novella di madonna Oretta e le due parti del *Decameron*." *Yale Italian Studies* (1973–1975): 27–39.

448. Sticca, Sandro. "Boccaccio and the Birth of the French Nouvelle." *Forum Italicum* 11 (1977): 218–47.

449. Tartaro, Achille. *Boccaccio.* Vol. 6. *Storia della critica*, edited by Giuseppe Petronio. Palermo: Palumbo, 1981.

450. Todorov, Tsvetan. *Grammaire du Décaméron.* The Hague and Paris: Mouton; New York: Humanities Press, 1969.

451. Tournoy, Gilbert, ed. *Boccaccio in Europe.* Proceedings of the Boccaccio Conference, 1975. Louvain: Leuven University Press, 1977.

452. Tusiani, Joseph. "The Poetry of Giovanni Boccaccio." *Thought* 50 (1975): 339–50.

453. Velli, Giuseppe. "*L'Ameto* e la pastorale: Il significato della forma." In *Il Boccaccio nella culture inglese e anglo-americana* (entry 344), pp. 67–80.

454. Waley, Pamela. "Fiammetta and Panfilo Continued." *Italian Studies* 24 (1969): 15–31.

455. ———. "The Nurse in Boccaccio's Fiammetta: Source and Invention." *Neophilologus* 56, no. 2 (1972): 164–74.

456. Wheelock, James T. S. "The Rhetoric Polarity in *Decameron* III:3." *Lingua e stile* 9 (1974): 257–74.

457. Wis, Roberto. "Il Boccaccio nella letteratura popolare della Svezia e della Finlandia." In *Il Boccaccio nelle culture e letterature nazionali* (entry 382), pp. 453–58.

458. Wright, Herbert G. *Boccaccio in England from Chaucer to Tennyson*. London: Athlone Press, 1957.

459. Zaboklicki, Krzysztof. "La fortuna del Boccaccio in Polonia." In *Il Boccaccio nelle culture e letterature nazionali* (entry 382), pp. 393–406.

460. Zorič, Mate. "Boccaccio nella cultura letteraria croata (dal romanticismo ad oggi)." In *Il Boccaccio nelle culture e letterature nazionali* (entry 382), pp. 317–49.

STUDIES: SPECIAL TOPICS AND MINOR WRITERS

461. *Il contributo dei giullari alla drammaturgia italiana delle origini*. Atti del Il Convegno di studio, 1977. Rome: Bulzoni, 1978.

462. Corsi, Giuseppe. "Madrigali e ballate inedite del Trecento." *Belfagor* 14 (1959): 329–40; 15 (1959): 72–81.

463. Faccioli, Emilio, comp. *Il teatro italiano*. Vol. 1. *Dalle origini al Quattrocento*. Turin: Einaudi, 1975.

464. Ferrero, Giuseppe Guido. *Poemi cavallereschi del Trecento*. Turin: UTET, 1965.

465. Getto, Giovanni. *Letteratura religiosa*. 2 vols. Florence: Sansoni, 1967.

466. Lanza, Antonio. *Studi sulla lirica del Trecento*. Rome: Bulzoni, 1978.

467. Rambaldi. *Laudi in volgare da un codice reggiano del secolo XIV e XV*. Reggio Emilia: Age, 1965.

468. Vecchi, Giuseppe. "Letteratura e musica nel Trecento." In *L'ars nova italiana del Trecento*. Secondo convegno internazionale, 1969. Certaldo: Centro di studi sull'ars nova italiana, 1970.

STUDIES: INDIVIDUAL AUTHORS

Antonio (Beccari) da Ferrara

469. Bellucci, Laura, ed. *Le rime di Maestro Antonio da Ferrara (Antonio Beccari)*. Bologna: Pàtron, 1972.
470. Blomme, R. "La 'disperata' di Antonio da Ferrara." *Handelingen van het xxxᵉ Vlaams Filogencongres*, 1977. Leuven: Secretariaat van de Vlaamse Filogencongressen, 1977, pp. 180–84.
471. Gallo, F. Alberto. "Antonio da Ferrara, Lancilotto Anguissola e il madrigale trecentesco." *Studi e Problemi di Critica Testuale* 12 (1976): 40–45.

Bonvesin de la Riva

472. Marri, Fabio. *Glossario al milanese di Bonvesin*. Bologna: Pàtron, 1977.

Cantari

473. Ageno, Franca B. "Cantari religiosi senesi del Trecento." *Romance Philology* 24 (1971): 478–88.
474. Branca, Vittore. "Nostalgie tardogotiche e gusto del fiabesco nella tradizione narrativa dei cantari." *Varia umanità* (1963): 88–108.
475. Delcorno, Branca, Daniela. "I cantari di Tristano." *Lettere Italiane* 23 (1971): 289–305.
476. Franceschetti, Antonio. "Rassegna sui cantari." *Lettere Italiane* 25 (1973): 556–74.

Caterina da Siena

477. Bizzicari, Alvaro. "Linguaggio e stile delle Lettere di Catarina da Siena." *Italica* 53 (1976): 320–46.
478. Busti, Mario. *Santa Caterina da Siena nel V centenario della canonizzazione*. Milan: Pro Cultura, 1962.
479. D'Urso, Giacinto. *Il genio di Santa Caterina*. Rome: edizioni cateriniane, 1971.
480. D'Urso, Giacinto, and Jesus Castellano. *Santa Caterina e Santa Teresa, dottori della Chiesa*. Naples: Edizioni domenicane, 1970.

481. Mazzamuto, Pietro. "Aspetti teologici e strutturali dell'epistolario cateriniano." In *Studi in onore di Alberto Chiari*, pp. 853–62. Brescia: Paideia editrice, 1973.

482. Perrin, J. M. *Catherine of Siena*. Translated by Paul Barrett. Westminster: Newman Press, 1965.

483. Pisani, Vittore. "Tradizione e poesia nella lingua di Santa Caterina da Siena." *Acme* 19 (1966): 243–69.

484. Radius, Emilio. *Santa Caterina da Siena*. Milan: Martello, 1970.

485. Rupp, Jean. *Catherine et Thérèse. Docteurs pour nos temps.* Paris: P. Lethielleux, 1971.

Cecco d'Ascoli

486. Alessandrini, Mario. *Cecco d'Ascoli*. Rome: 1955.

487. Sansoni, Giuseppe. "Considerazioni sul testo dell'Acerba." *Studi Mediolatini e Volgari* 18 (1970): 217–28.

Cino da Pistoia

488. Boggs, Edward Louis, III. "Cino da Pistoia: A Study of His Poetry." Ph.D. diss., 1977.

489. *Colloquio Cino da Pistoia, 1975.* Atti dei Convegni Lincei 18. Rome: Accademia Nazionale dei Lincei, 1976.

490. Libertini, Vincenzo. *Cino da Pistoia*. Lanciano: Itinerari Lanciani, 1974.

491. Paganelli, Gianluigi. *Discorso su Cino da Pistoia.* Pistoia: Pacinotti, 1958.

Francesco da Barberino

492. Goldin, Daniela. "Un gioco poetico di società e i 'Moteti' di Francesco da Barberino." *Giornale Storico della Letteratura Italiana* 150 (1973): 259–91.

493. ———. "Autotraduzione latina nei 'Documenti d'amore' di Francesco da Barberino." *Atti del R. Istituto veneto di Scienze* 133 (1974–1975): 371–92.

494. Mariuzzo, Gabriel. "Composizione e significato de *I documenti d'amore* di Francesco da Barberino." *Giornale Italiano di Filologia* 26 (1974): 217–51.

Jacopo Passavanti

495. Aurigemma, Marcello. "La fortuna critica dello Specchio di vera penitenza di Jacopo Passavanti." In *Studi in onore di Angelo Monteverdi*, 1:48–75. Modena: Tip-editrice modenese, 1959.
496. Auzzas, Ginetta. "Per il testo dello *Speculum della vera penitenza:* Due fonti manoscritte." *Lettere Italiane* 26 (1974): 261–87.
497. Cornagliotti, Anna. "Un nuovo codice dello *Specchio di vera penitenza.*" *Giornale Storico della Letteratura Italiana* 153 (1976): 376–86.

Antonio Pucci

498. Fasani, Remo. "Ancora per l'attribuzione del *Fiore* al Pucci." *Studi e Problemi di Critica Testuale* 6 (1973): 22–68.

Franco Sacchetti

499. Esch, Arnold. "Weitere historische Personen in Franco Sacchettis *Trecentonovelle.*" *Zeitschrift für Romanische Philologie* 90 (1974): 247–52.
500. Ageno, Franca. "Per il Testo del Trecentonovelle." *Giornale Storico della Letteratura Italiana* 134 (1957): 638–40.
501. Scrivano, Riccardo. "Aspetti della narrativa sacchettiana." *Rassegna della Letteratura Italiana* 44 (1960): 432–45.

Giovanni Sercambi

502. Robuschi Romagnoli, Pina. "Ancora sulla struttura del *Pecorone.*" *Studi in onore di Alberto Chiari*, pp. 1067–91. Brescia: Paideia, 1973.
503. Sinicropi, Giovanni. "Per la datazione delle novelle del Sercambi." *Giornale Storico della Letteratura Italiana* 141 (1964): 548–66.

LATIN LITERATURE

Fred J. Nichols*

To survey the current state of scholarship in fourteenth-century literature written in Latin is to undertake an enterprise very different from that of my colleagues surveying literatures in the vernacular languages. This is not just because the Latin literature of that century is an international literature spanning the confines of any single geographical area defined by language. Symptomatic of the problem is the fact that no survey or history or even reasonably full description of the Latin literature of the fourteenth century as a whole exists. Given this particular fact, it seems useful to explore why the study of this literature has been neglected, so that the reader will understand the reasons my survey of scholarship in the area consists so often of attention to works focusing on disciplines other than fourteenth-century Latin literature—as we understand the term *literature.*

To begin with, we must candidly admit that the quality of the literature in Latin in this century is not as high as that of the centuries preceding it or following it, nor is it as high as the quality of the vernacular literatures of its

*Fred J. Nichols is an Associate Professor of Comparative Literature at the Graduate Center of the City University of New York. He also teaches in the Summer Latin/Greek Institute at the Graduate Center and has taught previously at Yale University and New York University. He has published *An Anthology of Neo-Latin Poetry* as well as numerous articles on subjects ranging from Renaissance Latin punctuation to Goethe's *Faust.* His current research projects include studies of seventeenth-century Dutch literature and a translation of the work of the sixteenth-century black Neo-Latin poet Juan Latino.

time. A century in which the most notable long poems in Latin, for instance, are Petrarch's *Africa* and John Gower's *Vox Clamantis*, is not one of the great ages of long Latin poetry. The situation of lyric poetry is similar, as a glance at Raby's *Oxford Book of Medieval Latin Verse* will make clear. There is nothing like the great outpouring of effective and expressive Latin, in poetry and prose, that arose in the twelfth century and continued into the thirteenth. The richness of this production decidedly falls off just short of the fourteenth century. Those last great medieval Latin lyrics, the *Dies Irae* and the *Stabat Mater*, seem to have been written just before the fourteenth century. On the other hand, the *Imitation of Christ*, that late monument of medieval Latin prose, comes after it, and the Latin work produced by Petrarch and Boccaccio seems in a broader view to be a kind of prelude to the last brilliant age of creativity in Latin letters under the auspices of the humanists, which gathered its strength during the fifteenth century and reached a final flowering in the sixteenth and early seventeenth centuries. If such men as Petrarch and Boccaccio composed Latin works of intrinsic literary as well as historical importance in this period, what they wrote in Latin does not reach the heights they achieved in the vernacular, and nothing in the Latin of the time remotely approaches the accomplishment of Dante's *Divine Comedy* early in the century or Chaucer's *Canterbury Tales* toward the end of it. In comparison to other arts and sciences, the Latin literature of the time is deficient too. Far more important work in Latin goes on in philosophy, and even in music, than in literature in the stricter sense of the term.

A primary difficulty is that during the fourteenth century there are two kinds of Latin, which we may distinguish as medieval Latin and humanist Latin. I am aware that I tread on sensitive territory in making such a distinction, but it must be emphasized that a very sharp difference between these two kinds of Latin exists without much overlapping. On the one hand, medieval Latin continues the still vigorous traditions of preceding centuries and is marked by such features as rhymed verse with metrics based upon accent, and precise and highly developed terminology such as that of scholastic philosophy. The essential characteristic of this kind of writing is that it is based upon medieval procedures of versification, rhetoric, and coining of terms not identical to those of classical antiquity.

Humanist Latin, on the other hand, of which Petrarch is the most accomplished early practitioner (and in fact he was considered by later humanists to be the father of what they saw as their reborn Latinity), is defined by its intention of using the Latin language, both in poetry and prose, in strict conformity to ancient Roman principles of composition and rhetoric, principles that became clearer in our period with the discovery of such lost Roman authors as Quintilian. In this century, humanist Latin was largely confined to Italy, although there are glimmerings of it in the South of France, and traces of pre-humanist activity as far afield as England and Bohemia.

It should at once be said that the study of humanist Latin in our period has not been neglected if one expands the definition of Latin literature to include anything written in Latin, a definition that would have made more sense than our modern one to writers of the period. Both because of their importance in the history of ideas and because of the importance of what they wrote in the vernacular, the Latin works of Dante and Petrarch have been submitted to an intense scrutiny. I shall speak of this in more detail, but it should be noted that in spite of this interest in the earlier phases of humanism, much in the field of humanist Latin remains to be done, especially with the poetry, and with writers other than Dante and Petrarch. Standard surveys of Renaissance Latin literature, such as those of Grant and Van Tieghem, cover the fourteenth century in the most cursory manner.

The medieval Latin literature of the time, however, has been remarkably little studied, although this lack of attention has lately begun to be noticed. Jozef IJsewijn (138) has recently remarked that "the Latin literature dating from the waning of the Middle Ages is a rather neglected field in modern scholarship."[1] The situation has been described in detail by Marian Plezia (17): "So far no intrepid sailor has been found to cross safely the immense ocean of the thirteenth and fourteenth century literary production in spite—and perhaps just because—of the fact that the belles lettres took in that time indisputable second place as compared with the extraordinary abundance of learned or only didactic literature, in a considerable measure not yet published today but occupying still in form of manuscripts the shelves of numerous European libraries."[2]

As Plezia also notes, most histories of medieval Latin, such as the fundamental works of Max Manitius and J. de Ghellinck, come nowhere near as far as the fourteenth century. Works that do reach 1500, such as Raby's standard studies of medieval Latin religious and secular verse, or Helin's short survey of medieval Latin literature, do not contain extensive information about the period. Here an immense amount of work remains to be done.

It is interesting to speculate about the reasons for this neglect. When we survey the scholarship on medieval Latin literature as a whole, the farther back in time we go, the more there is that has been done. In the earlier period, there are fewer texts to begin with, as Plezia notes, and more is available in the way of reference works and secondary studies. As one progresses on into the Middle Ages, the number of texts increases, the aids to scholarship often

1. Jozef IJsewijn, *Companion to Neo-Latin Studies* (Amsterdam: North Holland, 1977), p. 16.
2. Marian Plezia, "Development Periods of Medieval Latin." In *Miscellanea Mediaevalia in memoriam Jan Frederik Niermeyer* (Groningen: Wolters, 1967), p. 31.

become sketchier, manuscripts become more difficult to read, and difficulties in general multiply. Yet none of this justifies the neglect of an area that is in fact the most vital interface between the Middle Ages and the Renaissance. Whether one wishes to stress what binds them together, or what distinguishes them, the coexistence of medieval and humanist Latin during the fourteenth century is a fact both inescapable and important. The history of medieval Latin literature will not be complete until we know, in detail, how and why it ended.

That task awaits medievalists. The history of Renaissance Latin literature is incomplete until we know how and why it began, and such investigations await specialists in the Renaissance. And no one, as far as I know, has attempted to examine the Latin literature of the fourteenth century in Europe as a whole. The result would certainly be very curious from our present point of view, based as it is mainly on a perception of Latin literature in terms of our understanding of vernacular literatures. Such an attempt to study the Latin literature of this century in its own terms, beginning with its understanding of its own centrality in European cultural life, would be disconcerting both to medievalists and Renaissance specialists, and all the more worth doing for just that reason.

This survey reflects the scattered state of studies in the Latin literature of the fourteenth century. Since so much of the work in this area has been done in studies of a broader compass, to give an accurate picture of recent developments, I shall mention a number of works that do not focus primarily or specifically on the century. And since the area is still rather neglected compared to the vernacular literatures of the same period, I shall begin by mentioning works pertaining to medieval or early Renaissance Latin that have an immediate usefulness even if they deal rather slightly with the fourteenth century. After considering such general works, my plan is first to survey work done on specifically literary texts in the narrower sense of that term: poetry, drama, and humanist Latin. I shall conclude by surveying in a more summary fashion the writing that was done in Latin because it was the language of serious intellectual thought in the time. My focus will be the philosophical and religious works that were the liveliest form of Latin writing in this century, at least outside of Italy.

GENERAL STUDIES AND REFERENCE WORKS

The approximate starting point for my survey is 1963, which is the last year covered in the extremely useful review of studies by Albert C. Freund in the volume edited by John Fisher entitled *The Medieval Literature of Western Europe: A Review of Research* (3). While I cannot, in the space I have, mention everything done in such a diffusely organized field of study, I have tried to select what I shall mention in such a way as to give a representative idea of work in the field.

The fastest way to get a view of what is being done at any given time is to consult the *Year's Work in Modern Language Studies* (23), which contains two sections relevant to Latin. The Medieval Latin section, done by W. F. Bolton and more recently by A. K. Bate, is even broken down into centuries. Although by no means a complete listing, this is the easiest way to get some idea of current developments. The Neo-Latin section by J. W. Binns, also covers, a bit more systematically, fourteenth-century scholarship in humanist Latin. A fundamental reference work for all medievalists is the *International Medieval Bibliography* (8), an annual publication that lists articles arranged by subject, and that extends to 1500. There is no separate section for Latin literature, however, and studies of individual Latin works are arranged geographically with works in the relevant national literatures. For an annotated list of journals, there is the *Serial Bibliographies for Medieval Studies* by Richard H. Rouse (19), which does have a section on studies of Latin. A. G. Rigg of the University of Toronto, one of the few scholars who has made something of a specialty of the Latin literature of this period outside of Italy, is preparing a bibliography of medieval Latin literature to appear as part of the series of Toronto Medieval Bibliographies.

A general reference work recently begun that will contain material of great interest for medieval Latin scholars is the *Lexikon des Mittelalters* (12), which also goes as far as 1500. Seven fascicles have appeared so far, taking us up to *Barmherzigkeit*. With articles of continued high quality, it will be an indispensable reference work.

There has been substantial activity in the area of general introductions to the study of medieval Latin. Here the neglect of the fourteenth century is to some extent understandable, but it is symptomatic and regrettable that so basic a work as Martin McGuire's *Introduction to Medieval Latin Studies: A Syllabus and Bibliographical Guide* (13) only goes as far as the twelfth century, thereby restricting its usefulness. An equally basic book, which, however, regrets the lack of scholarly work in the later period of medieval Latin, is Karl Strecker's *Introduction to Medieval Latin* (20). Although the work first appeared in German as long ago as 1929, the English translation by Robert B. Palmer appeared in a new, revised edition in 1971. Other recent works helpful to a student of fourteenth-century Latin are Karl Langosch's brief *Lateinisches Mittelalter: Einleitung in Sprache und Literatur* (9) and the collection of essays edited by Alf Önnerfors, *Mittellateinische Philologie: Beitrage zur Erforschung der mittelalterlichen Latinität* (15). A useful and fundamental work in a related field is R. C. van Caenegem's *Guide to the Sources of Medieval History* (21), which also extends to 1500 and covers such literary matters as letters, hagiography, and journals.

It is interesting to note in passing that some new material is available for those venturesome enough to teach medieval Latin literature with some coverage of the fourteenth century. An extremely handy article full of practical suggestions for one familiar with classical Latin who is teaching medieval Latin for the first time is John R. Clark's "Teaching Medieval Latin" (2). One textbook has appeared in recent years that does cover some fourteenth-century material, F. E. Harrison's *Millenium: A Latin Reader, 375–1374* (6). It is more typical that Dag Norberg's *Manuel pratique de latin médiéval* (14) does not.

While I don't intend to cover linguistics, one book of background interest to a literary scholar concerned with the changes in the use of Latin in the fourteenth century is Philippe Wolff's *Western Languages, A.D. 100–1500* (22). Relevant to the study of literature, although a subject in which a great deal needs to be done given the small amount of research underlying the traditional generalities, is the question of literacy in Latin. Here there is the recently published work of M. T. Clanchy, *From Memory to Written Record: England 1066–1307* (1), which gives a picture of Latin literacy at the beginning of the period that is useful even if relentlessly confined to England. Much more work remains to be done in this area.

EDITING TEXTS

Some materials have also been published discussing the problems of editing medieval texts. Recent work in this field has mainly been in the form of articles, and two proceedings of conferences devoted to the question have been published. *Probleme der Edition mittel- und neulateinischer Texte* (25) contains the records of a congress held at Bonn in 1973 edited by Ludwig Hödl and Dieter Wuttke, and *Editing Medieval Texts* (27), papers given at a conference in Toronto in 1976 edited by A. G. Rigg, includes Rigg's own article on editing Latin texts written in England. See also the helpful article by Louis J. Bataillon, "Problèmes posés par l'édition des textes latins médiévaux" (24). A good preliminary article on the subject of Latin paleography by James John appears in *Medieval Studies: An Introduction*, edited by James M. Powell (18). It should be noted that a new edition of Bernhard Bischoff's fundamental *Paläographie* (28) appeared in 1979. Also helpful for our century is S. Harrison Thomson's *Latin Bookhands of the Later Middle Ages, 1100–1500* (42), which contains texts with transcriptions. Useful too is the second volume of the *Geschichte der Textüberlieferung der antiken und mittelalterlichen Literatur* edited by Karl Langosch (11), the first chapter of which is a history by Langosch of the transmission of medieval Latin texts.

LEXICOGRAPHY

The field of lexicography has been active in recent years, although here too a bias against the later period restricts the usefulness of some major efforts. Perhaps the single best one-volume dictionary of medieval Latin is J. F. Niermeyer's *Mediae Latinitatis Lexicon Minus* (39), which gives French and English translations of Latin words, but it only goes as far as 1200. Someone working in the fourteenth century would also want to consult the *Lexicon Latinitatis Medii Aevi* by Albert Blaise (29), which is a Latin-French dictionary. An idiosyncratic work, it focuses on religious subjects, and although it is primarily a medieval Latin dictionary, it includes selected terms from later Latin writings right down to modern times. Among the writers whose Latin it glosses are Francis Bacon and Leibnitz.

One of the most monumental efforts currently being undertaken in medieval studies is the *Novum Glossarium Mediae Latinitatis* (40), being edited by Frans Blatt for the International Union of Academies. A first volume (*L* to *Nysus*) had already appeared in 1957, and two fascicles covering most of the letter *O* were published in 1975 and 1978. Once again, however, this work only extends to the year 1200, and no comparable international dictionary is under way for Latin after that date. Instead national projects under the sponsorship of individual national academies are involved in dictionary projects for the Latin of their own national areas. But here, too, the German *Mittellateinisches Wörterbuch* (38), a joint project of East German, West German, and Swiss academies, extends only to the end of the thirteenth century. Publication under the editorship of Otto Prinz began in 1967, and parts published thus far have reached the letter *C*.

Recently active dictionary projects that do cover the fourteenth century include the following works. R. E. Latham's *Revised Medieval Latin Word-List from British and Irish Sources* (34) is based on a 1934 word list by J. H. Baxter and C. Johnson. This is a preliminary step of Latham's *Dictionary of Medieval Latin from British Sources* (33), of which the first volume (A–B) has appeared. It extends to 1500, as does the Swedish dictionary project, the *Glossarium till Medeltidslatinet i Sverige* (31) by Ulla Westerbergh and more recently Eva Odelman; fascicles began to appear in 1968 and have reached the letter *H*. The Dutch project, the *Lexicon Latinitatis Nederlandicae Medii Aevi* (36) by J. W. Fuchs and Olga Weijers, published its first volume in 1977 and has reached the letter *C*. In Eastern Europe, the Polish *Lexicon Mediae et Infimae Latinitatis Polonorum* (37), under way since 1953 under the editorship of Marian Plezia, has in its most recent fascicle reached the word *Industria*. The first volume of *Lexicon Latinitatis Medii Aevi Iugoslaviae* (35), edited by Marko Kostrenčić, appeared in 1973 including the letters *A* to *K*; a fascicle reaching from *Q* well into *S* appeared in 1976. Although much is being done in this area, there is still much left to do, and a scholar working in a language that exhibits as many local peculiarities and idiosyncracies as fourteenth-century Latin is still likely to encounter lexical difficulties hard to resolve if he gets very far off the beaten track.

A useful and related reference work is Auguste Pelzer's *Abréviations latines médiévales* (41), a supplement to the indispensable Capelli dictionary of abbreviations. Also of interest here as an example of medieval lexicography is the study of a fourteenth-century Latin-German vocabulary by Klaus Grubmüller, *Vocabularius Ex quo* (32).

CATALOGUES OF MANUSCRIPTS

An even busier area of medieval studies than lexicography is the cataloging of texts and manuscripts, and a large number of extremely helpful works have been produced within the last twenty years, so many that I can only give some indication of what is most useful and most symptomatic. This work is of vital importance to the student of fourteenth century Latin literature in the virtual absence of such bibliographical work specifically focused on that century. We can only skim the surface of catalogues and lists of manuscripts. Perhaps the best known of such works is Paul Oskar Kristeller's *Iter Italicum* (46), explained by its subtitle as "a finding list of uncatalogued or incompletely catalogued humanistic manuscripts of the Renaissance in Italian and other libraries." It begins with 1300 and includes, among many others, Petrarch. The two volumes covering libraries in Italy appeared in 1963 and 1967. We are promised similar volumes for manuscripts in other countries.

Many catalogues of manuscripts for individual countries exist. The first two volumes of N. R. Ker's *Medieval MSS in British Libraries* (45) have been published, the first covering London, the second proceeding alphabetically from Abbotsford to Keele, and a third volume is to come. A monumental project on medieval manuscripts in France, by Charles Samaran and Robert Marichal, arranged by region, has appeared in six volumes (50). A similar Dutch project by G. I. Lieftinck, *Manuscripts datés conservés dans les Pays-Bas* (48) has completed its first volume, which deals with foreign manuscripts. For Belgium, the fourteenth century is covered in the first volume of *Manuscrits datés conservés en Belgique* (49), edited by François Masai and Martin Wittek. The first volume of the Swiss catalogue of dated manuscripts, under the general editorship of M. Burckhardt (43), covers the cantons of Aarau, Appenzell, and Basel. The first volume of a Swedish catalogue of dated manuscripts, by G. Hornwall and others, deals with the manuscripts in the University Library of Uppsala (44). And the first volume of an Italian catalogue, on the manuscripts at the National Library in Rome, has appeared (51). It should be noted that 1965 saw the publication of a revised third edition of the indefatigable Paul Oskar Kristeller's previously published *Latin Manuscript Books before 1600: A List of the Printed Catalogues and Unpublished Inventories of Extant Collections* (47).

LISTS AND INDEXES OF INDIVIDUAL WORKS

A basic research tool for historians, but useful for literary scholars as well, is the series *Typologie des sources du Moyen Âge occidental* (4), which has been published in separate fascicles under the general editorship of Léopold Genicot. This series consists of studies and bibliographies of genres useful to historians as sources. Of particular literary interest are Giles Constable's excellent "Letters and Letter Collections," G. Philippart's "Les Légendiers latins," and studies of martyrologies, *libri poenitentiales*, and funeral songs. An enormous project that produced its first volume in 1960 continues: the *Catalogus Translationum et Commentariorum* (54), begun by Paul Oskar Kristeller and now edited by F. Edward Cranz. This is a listing of manuscripts and editions of Latin commentaries on classical authors and of Latin translations of Greek authors, as well as brief essays that trace the *fortuna* of each classical author down to 1600. Three more volumes of this useful and usable work have appeared in the last decade.

A number of more specialized listings of works are often arranged, in an age of frequently anonymous authorship and uncertain titles, by the opening words, and all those I note include the fourteenth century. A revised edition of Hans Walther's *Initia carminum ac versuum Medii Aevi posterioris Latinorum* (61) lists 21,000 entries up to the year 1500 and is of obvious value for the study of fourteenth-century Latin poetry. We are promised a supplemental volume with an additional 10,000 entries. The same energetic scholar has produced *Lateinische Sprichwörterund Sentenzen des Mittelalters* (62),a similar compilation of Latin proverbs, arranged alphabetically in six volumes. An equally monumental undertaking is J. B. Schneyer's *Repertorium der lateinisches Sermones des Mittelalters* (57), which includes the first half of the fourteenth century. A total of nine volumes has been published, arranged by author when the author is known. A companion volume is Schneyer's *Wegweiser lateinischen Predigtreihen des Mittelalters* (58), a survey of series of medieval Latin sermons and a guide to their study.[3] Of great interest is Charles Lohr's listing of medieval Latin Aristotle commentaries that appeared as a series of articles in *Traditio* (56) and that will form part of the Aristotle section of the *Catalogus Translationum et Commentariorum*. A revised and expanded edition of Lynn Thorndike and Pearl Kibre's *Catalogue of Incipits of Mediaeval Scientific Writings in Latin* (59) has been pub-

---

3. Current work in the field can also be found in the *Medieval Sermon Newsletter*, edited by Gloria Cigman. Useful background is also contained in the work of Richard Rouse; see his *Preachers, Florilegia and Sermons* (82).

lished. Several scholars headed by Morton Bloomfield have recently compiled the *Incipits of Latin Works on the Virtues and Vices* (52), and in the same area is Frederick Tubach's *Index Exemplorum: A Handbook of Medieval Religious Tales* (60), which includes a detailed subject index.

LITERARY HISTORY AND CRITICISM OF MEDIEVAL LATIN

I shall turn now to studies primarily concerned with the critical and technical analysis of literary works. Reflecting the absolute division I have already discussed in research on the Latin of the period, I shall mention first works that focus on medieval Latin, then works concerned with humanist Latin.

I have observed that earlier standard histories of medieval Latin frequently neglected the fourteenth century. However that has not been the case with certain works in recent years. A new and ambitious history of medieval Latin literature is Franz Brunhölzl's *Geschichte der lateinischen Literatur des Mittelalters* (66). The first volume reaches only as far as the Carolingian period, but if the author holds to his promise, we will some day have a very effective survey of the Latin literature of the fourteenth century. In the meantime, we do have a solid preliminary study that stresses the vitality of the literature of the period: Brunhölzl's article "Die lateinische Literatur" in the volume on medieval literature entitled *Europäisches Spätmittelalter* edited by Willi Erzgraber (70). A handy introductory volume that also covers the area is W. T. H. Jackson's *Medieval Literature: A History and a Guide* (74), which has a short clear section on Latin. One earlier study that didn't altogether neglect the period was Maurice Helin's *History of Medieval Latin Literature*, which was published in French in 1943 and in English translation in 1949. The same author has more recently written a volume in the Que sais-je series entitled *La Littérature latine au Moyen Âge* (73), a witty and urbane introduction to a literature "qu'on ne lit plus" that includes the fourteenth century.

A number of works have appeared in recent years on more specific matters. One of the most interesting, Judson B. Allen's *The Friar as Critic: Literary Attitudes in the Later Middle Ages* (64), treats classicizing friars in the fourteenth century and is a relatively rare example of a book on the literary theory of this period.[4] One book that stops just short of the fourteenth century is Tore Janson's thorough *Prose Rhythm in Medieval Latin from the Ninth to the Thirteenth Century* (75), but it should be mentioned because much of the latter part of it is applicable to our century as well. Fourteenth-century works are mentioned in Paule Demats, *Fabula: Trois études de mythologie antique et médiévale* (67), in Siegfried Wenzel's thoughtful study, *The Sin of Sloth: "Acedia" in Medieval Thought and Literature* (88), and in John Block Friedman's stimulating *Orpheus in the Middle Ages* (71). The genre of the textual commentary is carefully studied in Bruno Sandkühler, *Die frühen Dantekommentare und ihr Verhältnis zur mittelalterlichen Kommentartradition* (83).

Absolutely fundamental in its own field and extremely useful to anyone interested in medieval Latin poetry is Joseph Szövérffy's *Annalen der lateinischen Hymnendichtung* (86). This is a detailed outline of medieval hymnody, and the second volume contains seventy pages on the fourteenth century and is the most extensive general treatment of Latin lyrics of the period that I have seen. The same author is also producing *Weltliche Dichtungen des lateinischen Mittelalters* (87). The first volume reaches

---

4. The same author has continued these studies in his just-published *The Ethical Poetics of the Later Middle Ages* (65). Also very recent is Alastair J. Minnis, *Medieval Theory of Authorship* (79).

to Carolingian times; its continuation to our century will be welcome and would remedy a large gap in fourteenth-century studies. In the realm of studies of the poetry of the period, another work that extends only to the thirteenth century, but whose conclusions apply to the fourteenth, is the *Einführung in die mittellateinische Verslehre* (76), a short but thorough survey by Paul Klopsch.

The specific study of the poetry in recent years has been an area in which two men have distinguished themselves, Peter Dronke and the indispensable A. G. Rigg. Dronke is best known for his provocative *Medieval Latin and the Rise of the European Love-Lyric* (68). The fact that he analyzes seven Latin poems of the fourteenth century and several others that date approximately from it shows that serious critical analysis can profitably be done in this little-studied material. Rigg, whose name we have already several times had occasion to mention, breaks new ground in his study of "Medieval Latin Poetic Anthologies" (81). Anthologies were popular in the fourteenth century, and as he notes, "a general history of the medieval verse anthology has yet to be written."[5] Certainly the best recent anthology of the poetry of the period is Henry Spitzmuller's *Poésie latine chrétienne du moyen âge* (84), which includes over 150 pages of fourteenth-century Latin poetry.

STUDIES OF INDIVIDUAL MEDIEVAL AUTHORS

Just how neglected the poetry has been is clear from the small number of editions and studies of individual poets and works there have been, and most of these, as we shall see, deal with only two of the authors of the time. This may be a result of the skimpy treatment of fourteenth-

---

5. A. G. Rigg, "Medieval Latin Poetic Anthologies," *Mediaeval Studies* 39 (1977): 281.

century verse in Raby's two works on medieval poetry, but Peter Dronke has, I might repeat, provided an example of the value of studying it. The two authors whose work has been dealt with thoroughly in recent years are both English. The first is Richard Ledrede (or Ledredge), Bishop of Ossory in Ireland from 1317 to 1360, a curious figure under whose reign the first trial for witchcraft took place in Ireland. He was also a poet, and sixty Latin hymns attributed to him are preserved in the Red Book of Ossory, a collection of official diocesan documents. These were edited no less than three times in two years by Edmund Colledge (96) and by Richard Leighton Greene (99) in 1974, and by Theo Stemmler (104) in 1975; the latter found much to correct in the first two. Each of these volumes was published in a different country, and one wonders if better communication would have prevented such curious concentration of effort in a field generally so neglected.

John Gower is a much better known figure than Ledrede, and his status as a poet in English has led to the interest in his Latin poetry, his major work being the *Vox Clamantis* in some ten thousand lines. Just before the period I am covering, Eric Stockton's translation of *The Major Latin Works of John Gower* (91) was published with introduction and annotation. J. A. W. Bennett's *Selections from John Gower* (89) includes some Latin verse, and the Latin poems are among those discussed in John H. Fisher's definitive study, *John Gower, Moral Philosopher and Friend of Chaucer* (90). A full and detailed bibliography of Gower including the Latin works by R. F. Yeager was published in *Mediaevalia* (95).

MEDIEVAL GRAMMAR AND RHETORIC

The study of medieval rhetoric has been greatly advanced by the energetic work of James J. Murphy, who has not neglected the fourteenth century, which is partic-

ularly important for the study of the subject. He has produced a fundamental bibliography (111) in the Toronto
Medieval Bibliographies series, which is annotated and
includes treatises on grammar, letter writing, and preaching. He has produced a general study, *Rhetoric in the Middle Ages* (112), and, more recently, has edited a collection
of essays by various hands, *Medieval Eloquence* (110). He
has also edited *Three Medieval Rhetorical Arts* (113), which
includes Robert Basevorn's *Forma Praedicandi*, dating from
the fourteenth century. Much material on the late medieval period is to be found in the collection of articles by
Harry Caplan, *Of Eloquence: Studies in Ancient and
Mediaeval Rhetoric* (107). Unfamiliar territory is covered
by Charles Faulhaber in his *Latin Rhetorical Theory in
Thirteenth and Fourteenth Century Castile* (108). A text
of great interest for the study of rhetoric from Bohemia
has been edited by Samuel Peter Jaffe, *Nicolaus Dybinus'
"Declaracio oracionis de beata Dorothea"* (109). This is a
long poem in honor of Saint Dorothy that is designed to
exhibit all the colors of rhetoric, a technically if not poetically satisfying feat.

Fourteenth-century texts are included in a book indispensable to any study of medieval levels of style, although it comes just before my starting date, *Die antike
Theorie der "genera dicendi" im lateinischen Mittelalter*
by Franz Quadlbauer (115). Closely related to rhetoric and
overlapping with philosophy are the speculative grammars produced by those late medieval grammarians known
as the *modistae*. These have been studied by G. L. Bursill-
Hall in *Speculative Grammars of the Middle Ages* (106).
The same author is also compiling "A Check-list of Incipits of Medieval Latin Grammatical Treatises" (105); the
first installment, A to G, has been published. I might add
that a series of critical editions of the works of the *modistae* and other medieval grammarians will appear in the
series Grammatica Speculativa at Stuttgart under the general editorship of J. Pinborg.

MEDIEVAL DRAMA

Fourteenth-century Latin drama is a restricted area because most of the activity in the religious drama of the time was already in the vernacular. There are a few Latin dramatic texts, however, and some pieces partly in the vernacular and partly in Latin, especially in German-speaking areas, where the transition to the vernacular occurred later. A new basic reference tool in medieval drama is Carl J. Stratman's *Bibliography of Medieval Drama* (122), the fundamental bibliography with nearly two thousand entries in Latin drama alone. A basic collection of Latin dramatic texts, including many of the fourteenth century, is contained in Walther Lipphardt's *Lateinischen Osterfeiern und Osterspiele* (117); intended to replace Karl Young's collection of texts in its area, five of the seven volumes have appeared.

One Latin dramatic text of the period is the Sulmona Passion fragment. This is discussed by Sandro Sticca in *The Latin Passion Play: Its Origin and Development* (120). Fourteenth-century *planctus* poems and their relationship to Latin drama are discussed by Sticca in an article entitled "The Literary Genesis of the Latin Passion Play" in the collection of essays edited by him entitled *The Medieval Drama* (121). A study of the bilingual plays of the period, including such works as the Vienna Easter play, is Wilfried Werner's *Studien zu den Passions- und Osterspielen des deutschen Mittelalters* (124). Larry E. West has done an English translation with critical introduction of such a bilingual play, *The Saint Gall Passion Play* (125).

GENERAL AND INTRODUCTORY STUDIES OF HUMANIST LATIN

Were I to have done this report as recently as ten years ago, I should have had to lament the relative neglect of Renaissance Latin studies as compared with medieval

Latin. In the last decade, however, there has been a sudden flowering of studies in Renaissance Latin in Europe and America, which has resulted in a large number of critical editions, translations, and critical and scholarly studies. One symptom of this new interest is the recent founding of the International Association for Neo-Latin Studies. (The term *Neo-Latin* has increasingly come to be used to refer to the Latin of the Renaissance and subsequent times.) Since Latin writers of the Renaissance saw Petrarch as the founder of the renewal of the Latin in which they themselves wrote, studies of Renaissance Latin generally begin with Petrarch and his contemporaries. This, combined with the recognized importance of works often literary in intention for intellectual history, has meant that a good deal of attention has been devoted to fourteenth-century humanist writing in Latin. While much remains to be done, especially in such areas as lexicography, one can now say, for the first time in several hundred years, that Renaissance Latin is not a neglected field.

The central figure in the renewal of the study of Renaissance Latin is Jozef IJsewijn of the University of Leuven in Belgium, and an indispensable work for use by the beginner and the specialist in the field is his *Companion to Neo-Latin Studies* (138). Another helpful guide is the essay on Neo-Latin literature by Lawrence V. Ryan in the companion volume to this one edited by William M. Jones entitled *The Present State of Scholarship in Sixteenth-Century Literature* (154). This essay surveys work in the entire field as well as in the sixteenth century, and anyone interested in more detail on developments in the area should begin with these two studies, which give a clear and effective overall view of what has and has not been done. The publication *Humanistica Lovaniensia*, revived as an annual volume devoted to Neo-Latin studies, contains an *Instrumentum Bibliographicum* listing new publications. In America, *Seventeenth Century News* includes

Neo-Latin News, which often covers current work in the field.

Several works concerned with Renaissance Latin poetry have begun with the fourteenth century. An extremely useful volume, unfortunately marred by the absence of texts in the original Latin, is W. Leonard Grant's *Neo-Latin Literature and the Pastoral* (137). Two recent anthologies include some fourteenth-century poetry, *Renaissance Latin Verse: An Anthology* (151), edited by Allessandro Perosa and John Sparrow, and my own *Anthology of Neo-Latin Poetry* (149).

The study of early Renaissance history, based for the fourteenth century as we have seen largely on writings in Latin, has flourished in recent decades, and here I am constrained to touch only the peaks. I shall begin by noting general studies of humanism in the period. Petrarch of course looms large in nearly all of them, but I shall defer discussing until somewhat later work that is concerned exclusively with him.

No one will quarrel with me, I think, if I give first place here to Paul Oskar Kristeller. In addition to the bibliographical work already alluded to, he has continued to produce a series of superbly accomplished and extremely valuable historical studies. Of his work in the last years, I note here *Eight Philosophers of the Italian Renaissance* (140), *Le Thomisme et la pensée italienne de la Renaissance* (143), in turn translated into English as one part of his *Medieval Aspects of Renaissance Learning* (141), and most recently, *Renaissance Thought and Its Sources* (142), a collection of his essays in revised and updated form edited by Michael Mooney. Several valuable essays on the period are to be found in *Florilegium Historiale*, the Wallace K. Ferguson festschrift edited by J. G. Rowe and others (153); especially noteworthy analyses of the early Renaissance quest for self-identity are the articles in the volume by Hans Baron and Marvin Becker. Another important collection of essays is the work of Ludwig Bertalot edited by Kristeller under the title *Studien zum italienischen und deutschen Humanismus* (132). Originally published between 1908 and 1946, the essays appear here in a useful collected format and include studies on Dante as a Latin author, Petrarch, and others in the fourteenth century.

A controversial recent book in this area is Walter Ullmann's *Medieval Foundations of Renaissance Humanism* (160), focusing on political thought. Rudolf Pfeiffer's *History of Classical Scholarship from 1300 to 1850* (152) is an excellent survey of an important aspect of the period, and a related study is Roberto Weiss, *The Spread of Italian Humanism* (161), with a good chapter on humanism before Petrarch. Another solid work is Jerrold Siegel's *Rhetoric and Philosophy in Renaissance Humanism: The Union of Eloquence and Wisdom* (156). This work discusses Petrarch and Salutati extensively, as does the first volume of Charles Trinkaus, *In Our Image and Likeness: Humanity and Divinity in Italian Humanist Thought* (159), which relates the early humanist emphasis on rhetoric to Augustinianism and nominalism. Here too I might mention the essays of Hans Baron collected in his *From Petrarch to Leonardo Bruni* (130), especially his study of Petrarch's *Secretum*.

A number of studies of more specialized topics exist within the area. The methods of humanist historiography are examined by Rüdiger Landfester in *Historia Magistra Vitae: Untersuchungen zur humanistischen Geschichtstheorie des 14. bis 16. Jahrhunderts* (144). There has been a recent full-length work on humanist activity at Padua, *Arts and Sciences at Padua: The "Studium" of Padua before 1350*, by Nancy G. Siraisi (158). A good selection of texts is contained in *The Earthly Republic: Italian Humanists on Government and Society* (139), edited by Benjamin C. Kohl and others. The use of rhetorical techniques in the correspondence of early Italian humanists has been studied by Gudrun Lindholm in her *Studien zum mittel-lateinischen Prosarhythmus* (146), and O. Herding and R. Stupperich edited a collection of studies of humanism in its context entitled *Die Humanisten in ihrer politischen und sozialen Umwelt* (136). An original and valuable interdisciplinary study is Michael Baxendall's *Giotto and the Orators* (131), which analyzes humanist reactions to painting.

EARLY HUMANISTS

In beginning to consider studies of individual humanists, we should recall Jozef IJsewijn's observation that Petrarch was not the first representative of the new Latin style he practiced.[6] That distinction goes to Lovato Lovati, at the very beginning of the fourteenth century, and his younger associate Albertino Mussato. One recent study of these men, in Modern Greek, ʽΟ προουμανιστικὸς κύκλὸς τῆς Παδούοϲ by A. C. Megas (180), is centered on their textual work on Seneca. M. Dazzi has studied Mussato alone in *Il Mussato preumanista, 1261–1329. L'ambiente e l'opera* (178). It was Mussato who wrote the first humanist tragedy, based on classical models. That play, the *Ecerinus*, has been translated with a critical introduction and facsimile reproduction of an earlier critical edition by Joseph R. Berrigan (177) in a volume that also includes a late fourteenth-century play, the *Achilles* of Antonio Loschi.

Dante

I mention among early humanists, with some trepidation, Dante Alighieri, all of whose extant Latin works seem to have been composed after 1300. One could well argue that Dante's Latin is medieval rather than humanist, but reasons of historical continuity at least place him

---

6. Jozef IJsewijn, *Companion to Neo-Latin Studies* (138), p. 16.

here. The attention devoted to anything written by Dante has of course been extremely intense, so I will mention here only a small proportion of what has been done recently. For a student of Dante's Latin, perhaps the most significant recent scholarly tool is the new *Enciclopedia dantesca* (167) edited by Umberto Bosco. It contains excellent and informed articles on the Latin works with very full bibliographies; I might especially note Pier Vincenzo Mengaldo on *De vulgari eloquentia* and Pier Giorgio Ricci on *Monarchia*. Also worth consulting is Giorgio Brugnoli's article on *Latino*, excellent on Dante's Latin. Recent years have seen a number of new editions, notably Ricci's edition of the *Monarchia* (166), as part of the finally revivified *Edizione Nazionale* of Dante's work. A new edition of Paget Toynbee's standard annotated edition of Dante's letters updated by C. G. Hardi (164) was published in 1966. Mengaldo has edited a useful edition of the *De Vulgari Eloquentia* (163). The first volume containing the introduction and text was published in 1968, but as far as I can discover, the second volume with the notes and commentary has not yet been published. There is also a new edition, with Italian translation, of the *Questio de Aqua et Terra* (175) by Severino Ragazzini and Luigi Pescasio. In addition there have been a number of articles on various aspects of Dante's work in Latin. I will confine myself to mentioning Cecil Grayson's "'Nobilior est vulgaris': Latin and Vernacular in Dante's Thought" (174) as an excellent if brief analysis of a thorny subject.

Petrarch

No writer in Latin of the time has been more thoroughly examined than Petrarch. Since the bulk of Petrarch's writing, including all of his prose, is in Latin, anyone approaching the author of the *Canzoniere* must be familiar with his Latin work. Petrarch no doubt thought he would be remembered mainly for his Latin writings, and although subsequent history has taken an ironic turn in that respect, we cannot say that Petrarch's Latin has been neglected in recent years. Here too I will be obliged to limit myself to what seem to me to be most interesting and significant among works focusing primarily on the Latin writings.

The period surveyed begins with Morris Bishop's urbane and witty biography *Petrarch and His World* (187). This book exemplifies the way in which a study of the man must depend upon the Latin writings because the full account of his own life that Petrarch left us is entirely in Latin. I should also mention that the definitive and invaluable studies of Ernest H. Wilkins have recently been gathered by Aldo S. Bernardo in *Studies on Petrarch and Boccaccio* (218). Of other general studies that deal with the Latin writings, there is the analysis of the life through the works of Arnaud Tripet, *Pétrarque, ou la connaissance de soi* (217); the excellent study by Charles Trinkaus of the way in which the experience of the poetry informs the philosophy, *The Poet as Philosopher: Petrarch and the Formation of Renaissance Consciousness* (216); and a coherent collection of essays focusing on a medieval aspect of Petrarch, Pietro Paolo Gerosa's *Umanesimo cristiano del Petrarca* (189). Petrarch's activity as historian has been much studied lately. Here we have the monograph-length article by Giuseppe Billanovich, "Il Petrarca e gli storici latini" (185), which deals with the manuscripts of ancient historians that Petrarch used; a recent study linking Petrarch's activity as historian to nominalism, Eckhard Kessler's *Petrarca und die Geschichte* (193); and a study of Petrarch the historian as seen by commentators in his own time and later, Werner Handschin's *Francesco Petrarca als Gestalt der Historiographie* (192).

Our survey of scholarship on individual works should begin by mentioning a new two-volume edition of Petrarch's *Opere latine* (207), without his letters, edited by Antonietta Bufano and others. Thomas G. Bergin and Alice

S. Wilson have recently published a graceful and useful translation of Petrarch's failed masterpiece, the *Africa* (197), which leads me to mention the excellent and thorough study of that work published at the threshold of the period I am surveying, Aldo S. Bernardo's *Petrarch, Scipio, and the "Africa"* (184). Professor Bergin has also translated Petrarch's pastorals, the *Bucolicum Carmen* (199), and there is a useful study of the development of the work, Nicholas Mann's long article, "The Making of Petrarch's *Bucolicum Carmen*" (194). There have been two books in the past decade on the *Secretum:* the exhaustive close reading by Francisco Rico in the first volume of his *Vida u obra de Petrarca* (212) and the *Allegoria retorica e poetica nel "Secretum" del Petrarca* by Oscar Giuliani (190). The slow progress of the *Edizione Nazionale* continued with the appearance of the first volume of *De Viris Illustribus*, edited by G. Martellotti (202); we still await the long-promised volume of the Latin poems in that series, in addition to the *Africa* that was published in 1926. *De Remediis Utriusque Fortunae* has been edited by Rudolf Schottlaender (201), and excerpts from that reflective work have been translated by Conrad H. Rawski in his *Four Dialogues for Scholars* (205). A late Middle English version of a part of the work has been edited together with the Latin text by F. N. M. Diekstra as *A Dialogue between Reason and Adversity* (203). Students of this particular work will also want to consult Nicholas Mann's "The Manuscripts of Petrarch's *De Remediis*" (195).

Petrarch's Latin correspondence is the richest of his time, and two English selections have appeared: Morris Bishop's well-chosen *Letters from Petrarch* (186) and David Thompson's helpful anthology of letters and other writings, *Petrarch: A Humanist Among Princes* (215). Aldo S. Bernardo has completed an English translation of the first eight books of the *Rerum Familiarum* (209), and his enormous project, a concordance to all of the *Familiari*, as they are called in Italian, is available in microfiche (183). And that particular collection of polemical letters called the *Sine Nomine* has not been neglected. A new edition by Ugo Dotti (210) as well as an English translation by Norman P. Zacour, *Petrarch's Book Without a Name* (198), were published in the mid-seventies.

Boccaccio

If the Latin work of Dante and Petrarch has been intensively studied in recent years, that of Boccaccio presents a curious contrast. There has been some activity here: a new edition of the well-known Book Fourteen of the *Genealogiae deorum gentilium* entitled *Boccaccio in Defence of Poetry* by Jeremiah Reedy in the Toronto Medieval Latin Texts series (219), a good selection of his Latin prose edited by P. G. Ricci in the volume of his works entitled *Opere in versi, Corbaccio, Tratatello in laude di Dante, Prose latine, Epistole* (220), and the new edition of the poet's complete works, including those in Latin, edited by Vittore Branca (221). On *De Mulieribus Claris*, there is also a study by Anna Cerbo in *Arcadia* (222), and an examination of textual problems by Guglielmo Zappacosta and Vittorio Zacaria in *Studi sul Boccaccio* (227). The first eclogue appears with an English translation by A. M. Prowse in *Allegorica* (225). The collection entitled *Boccaccio in Europe* (226), edited by Gilbert Tournoy, contains a number of articles on the Latin works. Enzo Esposito's *Boccacciana* (224), a bibliography of editions, translations, and criticism from 1939 to 1974, is helpful. But the work done on Boccaccio's Italian writings has not led to extensive study of his voluminous Latin works, which very much need sympathetic re-examination. Here is a curious lacuna where much of great interest remains to be done.

Other Humanist Authors

The most prominent humanist in Italy toward the end of the fourteenth century was Coluccio Salutati, who has not been neglected in recent years. His career has been effectively examined by Berthold Ullman in *The Human-ism of Coluccio Salutati* (236), and Eckhard Kessler has studied his place in his time's currents of thought in *Das Problem des frühen Humanismus: Seine philosophische Bedeutung bei Coluccio Salutati* (234). Armando Petrucci has focused on this author's use of rhetoric in *Coluccio Salutati* (235), and an important part of his public career is dealt with in Ronald G. Witt's *Coluccio Salutati and His Public Letters* (237).

Even minor humanists of the century have often been studied; much of this material is to be found in articles. Luciano Gargan's *Cultura e arte nel Veneto al tempo del Petrarca* (239) may stand as a book-length example; it deals with Oliviero Forzetta, a collector of books and manuscripts active at Treviso in the middle part of the century. Here too much remains to be done, work that will be facilitated by the bibliographical projects of Pro-fessor Kristeller already mentioned, but on the whole, the study of early humanism has recently been active and fruitful.

The Philosophical and Intellectual Context

I shall conclude by giving a brief sketch of activities in fourteenth-century Latin in fields not primarily literary. Here there has been a great deal of activity, particularly in the study of philosophy, as a result of the fact that the century has increasingly been seen as a productive one for philosophy. Editions and studies of such important figures as Duns Scotus and William of Ockham have been published, as nominalism has come to be understood as a philosophical movement valid in its own right and not merely as a falling away from the accomplishment of Thomas Aquinas and his contemporaries. Julius Weinberg has argued that the fourteenth century is one in which medieval logic accomplished its best work, work that was not to be equalled for centuries to come.[7] And an area of investigation only recently undertaken very systematically is the attempt to understand the great creative writers of the age in relation to our new understanding of the technical philosophy of the age. We have noted, for instance, Eckhard Kessler's study of Petrarch in relation to nominalism, and several recent articles have examined Chaucer in this light. From these studies, it would seem that literary scholars may profit by familiarity with the study of the philosophy of the time.

Work in this field has been intense in the last decades. Indeed, a full bibliography of studies of fourteenth-century philosophy in this time would probably be longer than a bibliography of works covering fourteenth-century Latin literature. I must, therefore, be content to indicate in a summary way the work recently done, focusing on the major figures, reminding the reader, however, that the work of editing, translating, and studying minor figures in this field is also continuing at an almost feverish rate. The prevalence of analytic and linguistic philosophies in American and British universities, although leading to a certain hostility to historical study, has also led to an awareness of similarities between scholastic and analytic philosophy, and the recent rise of structuralism has reinforced an interest in scholastic theories of language. These factors have fueled a widespread interest in America, England, France, and Germany in the work of fourteenth-century philosophers.

Fourteenth-century thought has been the special province of Gordon Leff of the University of York, and three of his works should be mentioned: *Heresy in the Later Middle Ages* (342), *Paris and Oxford Universities in the Thirteenth and Fourteenth Centuries* (269), and *The Dissolution of the Medieval Outlook* (268). These works fo-

7. Julius R. Weinberg, *A Short History of Medieval Philosophy* (Princeton, N.J.: Princeton University Press, 1964), p. 243.

cus on the relationship between institutions and ideas, between practice and belief, and view philosophical ideas as a response to situations. Another important worker in this area is Heiko Obermann, whose *Forerunners of the Reformation* (282) contains many extracts from Latin writings of our century. An excellent introduction to the philosophy of the period can be found in Julius Weinberg's *Short History of Medieval Philosophy* (327). Another clear and thorough survey is Martin Anton Schmidt's *Scholastik* (310), which will also appear as part of a larger volume on the history of the church being edited by Kurt Schmidt and Ernst Wolf. Collected essays of eminent early pioneers in this field have been published, among them the important studies of the Polish scholar Konstanty Michalski, *La Philosophie au XIVe siècle*, edited by Kurt Flasch (277) and the collected papers of Ernest A. Moody, *Studies in Medieval Philosophy, Science and Logic* (279). Valuable for the study of intellectual formation is Nicholas Orme's *English Schools in the Middle Ages* (292) and, for higher education, Helene Wieruszowski's *The Medieval University* (328). A clear and authoritative study of scholastic terminology is Alfonso Maierù's *Terminologia logica della tarda scolastica* (273). An excellent study of the logic of the period can be found in Jan Pinborg's *Logik und Semantik im Mittelalter* (297). It should be noted that the century will be extensively covered in the forthcoming *Cambridge History of Later Medieval Philosophy*.

The dominant figure in philosophy at the start of the fourteenth century was Duns Scotus, and although some of his work belongs to the preceding century, I begin with him because in recent years, the study of Scotus has been extremely productive. An interested investigator might first read the book edited by John K. Ryan and Bernardine M. Bonansea, *John Duns Scotus, 1265–1965* (309), which gives a good idea of the state of Scotus studies. An important text, the *Tractatus de Primo Principio*, has been edited by W. Kluxen (258), and an equally significant text, the *Quodlibetal Questions,* has been translated into English by F. Alluntis and A. B. Wolter (257). Of the several books on the man who personified scholasticism for subsequent centuries, I might note *Das Glaubensverständnis bei Johannes Duns Scotus* by Ludwig Walter (325).

Another philosopher active at the beginning of the century was the curious and indefatigable Catalan Ramon Lull. A standard edition of his *Opera Latina* (272) has been under way since 1959 under the direction of Friedrich Stegmüller of the Lullus-Institut at Freiburg im Breisgau, and volume 7 was published in 1975. A good introduction for someone unfamiliar with his thought is Miguel Cruz Hernández's *El pensamiento de Ramon Llull* (254). Lull was a familiar figure at the University of Paris at the beginning of the century, and J. N. Hillgarth has written a study of his fortunes and those of his disciples there, *Ramon Lull and Lullism in Fourteenth-Century France* (265).

The commanding philosophical presence of the century was William of Ockham, whose name has come to be inextricably linked with nominalism. Work on his thought and writings has been active in recent years, and of central importance is the critical edition of his theological and philosophical works, the *Opera Philosophica et Theologica* (285), which has been undertaken by the Franciscan Institute of St. Bonaventure University. The series began in 1967 and four volumes of an eventual twenty have been published. Translations have also been published: *Predestination, God's Foreknowledge and Future Contingents* by Marilyn McCord Adams and Norman Kretzmann (286), and *Ockham's Theory of Terms* (284) by Michael J. Loux. Of the numerous studies on the philosopher, Gordon Leff's *William of Ockham, the Metamorphosis of Scholastic Discourse* (271) is thorough and authoritative. Ockham's place in a broader philosophical tradition has been studied by Julius R. Weinberg in *Ockham, Descartes and Hume: Self-Knowledge, Substance and Causality* (326). Activity in this field from 1950 to 1967 can be traced in the "Ockham Bibliography" by J. P. Reilly (304).

Ockham's nominalism was adopted and developed by a number of followers. To a certain degree, the story of philosophy in the latter fourteenth century is the story of the reaction to his thought, and these developments too have been the object of recent work. The *Sophismata* of his more moderate French follower John Buridan have been edited by T. K. Scott (247). Prominent among Ockham's disciples at the end of the century was Pierre d'Ailly. His work has been studied by Francis Oakley in *The Political Thought of Pierre d'Ailly: The Voluntarist Tradition* (281), and a survey of the canon of his works by P. Glorieux can be found in "L'Oeuvre littéraire de Pierre d'Ailly" (263). The career of d'Ailly extended into the fifteenth century, as did that of his more famous pupil Jean Gerson, but both were active before the end of the fourteenth century. A new edition of the *Oeuvres complètes* of Gerson edited by P. Glorieux was published between 1960 and 1973 (261). His extensive and varied corpus has been examined from a number of points of view. Recently the emphasis has been on his thought on the Church. A good study of this subject is Louis B. Pascoe's *Jean Gerson: Principles of Church Reform* (295). An edition of his *De Jurisdictione Spirituali et Temporali* is included in G. H. M. Posthumus Meyjes, *Jean Gerson et l'assemblée de Vincennes* (298). A curious literary footnote to Gerson's career is the Latin eclogue he wrote in his youth, and this has been edited and studied by G. Ouy, "Gerson, émule de Pétrarque" (293).

As the work of the philosophers we have just reviewed indicates, it is difficult to draw a line betwen philosophical and religious thought in the fourteenth century, but I will now mention work on men better known for their religious thought. The first of these is the English mystic Richard Rolle of Hampole, who is not a neglected figure because he wrote in English as well as in Latin. His *Con-*

tra Amatores Mundi has been edited and translated for the first time by Paul F. Theiner (352), and his Latin work is treated in Mary Felicitas Madigan's *The "Passio Domini" Theme in The Works of Richard Rolle* (345). One of the most popular and influential religious writings of the century was the *Vita Christi* of Ludolph of Saxony. This work has been studied by Charles A. Conway in his *The "Vita Christi" of Ludolph of Saxony and Late Medieval Devotion Centered on the Incarnation* (333) and at very great length by Walter Baier in his three-volume *Untersuchungen zu den Passionsbetrachtungen in der "Vita Christi"* (330). Edmund Colledge has recently suggested that a modern critical edition of the *Vita Christi* is very much needed.[8]

A different kind of religious thinker was the reformer John Wyclif. Gustav Adolf Benrath argues that the roots of Wyclif's reforming impulse arose primarily out of his biblical studies in *Wyclif's Bibelkommentar* (331). A religious movement of the century in the Netherlands that has been extensively studied is the "Devotio Moderna." Albert Hyma, in an expanded edition of his *The Christian Renaissance* (339), sees it as a forerunner of the Reformation and even the Counter-Reformation. This view is sharply disputed by R. R. Post in his *The Modern Devotion* (348). Another religious current still strong in the fourteenth century has been studied in Marjorie Reeve's detailed and thoughtful *The Influence of Prophecy in the Later Middle Ages: A Study in Joachism* (349). Helpful to a study of the religious life of the time is the new *Medieval Heresies; A Bibliography 1960–1979* (332) by Carl T. Berkhout and Jeffrey B. Russell.

Other figures and aspects of the intellectual life of the time should be touched on briefly. One of the more curious figures of the century was the English book collector

---

8. Edmund Colledge, review of Walter Baier's *Untersuchungen, Speculum* 54 (1979): 545.

Richard de Bury, often seen as a forerunner of humanism. His *Philobiblon* is one of the three works examined by Christian K. Zacher in *Curiosity and Pilgrimage: The Literature of Discovery in Fourteenth-Century England* (329). The historical writing of the age is exemplified in the figure of Ranulf Higden, the English historian whose great work has been well studied in John Taylor's *The "Universal Chronicle" of Ranulf Higden* (321).

As our last major figure we might mention a multifaceted thinker much studied in recent years, Henry of Langenstein of Vienna. One aspect of his thought is effectively studied in P. Lang's *Die Christologie bei Heinrich von Langenstein* (341) and a different aspect in Nicholas Steneck's *Science and Creation in the Middle Ages* (350). Thomas Hohmann has edited one of his works, *Unterscheidung der Geister lateinisch und deutsch* (337), which gives not only the Latin but also a nearly contemporary verbatim German translation designed to be read in conjunction with the original. The canon of Langenstein's work is indexed by Hohmann in his "Initienregister der Werke Heinrichs von Langenstein" (338). Finally one last intellectual current might be mentioned, Bohemian prehumanism. This was the movement out of which John Huss was to come, although he belongs more to the fifteenth century. One can get an overall view of the movement in Eduard Winter, *Frühhumanismus. Seine Entwicklung in Böhem* (355), and a central figure has been studied by Reuben E. Weltsch in his *Archbishop John of Jenstein* (354), which includes excerpts from Jenstein's works.

The current state of studies in the Latin literature of the fourteenth century is thus a lively one, but the effort, as we have seen, is not equally distributed. A vast amount remains to be done, a task now somewhat easier because many basic scholarly tools are available that did not exist until recently. In particular, studies arising out of two changes of perspective would be most valuable. The first would be to see the Latin literature of the century in its own terms and not only in relation to a vernacular or to vernacular languages. The second, arising out of the first, would be to see the Latin literature of the century as a whole. The age was one of traveling scholars and writers in spite of immense practical difficulties, and therefore an age of lively intellectual interchange, much of which took place in Latin. If we can view what was written in Latin as having a central importance for the age in which it was written, we will see it in its own terms, and our knowledge of its particularities, and of the vernacular literary accomplishment that always has some relationship to it, will be clearer and more accurate.[9]

9. I would like to thank Charlotte Morse of Virginia Commonwealth University for innumerable comments and suggestions and Linda Voigts of the University of Missouri at Kansas City and Judson Allen of Marquette University for several additions to the bibliography.

Bibliography

General Studies and Reference Works

1. Clanchy, M. T. *From Memory to Written Record: England 1066–1307*. Cambridge, Mass.: Harvard University Press, 1979.
2. Clark, John R. "Teaching Medieval Latin." *Classical Journal* 75 (1979): 44–50.
3. Fisher, John H., ed. *The Medieval Literature of Western Europe: A Review of Research, Mainly 1930–1960*. New York: Published for the Modern Language Association of America by the New York University Press, 1966.
4. Genicot, Léopold, ed. *Typologie des sources du Moyen Âge occidental*. Turnhout: Brepols, 1972–.
5. Gössmann, Elizabeth. *Antiqui und Moderni im Mittelalter: Eine geschichtliche Standortbestimmung*. Munich: Schöningh, 1974. (Covers humanist as well as medieval writers.)
6. Harrison, Francis Edward. *Millenium: A Latin Reader, A.D. 374–1374*. Oxford: Oxford University Press, 1968.
7. Hay, Denys. *Annalists and Historians: Western Historiography from the Eighth to the Eighteenth Centuries*. New York: Barnes & Noble, 1977.
8. *International Medieval Bibliography*. Leeds: University of Leeds, 1967–.
9. Langosch, Karl. *Lateinisches Mittelalter: Einleitung in Sprache und Literatur*. Darmstadt: Wissenschaftliche Buchgesellschaft, 1963.
10. Langosch, Karl, ed. *Mittellateinische Dichtung. Ausgewählte Beiträge zu ihrer Erforschung*. Darmstadt: Wissenschaftliche Buchgesellschaft, 1969.
11. Langosch, Karl. "Überlieferungsgeschichte der mittellateinischen Literatur." In *Geschichte der Textüberlieferung der antiken und mittelalterlichen Literatur*, edited

by Michael Meier et al., vol. 2, pp. 9–185. Zurich: Atlantis Verlag, 1964.

12. *Lexikon des Mittelalters*. Munich and Zurich: Artemis, 1977–.

13. McGuire, Martin R. P., and Hermigild Dressler. *Introduction to Medieval Latin Studies: A Syllabus and Bibliographical Guide*. Washington, D.C.: The Catholic University of America Press, 1977.

14. Norberg, Dag. *Manuel pratique de latin médiéval*. Paris: Picard, 1968.

15. Önnerfors, Alf, ed. *Mittellateinische Philologie. Beiträge zur Erforschung der mittelalterlichen Latinität*. Darmstadt: Wissenschaftlicher Verlag, 1975.

16. Paladini, V., and M. de Marco. *Lingua e letteratura mediolatina*. Bologna: Pàtron, 1970.

17. Plezia, Marian. "Development Periods of Medieval Latin." In *Miscellanea Mediaevalia in memoriam Jan Frederik Niermeyer*, pp. 29–40. Groningen: Wolters, 1967.

18. Powell, James M., ed. *Medieval Studies: An Introduction*. Syracuse: Syracuse University Press, 1976.

19. Rouse, Richard H., et al. *Serial Bibliographies for Medieval Studies*. Berkeley: University of California Press, 1969.

20. Strecker, Karl. *Introduction to Medieval Latin*. Translated and revised by Robert B. Palmer. Dublin: Weidmann, 1971.

21. Van Caenegem, R. C., and F. L. Ganshoff. *Guide to the Sources of Medieval History*. Amsterdam and New York: North-Holland, 1978.

22. Wolff, Philippe. *Western Languages, A.D. 100–1500*. New York: McGraw-Hill, 1971.

23. *Year's Work in Modern Language Studies*. London: Oxford University Press. (Essay on Medieval Latin by W. R. Bolton, 1963–1967, and A. K. Bate since 1968; essay on Neo-Latin by J. W. Binns since 1970.)

EDITING TEXTS

24. Bataillon, Louis J. "Problèmes posés par l'édition critique des textes latins médiévaux." *Revue Philosophique de Louvain* 75 (1977): 234–50.

25. Hödl, Ludwig, and Dieter Wuttke, eds. *Probleme der Edi-*

tion mittel- und neulateinischer Texte. Kolloquium der Deutschen Forschungsgemeinschaft, Bonn, 1973. Boppard: Boldt, 1978.

26. Kleinhenz, Christopher, ed. *Medieval Manuscripts and Textual Criticism.* Chapel Hill: University of North Caro' .na, Department of Romance Languages, 1976.

27. Rigg, A. G., ed. *Editing Medieval Texts: English, French, and Latin Written in England.* New York and London: Garland, 1977.

LEXICOGRAPHY AND PALEOGRAPHY

28. Bischoff, Bernhard. *Paläographie des römischen Altertums und des abendländischen Mittelalters.* Berlin: E. Schmidt, 1979.

29. Blaise, Albert. *Lexicon Latinitatis Medii Aevi: praesertim ad res ecclesiasticas investigandas pertinens.* Turnhout: Brepols, 1975.

30. Busa, Robertus. *Index Thomisticus.* 39 vols. Stuttgart and Bad Cannstatt: Frommann-Holzboog, 1974–1979.

31. *Glossarium till Medeltidslatinet i Sverige.* Edited by Ulla Westerbergh and Eva Odelman. Stockholm: Kungl. Vitterhets, Historie och Antikvitets Akademien, 1968–.

32. Grubmüller, Klaus. *Vocabularius Ex quo: Untersuchungen zu lateinisch-deutschen Vokabularen des Spätmittelalters.* Munich: C. H. Beck, 1967.

33. Latham, Ronald Edward. *Dictionary of Medieval Latin from British Sources.* London and New York: Oxford University Press for the British Academy, 1975–.

34. ———. *Revised Medieval Latin Word-List from British and Irish Sources.* London: Oxford University Press for the British Academy, 1965.

35. *Lexicon Latinitatis medii Aevi Iugoslaviae.* Edited by Marko Kostrenčić et al. Zagreb: Institutum Historicum Academiae Scientarum et Artium Slavorum Meridionalium, 1973–.

36. *Lexicon Latinitatis Nederlandicae Medii Aevi.* Edited by J. W. Fuchs and Olga Weijers. Leiden: E. J. Brill, 1977–.

37. *Lexicon Mediae et Infimae Latinitatis Polonorum.* Warsaw: Polska Akademia Nauk, 1953–.

38. *Mittellateinisches Wörterbuch bis zum ausgehenden dreizehnten Jahrhundert.* Munich: C. H. Beck, 1967–.
39. Niermeyer, J. F. *Mediae Latinitatis Lexicon Minus.* Leiden: E. J. Brill, 1976.
40. *Novum Glossarium Mediae Latinitatis ab Anno DCCC usque ad Annum MCC.* Edited by Frans Blatt. Copenhagen: Munksgaard, 1957–.
41. Pelzer, Auguste. *Abréviations latines médiévales. Supplément au "Dizionario di abbreviature latine ed italiane" di Adriano Capelli.* Louvain: Publications Universitaires; Paris: Béatrice-Nauwelaerts, 1964.
42. Thomson, S. Harrison. *Latin Bookhands of the Later Middle Ages, 1100–1500.* London: Cambridge University Press, 1969.

CATALOGUES OF MANUSCRIPTS

43. Burckhardt, M., et al., eds. *Katalog der datierten Handschriften in der Schweiz in lateinischer Schrift vom Anfang des Mittelalters bis 1550.* Dietikon: Urs-Graf, 1977–.
44. Hornwall, G., J. O. Tjäder, and M. Hedlund. *Katalog der datierten Handschriften vor 1600 im Schweden.* Stockholm: Almqvist och Wiksell, 1977.
45. Ker, N. R. *Medieval Manuscripts in British Libraries.* Oxford: Clarendon Press, 1969–.
46. Kristeller, Paul Oskar. *Iter Italicum: A Finding List of Uncatalogued or Incompletely Catalogued Humanistic Mss of the Renaissance in Italian and Other Libraries.* London: Warburg Institute; Leiden: E.J. Brill, 1963–.
47. ———. *Latin Manuscript Books before 1600: A List of the Printed Catalogues and Unpublished Inventories of Extant Collections.* New York: Fordham University Press, 1965.
48. Lieftinck, G. I. *Manuscrits datés conservés dans les Pays-Bas: Catalogue paléographique des manuscrits en écriture latine portant des indications de date.* Amsterdam: North-Holland, 1964.
49. Masai, François, and Martin Wittek, eds. *Manuscrits datés*

conservés en Belgique. Brussels and Ghent: Editions scientifiques E. Story-Scientia, 1968–.

50. Samaran, Charles, and Robert Marichal. *Catalogue des manuscrits en écriture latine portant des indications de date, de lieu ou de copiste.* 6 vols. Paris: Centre national de la recherche scientifique, 1959–1967.

51. Università degli studi di Roma, Scuola speciale per archivisti e bibliotecari. *Catalogo dei manoscritti in scrittura latina datati o databili.* Turin: Bottega d'Erasmo, 1971–.

LISTS AND INDEXES OF INDIVIDUAL WORKS

52. Bloomfield, Morton W., et al. *Incipits of Latin Works on the Virtues and Vices, 1100–1500 A.D., Including a Section of Incipits of Works on the Pater Noster.* Cambridge, Mass.: Mediaeval Academy of America, 1979.

53. Brounts, A. "Un guide des sermonnaires latins médiévaux." *Scriptorium* 21 (1967): 296–307.

54. *Catalogus Translationum et Commentariorum. Mediaeval and Renaissance Latin Translations and Commentaries. Annotated Lists and Guides.* Edited by Paul Oskar Kristeller and F. Edward Cranz. Washington: The Catholic University of America Press, 1960–.

55. Grégoire, Réginald. *Les Homiliares du Moyen Âge.* Rome: Herder, 1966.

56. Lohr, Charles H. "Mediaeval Latin Aristotle Commentaries." *Traditio* 23 (1967): 313–413: 24 (1968): 149–245; 26 (1970): 135–216; 27 (1971): 251–351; 28 (1972): 281–396; 29 (1973): 93–197; 30 (1974): 119–44.

57. Schneyer, J. B. *Repertorium der lateinischen Sermones des Mittelalters für die Zeit von 1150–1350.* 9 vols. Munster: Aschendorffsche Verlagsbuchhandlung, 1969–1980.

58. ———. *Wegweiser zu lateinischen Predigtreihen des Mittelalters.* Munich: Verlag der Bayerischen Akademie der Wissenschaften in Kommission bei der C. H. Beck'schen Verlagsbuchhandlung, 1965.

59. Thorndike, Lynn, and Pearl Kibre. *A Catalogue of Incipits*

of Mediaeval Scientific Writings in Latin. London and Cambridge, Mass.: Mediaeval Academy of America, 1963.

60. Tubach, Frederick C. *Index Exemplorum: A Handbook of Medieval Religious Tales.* Helsinki: Suomalainen Tiedeakatamia, 1969.

61. Walther, Hans. *Initia carminum ac versuum Medii Aevi posterioris Latinorum. Alphabetisches Verzeichnis der Versanfange mittellateinischer Dichtungen.* 2d ed. rev. Göttingen: Vandenhoeck und Rupprecht, 1969.

62. ———. *Proverbia sententiaeque latinitatis medii aevi. Lateinische Sprichwörter und Sentenzen des Mittelalters in alphabetischer Anordnung.* 6 vols. Göttingen: Vandenhoeck und Rupprecht, 1963–1969.

63. Werner, Jakob. *Lateinische Sprichwörter und Sinnsprüche des Mittelalters aus Handschriften gesammelt.* Heidelberg: Carl Winter Verlag, 1966.

MEDIEVAL LATIN: LITERARY HISTORY AND CRITICISM

64. Allen, Judson Boyce. *The Friar as Critic: Literary Attitudes in the Later Middle Ages.* Nashville: Vanderbilt University Press, 1971.

65. ———. *The Ethical Poetic of the Later Middle Ages: A Decorum of Convenient Distinction.* Toronto: The University of Toronto Press, 1982.

66. Brunhölzl, Franz. *Geschichte der lateinischen Literatur des Mittelalters.* Munich: Wilhelm Fink, 1975–.

67. Demats, Paule. *Fabula: Trois études de mythographie antique et médiévale.* Geneva: Droz, 1973.

68. Dronke, Peter. *Medieval Latin and the Rise of the European Love-Lyric.* 2 vols. New York: Oxford University Press, 1968.

69. Dronke, Peter, and Jill Mann. "Chaucer and the Medieval Latin Poets." In *Geoffrey Chaucer,* edited by Derek Brewer, pp. 154–183. London: G. Bell and Sons, 1974.

70. Erzgräber, Willi, ed. *Europäisches Spätmittelalter.* Wiesbaden: Akademische Verlagsgesellschaft Athenaion, 1978.

71. Friedman, John Block. *Orpheus in the Middle Ages.* Cambridge, Mass.: Harvard University Press, 1970.

72. Gneuss, Helmut. "Latin Hymns in Medieval England: Fu-

ture Research." In *Chaucer and Middle English Studies in Honour of Rossell Hope Robbins*, edited by Beryl Rowland, pp. 407–24. Kent, Ohio: Kent State University Press, 1974.

73. Helin, Maurice. *La littérature latine au Moyen Âge.* Paris: Presses Universitaires de France, 1972.

74. Jackson, W. T. H. *Medieval Literature: A History and a Guide.* New York: Collier, 1966.

75. Janson, Tore. *Prose Rhythm in Medieval Latin from the Ninth to the Thirteenth Century.* Stockholm: Almqvist & Wiksell, 1975.

76. Klopsch, Paul. *Einführung in die mittellateinische Verslehre.* Darmstadt: Wissenschaftliche Buchgesellschaft, 1972.

77. Kranz, Gisbert. *Europas christliche Literatur von 500 bis 1500.* Munich, Paderborn, Vienna: Ferdinand Schöningh, 1968.

78. Minnis, Alastair J. "Discussions of 'authorial role' and 'literary form' in late-medieval scriptural exegesis." *Beiträge zur Geschichte der deutschen Sprache und Literatur (Tübingen)* 99 (1977): 37–65.

79. ———. *Medieval Theory of Authorship: Scholastic Literary Attitudes in the Later Middle Ages.* Berkeley and Los Angeles: University of California Press, 1982.

80. Öberg, Jan. "La Suède médiévale et les auteurs latins classiques." In *Hommages à André Boutemy*, edited by Guy Cambier. Brussels: Latomus, 1976.

81. Rigg, A. G. "Medieval Latin Poetic Anthologies." *Mediaeval Studies* 39 (1977): 281–330; 40 (1978): 387–407.

82. Rouse, Richard, and Mary A. Rouse. *Preachers, Florilegia and Sermons: Studies on the Manipulus Florum of Thomas of Ireland.* Toronto: Pontifical Institute of Mediaeval Studies, 1979.

83. Sandkühler, Bruno. *Die frühen Dantekommentare und ihr Verhältnis zur mittelalterlichen Kommentartradition.* Munich: Max Hueber, 1967.

84. Spitzmuller, Henry. *Poésie latine chrétienne du Moyen Âge. IIIe-XVe siècle.* Brussels: Descleé de Brouwer, 1971.

85. Suchomski, Joachim. *"Delectatio" und "Utilitas": Ein Bei-*

trag zum Verständnis mittelaltlicher komischer Literatur. Bern and Munich: Francke, 1975.

86. Szövérffy, Joseph. *Annalen der lateinischen Hymnendichtung.* 2 vols. Berlin: Schmidt, 1976.

87. ———. *Weltliche Dichtungen des lateinischen Mittelalters: Ein Handbuch.* Berlin: Schmidt, 1970–.

88. Wenzel, Siegfried. *The Sin of Sloth: "Acedia" in Medieval Thought and Literature.* Chapel Hill: University of North Carolina Press, 1967.

MEDIEVAL LATIN: INDIVIDUAL AUTHORS

John Gower

89. Bennett, Jack Arthur Walter, ed. *Selections from John Gower.* Oxford: Clarendon Press, 1968.

90. Fisher, John H. *John Gower, Moral Philosopher and Friend of Chaucer.* New York: New York University Press, 1964.

91. Gower, John. *The Major Latin Works of John Gower.* Translated by Eric Stockton. Seattle: University of Washington Press, 1962.

92. Itô, Masayoshi. *John Gower, The Medieval Poet.* Tokyo: Shinozaki Shorin, 1976.

93. Olsson, Kurt O. "Rhetoric, John Gower, and the Late Medieval *Exemplum.*" *Medievalia et Humanistica* 8 (1977): 185–200.

94. Peck, Russell A. *Kingship and Common Profit in Gower's "Confessio Amantis."* Carbondale: Southern Illinois University Press, 1978.

95. Yeager, R. F. "A Bibliography of John Gower Materials through 1975." *Mediaevalia* 3 (1977): 261–306.

Other Authors

96. Colledge, Edmund, ed. *The Latin Poems of Richard Ledredge, O.F.M., Bishop of Ossory, 1317–1360.* Toronto: Pontifical Institute of Mediaeval Studies, 1974.

97. Epstein, Marcy J. "*Ludovicus Decus Regnantium:* Perspectives on the Rhymed Office." *Speculum* 53 (1978): 283–334.

238 / Fourteenth-Century Literature

98. Godi, Marcello, ed. *Una redazione poetica latina medie-vale della storia "De Excidio Troiae" di Darete frigio.* Rome: Angelo Signorelli, 1967.
99. Greene, Richard Leighton, ed. *The Lyrics of the Red Book of Ossory.* Oxford: Basil Blackwell for the Society for the Study of Medieval Languages and Literature, 1974.
100. Licitra, Vicenzo. "Gerardo Anechini cantore dei Bian-chi." *Studi Medievali,* 3 ser., 10, fasc. 2 (1969): 399–459.
101. Meyvaert, Paul. "John Erghome and the *Vaticinium Rob-erti Bridlington.*" *Speculum* 41 (1966): 656–64.
102. Palma, Marco, ed. *Nicola Trevet: Commento alle "Troades" di Seneca.* Rome: Edizioni di storia e letteratura, 1977.
103. Rigg, A. G. "Two Latin Poems Against the Friars." *Me-diaeval Studies* 30 (1968): 106–18.
104. Stemmler, Theo, ed. *The Latin Hymns of Richard Ledrede.* Mannheim: English Department (Medieval Section), University of Mannheim, 1975.

See also entry 109.

GRAMMAR AND RHETORIC

105. Bursill-Hall, G. L. "A Check-list of Incipits of Medieval Latin Grammatical Treatises: A-G." *Traditio* 34 (78): 439–74.
106. ———. *Speculative Grammars of the Middle Ages: The Doctrine of "Partes orationis" of the Modistae.* The Hague: Mouton, 1971.
107. Caplan, Harry. *Of Eloquence: Studies in Ancient and Mediaeval Rhetoric.* Ithaca: Cornell University Press, 1970.
108. Faulhaber, Charles. *Latin Rhetorical Theory in Thir-teenth and Fourteenth Century Castile.* Berkeley: University of California Press, 1972.
109. Jaffe, Samuel Peter. *Nicolaus Dybinus' "Declaracio ora-cionis de beata Dorothea": Studies and Documents in the History of Late Medieval Rhetoric.* Wiesbaden: Franz Steiner, 1974.
110. Murphy, James J., ed. *Medieval Eloquence: Studies in the Theory and Practice of Medieval Rhetoric.* Berkeley: University of California Press, 1978.

111. ———. *Medieval Rhetoric: A Select Bibliography.* Toronto: University of Toronto Press, 1971.
112. ———. *Rhetoric in the Middle Ages: A History of Rhetorical Theory from St. Augustine to the Renaissance.* Berkeley: University of California Press, 1974.
113. ———, ed. *Three Medieval Rhetorical Arts.* Berkeley: University of California Press, 1971.
114. Pinborg, Jan. *Die Entwicklung der Sprachtheorie im Mittelalter.* Münster: Aschendorff, 1967.
115. Quadlbauer, Franz. *Die antike Theorie der genera dicendi im lateinischen Mittelalter.* Vienna: Hermann Böhlaus Nachf., 1962.
116. Thomas of Erfurt. *Grammatica speculativa.* Edited with translations and commentary by G. L. Bursill-Hall. London: Longman, 1972.

DRAMA

117. Lipphardt, Walther. *Lateinische Osterfeiern und Osterspiele.* Berlin: De Gruyter, 1975–.
118. Nagler, A. M. *The Medieval Religious Stage: Shapes and Phantoms.* New Haven and London: Yale University Press, 1976.
119. Stemmler, Theo. *Liturgische Feiern und geistliche Spiele: Studien zu Erscheinungsformen des Dramatischen im Mittelalter.* Tübingen: Max Niemeyer, 1970.
120. Sticca, Sandro. *The Latin Passion Play: Its Origin and Development.* Albany: State University of New York Press, 1970.
121. Sticca, Sandro, ed. *The Medieval Drama. Papers of the Third Annual Conference of the Center for Medieval and Early Renaissance Studies, State University of New York at Binghamton, 1969.* Albany: State University of New York Press, 1972.
122. Stratman, Carl Joseph. *Bibliography of Medieval Drama.* New York: Frederick Ungar, 1972.
123. Tydeman, William. *The Theatre in the Middle Ages: Western European Stage Conditions, c. 800–1576.* Cambridge: Cambridge University Press, 1978.
124. Werner, Wilfrid. *Studien zu den Passions- und Oster-*

spielen des deutschen Mittelalters in ihrem Übergang vom Latein zur Volkssprache. Berlin: Erich Schmidt Verlag, 1963.

125. West, Larry E. *The Saint Gall Passion Play.* Brookline and Leiden: Classical Folia Editions, 1976.

126. Wickham, Glynne. *The Medieval Theatre.* London: Weidenfeld and Nicolson, 1974.

127. Wimmer, R. *Deutsch und Latein im Osterspiel. Untersuchungen zu den volkssprachlichen Entsprechungstexten der lateinischen Strophenleider.* Munich: Beck, 1974.

HUMANIST LATIN

History, Criticism, and Anthologies

128. Arbesmann, Rudolph. "Der Augustinereremitenorden und der Beginn der humanistichen Bewegung." *Augustiniana* 14 (1964): 250–314, 603–39; 15 (1965): 259–293.

129. Baron, Hans. *The Crisis of the Early Italian Renaissance. Civic Humanism and Republican Liberty in an Age of Classicism and Tyranny.* Rev. ed. with epilogue. Princeton: Princeton University Press, 1966.

130. ———. *From Petrarch to Leonardo Bruni: Studies in Humanistic and Political Literature.* Chicago: University of Chicago Press, 1968.

131. Baxendall, Michael. *Giotto and the Orators: Humanist Observers of Painting in Italy and the Discovery of Pictorial Composition, 1350–1450.* New York: Oxford University Press, 1971.

132. Bertalot, Ludwig. *Studien zum italienischen und deutschen Humanismus.* Edited by Paul Oskar Kristeller. 2 vols. Rome: Storia e letteratura, 1975.

133. Billanovich, Giuseppe, František Čada, Augusto Campana, and Paul Oskar Kristeller. "Scuola di retorica e poesia bucolica nel trecento italiano." *Italia Medioevale e Umanistica* 4 (1961): 181–221; 6 (1963): 203–34; 7 (1964): 279–324.

134. Cecchini, E. "Giovanni del Virgilio, Dante, Boccaccio." *Italia Medioevale e Umanistica* 14 (1971): 25–56.

135. Di Stefano, Giuseppe. *La découverte de Plutarque en Occident. Aspects de la vie intellectuelle en Avignon au XIVe siècle.* Turin: Accademia delle Scienze, 1968.

136. Elm, Kaspar. "Mendikanten und Humanisten im Florenz des Tre- und Quattrocento. Zum Problem der Legitimierung humanisticher Studien in den Bettelorden." In *Die Humanisten in ihrer politischen und sozialen Umwelt,* edited by Otto Herding and Robert Stupperich, pp. 51–86. Boppard: Boldt, 1976.

137. Grant, W. Leonard. *Neo-Latin Literature and the Pastoral.* Chapel Hill: University of North Carolina Press, 1965.

138. IJsewijn, Jozef. *Companion to Neo-Latin Studies.* Amsterdam: North-Holland, 1977.

139. Kohl, Benjamin G., and Ronald G. Witt, eds. *The Earthly Republic: Italian Humanists on Government and Society.* Philadelphia: University of Pennsylvania Press, 1978.

140. Kristeller, Paul Oskar. *Eight Philosophers of the Italian Renaissance.* Stanford: Stanford University Press, 1964.

141. ———. *Medieval Aspects of Renaissance Learning.* Durham: Duke University Press, 1974.

142. ———. *Renaissance Thought and Its Sources.* New York: Columbia University Press, 1979.

143. ———. *Le Thomisme et la pensée italienne de la Renaissance.* Montreal: Institut d'Etudes Médiévales; Paris, J. Vrin, 1967.

144. Landfester, Rüdiger. *Historia Magistra Vitae. Untersuchungen zur humanistischen Geschichtstheorie des 14. bis 16. Jahrhunderts.* Geneva: Droz, 1972.

145. Levi, A. H. T., ed. *Humanism in France at the end of the Middle Ages and in the Early Renaissance.* New York: Barnes and Noble, 1970.

146. Lindholm, Gudrun. *Studien zum mittellateinischen Prosarhythmus: Seine Entwicklung und sein Abklingen in der Briefliteratur Italiens.* Stockholm: Almqvist & Wiksell, 1963.

147. Martellotti, G. "Dalla tenzone al carme bucolico: Giovanni del Virgilio, Dante, Boccaccio." *Italia Medioevale e Umanistica* 7 (1964): 325–36.

148. Molho, Anthony, and John A. Tedeschi, eds. *Renaissance Studies in Honor of Hans Baron.* DeKalb: Northern Illinois University Press; Florence: Sansoni, 1971.

149. Nichols, Fred J. *An Anthology of Neo-Latin Poetry.* New Haven: Yale University Press, 1979.

150. Ouy, Gilbert. "La Dialectique des rapports intellectuels franco-italiens et l'humanisme en France aux XIVe et XVIe siècles." In *Rapporti culturali ed economici fra Italia e Francia nei secoli dal XIV al XVI.* Rome: Giunta centrale per gli studi storici, 1979.

151. Perosa, Alessandro, and John Sparrow. *Renaissance Latin Verse: An Anthology.* Chapel Hill: University of North Carolina Press, 1979.

152. Pfeiffer, Rudolf. *History of Classical Scholarship from 1300 to 1850.* New York: Oxford University Press, 1976.

153. Rowe, J. G., and W. H. Stockdale, eds. *Florilegium Historiale: Essays Presented to Wallace K. Ferguson.* Toronto: University of Toronto Press, 1971.

154. Ryan, Lawrence V. "Neo-Latin Literature." In *The Present State of Scholarship in Sixteenth-Century Literature,* edited by William M. Jones, pp. 197–257. Columbia and London: University of Missouri Press, 1978.

155. Sabbadini, R. *Le scoperte dei codici latini e greci ne' secoli XIV e XV.* Rev. ed. edited by Eugenio Garin. Florence: Sansoni, 1967.

156. Siegel, Jerrold. *Rhetoric and Philosophy in Renaissance Humanism: The Union of Eloquence and Wisdom, Petrarch to Valla.* Princeton: Princeton University Press, 1968.

157. Simone, Franco. *The French Renaissance: Medieval Tradition and Italian Influence in Shaping the Renaissance in France.* London: Macmillan, 1969.

158. Siraisi, Nancy G. *Arts and Sciences at Padua: The Studium of Padua before 1350.* Toronto: Pontifical Institute of Mediaeval Studies, 1973.

159. Trinkaus, Charles. *In Our Image and Likeness: Humanity and Divinity in Italian Humanist Thought.* 2 vols. Chicago: University of Chicago Press, 1970.

160. Ullmann, Walter. *Medieval Foundations of Renaissance Humanism.* Ithaca: Cornell University Press, 1977.

161. Weiss, Roberto. *The Spread of Italian Humanism.* New York: Hillary House, 1964.

HUMANIST LATIN AUTHORS

Dante Alighieri

162. Alighieri, Dante. *Dante in Hell. The De Vulgari Eloquentia.* Edited and translated by Warman Welliver. Ravenna: Longo, 1980.
163. ———. *De Vulgari Eloquentia.* Edited by Pier Vincenzo Mengaldo. Padua: Antenore, 1968.
164. ———. *Epistolae (The Letters of Dante).* Edited by Paget Toynbee; rev. ed. with bibliographical appendix by C. G. Hardie. New York: Oxford University Press, 1966.
165. ———. *Literature in the Vernacular.* A translation of *De Vulgari Eloquentia* by Sally Purcell. Manchester: Carcanet, 1981.
166. ———. *Monarchia.* Edited by Pier Giorgio Ricci. Milan: Mondadori, 1965.
167. Bosco, Umberto, ed. *Enciclopedia dantesca.* 6 vols. Rome: Instituto della Enciclopedia italiana, 1970–1978.
168. Chiavacci Leonardi, A. "La *Monarchia* di Dante alla luce della *Commedia.*" *Studi Medievali* 18 (1977): 147–83.
169. Costanzo, J. F. "The *De Monarchia* of Dante Alighieri." *Thought* 43 (1968): 87–126.
170. Davie, Mark. "Dante's Latin *Eclogues.*" In *Papers of the Liverpool Latin Seminar, 1976. Classical Latin Poetry / Medieval Latin Poetry / Greek Poetry,* edited by Francis Cairns, pp. 183–98. Liverpool: Cairns, 1977.
171. Foster, Kenelm. *The Two Dantes and Other Studies.* Berkeley: University of California Press, 1977.
172. Gilbert, Allan. "Did Dante Dedicate the *Paradiso* to Can Grande della Scala?" *Italica* 43 (1966): 100–124.
173. Grayson, Cecil. *Cinque saggi su Dante.* Bologna: Pàtron, 1972.
174. ———. " 'Nobilior est vulgaris': Latin and Vernacular in Dante's Thought." In *Centenary Essays on Dante,* by members of the Oxford Dante Society. New York: Oxford University Press, 1965.

175. Ragazzini, Severino, and Luigi Pescasio, eds. *Questio de Aqua et Terra*. Mantua: Padus, 1978.
176. Rizzo, Stefano. "Il *De Vulgari eloquentia* e l'unità del pensiero linguistico di Dante." *Dante Studies* 87 (1969): 69–88.

See also entry 228.

Early Humanists

177. Berrigan, Joseph R. *Mussato's "Ecerinus" and Loschi's "Achilles."* Munich: Wilhelm Fink, 1976.
178. Dazzi, M. *Il Mussato preumanista, 1261–1329. L'ambiente e l'opera.* Venice: 1964.
179. Leclercq, Jean. "Textes contemporains de Dante sur des sujets qu'il a traités." In *Per la storia della cultura in Italia nel duecento e primo trecento: Omaggio a Dante nel VII centenario della nascita, Studi Medievali,* 3 ser. 6, fasc. 2 (1965): 491–535.
180. Megas, Anastasios C. 'Ο προουμανιστικὸς κύκλος τῆς Παδούας *(Lovato Lovati, Albertino Mussato)* καὶ οἱ τραγοδίες τοῦ *L. A. Seneca.* Thessalonica: Aristoteleion Panepistimion Thessalonikis, 1967.

Petrarch

181. Baron, Hans. "The Evolution of Petrarch's Thought: Reflections on the State of Petrarch Studies." *Bibliothèque d'humanisme et Renaissance* 24 (1962): 7–41.
182. Benedek, Thomas G. "The Medical Autobiography of Petrarch." *Bulletin of the History of Medicine* 41 (1967): 325–41.
183. Bernardo, Aldo S. *Concordance to the "Familiari" of Francesco Petrarca.* 47 microfiches. Albany: State University of New York Press, 1975.
184. ———. *Petrarch, Scipio and the "Africa."* Baltimore: Johns Hopkins University Press, 1962.
185. Billanovich, Giuseppe. "Il Petrarca e gli storici latini." In *Tra latino e volgare. Per Carlo Dionisotti,* edited by Gabriello Bernardoni Trezzini et al., 1:67–145. Padua: Antenore, 1974.

186. Bishop, Morris. *Letters from Petrarch.* Bloomington and London: Indiana University Press, 1966.

187. ———. *Petrarch and His World.* Bloomington: Indiana University Press, 1963.

188. Fenzi, E. "Scipione, Annibale e Alessandro nell'*Africa* del Petrarca." *Giornale storico della letteratura italiana* 148 (1971): 481–518.

189. Gerosa, Pietro Paolo. *Umanesimo cristiano del Petrarca: Influenza agostiniana; Attinenze medievali.* Turin: Bottega d'Erasmo, 1966.

190. Giuliani, Oscar. *Allegoria retorica e poetica nel "Secretum" del Petrarca.* Bologna: Pàtron, 1977.

191. Godi, C. "La 'Collatio laureationis' del Petrarca." *Italia Medioevale e Umanistica* 13 (1970): 1–27.

192. Handschin, Werner. *Francesco Petrarca als Gestalt der Historiographie: Seine Beurteilung in der Geschichtsschreibung vom Frühhumanismus bis zu Jacob Burckhardt.* Basel: Helbing und Lichtenhahn, 1964.

193. Kessler, Eckhard. *Petrarca und die Geschichte: Geschichtsschreibung, Rhetorik, Philosophie im Übergang vom Mittelalter zur Neuzeit.* Munich: Wilhelm Fink, 1978.

194. Mann, Nicholas. "The Making of Petrarch's *Bucolicum Carmen:* A Contribution to the History of the Text." *Italia Medioevale e Umanistica* 20 (1977): 127–82.

195. ———. "The Manuscripts of Petrarch's *De Remediis:* A Checklist." *Italia Medioevale e Umanistica* 14 (1971): 57–90.

196. Mariotti, Scevola. "La *Philologia* del Petrarca. In *Scritti medievali e umanistici,* pp. 115–30. Rome: Edizioni di storia e letteratura, 1976.

197. Petrarca, Francesco. *Petrarch's Africa.* Translated by Thomas G. Bergin and Alice S. Wilson. New Haven and London: Yale University Press, 1977.

198. ———. *Petrarch's Book without a Name. A Translation of the "Liber sine nomine."* Translated by Norman P. Zacour. Toronto: Pontifical Institute of Mediaeval Studies, 1973.

199. ———. *Petrarch's Bucolicum Carmen.* Translated by Thomas G. Bergin. New Haven and London: Yale University Press, 1974.

200. ———. *Collatio inter Scipionem, Alexandrum, Annibalem et Pyrhum.* Edited by Guido Martellotti. Philadelphia: University of Pennsylvania Libraries, 1974.

201. ———. *De Remediis Utriusque Fortunae.* Translation and commentary by Rudolf Schottlaender. Munich: Wilhelm Fink, 1975.

202. ———. *De Viris Illustribus, I.* Edited by Guido Martellotti. Florence: Sansoni, 1968.

203. ———. *A Dialogue between Reason and Adversity: A Late Middle English Version of Petrarch's "De Remediis."* Edited by F. N. M. Diekstra. New York: Humanities Press; Assen: Van Gorcum, 1968.

204. ———. *Epistole autografe.* Edited by Armando Petrucci. Padua: Antenore, 1968.

205. ———. *Four Dialogues for Scholars, from "De Remediis Utriusque Fortunae."* Edited and translated by Conrad H. Rawski. Cleveland: Press of Western Reserve University, 1966.

206. ———. *Opere.* 2 vols. Florence: Sansoni, 1975. (Reprints previously published standard texts.)

207. ———. *Opere latine.* 2 vols. Turin: UTET, 1975.

208. ———. *Poesie latine.* Edited by Guido Martellotti and Enrico Bianchi. Turin: Einaudi, 1976.

209. ———. *Rerum Familiarum Libri, I–VIII.* Translated by Aldo S. Bernardo. Albany: State University of New York Press, 1975.

210. ———. *Sine Nomine. Lettere polemiche e politiche.* Edited by Ugo Dotti. Bari, Laterza, 1974.

211. Rawski, Conrad H. "Petrarch's Dialogue on Music." *Speculum* 46 (1971): 302–17.

212. Rico, Francisco. *Vida u obra de Petrarca, I: Lectura del "Secretum."* Chapel Hill: University of North Carolina, Department of Romance Languages, 1974.

213. Scaglione, Aldo, ed. *Francis Petrarch, Six Centuries Later: A Symposium.* Chapel Hill: University of North Carolina, Department of Romance Languages, 1975.

214. Simone, Franco. "Il Petrarca e la cultura francese del suo tempo." *Studi francesi,* fasc. 41 (1970): 201–15; fasc. 42 (1970): 403–17.

215. Thompson, David, ed. *Petrarch: A Humanist among*

Princes. An Anthology of Petrarch's Letters and of Selections from His Other Works. New York: Harper and Row, 1971.

216. Trinkaus, Charles. *The Poet as Philosopher: Petrarch and the Formation of Renaissance Consciousness*. New Haven and London: Yale University Press, 1979.

217. Tripet, Arnaud. *Pétrarque, ou la connaissance de soi*. Geneva: Droz, 1967.

218. Wilkins, Ernest H. *Studies on Petrarch and Boccaccio*. Edited by Aldo S. Bernardo. Padua: Antenore, 1978.

See also entry 240.

Boccaccio

219. Boccaccio, Giovanni. *Boccaccio in Defence of Poetry: Genealogiae Deorum Gentilium Liber XIV*. Edited by Jeremiah Reedy. Toronto: Pontifical Institute of Mediaeval Studies, 1978.

220. ———. *Opere in versi, Corbaccio, Tratatello in laude di Dante, Prose latine, Epistole*. Edited by Pier Giorgio Ricci. Milan and Naples: Ricciardi, 1965.

221. ———. *Tutte le opere*. Edited by Vittore Branca. 12 vols. Verona: Mondadori, 1967–1976.

222. Cerbo, Anna. "Il *De mulieribus claris* di Giovanni Boccaccio." *Arcadia, Accademia Letteraria Italiana. Atti e memorie* 7 (1974): 51–75.

223. Di Benedetto, F. "Considerazioni sullo Zibaldone laurenziano del Boccaccio e restauro testuale della prima redazione del Faunus." *Italia Medioevale e Umanistica* 14 (1971): 91–130.

224. Esposito, Enzo. *Boccacciana. Bibliografia delle edizione e degli scritti critici (1939–1974)*. Ravenna: Longo, 1976.

225. Prowse, A. M. "The First Eclogue of Boccaccio." *Allegorica* 2 (1977): 172–81. (Text and translation.)

226. Tournoy, Gilbert, ed. *Boccaccio in Europe: Proceedings of the Boccaccio Conference, Louvain, 1975*. Louvain: Leuven University Press, 1977.

227. Zappacosta, Guglielmo, and Vittorio Zaccaria. "Per il testo del *De mulieribus claris*." *Studi sul Boccaccio* 7 (1973): 239–70.

See also entry 218.

Salutati

228. Aguzzi-Barbagli, Danilo. "Dante e la poetica di Coluccio Salutati." *Italica* 42 (1965): 108–31.

229. Billanovich, Giuseppe, and Gilbert Ouy. "La Première Correspondence échangée entre Jean de Montreuil et Coluccio Salutati." *Italia Medioevale e Umanistica* 7 (1964): 337–74.

230. Bonnell, Robert A. "Salutati—A View of Caesar and Rome." *Annuale Mediaevale* 8 (1967): 59–69.

231. Donovan, Richard S. "Salutati's Opinion of Non-Italian Latin Writers of the Middle Ages." *Studies in the Renaissance* 14 (1967): 185–201.

232. Herde, Peter. "Politik und Rhetorik in Florenz am Vorabend der Renaissance. Die ideologische Rechtfertigung der Florentiner Aussenpolitik durch Coluccio Salutati." *Archiv für Kulturgeschichte* 47 (1965): 141–220.

233. Jensen, R. C. "Coluccio Salutati's 'Lament of Phyllis.'" *Studies in Philology* 65 (1968): 109–23.

234. Kessler, Eckhard. *Das Problem des frühen Humanismus: Seine philosophische Bedeutung bei Coluccio Salutati.* Munich: Wilhelm Fink, 1968.

235. Petrucci, Armando. *Coluccio Salutati.* Rome: Istituto della Enciclopedia italiana, 1972.

236. Ullman, Berthold L. *The Humanism of Coluccio Salutati.* Padua: Antenore, 1963.

237. Witt, Ronald G. *Coluccio Salutati and His Public Letters.* Geneva: Droz, 1976.

238. ———. "Coluccio Salutati and the Conception of the *Poeta Theologus* in the Fourteenth Century." *Renaissance Quarterly* 30 (1977): 538–63.

See also entry 324.

Other Authors

239. Gargan, Luciano. *Cultura e arte nel Veneto al tempo del Petrarca.* Padua: Antenore, 1978.

240. Kohl, Benjamin G., and J. Day. "Giovanni Conversini's *Consolatio ad Donatum* on the Death of Petrarch." *Studies in the Renaissance* 21 (1974): 9–30.

241. McCall, John P. "The Writings of John of Legnano with a List of Manuscripts." *Traditio* 23 (1967): 415–37.

242. Ross, W. Braxton, Jr. "Giovanni Colonna, Historian at Avignon." *Speculum* 45 (1970): 533–63.

243. Schork, R. J., and John P. McCall. "A Lament on the Death of John of Legnano." *Studies in the Renaissance* 19 (1972): 180–95.

See also entry 177.

PHILOSOPHICAL AND INTELLECTUAL WRITINGS

244. Bauer, Martin. *Die Erkenntnislehre und der Conceptus entis nach vier Spätschriften des Johannes Gerson.* Meisenheim: Hain, 1973.

245. Bernstein, Alan E. *Pierre d'Ailly and the Blanchard Affair.* Leiden: E. J. Brill, 1978.

246. Bobik, Joseph. *The Commentary of Conrad of Prussia on the De Ente et Essentia of St. Thomas Aquinas.* The Hague: Nijhoff, 1974.

247. Buridan, John. *Sophismata.* Edited by T. K. Scott. Stuttgart: Frommann-Holzboog, 1977.

248. Burley, Walter. *De Fromis.* Edited by Frederick J. Down Scott. Munich: C. H. Beck, 1970.

249. Cheney, Christopher R. "Richard de Bury, Borrower of Books." *Speculum* 48 (1973): 325–28.

250. Clagett, Marshall. *Archimedes in the Middle Ages: I. The Arabo-Latin Tradition.* Madison: University of Wisconsin Press, 1964.

251. Combes, André. *Jean Gerson, commentateur dionysien: Pour l'histoire des courants doctrinaux à l'Université de Paris à la fin du XIVe siècle.* Paris: Vrin, 1973.

252. Constable, Giles. "Twelfth-Century Spirituality and the Late Middle Ages." In *Medieval and Renaissance Studies: Proceedings of the Southeastern Institute of Medieval and Renaissance Studies. Summer, 1969.* Chapel Hill: University of North Carolina Press, 1971.

253. Courtenay, William J. *Adam Wodeham: An Introduction to His Life and Writings.* Leiden: E. J. Brill, 1978.

254. Cruz Hernández, Miguel. *El pensamiento de Ramon Llull.* Madrid: Castalia, 1977.

255. Dettloff, W. *Die Entwicklung der Akzeptations- und Verdienstlehre von Duns Scotus bis Luther.* Münster, 1963.

256. Di Vona, Piero. *I principi del Defensor Pacis.* Naples: Morano, 1974.

257. Duns Scotus, John. *God and Creatures: The Quodlibetal Questions.* Translated by F. Alluntis and A. B. Wolter. Princeton: Princeton University Press, 1975.

258. ———. *Tractatus de Primo Principio.* Edited and translated by W. Kluxen. Darmstadt: Wissenschaftliche Buchgesellschaft, 1974.

259. ———. *A Treatise on God as First Principle.* Translated and edited by Allan B. Wolter. Chicago: Franciscan Herald Press, Forum Books, 1966.

260. Genet, Jean-Philippe, ed. *Four English Political Tracts of the Later Middle Ages.* London: Royal Historical Society, University College, London, 1977.

261. Gerson, Jean. *Oeuvres complètes.* Edited by P. Glorieux. 10 vols. Paris: Desclée et Cie., 1960–1973.

262. Gilbert, Neal W. "Richard de Bury and the *Quires of Yesterday's Sophisms.*" In *Philosophy and Humanism: Renaissance Essays in Honor of Paul Oskar Kristeller,* edited by Edward P. Mahoney, pp. 229–57. New York: Columbia University Press, 1976.

263. Glorieux, P. "L'Oeuvre littéraire de Pierre d'Ailly, Remarques et précisions." *Mélanges de science réligieuse* 22 (1965): 61–78.

264. Henry, Desmond Paul. *Medieval Logic and Metaphysics: A Modern Introduction.* London: Hutchinson, 1972.

265. Hillgarth, J. N. *Ramon Lull and Lullism in Fourteenth-Century France.* New York: Oxford University Press, 1971.

266. Hugonnard-Roche, Henri. *L'Oeuvre astronomique de Thémon Juif, maître parisien du XIVe siècle.* Geneva: Droz; Paris: Minard, 1973.

267. Lawson, John. *Medieval Education and the Reformation.* New York: Humanities Press, 1967.

268. Leff, Gordon. *The Dissolution of the Medieval Outlook: An Essay on Intellectual and Spiritual Change in the Fourteenth Century.* New York: Harper and Row, 1976.

269. ———. *Paris and Oxford Universities in the Thirteenth and Fourteenth Centuries: An Institutional and Intellectual History.* New York: John Wiley, 1968.

270. ———. *Richard FitzRalph, Commentator of the Sentences: A Study in Theological Orthodoxy.* Manchester: Manchester University Press, 1963.

271. ———. *William of Ockham: The Metamorphosis of Scholastic Discourse.* Manchester: Manchester University Press; Totowa, N.J.: Rowman and Littlefield, 1975.

272. Lullus, Raimondus. *Opera Latina.* Edited by Friedrich Stegmüller. Vols. 1–5. Palma de Mallorca: Maioricensis Schola Lullistica, 1959–1967. Vols. 7–. Turnhout: Brepols, 1975–.

273. Maierù, Alfonso. *Terminologia logica della tarda scolastica.* Rome: Ateneo, 1972.

274. Marsilius of Padua. *La Défenseur de la paix.* Edited and translated by Jeannine Quillet. Paris: Vrin, 1968.

275. McGrade, Arthur Stephen. *The Political Thought of William of Ockham: Personal and Institutional Principles.* New York: Cambridge University Press, 1974.

276. Menut, Albert D. "A Provisional Bibliography of Oresme's Writings." *Mediaeval Studies* 28 (1966): 279–99.

277. Michalski, Konstanty. *La Philosophie au XIVe siècle. Six études.* Edited by Kurt Flasch. Frankfurt: Minerva, 1969.

278. Miethke, Jürgen. *Ockhams Weg zur Sozialphilosophie.* Berlin: De Gruyter, 1969.

279. Moody, Ernest A. *Studies in Medieval Philosophy, Science, and Logic; Collected Papers 1933–1969.* Berkeley: University of California Press, 1975.

280. Murdoch, John E. "The Development of a Critical Temper: New Approaches and Modes of Analysis in Fourteenth Century Philosophy, Science, and Theology." In *Medieval and Renaissance Studies. Proceedings of the Southeastern Institute of Medieval and Renaissance Studies, Summer 1975,* edited by Siegfried Wenzel, pp. 51–79. Chapel Hill: University of North Carolina Press, 1975.

281. Oakley, Francis. *The Political Thought of Pierre d'Ailly: The Voluntarist Tradition.* New Haven and London: Yale University Press, 1964.

282. Oberman, Heiko A., ed. *Forerunners of the Reformation: The Shape of Late Medieval Thought.* New York: Holt, Rinehart and Winston, 1966. (A collection of documents.)

283. ———. "Some Notes on the Theology of Nominalism with Attention to its Relation to the Renaissance." *Harvard Theological Review* 53 (1960): 47–76.

284. Ockham, William of. *Ockham's Theory of Terms, Part I of the "Summa Logicae."* Translated by Michael J. Loux. Notre Dame and London: University of Notre Dame Press, 1974.

285. ———. *Opera Philosophica et Theologica.* St. Bonaventure, N.Y.: Franciscan Institute, 1967–.

286. ———. *Predestination, God's Foreknowledge, and Future Contingents.* Translated by Marilyn McCord Adams and Norman Kretzmann. New York: Appleton-Century-Crofts, 1969.

287. Oresme, Nicole. *De Proportionibus Proportionum, Ad Pauca Respicientes.* Edited and translated by Edward Grant. Madison: University of Wisconsin Press, 1966.

288. ———. *Le Livre de politiques d'Aristote.* Edited by Albert Douglas Menut. Philadelphia: American Philosophical Society, 1970.

289. ———. *Le Livre du ciel et du monde.* Edited by Albert D. Menut and Alexander J. Denomy. Translated by Albert D. Menut. Madison: University of Wisconsin Press, 1968.

290. ———. *Nicole Oresme and the Kinematics of Circular Motion. Tractatus de Commensurabilitate vel Incommensurabilitate Motum Celi.* Edited and translated by Edward Grant. Madison: University of Wisconsin Press, 1971.

291. ———. *Nicole Oresme and the Medieval Geometry of Qualities and Motions. A Treatise on the Uniformity and Difformity of Intensities Known as "Tractatus de Configurationibus Qualitatum et Motuum."* Edited and translated by Marshall Clagett. Madison: University of Wisconsin Press, 1968.

292. Orme, Nicholas. *English Schools in the Middle Ages.* London: Methuen, 1973.

293. Ouy, Gilbert. "Gerson, émule de Pétrarque. Le 'Pastorum carmen', poème de jeunesse de Gerson, et la renaissance de l'églogue en France à la fin du XIVe siècle." *Romania* 88 (1967): 175–231.

294. Paqué, Ruprecht. *Das Parisier Nominalistenstatut zur Entstehung des Realitätsbegriffs der neuzeitlichen Naturwissenschaft.* Berlin: De Gruyter, 1970.

295. Pascoe, Louis B. *Jean Gerson: Principles of Church Reform.* Leiden: E. J. Brill, 1973.

296. Pinborg, Jan, ed. *The Logic of John Buridan: Acts of the Third European Symposium on Medieval Logic and Semantics, Copenhagen, 1975.* Copenhagen: Museum Tusculanum, 1976.

297. ———. *Logik und Semantik im Mittelalter; Ein Überblick.* Stuttgart and Bad Cannstatt: Frommann-Holzboog, 1972.

298. Posthumus Meyjes, G. H. M. *Jean Gerson à l'assemblée de Vincennes (1329): ses conceptions de la juridiction temporelle de l'église. Accompagné d'une édition critique du "De jurisdictione spirituali et temporali."* Leiden: E. J. Brill, 1978.

299. Pratt, Robert A. "Some Latin Sources of the Nonnes Preest on Dreams." *Speculum* 52 (1977): 538–70. (Chiefly on Chaucer's use of Robert Holcot.)

300. Prentice, R. P. *The Basic Quidditative Metaphysics of Duns Scotus as Seen in His "De Primo Principio."* Rome: Antonianum, 1970.

301. Prentice, Robert. "The Fundamental Metaphysics of Scotus Presumed by the *De Primo Principio.*" *Antonianum* 44 (1969): 40–92, 227–308.

302. Quillet, Jeannine. *La Philosophie politique de Marsile de Padoue.* Paris: Vrin, 1970.

303. ———. *La Philosophie politique du "Songe du Vergier" (1378): Sources doctrinales.* Paris: Vrin, 1977.

304. Reilly, J. P. "Ockham Bibliography, 1950–1967." *Franciscan Studies* 28 (1968): 197–214.

305. Rouse, Richard H. "Bostonus Buriensis and the Author of the *Catalogus Scriptorum Ecclesiae.*" *Speculum* 41 (1966): 471–99.

306. Rowland, Beryl. "Bishop Bradwardine on the Artificial

Memory." *Journal of the Warburg and Courtauld Institutes* 41 (1978): 307–12.

307. ———. "Bishop Bradwardine, the Artificial Memory, and the *House of Fame.*" In *Chaucer at Albany,* edited by Rossell Hope Robbins, pp. 41–62. New York: Franklin, 1975.

308. Rubinstein, Nicolai. "Marsilius of Padua and Italian Political Thought of His Time." In *Europe in the Late Middle Ages,* edited by J. R. Hale et al., pp. 44–75. Evanston: Northwestern University Press, 1965.

309. Ryan, John K., and Bernardine M. Bonansea, eds. *John Duns Scotus, 1265–1965.* Washington: Catholic University of America Press, 1965.

310. Schmidt, Martin Anton. *Scholastik.* Göttingen: Vandenhoeck und Ruprecht, 1969.

311. Schneider, Richard. *Die Trinitätslehre in den "Quodlibeta" und "Quaestiones Disputatae" des Johannes von Neapel O. P. (†1336).* Munich: Ferdinand Schöningh, 1972.

312. Shapiro, Herman, and Frederick Scott. *Walter Burley's "De Sensibus."* Munich: Max Hueber, 1966.

313. Spade, Paul Vincent. *The Medieval Liar: A Catalogue of the Insolubilia Literature.* Toronto: Pontifical Institute of Mediaeval Studies, 1975.

314. ———. "Roger Swyneshed's *Obligationes:* Edition and Comments." *Archives d'Histoire Doctrinale et Littéraire du Moyen Âge,* Paris 44(1977): 243–85.

315. ———. *William Heytesbury on "Insoluble" Sentences: Chapter One of His "Rules for Solving Sophisms."* Toronto: Pontifical Institute of Mediaeval Studies, 1979.

316. Stow, G. B., Jr., ed. *Historia Vitae et Regni Ricardi Secundi.* Philadelphia: Pennsylvania University Press, 1977.

317. Sutton, Thomas of. *Contra Quodlibet Iohannis Duns Scoti.* Edited by Johannes Schneider. Munich: C. H. Beck, 1978.

318. ———. *Expositionis D. Thomae Aquinatis in Libros Aristotelis De Generatione et Corruptione Continuatio per Thomam de Sutona.* Edited by Francis E. Kelley. Munich: C. H. Beck, 1976.

319. ———. *Quaestiones Ordinariae.* Munich: C. H. Beck, 1977.

320. ———. *Quodlibeta.* Edited by Michael Schmaus and Maria Gonzalez-Haba. Munich: C. H. Beck, 1969.

321. Taylor, John. *The "Universal Chronicle" of Ranulf Higdon.* New York: Oxford University Press, 1966.

322. Trinkaus, Charles. "Erasmus, Augustine, and the Nominalists." *Archiv für Reformationsgeschichte* 67 (1976): 5–32.

323. Uña Juárez, Agustín. *La filosofia del siglo XIV: Contexto cultural de Walter Burley.* Madrid: Real Monasterio del Escorial, 1978.

324. Vasoli, C. "Pietro degli Alboini da Mantova, 'scolastico' della fine del Trecento e un' Epistola di Coluccio Salutati." In *Arte pensiero e cultura a Mantova nel primo Rinascimento in rapporto con la Toscana e con il Venetto: Atti del VI convegno internazionale di studi sul Rinascimento,* pp. 57–76. Florence: Sansoni, 1965.

325. Walter, Ludwig. *Das Glaubensverständnis bei Johannes Duns Scotus.* Paderborn: Ferdinand Schöningh, 1968.

326. Weinberg, Julius R. *Ockham, Descartes and Hume: Self-Knowledge, Substance and Causality.* Madison: University of Wisconsin Press, 1977.

327. Weinberg, Julius R. *A Short History of Medieval Philosophy.* Princeton: Princeton University Press, 1964.

328. Wieruszowski, Helene. *The Medieval University: Masters, Students, Learning.* Princeton: Van Nostrand, 1966.

329. Zacher, Christian K. *Curiosity and Pilgrimage: The Literature of Discovery in Fourteenth-Century England.* Baltimore: Johns Hopkins University Press, 1976.

RELIGIOUS WRITINGS

330. Baier, Walter. *Untersuchungen zu den Passionsbetrachtungen in der "Vita Christi" des Ludolph von Sachsen: Ein quellenkritischer Beitrag zu Leben und Werk Ludolfs und zur Geschichte der Passionstheologie.* 3 vols. Salzburg: Institut für Englische Sprache und Literatur, 1977.

331. Benrath, Gustav Adolf. *Wyclifs Bibelkommentar.* Berlin: De Gruyter, 1966.

332. Berkhout, Carl T., and Jeffrey B. Russell. *Medieval Heresies. A Bibliography 1960–1979.* Toronto: Pontifical Institute of Mediaeval Studies, 1981.

333. Conway, Charles Abbott, Jr. *The "Vita Christi" of Ludolph of Saxony and Late Medieval Devotion Centered on the Incarnation: A Descriptive Analysis.* Salzburg: Institut für Englische Sprache und Literatur, 1976.

334. Dykmans, Marc, ed. *Les Sermons de Jean XXII sur la vision béatifique.* Rome: Università Gregoriana, 1973.

335. Fleming, John V. *An Introduction to the Franciscan Literature of the Middle Ages.* Chicago: Franciscan Herald Press, 1977.

336. Fristedt, Sven L. *The Wycliffe Bible, III: Relationships of Trevisa and the Spanish Medieval Bibles.* Stockholm: Almqvist & Wiksell, 1973.

337. Hohmann, Thomas. *Heinrichs von Langenstein "Unterscheidung der Geister" lateinisch und deutsch: Texte und Untersuchungen zu Übersetzungsliteratur aus der Wiener Schule.* Munich: Artemis, 1977.

338. ———. "Initienregister der Werke Heinrichs von Langenstein." *Traditio* 32 (1976): 399–426.

339. Hyma, Albert. *The Christian Renaissance. A History of the "Devotio Moderna."* Hamden, Conn.: Archon, 1965.

340. Kadlec, Jaroslav. *Leben und Schriften des Prager Magisters Adalbert Rankonis de Ericinio.* Münster: Aschendorff, 1971.

341. Lang, Peter. *Die Christologie bei Heinrich von Langenstein: Eine Dogmenhistorische Untersuchung.* Freiburg, 1966.

342. Leff, Gordon. *Heresy in the Later Middle Ages.* 2 vols. New York: Barnes and Noble, 1967.

343. ———. "The Making of the Myth of a True Church in the Later Middle Ages." *Journal of Medieval and Renaissance Studies* 1 (1971): 1–15.

344. ———. "Wycliffe and the Augustinian Tradition with Special Reference to his *De Trinitate.*" *Medievalia et Humanistica*, n.s. 1 (1970): 29–39.

345. Madigan, Mary Felicitas. *The "Passio Domini" Theme in*

the Works of Richard Rolle: His Personal Contribution in its Religious, Cultural, and Literary Context. Salzburg: Institut für Englische Sprache und Literatur, 1978.

346. Oberman, Heiko A. "Fourteenth Century Religious Thought: A Premature Profile." *Speculum* 53 (1978): 80–93.

347. Patschovsky, A. *Die Anfänge einer ständigen Inquisition in Böhmen: Ein Prager Inquisitoren-Handbuch aus der ersten Hälfte des XIV. Jahrhunderts.* Berlin: De Gruyter, 1975.

348. Post, Regnerus Richardus. *The Modern Devotion: Confrontation with Reformation and Humanism.* Leiden: E. J. Brill, 1968.

349. Reeves, Marjorie. *The Influence of Prophecy in the Later Middle Ages: A Study in Joachism.* New York: Oxford University Press, 1969.

350. Steneck, Nicholas H. *Science and Creation in the Middle Ages: Henry of Langenstein (d. 1397) on Genesis.* Notre Dame: University of Notre Dame Press, 1976.

351. Suso, Henry. *Horologium Sapientiae.* Edited by Pius Künzle. Freiburg: Universitätsverlag, 1977.

352. Theiner, Paul F., ed. *The "Contra Amatores Mundi" of Richard Rolle of Hampole.* Berkeley: University of California Press, 1968.

353. Walsh, Katherine. *The "De Vita Evangelica" of Geoffrey Hardeby, O.E.S.A. (c. 1320–c. 1385): A Study in the Mendicant Controversies of the Fourteenth Century.* Rome: Institutum Historicum Augustinianum, 1972.

354. Weltsch, Ruben E. *Archbishop John of Jenstein, 1348–1400: Papalism, Humanism and Reform in Pre-Hussite Prague.* The Hague: Mouton, 1968.

355. Winter, Eduard. *Frühhumanismus. Seine Entwicklung in Böhmen und deren europäische Bedeutung für die Kirchenreformbestrebungen im 14. Jahrhundert.* Berlin: Akademie-Verlag, 1964.

SPANISH LITERATURE

James F. Burke*

The interaction of the Christian, the Jewish, and the Muslim cultures in the Iberian Peninsula in the Middle Ages resulted in literary works of a very distinctive character, which often lends a color to them very different from what is found in the rest of Western Europe. Scholars and critics during the last two decades have actively considered this unique body of literature.

I would suggest three important works for those who wish to familiarize themselves with the Spanish medieval era in general, each of which deals specifically with the fourteenth century. Angus Mackay's *Spain in the Middle Ages: From Frontier to Empire, 1000–1500* (16) summarizes those developments that made medieval Spain unique. Although it is primarily a study of history, it often contains remarks pertinent to literary developments. The best survey of literature is Alan Deyermond's *The Middle Ages* in the books initiated and edited by R. O. Jones

---

*James F. Burke is Professor of Spanish literature in the Department of Spanish and Portuguese at the University of Toronto, where he has taught since 1966. He is also cross-appointed to the Centre for Medieval Studies and to the Centre for Comparative Literature at that University. From 1976 to 1981 he was Associate Dean for the Humanities in the School of Graduate Studies at the University of Toronto. Besides medieval Castilian literature, he is also interested in Hispano-Arabic language and literature. Professor Burke has written a book on the *Libro del Cavallero Zifar—History and Vision: The Figural Structure of the Libro del Cavallero Zifar* and articles on Gonzalo de Berceo, the *Libro de buen amor,* Juan Manuel, and *La Celestina,* as well as on several of the dramas of the Spanish Golden Age.

259

called *A Literary History of Spain* (7). The work was subsequently revised, expanded, and translated into Spanish with updated bibliography (8). Finally, the first volume of Otis Green's study *Spain and the Western Tradition: The Castilian Mind in Literature from "El Cid" to Calderón* (55) combines a philosophical, historical, and literary approach in presenting the author's view of what the medieval Castilian world picture was. The title of Green's study suggests that I make clear that I only deal in this essay with literary works written in Castilian. The term *Spanish* is used as an equivalent.

A foremost expert on fourteenth-century Castilian is Alan Deyermond. As such, he is an excellent resource for any answers to serious questions of bibliography and can be contacted at Westfield College of the University of London. He always seems to find time to answer queries in a most kind and human fashion. Deyermond has just published a volume dedicated to the Middle Ages in the series *Historia y crítica de la literatura española* (6) edited by Francisco Rico. It is an anthology of criticism and scholarship of the last thirty years. The introductory passages contain detailed commentary on every work of note produced during the Castilian Middle Ages. It is expected that volumes in this series will be updated every two years. The existence of such an excellent compendium should prove to be quite a stimulus to work in our area. I should add at this point a word concerning what a great aid this study was to me in preparing this essay—an aid and often an embarrassment since more than once Deyermond had encountered something worthy of note that had eluded me.

La Corónica, which first appeared in the fall of 1972, is the newsletter of the Division of Spanish Medieval Language and Literature of the MLA. Periodically, it produces bibliographies that are generally most complete. In addition the editor often asks experts on a given point or subject to do a complete survey for the pages of *La Corónica.*

Articles are also published, and the speed with which they appear makes the journal an especially valuable forum for discussion.

The *Bibliografía de la literatura hispánica* compiled by José Simón Díaz (33) is, with its supplements, still extremely useful; however, it contains errors and must be utilized with care. Two of the three projected volumes of the *Repertorio de medievalismo hispánico* (31), edited by Emilio Sáez, have been published. They list alphabetically thousands of Hispanists and their most relevant studies. In regard to primary sources the *Bibliography of Old Spanish Texts* (25) done at the University of Wisconsin is invaluable. The *Checklist of Manuscripts Microfilmed for the Hill Monastic Manuscript Library II, Spain, Part 1* (76) gives access to all those Hispanic manuscripts that are available in the Collegeville, Minnesota, archive. Harold Jones's *Hispanic Manuscripts and Printed Books in the Barberini Collection* (75) is a guide to such material in the Vatican. Charles Faulhaber is now compiling a catalogue of the medieval manuscripts in the collection of the Hispanic Society of America.

While studies on medieval Spain have been active, I believe too much of this work has been oriented toward a historical or archaeological approach to the subject. Most of the effort has been directed toward source studies, manuscript surveys, and editions rather than toward critical analysis. We now need to begin to emphasize critical analysis and to direct the interests of students toward this end. Because of the completeness of Deyermond's recent survey, which certainly demonstrates the flourishing of the traditional modes, I am accentuating studies that deal more exclusively with literary criticism. Since there is no broad examination of the fourteenth century in this respect, I shall treat the relevant critical studies as I discuss the individual work. Luis Beltrán's *Razones de buen amor* (161), although an analysis of only one poem, *The Book of Good Love*, does provide a good example of this kind of study. This is a highly controversial, idiosyncratic study. Yet, I think that Beltrán does the field a great service in that he has not been afraid to plunge into the LBA and tell us what he thinks it means, often episode by episode. One may, and often does, reject his readings. The important point is that Beltrán has produced a full, book-length study that interprets the poem as a distinct entity rather than by artificially applying some variety of template criticism.

The appearance of the *Diccionario crítico-etimológico de la lengua castellana* of Juan Corominas in 1954–1957 (26) was an enormous aid to scholars. Since the dictionary is oriented toward discussions of the etymology and origin of a word, it is not dedicated to providing definition. A new edition of this work will appear very soon. It is therefore necessary to use it in concert with a number of other secondary dictionaries and glossaries. In addition, Corominas's new etymological dictionary of the Catalan language (27) will be an indispensable aid as scholars will be able to cross check difficult entries. The University of Wisconsin Medieval Spanish Seminary has been preparing for some years a computer-based *Dictionary of the Old Spanish Language* with a targeted completion date of 1985. The base for the work is original manuscripts of literary pieces. I fervently hope that this important dictionary will not be delayed beyond 1985 because it promises to be of inestimable value. Rafael Lapesa's *Historia de la lengua española* (41), updated most recently in 1980, remains the best guide to questions of language. One reviewer, however, has criticized the book because Lapesa still makes no reference to modern theoreticians and only briefly mentions advances made by scholars, such as Yacob Malkiel and his students, who are adherents to more traditional approaches. We, therefore, still wait and need a history of the Spanish language written by a linguist who will take into account all theories and schools. In addition we need more linguistic studies of texts from the century such as that one done by Herbert L. Baird, Jr., of the *Otas de Roma* (145).

We have been blessed with an abundance of editions of the important works from fourteenth-century Castile. Every major work and practically every secondary one either is or soon will be available. I think it more convenient to discuss the relevant editions and translations in the sections treating respective individual works. It is important to note that generally there is too much emphasis on editing original texts rather than on presenting full and extensive critical apparatus. In 1978, for example, two editions of Pedro López de Ayala's *Rimado de Palacio* were published, that of Jacques Joset (184) and the one of Michel García (183). I have no quarrel with either of these save to say that it is wasteful to produce more than one edition of such a work. In a recent review of two of the renderings of the *Conde Lucanor* of Juan Manuel (131), only one of his many works, Alan Deyermond has explained the great difficulties that any editor would face in attempting to produce a definitive critical edition of all these works. This formidable task is the kind that badly needs to be undertaken.

HISTORICAL BACKGROUND

Two scholars, J. N. Hillgarth and Joseph O'Callaghan, have recently produced excellent histories of medieval Spain that complement one another superbly. O'Callaghan's study (18), which is in a traditional historical style, stresses the manifest destiny of Spain as embodied particularly in the Castilian *reconquista*. Hillgarth (13), also a traditional historian, has great sympathy for the aspirations of the other subcultures of the Peninsula and therefore gives a more pluralistic point of view. Joaquín Gimeno Casalduero's *La imagen del monarca en la Castilla del siglo XIV* (12), although somewhat flawed, still gives a good view of political developments in the fourteenth century. Helen Nader's study *The Mendoza Family in the Spanish Renaissance, 1350–1550* (17), provides excellent background material for understanding the latter half of the fourteenth century. Particularly interesting for scholars of literature is the attention she devotes to Pedro López de Ayala.

Alberto Vàrvaro has written two extremely useful histories of medieval Spanish literature, the second of which was done with Carmelo Samonà (22, 23). The history written by Deyermond (7, 8) is well complemented in many aspects by the extensively revised fourth edition of Francisco López Estrada's *Introducción a la literatura medieval española* (15). Hans Flasche's *Geschichte der Spanischen Literatur,* published in 1977 (11), is uneven, the bibliography being almost useless since there appears to be no rationale for the choosing of the items that appear there. However, the book does contain interesting remarks and commentary of a comparative nature.

For more than seven hundred years a vibrant, fertile Islamic civilization existed in the Peninsula. It is impossible to understand any facet of medieval Spanish culture without an acquaintance with the Semitic influences at work there. Anwar Chejne's *Muslim Spain: Its History and Culture* (84) with its excellent bibliography perpetuates in convenient and readable form the ideas of earlier authorities and gives a panoramic view of the subject. Juan Vernet Gines's *La cultura hispanoárabe en oriente y occidente* (88) mixes comments about literary phenomena with remarks concerning history and culture. Oleg Grabar's *The Alhambra* (86) helps one to understand this landmark in the context of the vast Islamic civilization and also to have some perception of *mudéjar* art—art the Muslims left behind after the passing of the Reconquest.

From the perspective of so-called Western Civilization (it must be remembered that both the medieval Jewish and Muslim cultures fall within a Western tradition) María Rosa Lida de Malkiel's book *La tradición clásica en Es-*

paña (62) demonstrates how the Greco-Roman stream continued in the Peninsula. Otis Green's *Spain and the Western Tradition* (55) is written partially with the same purpose. Francisco Rico's article "Las letras latinas del siglo XII en Galicia, León y Castilla" (19) provides the setting for the Alphonsine revival of the thirteenth century and the flourishing of vernacular literature in the fourteenth. There has been a dearth of work in the field of medieval philosophy of Spain since the appearance of the now classic study by Tomás and Joaquín Carreras Artau, in two volumes, published in 1939 and 1942 (3). Green does concern himself, although not systematically, with philosophical themes and ideas in *Spain and the Western Tradition* (55). An important article by Michael Gerli published in *Romance Philology* (149) takes up again the didactic structure of the *Libro de buen amor* as related to the Augustinian tradition. One suspects that much of the literature of the fourteenth century should be examined in the light of the continuance of the ideas of St. Augustine as opposed to those of St. Thomas Aquinas. Another mode of thought surely of great significance and little understood by most literary scholars is Lullism. J. N. Hillgarth's study *Ramon Lull and Lullism in Fourteenth-Century France* (57) could prove to be of great use to future investigators interested in such influence in Spain. Mark D. Johnston is now completing a study called *Ramon Lull and the Medieval Trivium*, which analyzes Lull's treatment of grammar, rhetoric, and logic.

A book-length study by Sister Francis Gormly (54) and an article by Diego Catalán (47) provide us with ample information on the use of Holy Scripture in medieval Spanish literature. Two articles by Derek Lomax, the first on the effect of the Lateran reforms on Spanish literature (65) and the second (64) on those religious writers who were composing at the end of the thirteenth and the beginning of the fourteenth centuries, help us to understand the religious and spiritual ambience in which writers in the latter century were working. Lomax touches on education in the first of these articles. More study and investigation in the areas of religion and education would doubtless yield fruitful results. Professor Lomax has also contracted to write a history of the medieval Spanish Church that is scheduled to be published by Oxford University Press in 1983. Also useful in this respect is the five-volume *Historia de la Iglesia en España*, which is under the general editorship of Ricardo García-Villoslada. Volume 2, covering 711–c. 1400, has been edited by Francisco Javier Fernández Conde and should be published very soon (59).

THEMATIC STUDIES

During the past twenty years, a number of worthwhile studies have been published that have expanded our understanding of particular themes, images, and ideas and that are of signal importance for an adequate comprehension of medieval literature and culture. Robert Pring-Mill's explanation of the Lullian microcosm (71) not only aids in understanding this enigmatic figure but also clarifies the medieval world view. Francisco Rico's book (72) on the image of man as microcosm as reflected in literary, theological, and philosophical writings demonstrates how and why the idea of microcosm was such an important structuring device for the medieval literary consciousness. Susan J. McMullan's article "The World Picture in Medieval Spanish Literature" (66) has furthered even more our understanding in this regard. The concept of fortune, one always of compelling appeal for medieval writers, has been recently examined in Hispanic context by Ricardo Arias y Arias (42).

A number of extremely important studies related to medieval or renaissance Europe in general are particularly relevant to fourteenth-century Castilian literature. In practically every case, collateral study of Castilian literature would be well worth the effort. A good example of such is María Rosa Lida de Malkiel's appendix to Jorge Hernández Campos's Spanish translation of Howard Patch's *The Other World* (70). Terry Comito's *The Idea of the Garden in the Renaissance* (48) expands vastly our comprehension of this image. Victor and Edith Turner's *Image and Pilgrimage in Christian Culture* (73), written from the perspective of an anthropologist, clarifies why the idea of pilgrimage would have been so pervasive as a means for structuring a work. Barbara Nolan's *The Gothic Visionary Perspective* (68) discusses how medieval man in the Gothic period "saw" things and suggests how this visual happening was translated into art. A study by John Keller and Richard Kinkade, *Iconography and Narrative Art in Medieval Spanish Fiction* (58), should enhance our knowledge of connections between these areas.

One particularly troublesome problem is how imagery and thematic material were conveyed to a fictionalized "audience" in a period when literacy was the exception rather than the rule. Scholars have long believed that the sermon was of great importance in the development of medieval Spanish literature. Alan Deyermond has just presented an excellent *état de la question* with bibliography in the Spring 1980 issue of *La Corónica* (50). He suggests that we should add the medieval popular sermon to the list of oral-formulaic genres, an addition that could be far-reaching in our understanding of oral-formulaic theory. Pedro Cáthedra of the Autonomous University of Barcelona is now preparing a full bibliography of sermons for the Grant & Cutler Research Bibliographies and Checklists series. I would suggest that anyone investigating such issues take into account the ideas and theories of Walter J. Ong concerning the differences between a primarily oral culture, one evolving toward literacy, and finally one that is dominated by the image of print. His latest book *Interfaces of the Word* (69), a combination of previously published material and new studies, presents the thread of most of his arguments.

The problem of courtly love has always loomed large as a question in medieval Spanish literature. We are fortunate to have had Roger Boase's *The Origins and Meanings of Courtly Love* (44), which has a good bibliography and critical study of past and present scholarship on the subject. Boase suggests in a tentative manner that the origins of the phenomenon may lie in the Arabic tradition.

A new and fascinating field of study concerns how medieval legal theories affected literary composition. Steven D. Kirby, who wrote a study on these particular aspects of the *Libro de buen amor* (171), has written more generally on the subject in *La Corónica*, Spring 1980 (60). Kirby mentions the penetrating study of R. Howard Bloch, *Medieval French Literature and Law* (43), which suggests that the evolving legal tradition at least parallels and probably molds to some degree the emerging literary consciousness.

The field does need a good study of the aesthetical principles that governed the tastes of writers in medieval Spain, especially regarding the enigmatic works. Critics have long assumed that a close connection could be drawn between the *artes poeticae*, which are really comparable to school texts, and what appear to be in many cases rather sophisticated literary works. Charles Faulhaber's *Latin Rhetorical Theory in Thirteenth and Fourteenth Century Castile* (39) has raised serious doubts in regard to this supposition and has demonstrated the paucity of rhetorical texts in the area during this period. Mark Johnston's forthcoming study of Lull's rhetoric may prove helpful in this regard as it is not impossible that fourteenth-century writers could have drawn inspiration from Lull.

The interplay between history and literature, an aspect of great importance in the Middle Ages, has been more readily comprehensible lately due to the two works, Diego

Catalán's *De Alfonso X al Conde de Barcelos* (4) and Keith Whinnom's *Spanish Literary Historiography: Three Forms of Distortion* (24), which deals with the practice of historians of literature. One peculiarly medieval facet of the possible interrelations between history and literature is figuralism, the presentation of literary antitypes to historical types found principally in the Bible and classical sources. David W. Foster's *Christian Allegory in Early Hispanic Poetry* (52), an uneven work that must be used with care, is a study of the presentation in literature of the relationship between Old Testament type and New Testament antitype.

A number of studies have indicated the folkloric roots and associations of literary works from medieval Spanish literature. Few scholars, however, have understood the connection as well as Daniel Devoto and have explained it so perfectly as he has in his *Textos y contextos* (49). Devoto has seen that the popular oral and folkloric tradition parallels and interacts with the learned tradition and therefore is often as valuable or even more valuable in explaining the context of a difficult point in a literary work. Of interest here is the recent doctoral thesis of Egla Morales Blouin, "Ritual y canto: mito y símbolo en la lírica tradicional" (80). Morales Blouin relates the development of the traditional lyric in the Peninsula to a locus of themes and folkloric practices common not only in Spain but also across the rest of Europe. One would suspect that much more work is possible along this line, although it is clear that more fresh folkloric material will have to be assembled. The work of Julio Caro Baroja as presented in such studies as *El Carnaval* (77) and *Ritos y mitos equívocos* (78) has vastly expanded our knowledge and understanding of folk customs and usages and has noted the correlation between such customs and literary works.

One of the controversies that has excited a great deal of interest is that one between critics and scholars espousing the cause of neotraditionalism versus those favoring the approach of what one commentator has called "neoindividualism." Neotraditionalism, which is for the most part an approach to the understanding of the origins of the epic, was fostered in a number of works by the great Ramón Menéndez Pidal. Briefly, its principal points are that the epic was composed by a *juglar* or bard who was contemporary or near contemporary to the events being depicted. The resulting work then circulated by word of mouth and thus could easily have been altered and could thereby have undergone a process of "novelización." This mode of literary invention would obviously have required the knowledge of a great number of stock formulae whose existence could be verified in the resulting work. The neoindividualists, whose view is akin to that brought forth by Joseph Bédier in regard to the origins of the Old French epic, believe that the epics are deliberately conceived works, often created to support some cause dear to the hearts of their clerical authors. Charles Faulhaber, in a recent article in *Romance Philology* (51), has given an excellent summary of the quarrel. The longest and most complete work in the area in recent years, Alan Deyermond's study of the *Mocedades de Rodrigo* called *Epic Poetry and the Clergy* (142) is decidedly written from the neoindividualist perspective.

The controversy is important not only in regard to the epic but also to the *romance* or ballad and may relate to a number of other questions as well. Was Juan Ruiz, supposed author of the *Libro de buen amor,* really Archpriest of Hita, a small town near Guadalajara, or of *ficta* a Latin etymon that could have readily yielded Fita or Hita? Could this work be a product of a kind of goliardic neotraditionalism?

Recently the neotraditionalist, neoindividualist opposition appears to have been merging into the broader question of oral literature in general. In the Fall 1978 issue of *La Corónica,* Rina Benmayor has given a concise but extremely useful summary of the situation with a good bibliography (100). Samuel Armistead, who remains somewhat in doubt about the tenets of neoindividualism, has recently in a review article in *Romance Philology* (98) questioned whether individualist critics can and should project their theory of medieval epic upon the *romancero*. The field of medieval Spanish is fortunate to have a scholar, John Miletich, who is as conversant with the Slavic languages as with the Romance and is thereby able to deal firsthand not only with records of oral materials in these languages but also with the scholarship written in the Slavic tongues on the subject, much of which has never been translated. His article "Medieval Spanish Epic and European Narrative Traditions" in the Spring 1978 issue of *La Corónica* is extremely useful in this regard (102, see also 103–6). It would appear that the subject of oral literature could be one of the most fruitful fields for investigation for those with the wide training and talent necessary for success.

One of the most interesting problems having to do with medieval Spanish literature is the so-called Castro controversy. Américo Castro put forth the argument, perhaps best seen in *España en su historia* (83), that the distinction between Spain and the rest of Western civilization was the coexistence there during the Middle Ages of three major traditions—the Christian, the Jewish, and the Muslim. The discussion that has ensued has indeed been heated.

The early reaction of Sánchez-Albornoz against the tenets of Castro (87) has been followed by many others. José Luis Gómez Martínez in a book published in 1975 has given a good history of the controversy up to that point (85). Eugenio Asensio in *La España imaginada de Américo Castro* (81) demonstrated that a precise historical method was not always followed by Castro and his disciples in reaching conclusions. It seems to me that Vicente Cantarino in *Entre monjes y musulmanes: el conflicto que fue España* (82) may be getting close to the truth when he suggests that what characterized medieval Spain was the use which orthodox medieval Christianity made of certain intellectual values of Islam. The question is of crucial importance for an understanding of fourteenth-century Castilian literature because it has been suggested at one time or the other that almost all of the major works of the century are touched in some manner by either or both of the two Semitic cultures that shared this vital living space with the Christians. More research is needed on this subject.

As mentioned previously, for the most part the field of medieval Spanish studies has been conservative, preferring to engage in work that is largely historical in character and descriptive in nature. Stephen Gilman has most attempted to apply radically innovative approaches to the study of the literary works of the period (53), but he has not been greatly concerned with the fourteenth century. Julio Rodríguez-Puértolas has written two books (20, 21) from a sociohistorical approach, but neither has received much critical acclaim. He has also worked with Carlos Blanco Aguinaga and Iris M. Zavala on a three-volume *Historia social de la literatura española* (2), which applies Marxist criteria to literature, again without much success with the critics. One has remarked that the book makes banal the scheme of Marx. Another sociohistorical work is by Emmanuel Le Roy Ladurie titled *Montaillou* (61) and is based on the records of heresy trials in a small village of Languedoc in the Pyrenees. It is important because it took place at the end of the thirteenth and beginning of the fourteenth centuries in an area quite close to Spain. Armando Durán applied structuralist methods and technics in analyzing the romances of chivalry and the sentimental novel in his *Estructura y técnicas de la novela sentimental y caballeresca* (93). In this case also the critics have not been particularly laudatory. While reviewers have not responded particularly well to these books, all of them contain valuable insights and should be consulted. There are some very interesting developments in regard to individual works and authors, but I shall discuss these further along in the section dealing with works and authors.

Drama

The question of the drama in medieval Spain is shrouded with enigma and uncertainty. The *Auto de los reyes magos*, which consists of only 147 verses, is a play concerning the visit of the Wise Men to the Christ Child. It was composed toward the end of the twelfth century. Afterward, we have no examples of further dramatic pieces until the fifteenth century. (It must be noted that there are references in the legislation of the period that attempt to prohibit plays.) Scholars could rationalize the nonexistence of manuscripts containing secular plays by saying that they might not have been of sufficient interest to have inspired someone to record them. It is more difficult to explain why there would be no written traces of religious dramas if such were widely performed in Castilian-speaking areas. Richard Donovan's book *The Liturgical Drama in Spain* (89) demonstrates that almost no material has survived from Castile. C. Clifford Flanigan has pointed out that the liturgical drama seems to spring up in France soon after the dramatic, poetically inspired Gallican rite was replaced by the austere Roman liturgy with its aversion to literary features (90). Although officially the Mozarabic rite, fully as poetically ornate as the Gallican, was replaced in 1085, it is clear that features of it continued to be used for centuries. Perhaps these very features tended to satisfy the needs of the clergy and people for dramatic feeling and purpose so that no further development was necessary. The various articles of José Regueiro (92) provide information about the early drama such as it was, and a chapter by Ronald Surtz in a volume dedicated to the history of drama in Spain edited by Diez-

Borque to be published by Taurus will summarize the various theories having to do with the origins of drama.

Richard Kinkade recently presented a paper at the meeting of the Modern Language Association (résumé in *La Corónica*) (91) in which he suggests that works even from the *mester de clerecía* tradition could have been performed in church or elsewhere in the manner of what is today the theater in the round. A reader would have been reciting and prompting from either a pulpit or raised platform while mimes, appropriately masked and costumed, performed below. If Kinkade is correct, it would be necessary for us to rethink all our considerations having to do with the existence and interrelation of genres in the fourteenth century. Obviously the sphere comprising dramatic literature could be vastly expanded.

ROMANCES

Although we have few examples of the *romances* or the ballad from the fourteenth century, it seems certain that many were composed and circulating during that period. Consequently, by studying *romances* of later periods, we can hope to determine characteristics that survived from earlier eras as well as material that will shed light on works from the fourteenth century. For example, the themes and images studied in Edith Rogers's *The Perilous Hunt* (107) are all found at some point in the literature of the century. It is, of course, also likely that we may eventually encounter examples of ballads from the era.

In the Fall 1979 issue of *La Corónica*, Samuel Armistead has given us a bibliography that covers the field (98). The publication in 1979 of the proceedings of the second International Colloquium on the *romancero* (1977) entitled *El Romancero hoy: Historia, Comparatismo, Bibliografía crítica* (108), edited by three of the leading experts in the field, Armistead, Diego Catalán, and Antonio Sánchez Romeralo, is particularly valuable.

PROSE

Francisco López Estrada's *La prosa medieval (Orígenes—s. XIV)* (96) offers a good introduction to this genre for the period. Deyermond's surveys in his history of Spanish literature and in the book on history and criticism contain concise, relevant statements that frame the situation very well (6–8). María Jesús Lacarra (94), in her study of two works from the thirteenth century, also provides good background for the period.

ARTHURIAN

The Arthurian, post-Vulgate cycle now commonly referred to as the *Roman du Graal* reached Spain, although the original version in which it appeared is now lost. Fanni Bogdanow in *The Romance of the Grail* (46) utilized a great deal of Hispanic material in her description of the nature of the *Roman du Graal*. There are manuscripts of the Spanish Tristan and Lancelot stories surviving from the midfourteenth century. We are extremely fortunate that Harvey Sharrer has prepared an excellent bibliography (32) of this complex material. More important than the Arthurian material is the indigenous work in Castilian that appeared at roughly the same time and that may have been inspired or influenced by it. The *Libro del Cavallero Zifar* (c. 1300) is a carefully constructed book. I argued in *History and Vision* (115) that an understanding of the work requires that it be seen as composed figurally; its characters should be seen as antitypes to important figures in Sacred History. R. G. Keightley has continued this line of investigation (118, 119). Roger Walker wrote another noteworthy book-length study of the *Zifar* (120), which concerns *Tradition and Technique in "El Libro del Cavallero Zifar."* The *Zifar* fortunately continues to receive critical attention. This is one major work for which a readily available, scholarly edition is badly needed. There are problems with the Charles Wagner edition (201), which is difficult to secure in any event. Both Marilyn Olsen and J. González Muela are at present preparing such an edition. Charles L. Nelson's translation of the *Zifar*, which is in press, will make this work available to readers who do not read Old Spanish.

The *Gran conquista de Ultramar*, a fictionalized chronicle account of the Crusades, was probably written a few years after the *Zifar*. A version of the Swan Knight legend is incorporated within it. Hans Ulrich Gumbrecht's study adheres to the methods of *Rezeptionsgeschichte* in discussing why the Swan Knight legend and three other Old French texts would have been chosen for translation (56). The *Gran conquista* is by no means as fine a work as the *Zifar*, but I still suspect that it may be worthy of study from a number of points of view.

The famous *Amadís de Gaula* did not appear until 1508 in a version recast around 1492 by Garcí Rodríguez de Montalvo, but it almost surely dates from the earlier part of the fourteenth century. The study of Frank Pierce (112) in the Twayne series offers not only a good introduction to the *Amadís* but also numerous valuable remarks about the work. Cacho Blecua (110) approaches the book in a most satisfactory fashion. He analyzes the *Amadís* from the mythico-folkloric perspective, utilizing many of the latest theories concerning the evolution of the structure of a literary piece. He also deals with those traditional problems concerning the work which have perplexed scholars for years. Edwin B. Place has edited the Montalvo version of the *Amadís*, which is available in four volumes (192). It is a good, serviceable edition, which makes the *Amadís* readily accessible, but Place has by no means resolved all the problems involved, and more textual study and criticism are needed.

There are several chronicles dating from the fourteenth century that are of consummate interest from the point of view of history and historiography but which would not necessarily attract the attention of the student of literature. Diego Catalán has been the principal investigator who has not only prepared good editions of these works but has also studied them critically.

JUAN MANUEL

The major author of prose in this century is the Infante Don Juan Manuel, who, in spite of a life filled with adventure and intrigue, managed to write a large number of works, six of which unfortunately have been lost. The short book of Tracy Sturcken (134), again in the Twayne series, gives a good, up-to-date introduction to the subject of Juan Manuel in general. Daniel Devoto produced in 1972 what he was pleased to call *Introducción al estudio de Don Juan Manuel y en particular de "El conde Lucanor": una bibliografía* (130) which lists all relevant work on this author and is filled with numerous insightful comments in regard to the secondary literature as well as to basic works. Juan Manuel is one of those few fortunate authors or works that have been blessed by a *Studies* volume (140) produced by Támesis Books. Támesis is an editorial consortium headed by two eminent Hispanists. Among its publications are high-quality books in this field, which might be too specialized to interest financially harried university presses and the like. An editor who is particularly knowledgeable on a subject assembles articles from among well-known scholars in the field; those articles represent the latest views, ideas, and trends relating to an author or work. In the best instances the result is a convenient, readily accessible compendium of the latest thoughts on the subject at hand. The work on Juan Manuel, edited by Ian Macpherson, is an example of one of these best instances. One could suggest that this is a particularly appropriate and beneficial format and that therefore periodic *Studies* volumes, once a decade for example, would provide a needed stimulus for the field. We possess good, serviceable editions of the major works of this author, but a complete critical edition of all the works is sorely wanting.

The *Conde Lucanor* is the best known of all Juan Manuel's efforts. It is a strange book consisting of a frame-tale section with fifty-one traditionally recognized *exempla* followed by four other shorter sections. The first three of these are composed basically of a series of *sententiae* or proverbial sayings. The final part contains doctrinal teachings and philosophical musings that must in some fashion refer back to the initial section. Most of the studies of the *Conde Lucanor* have either been source oriented or have attempted to demonstrate what the author did with his sources. Such works have given us invaluable information concerning the origins of the creative process in Juan Manuel. The best example is Reinaldo Ayerbe-Chaux's *El Conde Lucanor: Materia tradicional y originalidad creadora*, which studies analogues to the stories in the *Conde Lucanor* (129).

Ian Macpherson in an article in *Romance Philology* (137) examined the didactic rationale that inspired the composition of the *Conde Lucanor*, but perhaps too much from a modern moral perspective. In 1973 he discussed Juan Manuel's attitude toward his own work in a good essay on literary historiography (138). Peter Dunn, a scholar who can usually be depended upon for resourceful application of advanced critical theories to medieval Spanish works, has given us a particularly useful article in the *Studies* volume on the structure of the *Conde Lucanor* because he has understood that among other things the book as a framed collection depends upon the axes of language discussed by Yacovsen, the metaphoric and the metonymic (136). Antonio Carreño (135) has applied ethical-social theories to the work in a study of the function of shame as an important factor in the honor code. The fact that the article in slightly varied form has appeared in at least three other journals should not detract from its usefulness. Two good editions, those of Blecua (187) and Orduna (188), readily available now provide us with excellent working copies of the *Conde Lucanor*. Orduna's introduction is on the whole the more detailed and informative of the two. Ayerbe Chaux hopes to surmount the not inconsiderable difficulties that one encounters with manuscripts in order to provide us with a definitive edition of the *Conde Lucanor*.

Probably the second most important work of Juan Manuel is the *Libro de los estados*, an adaptation of the Barlaam and Josaphat legend so popular in the Middle Ages. As might be inferred from the title, it is a justification of the accepted hierarchical structure of the Middle Ages and shows man, especially the nobleman, how to best fulfill his assigned role within this hierarchy. Brian Tate and Ian Macpherson have given us a good edition of this work (189). This message, one central to the writings of Juan Manuel, is basic to the medieval world view. One suspects that its presentation in the books of Juan Manuel is not nearly as simple as one might think. What is needed for the works of Juan Manuel in order to clarify this kind of problem is a study along the lines of the one done by Cacho Blecua in regard to the *Amadís*. José Romera Castillo's *Estudios sobre "El Conde Lucanor"* (141), which looks at the work from the perspective of structuralism and semiotics, is an interesting and valuable step in the right direction. Ian Macpherson's recent *Juan Manuel: A Selection* provides a good introduction to his work plus excellent examples that are a broad representation of his work (186).

The *Historia troyana polimétrica* is, as is obvious from the title, a piece that acclimatizes the Trojan material to the Hispanic Peninsula. It is a rather strange work in that there exists within its fabric a kind of opposition between the lyric and the narrative modes that is related to the difference between prose and poetry. Even the date of the book has been in dispute: some scholars suggest the late thirteenth century while others argue for the fourteenth. Marina Scordilis Brownlee, in the Fall 1978 *La Corónica* (113), has provided an excellent reappraisal of the *Historia* with bibliography. She has also signaled many of the important critical problems that exist in the work.

JUAN RUIZ

The most important literary creation from the fourteenth century in Spain is the enigmatic *Libro de buen amor*, the most complete version of which has been traditionally thought to date from 1343. The book has been extensively studied for years, but interest has largely centered on certain traditional problems, and traditional approaches have been employed to solve these problems. Recently a number of exciting new ventures have been launched that are beginning to focus the latest critical modes of inquiry upon the poem.

Probably the greatest impetus to *Libro de buen amor* studies in the last twenty years occurred in 1965 with the publication by Anthony Zahareas of *The Art of Juan Ruiz* (156). Zahareas was interested in differentiating the characteristics of the style of the poet and in the hope of shedding light on this question applied modern critical approaches to the work. Since then four other important points, posed in part by earlier critics, have continued to be researched and hotly debated in a variety of ways. Does the *Libro de buen amor* really have a unifying structure and if so, what is it? Closely allied to this point is whether the author deliberately made distinct the version from 1330 and the one from 1343. The poet claims that he has a serious, didactic aim in writing the book. Is he serious? Is this a *mudéjar* poem? Is it a product of the kind of unique interaction of Christian-Muslim culture that Castro sees in the Peninsula? Finally there is the question of love. What is *buen amor*? How does the Archpriest's understanding of love relate to general medieval philosophical considerations on the subject?

G. B. Gybbon-Monypenny initiated the Támesis *Studies* in 1944 with a volume devoted to the *Libro de buen amor* (150). Here, Gybbon-Monypenny argues that the avowed purpose of the book must be didactic, while Janet Chapman and Alan Deyermond (166, 167) suggest that the very important introductory sermon in prose should be seen as parodic in intent. The studies in this volume are far too extensive to be traced in this brief paper. All of the four important points mentioned above as well as many others are either dealt with or alluded to in this volume. The same is true for the *Actas* of the First International Congress of the Archpriest of Hita in 1973, which was conceived and sponsored by Manuel Criado de Val (147). Although the quality of the *Actas* as a whole is somewhat uneven, the volume greatly enriches our knowledge of the poet and his work. This congress was enlivened by a series of spectacles such as medieval-style banquets in Hita, a refreshing and effective approach to what could have been a dull scholarly gathering.

Alan Deyermond had by this time realized that many of the tentative conclusions and suggestions made by Félix Lecoy in his *Recherches* in 1938 were not only still valid but also could serve as starting points for new studies. After consulting with colleagues, he reedited Lecoy with an enriched bibliography. The revised edition was published in 1974 (152).

Eric Naylor, Gybbon-Monypenny, and Deyermond published a complete bibliography of *Libro de buen amor* studies from 1973 through 1979 in the Spring 1979 *La Corónica* (30). Mary-Anne Vetterling is now producing a *Computerized Bibliography for the Libro de buen amor,* which will be continually updated and revised (35). The first edition is now available. Needless to say, this sort of effort would prove to be invaluable in the case of any major author or work that receives a great deal of critical attention.

There have been in the past few years some particularly interesting developments either in regard to the four questions mentioned previously or to new topics. Alicia de Ferraresi's study *De amor y poesía en la España medieval* (148) sees the *Libro de buen amor* as a development of an idea of disillusionment with *fin' amors / buen amor* and as an attack on the *religio amoris*. Colbert Nepaulsingh has looked at the structure of the book, first the prologue (173) in terms of rhetoric and later (174) the entire book as a kind of juxtaposition of contraries. A study by Olga Impey also aids us in understanding how the structure of the *Libro de buen amor* is arranged (168). Nicolás Alvarez has examined the whole Don Amor in Toledo section in the light of similar circumstances in the *Libro de Alixandre* and reaches the conclusion that Juan Ruiz is parodying the *Alixandre* (159). In another article to be published in 1981 he has looked at the sermon prologue and by examining it closely in the terms of rhetoric has reached the conclusion that it consists of a series of binary opposites ultimately pointing toward *buen amor* (158). Steven Kirby has analyzed the episode where the fox and the wolf put a lawsuit before the judge Sir Ape and has shown that it is a learned exercise in forensic discourse aimed at showing off the poet's formidable knowledge of rhetoric (171). Any parodic intent would be completely secondary. This article plainly demonstrates the importance that the legal context has for the proper understanding of the *Libro de buen amor.* Emilio Sáez and José Trenchs in a brief article in the *Actas* of the *Libro de buen amor* Congress have attempted to identify the poet with a certain Juan Ruiz de Cisneros (153). Such an identification is interesting as this individual's knowledge of Islamic civilization is beyond doubt. John Walsh (155) has disclosed another aspect of the Archpriest's poetry in proving that the poem echoes again and again the diction and forms of previous works. For this reason he suspects that the intent of the *Libro de buen amor* could be that of a "full parody." I argue in a brief article in *La Corónica* that modern techniques of analysis such as those used by the deconstructive critics have shown that the work of a writer always reflects the literary code as expressed in previous authors and that, therefore, the presence of such echoes does not necessarily indicate the presence of parody (164). M. K. Read has approached the theme of alienation in the *Libro de buen amor* from a linguistic perspective suggesting that the work may reflect the crisis generated by the struggle between the realist and the nominalist view of language (175). L. Jenaro-MacLennan in an article (169) has studied stanzas 69–70, the meaning of which is central to a proper understanding of the work. He suspects that the key phrase "qual puntares," "as you may point," may not refer to music, as most have suspected, but to the *artes punctandi*, documents that showed how to punctuate correctly particularly in the legal context. Finally, those interested in the poem anxiously await the publication of a book by Henry A. Kelly in which he argues, I am told, based upon his knowledge of ecclesiastical procedures, that the date 1381 given in Manuscript S, stanza 1634, must be taken at face value and not as thirty-eight years earlier as it would be if the date is struck according to the Spanish era. Finally I would again mention the interesting and provocative, highly controversial study of the Luis Beltrán (161) that, if nothing else, has proved to be most stimulating.

There have been a number of editions of the *Libro de buen amor* in the last twenty years, all of which have contributed in one way or the other to our knowledge. Three deserve mention for special reasons. The one of Corominas (195) must be used with care because of readings that he has arbitrarily chosen. He does, however, have very good notes relating to the language of the text. The edition and English paraphrase of Raymond S. Willis

(196) has an extremely good introduction. The best text available, with careful notes, and certainly the least expensive, is that of Jacques Joset in the Clásicos Castellanos series (194). Joset has utilized to advantage all the editorial work done previously and has produced an edition with a remarkably balanced perspective. The best translation is that of Saralyn Daly done to accompany an edition of the book by Anthony Zahareas (193). This translation based on Manuscript S has won a prize from the Modern Language Association of America and serves as a good companion to the Willis effort, which centers on G. Three concordances to the *Libro de buen amor* were published between 1972 and 1977, the best of which is that of Rigo Mignani, Mario Di Cesare, and George F. Jones (29). Di Cesare and Mignani have put the computer-stored data employed in producing the concordance to extremely interesting use. Under the title *Ruiziana: Research Materials for the Study of the Libro de buen amor* (28) they have produced on microfiche packets containing such useful information as a complete vocabulary and concordance, graphemic distribution, and line-by-line merger for all three manuscripts. The *Ruiziana* first appeared in 1977, but because of some problem was not widely distributed. It is to be reissued during 1981.

OTHER WORKS

The *Poema de Alfonso XI*, written in midcentury, which relates the life of this monarch from the time he rose to the throne to the capture from the Muslims of Algeciras in 1344, has suffered from neglect during the past twenty years. It is ready for a truly critical edition beyond that of Yo Ten Cate (199), and for investigation that would clarify its relation to various chronicles. One suspects again that the new critical methods could aid in throwing light on this work.

The *Proverbios morales* of Rabbi Shem Tov ben Titzhak

Ardutiel known as Sem Tob or Santob de Carrión in Spanish is a delightful little work the meaning of which has long been debated. T. A. Perry provides a superb "The Present State of Shem Tov Studies" in *La Corónica*, with complete bibliography (177). There is no critical edition that takes into account all manuscripts and theories, so González Llubera's 1947 effort still stands (198). I would agree with Perry that the popularized version of Guzmán Alvarez (197) can be used for general reading as long as more scholarly work, the editing of a new manuscript by López Grigera for example, is taken into account for serious study (176). A very useful general approach to Sem Tob is Sanford Shepard's *Shem Tov, His World and His Works* (179), which gives background, provides résumés of critical material, and discusses the author's other works such as the *Battle of the Pen and the Scissors*. Carlos Polit's study, which deals with aspects of expressive originality in the *Proverbios morales* and which demonstrates that there exists a progression of themes in the book, should also be noted (178).

The last major work of the fourteenth century, written for the most part in *cuaderna vía* (the fourfold way), is the *Rimado de Palacio* of Pedro López de Ayala who was for a time chancellor of Castile. We are fortunate again that someone, this time José Luis Coy, has given us in *La Corónica* a critical update on the state of work on the *Rimado de Palacio* (123). Strong (127) has studied the first part of the poem, pointing out that it is modeled on the form of a confession, and has also studied the prayers and lyrics in the piece (128). Coy (122) has given us pertinent information concerning the chronology of López de Ayala's productions and has shown (121), by studying the notes in the margins of a manuscript translation of the *Moralia* on Job of St. Gregory, how the poet adapted this work as the last part of the *Rimado*. Kinkade (125) has looked at the influence that the Order of St. Jerome exercised on the works of López de Ayala. It has now been effectively demonstrated that the poet cannot be considered a precursor of the Renaissance particularly if considered in comparison with the emerging poets of the *Cancionero de Baena*. We have had (as mentioned before) a veritable *embarras de richesses* in regard to editions of the *Rimado*, with those of García and Joset, which both appeared in 1978 (183, 184), now complemented by that of Germán Orduna, 1980 (185), and with a further one projected by Coy. Certainly it would appear that scholars should now devote their efforts to attempting to understand what this work means.

Two other works merit mention. One is the edition of the fourteenth-century translation of Paul the Deacon's *Vida de Santa Maria Egipciaca* done by B. Bussell Thompson and John K. Walsh (200). This particular prose version may not be as interesting as other forms of the legend, but it demonstrates the continuation and popularity of the story. In addition Thompson and Walsh have done a very informative introduction. William Weisinger Johnson has given us a transcription and comparison of the manuscripts of the *Poema de José*, an *aljamiado* work, that is, one composed in Romance but written in Arabic characters (182). This poem of only 312 stanzas tells part of the story of Joseph and, although no outstanding masterpiece, does serve as an early example of what will later be a more important literary type.

Finally I should mention the *Mocedades de Rodrigo*, a poem in the epic tradition about the youth of the Cid that was composed in the latter half of the fourteenth century. Deyermond has written a book-length study of the work (142) in which he demonstrates among other things that it is a poem of learned authorship probably composed as propaganda for the Diocese of Palencia. Although he does not believe that this is a particularly good piece, one suspects that more study is also indicated. Ruth House Webber has recently argued that the language base of the poem was a traditional one that deteriorated and was then overlaid by editorial changes and emendations (144).

If the tendencies that have existed in the field toward historical and editorial work can be balanced by more critical studies, it can be predicted that fourteenth-century studies in Castilian will continue to flourish. The literary works of the century lay the foundation for the great masterpieces of the Spanish Renaissance and Golden Age. A proper critical understanding and appreciation of these works is essential not only because of the value inherent in them but also because of what proceeds from them.

BIBLIOGRAPHY

LITERARY HISTORIES, PHILOSOPHY, AND HISTORIOGRAPHY

1. Alborg, Juan Luis. *Historia de la literatura española.* Vol. 1. *Edad Media y Renacimiento.* 2d ed. Madrid: Gredos, 1970.
2. Blanco Aguinaga, Carlos, Julio Rodríguez-Puértolas, and Iris M. Zavala. *Historia social de la literatura española (en lengua castellana),* vols. 1–. Madrid: Castalia, 1978–.
3. Carreras Artau, Tomás, and Joaquín Carreras Artau. *Historia de la filosofía española. Filosofía cristiana de los siglos XIII al XV.* 2 vols. Madrid: Academia de Ciencias Exactas, Físicas y Naturales, 1939–1942.
4. Catalán Menéndez Pidal, Diego. *De Alfonso X al Conde de Barcelos: cuatro estudios sobre el nacimiento de la historiografía romance en Castilla y Portugal.* Madrid: Seminario Menéndez Pidal and Gredos, 1962.
5. Criado de Val, Manuel. *Historia de Hita y su Arcipreste: vida y muerte de una villa mozárabe.* Madrid: Editora Nacional, 1976.
6. Deyermond, Alan D. *Edad Media.* In *Historia y crítica de la literatura española,* edited by Francisco Rico, vol. 1. Barcelona: Editorial Crítica, 1980.
7. ———. *A Literary History of Spain: The Middle Ages.* Edited by R. O. Jones. London: Ernest Benn, 1971.
8. ———. *Historia de la literatura española,* vol. 1. *La Edad Media.* Letras e Ideas: Instrumenta, 1. Barcelona: Ariel, 1973.
9. ———. "The Lost Genre of Medieval Spanish Literature." *Hispanic Review* 43 (1975): 231–59.
10. ———. "The Lost Literature of Medieval Spain: Excerpts from a Tentative Catalogue." *La Corónica* 5 (1976–1977): 93–100.
11. Flasche, Hans. *Geschichte der Spanischen Literatur. Er-*

ster Band: Von den Anfängen bis zum Ausgang des fünfzehnten Jahrhunderts. Bern and Munich: Francke Verlag, 1977.

12. Gimeno Casalduero, Joaquín. *La imagen del monarca en la Castilla del siglo XIV: Pedro el Cruel, Enrique II y Juan I.* Madrid: Revista de Occidente, 1972.

13. Hillgarth, J. N. *The Spanish Kingdoms, 1250–1516. Precarious Balance, 1250–1410,* vol 1; *Castilian Hegemony, 1410–1516,* vol. 2. Oxford: Oxford University Press, 1976.

14. Kinkade, Richard P. "Sancho IV: Puente literario entre Alfonso el Sabio y Juan Manuel." *PMLA* 87 (1972): 1039–51.

15. López Estrada, Francisco. *Introducción a la literatura medieval española.* 4th ed., rev. Madrid: Gredos, 1979.

16. Mackay, Angus. *Spain in the Middle Ages: From Frontier to Empire, 1000–1500.* London: Macmillan, 1977.

17. Nader, Helen. *The Mendoza Family in the Spanish Renaissance 1350–1550.* New Brunswick, N.J.: Rutgers University Press, 1979.

18. O'Callaghan, Joseph F. *A History of Medieval Spain.* Ithaca and London: Cornell University Press, 1975.

19. Rico, Francisco. "Las letras latinas del siglo XII en Galicia, León y Castilla." *Abaco* 2 (1969): 9–91.

20. Rodríguez-Puértolas, Julio. *De la Edad Media a la edad conflictiva.* Madrid: Gredos, 1972.

21. ———. *Literatura, historia, alienación.* Barcelona: Editorial Labor, 1976.

22. Vàrvaro, Alberto. *Manuale di filologia spagnola medievale. II. Letteratura.* (Romanica Neopolitana, 4.) Naples: Liguori, 1969.

23. Vàrvaro, Alberto, and Carmelo Samonà. *La letteratura spagnola dal Cid ai Re Cattolici. Le Letterature del mondo,* 6. Milan: Sansoni, 1972.

24. Whinnom, Keith. *Spanish Literary Historiography: Three Forms of Distortion.* Exeter: University of Exeter, 1967.

BIBLIOGRAPHIES, DICTIONARIES, AND CONCORDANCES

25. Cárdenas, Anthony, Jean Gilkinson, John Nitti, and Ellen Anderson. *Bibliography of Old Spanish Texts.* 2d ed. Madison: Hispanic Seminary of Medieval Studies, 1977.

26. Corominas, Juan. *Diccionario crítico-etimológico de la lengua castellana.* 4 vols. Madrid: Gredos; Bern: Francke, 1954–1957.
27. ———. *Diccionari etimològic i complementari de la llengua catalana,* with the collaboration of Joseph Gulsoy and Max Cahner, vol. 1 (A–Bl), 1980; vol. 2 (Bl–C), 1981. Barcelona: Curial Edicions Catalanes, 1980–.
28. Mignani, Rigo, and Mario Di Cesare. *Ruiziana: Research materials for the study of the Libro de buen amor.* Albany: State University of New York Press, 1977.
29. Mignani, Rigo, Mario Di Cesare, and George F. Jones. *A Concordance to Juan Ruiz: "Libro de buen amor."* Albany: State University of New York Press, 1977.
30. Naylor, Eric W., G. B. Gybbon-Monypenny, and Alan D. Deyermond. "Bibliography of the *Libro de buen amor* since 1973." *La Corónica* 7 (1978–1979): 123–35.
31. Sáez, Emilio, and Mercè Rossell. *Repertorio de medievalismo hispánico (1955–1975).* Barcelona: "El Albir," Vol. 1, 1976, Vol. 2, 1978; Vol. 3 not yet published.
32. Sharrer, Harvey L. *A Critical Bibliography of Hispanic Arthurian Material.* Volume 1. *Texts: The Prose Romance Cycles.* Research Bibliographies and Checklists, 3. London: Grant and Cutler, 1977.
33. Simón Díaz, José. *Bibliografía de la literatura hispánica,* III. 2d ed. Madrid: CSIC, 1963–1965. (Supplements are published in the *Revista de Literatura.)*
34. ———. *Manual de bibliografía de la literatura española.* Barcelona: Gustavo Gili, 1963. (Supplement 1, 1966; Supplement 2, 1972.)
35. Vetterling, Mary-Anne. *A Computerized Bibliography of the "Libro de buen amor."* Boston: Mary-Anne Vetterling, 1981.

LANGUAGE, PROSODY, RHETORIC, AND PALEOGRAPHY

36. Baehr, Rudolf. *Manual de versificación española.* Madrid: Gredos, 1970.
37. Baldinger, Kurt. *La formación de los dominios lingüísticos en la península ibérica.* Translated by Emilio Lledó

and Montserrat Macau. German edition, 1958; Madrid: Gredos, 1963.

38. Bustos Tovar, José Jesús de. *Contribución al estudio del cultismo léxico medieval.* Anejos del *Boletín de la Real Academia Española,* 27. Madrid: Real Academia Española, 1974.

39. Faulhaber, Charles. *Latin Rhetorical Theory in Thirteenth and Fourteenth Century Castile.* Publications in Modern Philology, 103. Berkeley: University of California Press, 1972.

40. ———. "Retóricas clásicas y medievales en bibliotecas castellanas." *Abaco* 4 (1973): 151–300.

41. Lapesa, Rafael. *Historia de la lengua española.* 8th ed. Madrid: Gredos, 1980.

BACKGROUND STUDIES

42. Arias y Arias, Ricardo. *El concepto del destino en la literatura medieval española.* Madrid: Insula, 1970.

43. Bloch, R. Howard. *Medieval French Literature and Law.* Berkeley, Los Angeles, and London: University of California Press, 1977.

44. Boase, Roger. *The Origin and Meaning of Courtly Love: A Critical Study of European Scholarship.* Manchester: University Press, 1977.

45. ———. *The Troubadour Revival: A Study of Social Change and Traditionalism in Late Medieval Spain.* London: Routledge, 1978.

46. Bogdanow, Fanni. *The Romance of the Grail: A Study of the Structure and Genesis of a Thirteenth-Century Arthurian Prose Romance.* Manchester: Manchester University Press, 1966.

47. Catalán Menéndez Pidal, Diego. "La Biblia en la literatura medieval española." *Hispanic Review* 33 (1965): 310–18.

48. Comito, Terry. *The Idea of the Garden in the Renaissance.* New Brunswick, N.J.: Rutgers University Press, 1978.

49. Devoto, Daniel. *Textos y contextos: Estudios sobre la tradición.* Biblioteca Románica Hispánica II. Estudios y Ensayos, 212. Madrid: Gredos, 1974.

50. Deyermond, Alan. "The Sermon and Its Uses in Medieval Castilian Literature." *La Corónica* 8 (1979–1980): 127–45.

51. Faulhaber, Charles. "Neo-traditionalism, Formulism, Individualism, and Recent Studies on the Spanish Epic." *Romance Philology* 30 (1976–1977): 83–101.

52. Foster, David W. *Christian Allegory in Early Hispanic Poetry.* Studies in Languages, 4. Lexington: University Press of Kentucky, 1970.

53. Gilman, Stephen. *The Spain of Fernando de Rojas: The Intellectual and Social Landscape of "La Celestina."* Princeton: Princeton University Press, 1972.

54. Gormly, Sister Francis. *The Use of the Bible in Representative Works of Medieval Spanish Literature, 1250–1300.* Studies in Romance Languages and Literatures, vol. 46. Washington, D.C.: Catholic University of America, 1962.

55. Green, Otis H. *Spain and the Western Tradition: The Castilian Mind in Literature from "El Cid" to Calderón.* 4 vols. Madison: University of Wisconsin Press, 1963–1966.

56. Gumbrecht, Hans Ulrich. "Literary Translation and Its Social Conditioning in the Middle Ages: Four Spanish Romance Texts of the 13th Century." Translated by Helga Bennett. *Yale French Studies* 51 (1975): 205–22.

57. Hillgarth, J. N. *Ramon Lull and Lullism in Fourteenth-Century France.* Oxford: Oxford University Press, 1971.

58. Keller, John, and Richard P. Kinkade. *Iconography and Narrative Art in Medieval Spanish Fiction.* Lexington: University Press of Kentucky, in press.

59. *Historia de la Iglesia en España.* Edited by Ricardo García-Villoslada. Biblioteca de Autores Cristianos. 5 vols. Madrid: La Editorial Católica, 1979–.

60. Kirby, Steven D. "Legal Doctrine and Procedure as Approaches to Medieval Hispanic Literature." *La Corónica* 8 (1979–1980): 164–71.

61. Le Roy Ladurie, Emmanuel. *Montaillou: The Promised Land of Error.* Translated by Barbara Bray. French edition, 1975; New York: Vintage Books, 1979; London: Penguin Books, 1980.

62. Lida de Malkiel, María Rosa. *La tradición clásica en España.* Letras e Ideas: Maior, 4. Barcelona: Ariel, 1975.

63. Liria Montañés, Pilar. *Libro de las maravillas del mundo*

de Juan de Mandevilla. Zaragoza: Caja de Ahorros de Zaragoza, Aragón y Rioja, 1979.

64. Lomax, Derek. "Algunos autores religiosos, 1205–1350." *Journal of Hispanic Philology* 2 (1977–1978): 81–90.

65. ———. "The Lateran Reforms and Spanish Literature." *Iberoromania* 1 (1969): 299–313.

66. McMullan, Susan J. "The World Picture in Medieval Spanish Literature." *Annali dell'Istituto Universitario Orientale di Napoli, Sezione Romanza* 13 (1971): 27–105.

67. Mendoza Negrillo, Juan de Dios. *Fortuna y Providencia en la literatura castellana del siglo XV. Anejo del Boletín de la Real Academia Española,* vol. 7. Madrid: Real Academia Española, 1973.

68. Nolan, Barbara. *The Gothic Visionary Perspective.* Princeton, N.J.: Princeton University Press, 1977.

69. Ong, Walter J. *Interfaces of the Word: Studies in the Evolution of Consciousness and Culture.* Ithaca and London: Cornell University Press, 1977.

70. Patch, Howard R. *El otro mundo en la literatura medieval.* Translated by Jorge Hernández Campos, with an appendix, "La visión de trasmundo en las literaturas hispánicas" by María Rosa Lida de Malkiel, pp. 371–449. Mexico: Fondo de Cultura Económica, 1956.

71. Pring-Mill, Robert. *El microcosmos lulliá.* Palma de Mallorca: Moll; Oxford: Dolphin, 1961.

72. Rico, Francisco. *El pequeño mundo del hombre: varia fortuna de una idea en las letras españolas.* Madrid: Castalia, 1970.

73. Turner, Victor, and Edith Turner. *Image and Pilgrimage in Christian Culture.* New York: Columbia University Press, 1978.

MANUSCRIPT STUDIES

74. Catalán Menéndez Pidal, Diego. *La tradición manuscrita en la "Crónica de Alfonso XI."* Biblioteca Románica Hispánica II. Estudios y Ensayos, 211. Madrid: Gredos, 1974.

75. Jones, Harold. *Hispanic Manuscripts and Printed Books in the Barberini Collection,* 2 vols. Studi e Testi 280–281. Vatican City: Biblioteca Apostolica Vaticana, 1978.

76. Plante, Julian G. *Checklist of Manuscripts Microfilmed for the Hill Monastic Manuscript Library II, Spain,* Part 1. Collegeville, Minn.: Library 19, 1978.

Folklore

77. Caro Baroja, Julio. *El Carnaval: análisis histórico-cultural.* Madrid: Taurus, 1965.
78. ———. *Ritos y mitos equívocos.* Biblioteca de Estudios Críticos—Sección de Antropología. Madrid: Ediciones Istmo, 1974.
79. Frenk Alatorre, Margit. *Entre folklore y literatura (Lírica hispánica antigua).* Mexico: El Colegio de México, 1971.
80. Morales Blouin, Egla. "Ritual y canto: mito y símbolo en la lírica tradicional ibérica." Ph.D. diss., Georgetown University, 1979.

Muslim Spain and Castro Controversy

81. Asensio, Eugenio. *La España imaginada de Américo Castro.* Barcelona: El Albir, 1976.
82. Cantarino, Vicente. *Entre monjes y musulmanes: El conflicto que fue España.* Madrid: Alhambra, 1978.
83. Castro, Américo. *España en su historia: cristianos, moros y judíos.* Buenos Aires: Losada, 1948. 2d ed.: *La realidad histórica de España.* Mexico: Porrúa, 1954.
84. Chejne, Anwar G. *Muslim Spain: Its History and Culture.* Minneapolis: University of Minnesota Press, 1974.
85. Gómez Martínez, José Luis. *Américo Castro y los orígenes de los españoles: historia de una polémica.* Madrid: Gredos, 1975.
86. Grabar, Oleg. *The Alhambra.* Cambridge, Mass.: Harvard University Press; London: Allen Lane, 1978.
87. Sánchez-Albornoz, Claudio. *España, un enigma histórico.* Buenos Aires: Sudamericana, 1956.
88. Vernet Gines, Juan. *La cultura hispanoárabe en oriente y occidente.* Barcelona and Caracas: Ariel, 1978.

DRAMA

89. Donovan, Richard B. *The Liturgical Drama in Medieval Spain.* Toronto: Pontifical Institute of Mediaeval Studies, 1958.
90. Flanagin, C. Clifford. "The Roman Rite and the Origins of the Liturgical Drama." *University of Toronto Quarterly* 43 (1974): 263–84.
91. Kinkade, Richard P. Summary of paper "Sermon in the Round: The *Mester de Clerecía* as Dramatic Art," delivered at a special session of the MLA, December 1980. *La Corónica* 9 (1980–1981): 9.
92. Regueiro, José. "El Auto de los Reyes Magos y el teatro litúrgico medieval." *Hispanic Review* 45 (1977): 149–64.

PROSE

93. Durán, Armando. *Estructura y técnicas de la novela sentimental y caballeresca.* Madrid: Gredos, 1973.
94. Lacarra, María Jesús. *Cuentística medieval en España: los orígenes.* Publicaciones del Departamento de Literatura Española. Zaragoza: 1979.
95. Lida de Malkiel, María Rosa. "Arthurian Literature in Spain and Portugal." In *Arthurian Literature in the Middle Ages: A Collaborative History,* edited by Roger S. Loomis, pp. 406–18. Oxford: Clarendon, 1959.
96. López Estrada, Francisco. *La prosa medieval (Orígenes—s. XIV).* Literatura Española en Imágenes, vol. 6. Madrid: La Muralla, 1973.

BALLAD (ROMANCE)

97. Alvar, Manuel. *El Romancero, Tradicionalidad y pervivencia.* Barcelona: Planeta, 1970.
98. Armistead, Samuel G. "Neo-individualism and the *Romancero.*" *Romance Philology* 33 (1979–1980): 172–81.
99. ———. "*Romancero* Studies: 1977–1979." *La Corónica* 8 (1979–1980): 57–66.

100. Benmayor, Rina. "New Directions in the Study of Oral Literature." *La Corónica* 7 (1978–1979): 39–42.
101. Catalán Menéndez Pidal, Diego. "La novela medieval y el romancero oral moderno." In *Por campos del romancero: estudios sobre la tradición oral moderna*, pp. 77–117. Madrid: Gredos, 1970.
102. Miletich, John. "Medieval Spanish Epic and European Narrative Traditions." *La Corónica* 6 (1977–1978): 90–96.
103. ———. "Oral-Traditional Style and Learned Literature: A New Perspective." *PTL: A Journal for Descriptive Poetics and Theory of Literature* 3 (1978): 345–56.
104. ———. "The Quest for the 'Formula': A Comparative Reappraisal." *Modern Philology* 74 (1976): 111–23.
105. ———. "South Slavic and Hispanic Versified Narrative: A Progress Report on One Approach." In *El Romancero hoy: Historia, Comparatismo, Bibliografía crítica*, edited by Samuel G. Armistead, Antonio Sánchez Romeralo, and Diego Catalán, pp. 131–35. Madrid: Gráficas Cóndor, 1979.
106. ———. "The South Slavic *Bulgarštica* and the Spanish *Romance*: A New Approach to Typology." *International Journal of Slavic Linguistics and Poetics* 21 (1975): 51–69.
107. Rogers, Edith Randam. *The Perilous Hunt: Symbols in Hispanic and European Balladry*. Lexington: The University Press of Kentucky, 1980.
108. *El Romancero hoy: Historia, Comparatismo, Bibliografía crítica*. Edited by Samuel Armistead, Antonio Sánchez Romeralo, and Diego Catalán. 3 vols. Madrid: Cátedra—Seminario Menéndez Pidal, 1979.

FESTSCHRIFTS

109. Jones, Joseph R. *Medieval, Renaissance and Folklore Studies in Honor of John Esten Keller*. Newark, Del.: Juan de la Cuesta—Hispanic Monographs, 1980.

INDIVIDUAL WORKS AND AUTHORS: AMADÍS DE GAULA

110. Cacho Blecua, Juan Manuel. *Amadís: heroísmo mítico cortesano*. Madrid: Cupsa, 1979.

111. Lida de Malkiel, María Rosa. "El desenlace del *Amadís primitivo.*" *Romance Philology* 6 (1952–1953): 283–89.
112. Pierce, Frank. *Amadís de Gaula.* Twayne's World Authors Series, 372. Boston: Twayne, 1976.

HISTORIA TROYANA POLIMÉTRICA

113. Brownlee, Marina Scordilis. "Towards a Reappraisal of the *Historia Troyana Polimétrica.*" *La Corónica* 7 (1978–1979): 13–17.
114. ———. "Undetected Verses in the *Historia Troyana en Prosa y Verso.*" *Romania* 100 (1979): 270–72.

LIBRO DEL CAVALLERO ZIFAR

115. Burke, James F. *History and Vision: The Figural Structure of the "Libro del Cavallero Zifar.*" London: Támesis, 1972.
116. Hernández, Francisco. "Ferrán Martínez, 'escrivano del rey,' canónigo de Toledo, y autor del *Libro del Cavallero Zifar.*" *Revista de Archivos, Bibliotecas y Museos* 81 (1978): 289–325.
117. ———. "Noticias sobre Jofré de Loaisa y Ferrán Martínez." *Revista Canadiense de Estudios Hispánicos* 4 (1980): 281–309.
118. Keightley, Ronald J. "Models and Meanings for the *Libro del Cavallero Zifar.*" *Mosaic* 12 (1979): 55–73.
119. ———. "The Story of Zifar and the Structure of the *Libro del Cavallero Zifar.*" *Modern Language Review* 73 (1978): 308–27.
120. Walker, Roger M. *Tradition and Technique in "El Libro del Cavallero Zifar.*" London: Támesis, 1974.

PEDRO LÓPEZ DE AYALA

121. Coy, José Luis. " 'Busco por que lea algunt libro notado': De las notas de los *Morales* al texto del *Rimado del Palacio.*" *Romance Philology* 30 (1976–1977): 454–69.
122. ———. "Para la cronología de las obras del Canciller Ay-

ala: la fecha de la traducción de los *Morales de San Gre-gorio." Romance Notes* 18 (1977): 141–45.

123. ———. "El Rimado de Palacio: Historia de la tradición y crítica del texto." *La Corónica* 6 (1977–1978): 82–90.

124. Gregory, Strong E. "Magna Moralia." In *Homenaje a Don Agapito Rey*, pp. 131–48. Bloomington: Indiana University Press, 1980.

125. Kinkade, Richard P. "On Dating the *Rimado de Palacio." Kentucky Romance Quarterly* 18 (1971): 17–36.

126. ———. "Pedro López de Ayala and the Order of St. Jerome." *Symposium* 26 (1972): 161–80.

127. Strong, E. B. "The *Rimado de Palacio:* López de Ayala's Rimed Confession." *Hispanic Review* 37 (1969): 439–51.

128. ———. "Some Features of the Prayers and Lyrics in the *Rimado de Palacio." Forum for Modern Language Studies* 12 (1976): 156–62.

JUAN MANUEL

General Discussion

129. Ayerbe-Chaux, Reinaldo. *"El conde Lucanor": materia tradicional y originalidad creadora.* Madrid: Porrúa Turanzas, 1975.

130. Devoto, Daniel. *Introducción al estudio de Don Juan Manuel y en particular de "El conde Lucanor": una bibliografía.* Madrid: Castalia, 1972.

131. Deyermond, Alan D. *El Conde Lucanor o Libro de los enxiemplos del conde Lucanor et de Patronio.* Edited by José Manuel Blecua. Madrid: Clásicos Castalia, 1969. *Libro del conde Lucanor et de Patronio,* edited by Germán Orduna. Buenos Aires: Huemul, 1972. *Romance Philology* 31 (1977–1978): 618–30.

132. England, John. *"Exemplo* 51 of *El conde Lucanor:* The Problem of Authorship." *Bulletin of Hispanic Studies* 51 (1974): 16–27.

133. Keller, John E. "A Feasible Source of the Dénouements of the *Exemplos* in *El Conde Lucanor." American Notes & Queries* 14 (1975): 34–37.

134. Sturcken, H. Tracy. *Don Juan Manuel.* Twayne's World Authors Series, vol. 303. New York: Twayne, 1974.

Commentary and Criticism

135. Carreño, Antonio. "La vergüenza como constante social y narrativa en Don Juan Manuel: El 'Ejemplo L' de 'El Conde Lucanor.'" *Revista de Archivos, Bibliotecas y Museos* 80 (1977): 3–20.

136. Dunn, Peter. "The Structures of Didacticism: Private Myths and Public Functions." In *Juan Manuel Studies,* edited by Ian Macpherson, pp. 53–67. London: Támesis, 1977.

137. Macpherson, Ian. "Dios y el mundo: the Didacticism of *El Conde Lucanor.*" *Romance Philology* 24 (1970–1971): 26–38.

138. ———. "Don Juan Manuel: The Literary Process." *Studies in Philology* 70 (1973): 1–18.

139. ———. *Juan Manuel: A Selection.* London: Támesis, 1980.

140. Macpherson, Ian, ed. *Juan Manuel Studies.* London: Támesis, 1977.

141. Romera Castillo, José. *Estudios sobre "El conde Lucanor."* Madrid: Departamento de Filología Hispánica, Universidad Nacional de Educación a Distancia, 1980.

MOCEDADES DE RODRIGO

142. Deyermond, Alan D. *Epic Poetry and the Clergy: Studies on the "Mocedades de Rodrigo."* London: Támesis, 1968.

143. Geary, John Steven. *Formulaic Diction in the Poema de Fernan González and the Mocedades de Rodrigo—A Computer Aided Analysis.* Madrid: Studia Humanitatis, 1980.

144. Webber, Ruth House. "Formulaic Language in the *Mocedades de Rodrigo.*" *Hispanic Review* 48 (1980): 195–211.

OTAS DE ROMA

145. Baird, Herbert L., Jr. *Análisis lingüístico y filológico de Otas de Roma.* Anejos del Boletín de la RAE, 33. Madrid: 1976.

POEMA DE ALFONSO XI

146. Catalán Menéndez Pidal, Diego. *Poema de Alfonso XI: fuentes, dialecto, estilo.* Madrid: Gredos, 1953.

JUAN RUIZ

General Discussion

147. Criado de Val, Manuel, ed. *El Arcipreste de Hita: el libro, el autor, la tierra, la época. Actas del I Congreso Internacional sobre el Arcipreste de Hita.* Barcelona: SERESA, 1973.
148. de Ferraresi, Alicia C. *De amor y poesía en la España medieval: prólogo a Juan Ruiz.* Mexico: El Colegio de México, 1976.
149. Gerli, Michael. "*Recta voluntas est bonus amor:* St. Augustine and the Didactic Tradition." *Romance Philology* 25 (1981–1982): 500–508.
150. Gybbon-Monypenny, G. B., ed. "*Libro de buen amor*" *Studies.* London: Támesis, 1970.
151. Kinkade, Richard P. "*Ioculatores Dei: El libro de buen amor* y la rivalidad entre juglares y predicadores." In *El Arcipreste de Hita: el libro, el autor, la tierra, la época. Actas del I Congreso Internacional sobre el Arcipreste de Hita,* edited by Manuel Criado de Val, pp. 115–28. Barcelona: SERESA, 1973.
152. Lecoy, Félix. *Recherches sur le Libro de buen amor de Juan Ruiz, archiprêtre de Hita.* 2d ed., with supplements by Alan Deyermond. Farnborough: Gregg International, 1974.
153. Sáez, Emilio, and José Trenchs. "Juan Ruiz de Cisneros (1295/1296–1351/1352) Autor del *Buen Amor.*" In *El Arcipreste de Hita: el libro, el autor, la tierra, la época. Actas del I Congreso Internacional sobre el Arcipreste de Hita,* edited by Manuel Criado de Val, pp. 365–68. Barcelona: SERESA, 1973.
154. Ullman, Pierre L. "Juan Ruiz's Prologue." *Modern Language Notes* 82 (1967): 149–70.
155. Walsh, John K. "Juan Ruiz and the *Mester de Clerezía:*

Lost Context and Lost Parody in the *Libro de buen amor.*" *Romance Philology* 33 (1979): 62–86.

156. Zahareas, Anthony N. *The Art of Juan Ruiz, Archpriest of Hita.* Madrid: Estudios de Literatura Española, 1965.

157. ———. "Juan Ruiz's Envoi: The Moral and Artistic Prose." *Modern Language Notes* 49 (1964): 206–11.

Commentary and Criticism

158. Alvarez, Nicolás Emilio. "Análisis estructuralista del Prefacio del *Libro de buen amor.*" To be published in *Kentucky Romance Quarterly* 28 (1981).

159. ———. "El epílogo del *Libro de buen amor.*" In *Medieval, Renaissance and Folklore Studies in Honor of John Esten Keller,* pp. 141–50. Newark, Del.: Juan de la Cuesta—Hispanic Monographs, 1980.

160. ———. "El recibimiento y la tienda de Don Amor en el *Libro de buen amor* a luz del *Libro de Alexandre.*" *Bulletin of Hispanic Studies* 53 (1976): 1–14.

161. Beltrán, Luis. *Razones de buen amor: oposiciones y convergencias en el libro del Arcipreste de Hita.* Colección Pensamiento Literario Español 5. Madrid: Fundación March y Castalia, 1977.

162. Burke, James F. "Again *Cruz,* the Baker-girl; *Libro de buen amor.* ss. 115–120." *Revista Canadiense de Estudios Hispánicos* 4 (1980): 253–70.

163. ———. "Juan Ruiz, the *Serranas,* and the Rites of Spring." *The Journal of Medieval and Renaissance Studies* 5 (1975): 13–35.

164. ———. "The *Libro de buen amor* and the Medieval Meditative Sermon Tradition." *La Corónica* 9 (1980–1981): 122–27.

165. ———. "Love's Double Cross: Language Play as Structure in the *Libro de buen amor.*" *University of Toronto Quarterly* 43 (1974): 231–62.

166. Chapman, Janet A. "Juan Ruiz's Learned Sermon." In *Libro de buen amor Studies,* edited by G. B. Gybbon-Monypenny, pp. 29–50. London: Támesis, 1970.

167. Deyermond, Alan D. "Some Aspects of Parody in the *Libro de buen amor.*" In *Libro de buen amor Studies,*

edited by G. B. Gybbon-Monypenny, pp. 53–78. London: Támesis, 1970.

168. Impey, Olga. "Parvitas y brevitas en el *Libro de buen amor.*" *Kentucky Romance Quarterly* 22 (1975): 193–207.

169. Jenaro-MacLennan, L. "*Libro de buen amor* 69–70, Notas de crítica textual." *Medioevo Romanzo* 4 (1977): 350–67.

170. Kinkade, Richard P. "Intellectum Tibi Dabo . . . : The Function of the Free Will in the *Libro de buen amor.*" *Bulletin of Hispanic Studies* 47 (1970): 296–315.

171. Kirby, Steven D. "Juan Ruiz and Don Ximio: The Archpriest's Art of Declamation." *Bulletin of Hispanic Studies* 55 (1978): 283–87.

172. Lida de Malkiel, Rosa María. *Two Spanish Masterpieces: The Book of Good Love and the Celestina.* Urbana: University of Illinois Press, 1961.

173. Nepaulsingh, Colbert. "The Rhetorical Structure of the Prologues to the *Libro de buen amor* and the *Celestina.*" *Bulletin of Hispanic Studies* 51 (1974): 325–34.

174. ———. "The Structure of the *Libro de buen amor.*" *Neophilologus* 61 (1977): 58–73.

175. Read, M. K. "Man Against Language: A Linguistic Perspective on the Theme of Alienation in the *Libro de buen amor.*" *MLN* 96 (1981): 236–60.

SEM TOB

176. López Grigera, Luisa. "Un nuevo códice de los 'Proverbios morales' de Sem Tob." *Boletín de la Real Academia Española* 56 (1976): 221–81.

177. Perry, T. Anthony. "The Present State of Shem Tov Studies." *La Corónica* 7 (1978–1979): 34–38.

178. Polit, Carlos E. "La originalidad expresiva de Sem Tob." *Revista de Estudios Hispánicos* 12 (1978): 135–54.

179. Shepard, Sanford. *Shem Tov, His World and His Works.* Miami: Ediciones Universal, 1978.

EDITIONS

181. de Gayangos, Pascual, ed. *Gran conquista de Ultramar.* Biblioteca de Autores Españoles, 44.

182. Johnson, William Weisiger. *Poema de José: Transcription and Comparison of the Extant Manuscripts.* Romance Monographs, 6. University: University Press of Mississippi, 1974.

183. López de Ayala, Pero. *Rimado de Palacio.* Edited by Michel García. 2 vols. Madrid: Gredos, 1978.

184. ———. *Rimado de Palacio.* Edited by Jacques Joset. 2 vols. Madrid: Alhambra, 1978.

185. ———. *Rimado de Palacio.* Edited by Germán Orduna. Pisa: Giardini, 1980.

186. Macpherson, Ian, ed. *Juan Manuel: A Selection.* London: Támesis, 1980.

187. Manuel, Don Juan. *El conde Lucanor.* Edited by J. M. Blecua. Madrid: Clásicos Castalia, 1969.

188. ———. *Libro del conde Lucanor et de Patronio.* Edited by Germán Orduna. Buenos Aires: Huemul, 1972.

189. ———. *Libro de los estados.* Edited by R. B. Tate and Ian Macpherson. Oxford: Clarendon, 1974.

190. ———. *Libro infinido y Tratado de la Asunción.* Edited by José María Blecua. Colección Filológica, 2. Granada: Universidad, 1952.

191. Menéndez, Pidal R., and E. Varón Vallejo, eds. *Historia troyana en prosa y verso.* Revista de Filología Española, Anejo 18. Madrid: Junta para la Ampliación de Estudios, 1934.

192. Place, Edwin, ed. *Amadís de Gaula.* 4 vols. Madrid: CSIC, 1959–1969.

193. Ruiz, Juan. *The Book of True Love.* Edited by Anthony N. Zahareas. Translated by Saralyn R. Daly. University Park: Pennsylvania State University Press, 1978.

194. ———. *Libro de buen amor.* Edited by Jacques Joset. Clásicos Castellanos, 14 and 17. Madrid: Espasa-Calpe, 1974.

195. ———. *Libro de buen amor: edición crítica.* Edited by Juan Corominas. Madrid: Gredos, 1967.

196. ———. *Libro de buen amor.* With introduction and English paraphrase by Raymond S. Willis. Princeton: Princeton University Press, 1972.

197. Sem Tob de Carrión. *Proverbios morales.* Edited by Guzmán Alvarez. Salamanca: Anaya, 1970.

198. ———. *Proverbios morales.* Edited by Ignacio González Llubera. Cambridge: Cambridge University Press, 1947.
199. Ten Cate, Yo, ed. *Poema de Alfonso XI.* Revista de Filología Española, Anejo 65. Madrid: CSIC, 1956.
200. Thompson, B. Bussell, and John K. Walsh, eds. *Vida de Santa Maria Egipciaca.* EHT, 17. Exeter: University of Exeter, 1977.
201. Wagner, Charles P., ed. *El libro del Cauallero Zifar (El libro del cauallero de Dios).* Ann Arbor: University of Michigan, 1929.

TRANSLATION

202. Place, Edwin, and Herbert C. Behm, trans. *Amadís de Gaula: A Novel of Chivalry of the 14th Century Presumably First Written in Spanish.* 2 vols. Studies in Romance Languages, 11. Lexington: University Press of Kentucky, 1974–1975.

INDEX

This index is to the essays only and does not include the bibliographies or chronology. Besides being a list of all medieval authors and works referred to, the index also cites all significant topics, particularly those that may be of common interest to students of any of the six literatures. Numbers in bold face indicate a major discussion of an author, topic, or work.

A

Abstracts, need for in the humanities, 4

Ailly, Pierre d': as chancellor, xxiii; bishop and cardinal, xxiii; and Ockham, 226; mentioned, xxi

Alexander romances, xvii, 24, 61. *See also* Romance

Aljamiado literature, xvi–xvii, 286

Allegory: as a genre, xix; in Dante, 6; in Langland, 6, 20; in *Gawain and the Green Knight*, 18; truth of, 58; of virtues, 64; French, **72–75;** in dream visions, 74; in *Minnereden*, 106; in the *Decameron*, 155–56; in Spanish literature, 269; mentioned, 7

Alliterative revival in English literature, 7–8

Amadís de Gaula, xvii, **276,** 279

Ambiguity, in Chaucer, 11

Analytic philosophy, and scholasticism, 223

Anglo-Norman literature, **75**

Animal imagery, in Chaucer, 12

Anthologies, medieval Latin, 210

Anticlericalism, xiii

Antonio de' Beccari da Ferrara, **158**

Apocalyptic poetry, in Langland, 6

Archaeological studies, of Spanish literature, 261

Archetypal criticism, of the *Decameron*, 155–56

Ariosto, and Boccaccio, 152

Aristotle, Latin commentaries on, 207

Art, medieval, exhibits, 118

Arthurian romance: English, 23–24; influence, 62; German, 103; Spanish, **275–76;** mentioned, 3. *See also* Romance

Assembly of Ladies, The, 21

Astrology: and Cecco d'Ascoli, xxiv; in Chaucer, 12

Auchinleck manuscript, 5

Audiences: and poets, 2; emergence of bourgeois, 8; of *Gawain and the Green Knight*, 17; for French lyrics, 62; and self-improvement, 106; manipulation of, 155; and literacy, 267

Augustine of Hippo, Saint, and Petrarch, 143

Augustinianism: and humanism, 216; in Ruiz, 265

Authors: multilingual, xvi; occupations of, xxii–xxiv; travels of, xxiv–xxv; fortunes of, xxv; life-spans, xxv–xxvi; at work, 6–7; rise of citizen authors, 56; German, 98–99; self-effacement, 105–6; classical, 206–7

CHRONOLOGY

ENGLISH	FRENCH

Northern Homily Cycle **1300** Jean de Joinville (1225–1317) **1300**
(verse sermons) (chronicle)
Le Roman de Fauvel (1310–1314)
(moral satire)
Robert Mannyng (1283–1338) *Les Voeux du paon* (1312)
(didactic verse tales; chronicles) (Alexander romance)
Perceforest (1320)
Interludium de clerico et puella (grail romance)
(secular verse play) Guillaume de Digulleville
(c. 1293–after 1380)
(allegorical verse)
Beginnings of dramatic **1325** Nicole Bozon (dates unknown) **1325**
cycles (moral tales)
Ovide moralisé (1328)
Sir Orfeo (c. 1330) (allegorical narrative)
(verse romance) Jean Dupin (1302–1374)
Le Livre de Mandevie
(dream allegory)
Ywain and Gawain (c. 1300– *Le Restor du paon* (before 1338)
1350) (verse romance) (Alexander romance)
Le Parfait du paon (1340)
(Alexander romance)
Richard Rolle (1300–1349) Jean de Condé (fl. 1313–1340)
(religious instruction, lyrics) (poetry, romances, fabliaux)
Les Miracles de Notre-Dame
(1339–1382) (miracle plays)
Libeaus Desconus **1350** Guillaume de Machaut **1350**
(c. 1325–1350) (verse romance) (1300–1377)
Winner and Waster (c. 1352) (didactic verse, debates, lyrics)
(verse debate) *Baudouin de Sebourc* (1350)
Morte Arthure (c. 1360) (chanson de geste)
(alliterative romance/epic) *Bérinus* (1350–1370)
John Wyclif (1320–1384) (prose romance)
(sermons, translations) Jean de Mandeville
Gawain-poet (dates unknown) (dates unknown)
Pearl (dream vision) (travel narrative)
Sir Gawain and the Green Geoffrey de la Tour Landry
Knight (verse romance) (c. 1325–after 1389)
William Langland (1330?–1386?) (educational treatise)
Piers Plowman (dream vision) Jean Froissart (c. 1337–1404)
(chronicles, narrative verse)
Geoffrey Chaucer **1375** Nicole Oresme(c. 1320–1382) **1375**
(1340–1400) (verse tales, dream (theology, finance, astronomy)
visions, romance, lyrics) John Gower (1330?–1408?)
John Gower (1330?–1408?) (moral allegory)
(verse tales) Eustache Deschamps (1346–1407)
The Cloud of Unknowing (lyric poetry, satire, poetics)
(devotional prose) Phillipe de Mézières (1327–1405)
Julian of Norwich (1343–1443) *Le Songe du vieil pelerin*
(devotional prose) (1389) (allegorical voyage)
Walter Hilton (? –1396) *Le Ménagier de Paris* (1392)
(religious instruction) (educational treatise)
Margery Kempe (c. 1373–c. 1439) *L'Estoire de Griseldis* (1395)
(autobiography) (drama)
Le Morte Arthur (c. 1400) **1400** Jean Gerson (1363–1429) **1400**
(stanzaic romance) (sermons)

GERMAN		ITALIAN	
Heinrich von Meissen ("Frauenlob") (c. 1260–1318) (lyric poetry)	**1300**	Bonvesin de la Riva (1240–c. 1315) (moral verse) Dante (1265–1321) *Commedia* (c. 1307–1321)	**1300**
Meister Eckhart (c. 1260–1328) (sermons, religious tracts)		Dino Compagni (c. 1255–1324) (chronicles)	
Innsbruck Easter Play *Vienna Passion Play* *St. Gall Passion Play*		Cecco d'Ascoli (1269–1327) (encyclopedia)	
Johannes Tauler (c. 1300–1361) (sermons)	**1325**		**1325**
Heinrich Seuse (c. 1295–1366) (autobiography, religious tracts and dialogues, letters)		Cino da Pistoia (1270–c. 1337) (lyrics, jurisprudence)	
Ulrich Boner (c. 1305–after 1350) *Der Edelstein* (c. 1340) (verse fables)		Giovanni Villani (1275–1348) (chronicles) Francesco da Barberino (1264–1348) (allegorical verse) Jacopo Passavanti (1302–1357)	
Hadamar von Laber (c. 1300–after 1354) (love allegory in verse)	**1350**	(moral treatises) Petrarch (1304–1374) (sonnets, allegorical verse)	**1350**
Heinrich der Teichner (c. 1300–before 1377) (didactic poetry)		Fazio degli Uberti (1305–1368) (didactic verse) Antonio Pucci	
Heinrich von Mügeln (c. 1325–after 1392) (allegorical and lyric poetry, chronicles, translations)		(c. 1310–1388) (lyrics) Boccaccio (1313–1375) (romances, epic, allegory, idyll, biography, prose tales)	
Konrad von Megenberg (c. 1309–1374) (natural history)		Antonio de' Beccari da Ferrara (1315–1371?) (lyrics and satirical verse)	
Heinrich von Langenstein (c. 1325–1397) (religious tracts, translations)	**1375**	St. Catherine of Siena (1347–1380) (autobiography, letters)	**1375**
Heinrich von St. Gallen (c. 1345/1350–after 1397) (religious tracts, sermons)			
Marquard von Lindau (?–1392) (religious tracts)			
Hugo von Montfort (1357–1423) (lyric poetry, discourses)			
Oswald von Wolkenstein (1377–1445) (lyric poetry)			
Heinrich Wittenwiler (c. 1350–1436?) *Der Ring* (comic/didactic epic)		Franco Sacchetti (1330–1400) (prose tales and poetry)	
Johannes von Tepl (c. 1350– 1414) *Der Ackermann aus Böhmen* (prose dialogue)	**1400**	Giovanni Sercambi (1348–1424) (prose tales)	**1400**

LATIN		SPANISH	
Lovato Lovati (1241–1309) (commentary on Senecan metrics)	**1300**	*Historia troyana polimétrica.* (prose/verse romance)	**1300**
Ramon Lull (1235?–1316) (philosophy and theology)		Ramon Lull (1235?–1316?) (lyrics, prose romance, devotional writings)	
Duns Scotus (1266–1308) (philosophy)		*Libro de caballero Zifar* (c. 1310) (prose romance)	
Dante Alighieri (1265–1321) (technical treatises, poetry, letters)		*Gran conquista de ultramar* (fictionalized prose chronicle)	
Albertino Mussato (1261–1329) *Ecerinus* (first humanist tragedy)		c. 1320 *et seq:* beginnings of ballad tradition ? *Amadís de Gaula* (romance)	
Richard de Bury (1281–1345) *Philobiblon* (treatise on books)	**1325**	Juan Manuel (1282–1349) *Libro de los estados* (c. 1330) (didactic prose)	**1325**
Richard Rolle (1300–1349) (devotional and mystical treatises)		*Conde Lucanor* (c. 1330–1335) (prose tales)	
William of Ockham (c. 1300–1350) (philosophy)		Juan Ruiz (1280–1350) *El libro de buen amor* (1330–1343)	
Ranulf Higden (?–1364) *Polychronicon* (universal history)		(lyrics/*exempla*/parody/ pseudo-autobiography) Rodrigo Yáñez (fl. 1348)	
Petrarch (1304–1374) (autobiographical, didactic, and technical treatises, verse, letters)		*Poema de Alfonso XI* (1348) (verse chronicle)	
Boccaccio (1313–1375) (mythology, didactic treatises, verse, letters)			
Ludolph of Saxony (1295–1377) *Vita Christi*	**1350**	Santob de Carrión (c. 1290–c. 1369) *Proverbios morales* (c. 1351) (didactic verse)	**1350**
John Wyclif (c. 1328–1384) (religious and theological treatises)			
Henry of Langenstein (c. 1325–1397) (theology and natural history)			
John Gower (1330?–1408?) *Vox Clamantis* (dream vision)			
Coluccio Salutati (1331–1406) (humanist and scholarly treatises, letters)			
Pierre d'Ailly (1350–1420) (philosophy)	**1375**	*Las mocedades de Rodrigo* (epic verse)	**1375**
Antonio Loschi (c. 1363–1441) *Achilles* (classical tragedy)		Pedro López de Ayala (1332–1407?) *El rimado de palacio* (mixed verse)	
Jean Gerson (1363–1429) (religion and philosophy)	**1400**	*Poema de José* (religious narrative verse)	**1400**